PERSPECTIVES ON BEHAVIORAL INHIBITION

The John D. and Catherine T. MacArthur Foundation
Series on Mental Health and Development

PERSPECTIVES ON BEHAVIORAL INHIBITION

Edited by

J. Steven Reznick

THE UNIVERSITY OF CHICAGO PRESS / CHICAGO AND LONDON

J. Steven Reznick is assistant professor of psychology at Yale University and lecturer at the Child Study Center of the Yale School of Medicine. He is a fellow of the Bush Center in Child Development and Social Policy.

The University of Chicago Press, Chicago 60637
The University of Chicago Press, Ltd., London
© 1989 by The University of Chicago
All rights reserved. Published 1989
Printed in the United States of America

98 97 96 95 94 93 92 91 90 89   54321

Portions of Chapter 12 have appeared in Myrna M. Weissman's article "Family Genetic Studies of Psychiatric Disorders," *Archives of General Psychiatry* 43 (November 1986): 11061–11116. Copyright 1986, American Medical Association.

Figures in Chapter 14 appeared in: James A. McCubbin, John S. Kizer, and Morris A. Lipton, "Naltrexone Prevents Footshock-induced Performance Deficits in Rats," *Life Sciences* 34 (1984): 2057–2066. Reprinted with permission. Copyright 1984, Pergamon Press, Inc. James A. McCubbin, Richard S. Surwit, and Redford B. Williams, "Endogenous Opiate Peptides, Stress Reactivity, and Risk for Hypertension," *Hypertension* 7, no. 5 (1985): 808–811. By permission of the American Heart Association, Inc. James A. McCubbin, Richard S. Surwit, and Redford B. Williams, "Naloxone and Blood Pressure Responses during Different Types of Stress," *Psychosomatic Medicine* 50 (1988): 8–14. Reprinted by permission of Elsevier Science Publishing Co., Inc. Copyright 1988 by the American Psychosomatic Society, Inc.

Library of Congress Cataloging-in-Publication Data

Perspectives on behavioral inhibition / edited by J. Steven Reznick.
    p.   cm.—(The John D. and Catherine T. MacArthur Foundation series on mental health and development)
    Papers originally presented at a conference held Nov. 1986 in Cambridge, Mass., sponsored by the John D. and Catherine T. MacArthur Foundation.
    Includes index.
    ISBN 0-226-71040-8 (alk. paper)
    1. Timidity—Physiological aspects—Congresses. 2. Timidity in children—Physiological aspects—Congresses. 3. Psychophysiology—Congresses. I. Reznick, J. Steven. II. John D. and Catherine T. MacArthur Foundation. III. Series.
QP402.P48 1989
155.2'32—dc20   89-32463
                                                          CIP

The University of Chicago Press gratefully acknowledges a subvention from the John D. and Catherine T. MacArthur Foundation in partial support of the costs of production of this volume.

⊗ The paper used in this publication meets the minimum requirements of the American National Standard for Information Sciences—Permanence of Paper for Printed Library Materials, ANSI Z39.48-1984.

Contents

Contributors

Robert E. Adamec   Memorial University, Newfoundland
Doreen Arcus   Harvard University
Joseph Biederman   Massachusetts General Hospital
Nathan A. Fox   University of Maryland
Michelle Gersten   Massachusetts General Hospital
    (now at Mount Sinai School of Medicine)
Jane L. Gibbons   Harvard University
C. P. Gruber   Brown University
Maureen O. Johnson   Harvard University
Jerome Kagan   Harvard University
L. L. LaGasse   Brown University
L. P. Lipsitt   Brown University
Kathleen McCartney   Harvard University
    (now at University of New Hampshire)
James A. McCubbin   Duke University Medical Center
    (now at University of Kentucky)
Paula M. McDonough   Harvard University
Robert Plomin   Pennsylvania State University
J. Steven Reznick   Harvard University
    (now at Yale University)
Jerrold F. Rosenbaum   Massachusetts General Hospital
Mary Klevjord Rothbart   University of Oregon
Nancy Snidman   Harvard University
Cannie Stark-Adamec   Univerity of Regina, Saskatchewan
Joan Stevenson-Hinde   Cambridge University
Clare Stocker   Pennsylvania State University
Myrna M. Weissman   Yale University
    (now at College of Physicians and Surgeons of Columbia
    University)

Preface

Various political and cultural forces tend to segregate psychologists (and others interested in behavior) into areas (e.g., developmental, clinical, and behavioral genetics) and topical themes within area (e.g., cognitive development, social development, and motor development). Patterns of communication, administrative pressures, and assorted "group" processes then reify these borders, making intermural communication and collaboration difficult. This volume is an attempt to overcome these forces and unite a group of researchers who share an interest in a common problem.

Humans, as do many other species, appear to experience a state of uncertainty when confronted with novel or unexpected situations or events (e.g., a child or an adult—or a cat or a rat—entering an unfamiliar room, encountering a new object, or meeting a stranger). Individuals differ in their perception of and/or response to uncertainty. At one extreme, uncertainty is handled easily and quickly, and there is no evidence that the organism is aware of the uncertainty or perturbed in any way. At the other extreme, uncertainty may be debilitating, causing the organism to freeze or even retreat. This response dimension parallels Schneirla's concept of approach-withdrawal and will vary as a function of the situation and the individual.

Interest in response to uncertainty has a long history in psychology, dating back to Jung and Pavlov (see Kagan, chap. 1, in this vol.). More recently, a group of researchers associated with the Harvard Infant Study have initiated a series of studies that focus on developmental and biological aspects of this phenomenon. We label extreme withdrawal to uncertainty "inhibition" and have explored factors affecting the preservation of a tendency toward inhibition, particularly biological mediation (see the chapters in this volume by Kagan, chap. 1, Snidman, chap. 3, Gersten, chap. 4, and Reznick et al., chap. 2).

In the course of our work on this topic, we have been impressed with its wide appeal and the variety of researchers who pursue it. This widespread interest reflects the biological significance of inhibition, its robustness, and its clinical implications. Our pursuit of these diverse literatures has also made it apparent that there is little communication between scholars who approach this problem from different perspectives.

To rectify this situation, we organized a conference, "Perspectives on Behavioral Inhibition," sponsored by the John D. and Catherine T. MacArthur Foundation, held in Cambridge, Massachusetts, in November 1986. The participants were researchers from a variety of disciplines and specializations, all interested in behavioral inhibition. To further the collaborative theme of the conference, we have assembled a collection of the papers presented and contributions by participants. We regard this volume as a sampling of state-of-the-art study for behavioral inhibition in children: it spans the range of knowledge that a serious scholar should be familiar with to pursue this topic.

We are grateful to many people who have aided this project. The John D. and Catherine T. MacArthur Foundation's Network on the Transition from Infancy to Childhood supported the conference and the preparation of this volume. Nancy Reisman orchestrated the conference with help from staff members of the Harvard Infant Study. Jerome Kagan and three anonymous reviewers helped shape the papers. Helen Snively assisted with editing.

1 The Concept of Behavioral Inhibition to the Unfamiliar

JEROME KAGAN

Although explanations of the stable sources of behavioral variation among children and adults have varied with time and culture, few societies have failed to recognize that the adults in a community differ in their habitual reactions to people, to responsibility, to challenge, and to frustration. Most of the explanations can be assigned to a space defined by a contrast between accounts that pit the power of endogenous qualities, whether genetic, prenatal, or occult, against the power of the environment, whether climate, diet, family experience, or position in the society. However, within each of these complementary types of interpretations, one can compare categories of people or compare people on continuous dimensions.

The ancients preferred categories of humans—choleric, sanguine, melancholic—while twentieth-century psychologists have preferred dimensions. Although Galen described an adult who was prone to display anger toward friends as possessing an inherently choleric mood, most American and European psychologists during this century have described the same person as having acquired a stronger hostility motive than his neighbor. The shift from stable categories of people to malleable psychological dimensions represents the most important historical change in descriptions of human personality, at least in the West, over the past 1,500 years.

It is reasonably accurate to suggest that Freud's ideas represented the sharpest change away from the views of the past. Freud made developmental experiences in the family the major source of individual variation and, equally important, chose constructs that were continuous dimensions present in all people to differing degrees. Anxiety, repression, projection, cathexis, and fixation are characteristic of all children and adults. The varied behavioral phenotypes are a function of differences in the intensity, or strength, of the major

Preparation for this paper was supported in part by grants from the John D. and Catherine T. MacArthur Foundation, and the National Institute of Mental Health, U.S. Public Health Service.

1

dimensions. Over the last seventy years, students of human personality have elaborated the belief that adult personalities are the product of the differential strength of correlated dispositions acquired over a lifetime of social encounters. Very few theorists have questioned that assumption, even though it is historically unique. Only recently has there been a renascence of the supposition that the biological qualities of children make a contribution to personality formation and, further, that there is utility to conceptualizing some components of personality as qualitative categories rather than continuous dimensions.

The history of personality study in children in this century can be divided into three phases. The first was a derivative of the psychoanalytic emphasis on motives. Children differed from each other in the differential strength of the basic motives, such as dependency, hostility, achievement, and dominance, as a result of experience. The profiles created by these motives defined a child's personality. Despite the popularity of this frame, its proponents failed to develop a methodology capable of evaluating the hypothetical motives. Investigators were forced to rely on the frequency of behaviors that they assumed reflected the motives of the hierarchy. But this assumption was flawed, and the conceptual strategy and its accompanying methodology were gradually replaced during the 1960s with a view that originated in cognitive and social psychology. The new view asserts that the origins of action are sets of acquired beliefs about the self and others that monitor behavior and persona. The idea of a self-concept is quintessential in this system. Investigators favoring this view rely for evidence on questionnaires administered to children or their parents and teachers. Unfortunately, these methods have serious validity problems.

The most recent phase represents a return to nineteenth-century temperamental categories. Scientists supporting this view do not contend that motives and beliefs are irrelevant. They suggest only that children are born with biases that predispose them to acquire different sets of motives, beliefs, and actions. Further, some of these temperamental biases are conceived of as qualitative rather than quantitative. It is not clear how many significant temperamental constructs will be discovered in the next half-century. The one that has attracted the most attention thus far is related to the concept of approach versus withdrawal when faced with novel and challenging events.

One of the few obvious behavioral differences among humans that is not correlated with social class is the initial reaction to unfamiliar or challenging situations for which the person does not have an immediate coping reaction. Some children and adults become quiet and restrained, assessing the situation and their resources before acting. Others act spontaneously as if the distinctions between familiar and novel were of minimal psychological consequence. The situation that reveals this quality most often in children and adults is an encounter with unfamiliar people, especially if the context is evaluative. Of course, it is rare to find many people who are consistently shy and affectively restrained or outgoing and spontaneous in every social context. There is, however, a small group of children—estimated to be about 10–15 percent—who consistently bring one or the other of these behavioral styles to such situations (see Cranach et al. 1978).

Almost every commentator on human nature, from Hippocrates to modern personologists, has noted these two contrasting characteristics, and empirical indices of these constructs are among the most stable and heritable in contemporary psychology (Conley 1985; Floderus-Myrhed, Pedersen, & Rasmuson 1980; Loehlin 1982; Plomin 1986). Further, many theorists have assumed that physiological processes make a partial contribution to the two styles (Thomas and Chess 1977). Jung's (1924) complementary categories of introversion and extraversion, which represent the most complete elaboration of this idea, must have been congenial to European and American minds for these terms continue to be the most popular names for these classes of behavior.

Jung's Conception

Jung regarded introversion and extraversion as complementary processes, similar to the Chinese conceptualization of the relation between yin and yang. Every adult's animus (or anima) possesses one of these biases as its primary quality, but each person also tries to achieve a psychological balance by adopting, in surface behavior, qualities that define the complementary type, which Jung called the persona. Gellhorn (1967) invented the terms "ergotrophic" and "trophotrophic," which came close to being physiological parallels to introversion and extraversion, to describe the complementary relation between the activity of the sympathetic and the parasympathetic nervous systems.

Jung chose the targets of a person's interests as a distinctive feature differentiating the two types. The extravert is concerned with people and objects; the introvert chooses to concentrate on thoughts, fantasy, and feelings. Jung wrote, "The names and forms in which the mechanism of introversion and extraversion has been conceived are extremely diverse, and are, as a rule, adapted only to the standpoint of the individual observer. Notwithstanding the diversity of the formulations, the common basis or fundamental idea shines constantly through; namely, in the one case an outward movement of interest toward the object, and in the other a movement of interest away from the object, towards subject and his own psychological processes" (Jung 1924, 11).

Intrapsychic processes take precedence over motivation and action in Jung's list of the four psychological features that distinguish introverts from extraverts: thinking, feeling, sensation, and intuition. The major difference between introverts and extraverts is in the quality of their consciousness, not in their everyday behaviors. Perhaps that is one reason why American psychologists have ignored Jung, for Watson and the behaviorists that followed him took exactly the opposite position. Jung believed that inheritance of a strong or a weak nervous system would explain the two types. Although it is unclear whether Jung borrowed this idea from Pavlov, he obviously appropriated Freud's concept of libidinal energy, while changing its primary function. Introverts, Jung suggested, have more intense primary forces and so appear more tense than extraverts. Because introverts have more libido available to be aroused by challenge or novelty, the secondary, or assimilative, function requires a longer time to recover. Thus, the brain of the extravert possesses a "higher restitutive capacity than that of the introvert" (Jung 1924, 355). (For a modern version of this view, see Strelau [1985]). Modern investigators might rephrase this idea and say that both central nervous system arousal following encounter with unfamiliar events and time to assimilate these experiences are enhanced in introverts. As we shall see, Jung's speculation was prescient, for the children we call inhibited show greater arousal of the sympathetic and hypothalamic-pituitary-adrenal axis following challenge and unfamiliarity and require more time to adapt to unfamiliar situations than uninhibited children do. Although Jung did not wish to underestimate the importance of parental behavior in sculpting a child's future profile, he believed "that the decisive factor must be looked for in the disposition of the child" (Jung 1924, 415), a hypothesis that is now being verified in many laboratories.

Animal Work

Comparative psychologists and zoologists have noticed two contrasting clusters of behaviors, similar to Jung's concepts, that differentiate among species or within strains of closely related animals. Schneirla (1965), who named the contrast "approach-withdrawal," implied that the balance between the two processes might distinguish among animals from the same or similar strains. Like Jung, Schneirla also tied withdrawal to sympathetic arousal but believed that prenatal experiences (rather than genetics) produced the bias favoring one or the other of these dispositions. The facts supporting this class of differences are persuasive. Dogs, mice, rats, wolves, cats, cows, monkeys, and even paradise fish differ intraspecifically in the tendency to approach or to avoid novelty (Royce 1955; Murphey, Duarte, and Penendo 1980; Blanchard, Flannelly, and Blanchard 1986; McDonald 1983; Csanyi and Gervai 1986; Dantzer and Mormede 1985; Adamec and Stark-Adamec 1986; Cooper, Schmidt, and Barrett 1983). Both Suomi (1987) and Stevenson-Hinde, Stillwell-Barnes, and Zunz (1980) have reported that laboratory-reared rhesus monkeys differ in degree of fearfulness and maintain these differences from infancy through puberty. In addition, the physiological differences between the fearful and the less fearful monkeys in Suomi's work are similar to those I shall report for inhibited and uninhibited children. The most extensive study of the genetic origins of these qualities was published over 20 years ago. Scott and Fuller (1965) studied five breeds of dogs—basenji, beagle, cocker spaniel, Shetland sheepdog, and fox terrier—in the Jackson Laboratories in Bar Harbor, Maine. Over 250 puppies from the five breeds were studied longitudinally from birth, with some puppies cross-fostered to mothers from a different breed. An additional group of about 200 dogs was the product of matings between breeds, including back-crosses. In one of the more sensitive assessment procedures, a handler took the puppy from a holding cage and returned it to the common room. The handler then placed the puppy 1 or 2 feet away, stood still, and noted the animal's behavior. The handler then slowly turned and walked toward the puppy, squatted down, held out his hand, stroked the puppy, and, finally, picked it up. The puppies classed as timid ran to the corner of the room, crouched down, and gave a high-pitched yelp early in this sequence. The five breeds differed dramatically in the degree of timidity shown in this situation, with basenjis, terriers, and shelties being much more timid than beagles and cocker spaniels. However, the rearing environment made a significant contribution to this behavior, for, if the puppies of the various breeds were raised in a home rather than in the laboratory, they showed less extreme signs of timidity.

Differences among the five breeds in resting heart rate revealed a correlation between timidity and a high heart rate. Basenjis had the highest heart rates, cocker spaniels had the lowest, and beagles, shelties, and terriers were in the middle. Further, the rank order of the five breeds on a measure of "disposition to escape" was very similar to the rank order for the heart-rate scores, with basenjis highest on both variables and cocker spaniels lowest. A factor analysis of the data from a large sample of dogs from all the breeds revealed a factor characterized by a high heart rate and behavioral timidity. An earlier analysis of similar data from the Bar Harbor laboratory revealed a major factor defined by early freezing, withdrawal from novelty, and high blood pressure (Royce 1955). Years later, Goddard and Beilharz (1985) studied puppies from four different breeds (Labrador, Australian kelpie, boxer, and German shepherd) and found that a factor defined by avoidance of unfamiliar objects on a noisy street significantly differentiated the four breeds, with the German shepherds most and the Labradors least fearful of novelty.

A series of studies of defensive versus aggressive cats, summarized by Adamec and Stark-Adamec (1986), provides some clues to the possible neural bases for these differences (see Adamec and Stark-Adamec, chap. 5, in this vol.). Ordinary house cats (*Felis catus*) vary in their disposition to retreat from or approach unfamiliar rooms and humans as well as to avoid or attack rats. A small group, about 15 percent, shows prolonged inhibition of approach to

novel events and people and also fails to attack rats, while a larger complementary group, about 40 percent, shows no tendency to retreat from novel
objects and typically attacks rats. As Adamec and Stark-Adamec (chap. 5, in
this vol.) note, the avoidant-defensive cats show greater neural activity in the
basomedial amygdala to the introduction of a rat as well as larger evoked
potentials in the ventromedial hypothalamus following stimulation of the basomedial amygdala, implying greater synaptic transmission from the amygdala to the hypothalamus. By contrast, electrical stimulation of the basomedial amygdala of aggressive cats produces larger potentials in the ventral
hippocampus. These facts imply, although they do not prove, that the connections between the amygdala and the hypothalamus and sympathetic chain are
more excitable in defensive cats while the connections between the amygdala
and the motor actions serving attack are more excitable in the nondefensive
cats (for differences in physiological responsiveness between squirrel and titi
monkeys, see Cubicciotti et al. [1986], and for the reaction of the amygdala
to novelty, see Kling, Lloyd, and Perryman [1987] and Dunn and Everitt
[1988]).

Inhibited and Uninhibited Children

No one disputes that some 2-year-olds are consistently shy, timid, and wary
when they first encounter unfamiliar contexts while others are immediately
sociable with strangers and exploratory in the same unfamiliar contexts.
These sets of qualities were the only ones preserved from the first 3 years of
life through childhood and adolescence in the Fels Research Institute's longitudinal population (Kagan and Moss 1962). A subsequent longitudinal study
with infants and children from Caucasian and Chinese families living in and
near Boston found that behavioral timidity in unfamiliar situations and a
stable heart rate, which were correlated, were the best-preserved characteristics from 3 through 29 months of age (Kagan, Kearsley, and Zelazo 1978; see
also Plomin and Rowe 1979). It is important to emphasize that the defining
feature of this classification is initial behavior to unfamiliar and challenging
events and not habitual behavior in familiar contexts, a fact also emphasized
by Suomi (1987) in his study of comparable differences in rhesus monkeys.
     Steven Reznick, Nancy Snidman, Cynthia Garcia-Coll and I, along with
other members of our laboratory, have been following two longitudinal cohorts of children selected to be extreme on initial behavioral timidity to the
unfamiliar (called "inhibited") or lack of timidity (called "uninhibited") at
either 21 or 31 months of age. Nancy Snidman (chap. 3, in this vol.) reports
some of the data for the second cohort selected at 31 months. I shall summarize the data from the first cohort of 58 children selected at 21 months of age.

Most of the major findings to be reported for the first cohort have been replicated in the second group of children selected at 31 months with slightly different procedures. The initial selection of the children in cohort 1 and the follow-up assessments at age 4 (43 children), 5½ (46 children), and 7½ years (41 children) were a collaborative effort with Reznick, Snidman and Garcia-Coll (see Garcia-Coll, Kagan, and Reznick 1984; Kagan et al. 1984; Reznick et al. 1986; Kagan, Reznick, and Snidman 1988; and Snidman 1984).

Preservation of Social Behavior

There was moderate preservation of inhibited and uninhibited behavior in unfamiliar contexts from 21 months through 7½ years (correlation was .67, $p < .001$). Three-fourths of the children classified as either inhibited or uninhibited at 21 months retained their appropriate behavioral classifications when they were seen at 7½ years in both peer play and laboratory contexts. It is of interest that, when volunteer cross-sectional samples of 14- and 20-month-old children (16 children in each group), not selected to be extreme in social behavior, were seen for a 45-minute laboratory and play session on two occasions 2 weeks apart, the stability coefficients for inhibited behavior as well as heart rate were moderately high. The index of inhibited behavior was based on each child's reaction to an unfamiliar room, an unfamiliar adult, and a novel toy. The specific variables were latency to vocalize, latency to approach the unfamiliar object or person, and time proximal to the mother. The stability correlations for inhibited behavior were .40 for all 32 children (.47 for the younger and .32 for the older 20-month-olds). The stability of heart rate and heart-rate variability were .62 and .29, respectively, for the younger children; .58 and .69 for the older children; and .64 and .57 for all 32 children. Thus, even for an unselected sample of young children, the critical behavioral and heart-rate variables that provide a referential definition of inhibition are moderately stable over short intervals, suggesting that these reactions are not transient.

The qualities of inhibition and lack of inhibition also generalized to an ecologically natural context. Children classed as inhibited at 21 months were more isolated, withdrawn, and quiet than uninhibited children when they were observed in their kindergarten classrooms at 5½ years of age, $r = .34$, $p < .05$ (Gersten 1986, and chap. 4, in this vol.). Additionally, inhibited children had more fears than uninhibited children at all ages, especially those who also had high heart rates. Eight inhibited children had lost their initially extreme form of shyness and timidity at 7½, but only three of these eight (two boys and one girl) had acquired an external demeanor that resembled that of the typical uninhibited child. However, only two originally uninhibited children—both girls—had become extremely shy and timid at 7½ years.

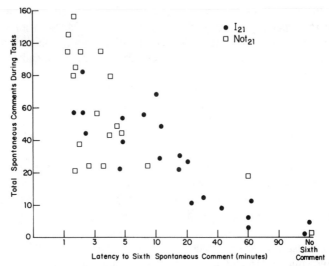

Fig. 1. Latency to sixth spontaneous comment and total spontaneous comments to examiner.

Thus, sex-role values surrounding fear and timidity may be influencing the probability that a particular child will move from one behavioral category to the other.

An extremely sensitive index of inhibition can be seen at age 4 when a child meets an unfamiliar peer of the same sex and age in a play situation with both mothers present. The inhibited children stay close to their mothers, remain quiet, and do not initiate play with the other child. However, by 5–6 years of age, a dyadic context is less sensitive because most children have learned how to interact with a single, unfamiliar child. At this age, behavior with an unfamiliar adult in a testing situation discriminates the two groups. Figure 1 shows that at 7½ years most of the formerly inhibited children waited a long time before making their sixth spontaneous comment to a friendly female examiner and, additionally, made very few spontaneous comments across the 90-minute testing session. One-third of the formerly inhibited children, but only one formerly uninhibited child, were extremely quiet, while 40 percent of the uninhibited children, but only one inhibited child, spoke early and frequently.

Inhibited children were also quiet at 7½ years when they were with a large group of unfamiliar children. At the 7½-year assessment, groups of eight or nine children of the same sex and age, and unfamiliar with each other, came to a large playroom. After an introductory period of 10 minutes without supervision, two adults entered and introduced a series of games (races, spelling contest). The entire session lasted about 90 minutes, with 3-minute intervals of free play between each structured play bout. A videotape record of the entire session was made, and individual observers—one observer per child—

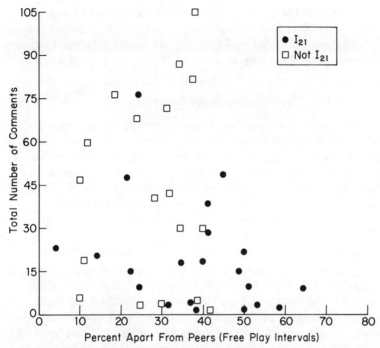

Fig. 2. Total comments and time distant from peers in free play.

narrated that child's behavior onto an audiotape from behind a one-way vision screen. The two variables that best discriminated inhibited from uninhibited children were, first, the total number of spontaneous utterances across all the episodes and, second, the amount of time the child stood apart from other children during the free-play intervals between the structured games, defined as the proportion of time each child was greater than an arm's length from any other child. The intercoder reliabilities for the two variables were .92 for utterances and .85 for distance from another. The formerly inhibited children were more often distant from any other child, $t(1,37) = 2.27, p < .05$, and much less likely to talk either to another child or to the two women monitoring the session, $t(1,37) = 2.69, p < .01$ (see fig. 2).

As noted above, only three formerly inhibited children were similar to the modal uninhibited child, and only two formerly uninhibited children, both girls, resembled the modal inhibited child. Thus, one of the salient attributes of the adult introvert—an initial period of quiet in an unfamiliar social setting—is also a salient characteristic of 7-year-old children who were selected to be inhibited when they were 21 months old. When the laboratory index of inhibition (long latency to talk and few spontaneous comments) was combined with the peer play index (playing apart from peers and not talking) to create a single aggregate index of inhibition, 77 percent of the children classified as inhibited at 21 months were above the median on this aggregate index, in contrast to 26 percent of the children originally classified as uninhibited at 21 months ($t[1,37] = 3.88, p < .001$, for the difference between the two groups on the aggregate index).

Cognitive Performance and Inhibition

Some cognitive functions are more easily disrupted by task-related stress in inhibited than in uninhibited children. Deterioration in recognition- and recall-memory performance is a sensitive psychological index of the uncertainty created in a child by an evaluating adult and the possibility of task failure (Messer 1968). At 5½ years of age, significantly more inhibited than uninhibited children showed a loss in accuracy of recognition memory following a series of difficult cognitive tests. At 7½ years of age, we replaced the recognition-memory test with a specific test of recall memory. After the child had received electrodes for the recording of heart rate and had remained quiet for a 1-minute baseline heart-rate recording, a prestress memory-recall task was administered. The child listened to a male voice narrate a 3-minute story about a boy and a girl. When the story was over, the child was given a set of 18 colored pictures—each about 3 × 3 inches—and asked to arrange the pictures so that they matched the chronology of the story just heard. (Each child was given an initial practice story to acquaint him or her with the requirements of the task.) Subsequently, the child was administered four different, difficult, cognitive tasks that involved some failure, followed by a parallel version of the recall-memory test. The child then heard a narration that was a continuation of the initial prestress story and, at its completion, was given another set of 18 pictures and asked to arrange them to match the chronology of the story. A significantly larger proportion of inhibited than uninhibited children showed poorer performance on the second than on the initial recall-memory test (59 percent vs. 31 percent, $\chi^2 = 3.1, p < .05$), suggesting that the intervening cognitive tests generated more uncertainty/arousal in the inhibited children (for a parallel phenomenon, see Doerr and Hokanson 1965).

A second procedure administered at 7½ years suggests that task-generated uncertainty also impairs the inhibited child's ability to make fine perceptual discriminations. Following a set of appropriate practice items, each child was shown a series of 32 pairs of chromatic pictures of people or objects. The child was told that some of the pairs were identical and that some differed in a very subtle way (e.g., a button missing on a shirt, an altered angle of a person's foot). The child had to decide if the pair of pictures projected on the screen was identical or different and, if different, to indicate the nature of the difference. Half the pictures were similar and half different; half were neutral in content, and half had an affective content that involved fear or anxiety (a person bleeding, a person tied with rope). If inhibited children have a lower threshold of arousal to uncertainty, they should show impaired discrimination on the affective scenes but not necessarily on the neutral scenes; the uninhibited children should perform equally well on both sets. This prediction was affirmed, for more inhibited than uninhibited children made more errors on the affective than on the neutral scenes (73 percent vs. 36 percent, $\chi^2 = 5.4$, $p < .05$). Moreover, 40 percent of the inhibited but only 10 percent of the uninhibited children showed both indexes of reaction to stress (i.e., more errors on the second story and more errors on the affective pictures). These procedures may also help to discriminate between temperamentally inhibited children who have become more sociable by 7½ years and temperamentally uninhibited children. Although a small number of formerly inhibited children showed sociable behavior with the examiner and peers, all made more errors on the affect than on the neutral scenes. By contrast, neither of the two formerly uninhibited girls whose external demeanor had become timid and shy showed an increase in errors on the second recall story or an excess of affect over neutral erorrs on the discrimination task.

The Physiology of Inhibition

As noted earlier, the differences in approach versus withdrawal behavior among closely related strains of animals are often correlated with physiological differences that suggest greater limbic arousal in the timid animals. As Adamec and Stark-Adamec (chap. 5, in this vol.) note, defensive cats show larger evoked potentials in the ventromedial hypothalamus following stimulation of the basomedial amygdala, implying greater transsynaptic excitability in this circuit, which presumably mediates defensive withdrawal in the animals. If these neural effects are also characteristic of inhibited children, there should be more signs of arousal in the peripheral systems that originate in the amygdala and hypothalamus in inhibited than in uninhibited children. Three of these systems are the sympathetic chain, the corpus striatum and its influence on skeletal muscles, and the hypothalamic-pituitary-adrenal axis.

Five potential indexes of sympathetic activity are a high and stable heart rate, acceleration of heart rate to cognitive stress, pupillary dilation, and total norepinephrine activity. At the first three evaluations (21 months, 4 years, 5½ years) inhibited children had higher and more stable heart rates than uninhibited children did. They also showed a tendency for cardiac acceleration across a series of cognitive tests, which Cohen (1974) suggests is an index of sympathetic tone on the heart (for a similar difference between introverts and extraverts, see Hinton and Craske [1977] and Giordani, Manuck, and Farmer [1981]). At 5½ years, the inhibited children had larger pupillary dilations to cognitive tasks and greater norepinephrine activity, as indexed by mass fragmentography of a urine sample obtained at the end of a laboratory session (see Reznick et al. 1986).

Additionally, Coster (1986) has found that inhibited children show less variability in the acoustic quality of their vocal utterances under cognitive stress, suggesting greater skeletal muscle tension in the vocal cords and laryngeal muscles (see Fridlund et al. 1986). Finally, radioimmunoassay of salivary cortisol at 5½ years revealed higher levels among inhibited children, both at home in the early morning as well as in the laboratory.

When we averaged the standard scores for eight peripheral physiological variables gathered at 5½ years of age to create an aggregate index of limbic arousal (heart rate, heart-rate variability, pupillary dilation, norepinephrine, cortisol level at home, cortisol level in the laboratory, variability of vocal utterences under cognitive stress, and the standard deviation of the fundamental frequency values of vocal utterances), there was a substantial, positive relation with the concurrent index of inhibition at 5½ years, $r = .58$, $p < .01$, as well as with the original index of inhibition gathered at 21 months, $r = .70, p < .001$ (see Kagan, Reznick, and Snidman 1987).

The correlation between the aggregate index of limbic-hypothalamic excitability and inhibited behavior and the stability of both behavior and heart rate and heart-rate variability suggest that more inhibited than uninhibited children may be born with a lower threshold of limbic-hypothalamic activation to unfamiliarity and challenge and, consequently, react with quieting and withdrawal to the slight increases in uncertainty that do not usually generate limbic-hypothalamic activity in the average child (for relevant data on adults, see Williams [1983], and, for comparable data on monkeys, Suomi [1987]).

Although there was a positive correlation between inhibited behavior and each of the eight peripheral physiological variables composing the aggregate index, the individual correlations were modest, ranging from .2 to .3. This fact suggests that factors local to each of the stress circuits exert considerable control over the level of activity in that circuit (for similar findings, see Kelley, Brown, and Shaffer [1970], Curtis et al. [1978], Fahrenberg et al. [1986], Nesse et al. [1985], Cubicciotti et al. [1986], and Levis and Smith [1987]). Indeed, the correlation between siblings for resting heart rate is modest—only .3 (Ditto 1987). Behavioral inhibition is not caused by high sympathetic tone or greater cortisol secretion. Rather, both the behavior and the peripheral physiological reactions are consequences of amygdala-hypothalamic arousal to unfamiliarity and challenge (see Gray 1982). Thus, there need not be a high correlation between behavioral signs of defensiveness and separate physiological reactions, even though specific sites in limbic structures and the hypothalamus mediate both reactions.

This suggestion is supported by the fact that changes in behavior over time are accompanied by appropriate changes in heart rate. For each of the 41

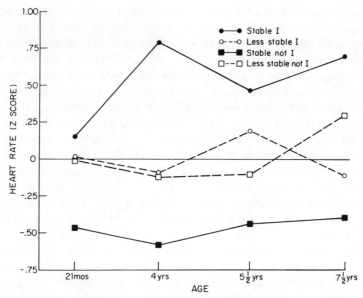

Fig. 3. Mean heart rate for four groups of children on each assessment.

children seen at 7½ years of age, we computed a z-score for the single index of inhibition obtained at each of the four assessments and a z-score for each child's heart rate at each age. We examined the four indexes of inhibited behavior for each child and determined whether that child (1) remained above the median ($z > 0$) for inhibited behavior at all four ages, (2) was below the median for inhibited behavior at all four ages, (3) showed a generally linear increase in inhibited behavior over the four assessments, or (4) showed a generally linear decrease in inhibition over the four ages. This categorization yielded 12 originally inhibited children who remained inhibited or showed increasing inhibited behavior over time and 10 inhibited children who showed a decrease in the magnitude of the behavioral index across the four longitudinal assessments. Among the original group of uninhibited children, 12 remained uninhibited or showed an increase in uninhibited behavior, while seven showed an increase in inhibited behavior over the four assessments.

We also classified each child's four heart-rate indexes as either (1) above the median for heart rate at all four ages or showing an increase in heart rate over the four assessments with a final heart rate at 7½ years above the median or (2) showing a decrease in heart rate over the four ages or remaining below the median heart-rate value at all four ages.

Figure 3 shows the mean heart rate (z-score) for the four groups of children at each of the four ages. Among the inhibited children, 11 of the 12 who remained inhibited showed a consistently high or an increasing heart rate over the four assessments, in contrast to three of 10 inhibited children who become less inhibited over time. Among the uninhibited children, five of seven who became more inhibited had high or rising heart rates, in contrast to three of 12 uninhibited children who remained uninhibited. When we contrasted the consistently innhibited or changing uninhibited children, on the one hand, with the consistently uninhibited and changing inhibited children, on the other, with respect to heart-rate pattern, the resulting χ^2 was 6.2 ($p < .05$). At every age, the consistently inhibited children had significantly higher heart rates than the consistently uninhibited children, and these two groups had, respectively, the highest and lowest heart rates. For the two groups that were less consistent over time, the inhibited children who became less inhibited showed a drop in heart rate between 5½ and 7½ years, while the uninhibited children who became inhibited showed a rise in heart rate over those two ages. (these differences were not statistically significant). This finding suggests that heart rate tracks behavior. As an uninhibited child becomes more inhibited, his or her heart rate rises, and, as an inhibited child becomes less inhibited, his or her heart rate becomes lower, implying that changes in the psychological state of the child are producing the correlated variation in both behavior and heart rate.

We do not conceive of the psychological or physiological states mediating inhibited or uninhibited behavior as essences, even though our constructs have that implication. Unfortunately, the use of noun phrases like "inhibited to the unfamiliar" tempts readers to conceive of the referent as a unitary, stable characteristic—like the shape of the moon—rather than as a family of related states that are malleable to change and actualized in different forms, depending on the procedural probe (for an example of habituation of the pituitary-adrenal response to stress in rats, see Armario et al. [1986]). Although we believe that some infants are born with a low threshold for limbic-hypo-thalamic arousal to challenge and novelty, a benevolent, minimally stressful environment over the first few years can reduce the likelihood that such children will develop inhibited behaviors. Further, the power of a specific situation to generate limbic-hypothalamic arousal and inhibited behavior varies with development. The entrance of an unfamiliar adult when a child is in an unfamiliar room is a powerful incentive at 2 years of age but a poor one at 4. An unfamiliar child is a much better incentive, and at 7 years a group of unfamiliar peers is necessary to generate sufficient uncertainty to produce the behavioral differences between inhibited and uninhibited children.

Final Speculations

In this last section, I consider some frankly speculative ideas that flow from the data summarized.

Preparedness and Inhibition

First, the concept of preparedness, a dividend of the recent influence of biology and ethology on the social sciences, offers an explanation of inhibited behavior that contrasts with the traditional emphasis on conditioning. "Preparedness" refers to biological structures and processes, present at birth or products of maturation, biasing the organism to react to events in particular ways. Newborn infants, for example, orient to visual arrays with a great deal of contour; newborn goslings follow moving objects. Although the idea of preparedness was proposed to explain behavioral differences between species, not intraspecific variation, this concept can enhance our understanding of the emergence and maintenance of temperamental inhibition. Without saying so, Adamec and Stark-Adamec (chap. 5, in this vol.) imply that defensive and aggressive cats are prepared to issue different behaviors to novelty.

Encounters with unexpected or novel events, such as the entrance of a stranger or a visit to an unfamiliar school or home, are frequent experiences in the lives of most children. All observers of young children have noted that the usual, prepared reaction to such events is a brief period of quiet staring at the source of unfamiliarity and seeking proximity to a familiar person. However, a small group of children (we estimate about 10 percent) are biased by their physiology to become extremely quiet and, sometimes, distressed to a much larger proportion of such events than are most children. For the former, the prepared reaction to novelty that is characteristic of all children is exaggerated. We believe this exaggerated reaction is a result of lower thresholds of excitability in selected limbic-hypothalamic sites. But, even if this particular explanation proves to be incorrect, it is useful to contrast it with the traditional account that relys on learning.

Psychologists used to explain consistent withdrawal and shyness in a 5-year-old by suggesting that these behaviors began as conditioned responses. Interactions with certain people or encounters with events led to an unpleasant state of fear or pain, and the child avoided such events in order to reduce the unpleasant state. The act of withdrawal was reinforced by reduction or removal of the unpleasant state.

Consider the following concrete, common phenomenon. A 2-year-old enters an unfamiliar room with his mother but stays close to her for 20 minutes rather than exploring the room full of attractive toys, as a majority of children would have done. The traditional psychological explanation interprets the act of remaining proximal to the mother as an instrumentally conditioned response. In the past, the child happened to remain close to the mother in an unfamiliar place, and that act led to a state that was reinforcing. Presumably, the reinforcing state of affairs was a reduction in the degree of uncertainty or fear, although that extra statement is not always present in modern behavioral essays.

A second possibility is that the behavior is a classically conditioned response. The novelty of the room is the unconditioned stimulus that creates a brain state that elicits inhibition of exploration and seeking a target of attachment. The problem with this explanation is that novelty is not a specific external stimulus but a relation between an external array and the child's schemata. Further, it is not clear what the conditioned stimulus might be in such a paradigm, for there is no stable object or feature in the room that could become a signal for future inhibition in other unfamiliar places.

The explanation that relies on individual differences in preparedness for inhibition holds that an unfamiliar room, which is not a threatening stimulus for most children, produces simultaneously both amygdala-hypothalamic arousal and inhibition of action in a small proportion of children. Hence, these children stay close to the mother and become quiet. It is possible, of course, that, although the initial tendency to become quiet and to remain proximal to the mother is a prepared response, repetition of these behaviors over a period of years might be maintained by the principles of instrumental conditioning. Further, instrumental learning might be involved in the attempts of older inhibited children to control their state of fear and inhibit their usual inclination to withdraw. As the child successfully inhibits uncertainty and avoidance and, instead, initiates interaction with others, the uncertainty is extinguished, and, as has been shown, some of the peripheral physiological signs can disappear.

Recent work on the neurophysiological circuits involved in classically conditioned responses forms a link between traditional conditioning theory and the idea of biologic preparedness. Rather than manipulate the parameters of the unconditioned and conditioned stimuli (as investigators did 30 years earlier), the new scientists use lesions and electrical recordings to study the circuits and structures of the nervous system that mediate the classically conditioned response. For example, Thompson and his colleagues (Thompson et al. 1987) suggest that two different parallel circuits are involved in the conditioning of the nictitating membrane reflex to a tone. The conditioned stimulus acquires the power to elicit both the state of fear and the skeletal motor response. These two links are regarded as separate, although the first facilitates the second. This conception differs from earlier accounts that assumed a linear process in which the conditioned stimulus first acquired the capacity to elicit a central state (e.g., fear), which, subsequently, elicited the reflex.

The more important change wrought by the modern work is the omission of any reference to reinforcement or reward. The deepest philosophical assumption in conditioning theory is that there is a purpose for a response and a goal to be obtained for its display. It is assumed, implicitly, that organisms will not issue a response if there is no advantage to be gained from the action. Traditional theorists wrote that a reflex (e.g., leg withdrawal to shock) reduced the unpleasant state of fear or pain produced by the unconditioned stimulus. The new theorists see no need for such language. They postulate that both the physiological and the behavioral phenomena occur because of the way in which the nervous system is constructed. A more satisfying explanation will have to involve propositions stated in biological language, not propositions that rely on concepts such as effort, reinforcement, pleasure, or pain.

This profound change in philosophical presuppositions is analogous to the change in the sixteenth and seventeenth centuries that followed the use of mathematical descriptions of physical phenomena, such as the velocity of falling bodies. These mathematical descriptions replaced explanations that relied on concepts referring to obscure forces imposed from without or residing within the object. As the neurosciences gradually move into areas that have been primarily psychological, the substitution of descriptions with biological language for sentences containing terms like "motive," "pleasure," "pain," and "reinforcement" will become more frequent. I do not claim this development is to be celebrated; I suggest only that use of physiological descriptions will alter the philosophical assumptions and everyday conceptions of these psychological phenomena, just as the language of artificial intelligence is changing the community's view of human thought by bleaching it of emotion and exaggerating its propositional and logical qualities.

A Possible Role for Norepinephrine

A second speculation involves the potential influence of central norepinephrine. Inhibited children who also had a consistently high and stable heart rate had the greatest number of specific fears at every age (e.g., large animals, the dark, violent shows on television). Even though this fact may seem intuitively reasonable, its explanation is not immediately obvious. One possibility is that inhibited children have higher tonic levels of limbic-hypothalamic arousal that facilitate the conditioning of a fear reaction toward specific objects or events. One potential basis for the greater arousal is higher levels of central norepinephrine, most of which is produced by the locus ceruleus, located near the pons in the brain stem (Redmond 1986). One indirect index of central norepinephrine is detection thresholds for sensory events because studies with animals indicate that stimulation of the locus ceruleus is followed by suppression of background activity of neurons in sensory areas and, as a consequence, enhancement of the signal-to-noise ratio (Aston-Jones 1985; Segal 1985).

Because Eysenck's theory of introversion-extraversion was based on the premise of greater cortical arousal in introverts, investigators following that tradition compared the performances of introverts and extraverts on perceptual vigilance tasks. In some of these studies, introverts performed better when they had to detect an infrequent, and often subtle, signal embedded in a background. For example, following a light signal, introverts detected low-frequency auditory signals (500 hertz) better than extraverts, although there was no difference between the groups in detection of 8,000-hertz sounds (Stelmack and Campbell 1974). In a later study, Stelmack, Achorn, and Michaud (1977) reported that introverts showed a larger amplitude of the N1-P2 component of the auditory-evoked response to 500-hertz but not to 8,000-hertz tones. Additionally, Hockey (1986) reported better performance for introverts than extraverts when subjects had to detect the infrequent occurrence of a slight increase in the brightness of a circle on a black background. Because extremely shy behavior with peers is a central characteristic of inhibited children, it is likely that a proportion of them will become introverted adults. If the superior detection performance of introverts is due to higher levels of central norepinephrine, it is at least possible that inhibited children, too, are secreting more central norepinephrine than uninhibited children are. As a consequence, they may be more likely to establish a conditioned fear reaction to unfamiliar events. It is important to note that levels of dopamine-beta hydroxylase (DBH), an enzyme mediating the final metabolic step in the production of norepinephrine, is controlled by a single gene locus (Dunnette and Weinshilboum 1982 and that DBH activity is highly heritable (Weinshilboum 1979).

Kindling and Inhibition

A third speculation is prompted by the fact that there was a noticeable change in the consistency of inhibited and uninhibited behavior between 5½ and 7½ years of age. Children who remained inhibited at 7½ years were much more consistent across all assessment contexts than they had been two years earlier. And it was the consistently inhibited children who showed the physiological signs noted earlier. Some theorists have reported that there is more robust preservation of personality characteristics after age 6 than before school entrance (see Kagan and Moss 1962). This fact invites the hypothesis of biological changes occurring between 5 and 7 years of age that mediate stabilization of the qualities of inhibition and lack of inhibition.

One of the processes that might contribute to the stabilization of inhibited behavior involves the concept of kindling (Adamec and Stark-Adamec 1986; Post, Rubinow, and Ballenger 1986). Briefly, a short daily burst of electrical stimulation to the amygdala of rats or cats eventually leads to permanent sensitization of this structure. After 30–60 days of daily 1-second bursts of stimulation, animals begin to show spontaneous limbic convulsions even though the electrical stimulation has ceased. Consider a speculation based on generalizing these facts from the animal laboratory to inhibited children. If inhibited children possess a more excitable circuit from the amygdala to the hypothalamus, a frightening environmental event might function as a kindling stimulus. The anxiety-arousing events might include thunderstorms, marital quarrels, attacks from a sibling or older child, or violent television shows. Such events, occurring several times a week over 5–6 years, might kindle the limbic system of inhibited children and make them susceptible to spontaneous attacks of anxiety. The children who had remained behaviorally inhibited at 7½ years were the only ones likely to display unprovoked bouts of anxiety. On a particular day, a child might refuse to go to school or a party or be reluctant to go upstairs to the bedroom at night. Many adult panic patients report that they were shy, timid, inhibited children, and a sudden panic attack in a department store might be regarded as analogous to a spontaneous limbic seizure in a kindled animal.

Final Comment

I do not suggest that all newborn infants born with an easily excited limbic-hypothalamic circuit will grow up to be inhibited children. The vulnerability to inhibited behavior requires environmental stressors in order to actualize the temperamental disposition. Some possible stressors include hospitalization early in life, chronic parental quarreling, a long illness in a family member, or economic privation. These stressors were not frequent in our sample. However, in both our longitudinal cohorts, inhibited children were more likely to be later born, and uninhibited children were more likely to be firstborn. This fact suggests that, for infants born with a biology favoring the development of inhibition, the presence of an older sibling, who unexpectedly seizes a toy and teases or yells at the infant, might provide the daily stress necessary to actualize the original biologic quality. However, firstborn children possessing the temperamental characteristics associated with inhibition but living in a minimally stressful environment are less likely to become behaviorally inhibited during later childhood.[1]

One reason there are not more robust generalizations from many years of study of the relation between family practices and child behavior is that some psychologists have been indifferent to the infant's temperament and failed to evaluate the interaction between the infant's temperamental qualities and parental behavior with respect to some delimited behavioral profile. The suggestion that later-born status is associated with inhibited behavior only for children born with amygdala-hypothalamic excitability is one example of this principle. Sackett et al. (1981) have shown that closely related strains of macaque monkey infants react differently after release from an initial 6 months of isolation. Rhesus monkeys emerge from the isolation showing extreme social withdrawal, while crabeaters do not, even though crabeaters show some behavioral consequences of the early isolation. Human infants, too, react dif-

1. It is of interest that Adamec and Stark-Adamec (chap. 5, in this vol.) report that a kitten who is potentially vulnerable to becoming a defensive cat is unlikely as an adult to be fearful with rats if it witnesses the killing of rats during the final months of the first year.

ferently to the same potentially stressful exogenous events. As psychologists begin to assess the interaction between experience and temperament, they will come closer to a synthesis of inherent biological states and environmental events. A similar synthesis has been unusually productive for evolutionary biology.

References

Adamec, R. E., and Stark-Adamec, C. 1986. Limbic hyperfunction, limbic epilepsy, and interictal behavior. In *The limbic system,* ed. B. K. Doane and K. E. Livingston, 129–45. New York: Raven.

Armario, A.; Lopez-Calderon, A.; Jolin, T.; and Balasch, J. 1986. Response of anterior pituitary hormones to chronic stress: The specificity of adaptation. *Neuroscience and Biobehavioral Reviews* 10:245–50.

Aston-Jones, G. 1985. Behavioral functions of locus coeruleus derived from cellular attributes. *Physiological Psychology* 13:118–26.

Blanchard, R. T.; Flannelly, K. J.; and Blanchard, D. C. 1986. Defensive behaviors of laboratory and wild Rattus Norvegicus. *Journal of Comparative Psychology* 100:101–07.

Cohen, D. H., 1974. The neural pathways and informational flow mediating a conditioned autonomic response. In *Limbic and autonomic nervous system research,* ed. L. V. DiCara, 223–75. New York: Plenum.

Conley, J. J. 1985. Longitudinal stability of personality traits: A multi-trait multimethod multi-occasion analysis. *Journal of Personality and Social Psychology* 49:1266–82.

Cooper, D. O.; Schmidt, D. E.; and Barrett, R. J. 1983. Strain specific cholinergic changes in response to stress. *Pharmacology, Biochemistry and Behavior* 19:457–62.

Coster, W. 1986. Aspects of voice and conversation in behaviorally inhibited and uninhibited children. Ph.D. diss., Harvard University.

Cranach, B. V.; Grote-Dham, R.; Huffner, U.; Marte, F.; Reisbeck, G.; and Mittelstadt, M. 1978. Das social Gehemmte im Kindergarten. *Praxis der Kinderpsychologie und Kinderpsychiatrie* 27:167–79.

Csanyi, V., and Gervai, J. 1986. Behavior-genetic analysis of the paradise fish (macropodus opercularis): 2. Passive avoidance learning in inbred strains. *Behavior Genetics* 16:553–57.

Cubicciotti, D. D.; Mendoza, S. P.; Mason, W. A.; and Sassenrath, E. N. 1986. Differences between *Saimiri sciureus* and *Callicebus moloch* in physiological responsiveness. *Journal of Comparative Psychology* 100:385–91.

Curtis, G. C.; Nesse, R.; Buxton, M.; and Lippman, D. 1978. Anxiety and plasma cortisol at the crest of the circadian cycle. *Psychosomatic Medicine* 40:368–78.

Dantzer, R., and Mormede, P. 1985. Stress in domestic animals. In *Animal stress,* ed. G. P. Moberg, 81–95. Bethesda, Md.: American Physiological Society.

Ditto, W. B. 1987. Sibling similarities in cardiovascular reactivity to stress. *Psychophysiology* 24:353–60.

Doerr, H. O., and Hokanson, J. E. 1965. The relation between heart rate and performance in children. *Journal of Personality and Social Psychology* 2:70–76.

Dunn, L. T., and Everitt, B. J. 1988. Double dissociations of the effects of amygdala and insular cortex lesions on conditioned taste aversion, passive avoidance, and neophobia in the rat using the excitotoxin Ibotenic acid. *Behavioral Neuroscience* 102:3–23.

Dunnette, J., and Weinshilboum, R. 1982. Family studies of plasma Dopamine-beta hydroxylase. *American Journal of Human Genetics* 34:84–99.

Fahrenberg, J.; Foerster, F.; Schneider, H. J.; Muller, W.; and Myrtek, M. 1986. Predictability of individual differences in activation processes in a field setting based on laboratory measures. *Psychophysiology* 23:323–33.

Floderus-Myrhed, B.; Pedersen, N.; and Rasmuson, I. 1980. Assessment of heritability for personality based on a short form of the Eysenck Personality Inventory. *Behavior Genetics* 10:153–62.

Fox, N. A., and Davidson, R. J. 1987. EEG asymmetry in ten month old infants in response to approach of a stranger and maternal separation. *Developmental Psychology* 23:233–40.

Fridlund, A. J.; Hatfield, M. E.; Cottam, G. L.; and Fowler, S. C. 1986. Anxiety and striate-muscle activation: Evidence from the electromyographic pattern analysis. *Journal of Abnormal Psychology* 95:228–36.

Garcia-Coll, C.; Kagan, J.; and Reznick, J. S. 1984. Behavioral inhibition in young children. *Child Development* 55:1005–19.

Gellhorn, E. 1967. *Principles of autonomic somatic integration.* Minneapolis: University of Minnesota Press.

Gersten, M. 1986. The contribution of temperament to behavior in natural contexts. Ed.D. diss., Harvard University, Graduate School of Education.

Giordani, B.; Manuck, S. B.; and Farmer, J. C. 1981. Stability of behaviorally induced heart rate changes in children after one week. *Child Development* 52:533–37.

Goddard, M. E., and Beilharz, R. G. 1985. A multi-variate analysis of the genetics of fearfulness in potential guide dogs. *Behavior Genetics* 15:69–89.

Gray, J. A. 1982. *The neuropsychology of anxiety.* Oxford: Clarendon.

Hinton, J. W., and Craske, B. 1977. Differential effects of test stress on the heart rates of extraverts and introverts. *Biological Psychology* 5:23–28.

Hockey, R. 1986. Temperament differences in vigilance performance as a function of variations in the suitability of ambient noise level. In *The biological basis of personality and behavior,* ed. J. Strelau, F. H. Farley, and A. Gale, 2:163–71. Washington, D.C.: Hemisphere.

Jung, C. G. 1924. *Psychological types.* New York: Harcourt Brace.

Kagan, J.; Kearsley, R.; and Zelazo, P. 1978. *Infancy: Its place in human development.* Cambridge, Mass.: Harvard University Press.

Kagan, J. and Moss, H. A. 1962. *Birth to maturity.* New York: Wiley.

Kagan, J.; Reznick, J. S.; Clarke, C.; Snidman, N.; and Garcia-Coll, C. 1984. Behavioral inhibition to the unfamiliar. *Child Development* 55:2212–25.

Kagan, J.; Reznick, J. S.; and Snidman, N. 1987. The physiology and psychology of behavioral inhibition in children. *Child Development* 58:1459–73.

Kagan, J.; Reznick, J. S.; and Snidman, N. 1988. Biological bases of childhood shyness. *Science* 240:167–71.

Kelley, D.; Brown, C. C.; and Shaffer, J. W. 1970. A comparison of physiological and psychological measurements on anxious patients and normal controls. *Psychophysiology* 6:429–41.

Kling, A. S.; Lloyd, R. L.; and Perryman, K. M. 1987. Slow wave changes in amygdala to visual, auditory, and social stimuli following lesions of inferior temporal cortex in squirrel monkey (Saimiri sciureus). *Behavioral and Neural Biology* 47:54–72.

Levis, D. J. and Smith, J. E. 1987. Getting individual differences in autonomic reactivity to work for instead of against you. *Psychophysiology* 24:346–52.

Loehlin, J. C. 1982. Are personality traits differentially heritable? *Behavior Genetics* 12:417–28.

McDonald, K. 1983. Stability of individual differences in behavior in a litter of wolf cubs. *Journal of Comparative Psychology* 97:99–106.

Messer, S. B. 1968. The effect of anxiety over intellectual performance on reflective and impulsive children. Ph.D. diss., Harvard University.

Murphey, R. M.; Duarte, F. A. M.; and Penendo, M. C. T. 1980. Approachability of bovine cattle in pastures: Breed comparisons and a breed × treatment analysis. *Behavior Genetics* 10:170–81.

Nesse, R. M.; Curtis, G. C.; Thyer, B. A.; McCann, D. S.; Huber-Smith, M.; and Knopf, R. F. 1985. Endocrine and cardiovascular responses during phobic anxiety. *Psychomatic Medicine* 47:320–32.

Plomin, R. 1986. *Development, genetics and psychology.* Hillsdale, N.J.: Erlbaum.

Plomin, R., and Rowe, D. C. 1979. Genetic and environmental etiology of social behavior in infancy. *Developmental Psychology* 15:62–72.

Post, R. M.; Rubinow, D. R.; and Ballenger, J. C. 1986. Conditioning and sensitization in the longitudinal course of affective illness. *British Journal of Psychiatry* 149:191–201.

Redmond, D. E. 1986. The possible role of locus coeruleus noradrenergic activity in anxiety-panic. In *Proceedings of the 15th collegium internationale Neuro-Psychopharmacologicum Congress,* ed. W. E. Bunney, E. Costa, and S. G. Potkin, 40–42. New York: Raven.

Reznick, J. S.; Kagan, J.; Snidman, N.; Gersten, M.; Baak, K.; and Rosenberg, A. 1986. Inhibited and uninhibited behavior: A follow-up study. *Child Development* 51:660–80.

Royce, J. R. 1955. A factorial study of emotionality in the dog. *Psychological Monographs,* vol. 69, no. 22, whole no. 407.

Sackett, G. P.; Ruppenthal, G. C.; Fahrenbruch, C. H.; Holm, R. A.; and Greenough, W. T. 1981. Social isolation rearing effects in monkeys vary with genotype. *Developmental Psychology* 17:313–18.

Schneirla, T. C. 1965. Aspects of stimulation and organization in approach-withdrawal processes underlying vertebrate development. In *Advances in the study of behavior,* ed. D. S. Lehrman, R. A. Hinde, and E. Shaw, 1:1–74. New York: Academic Press.

Scott, J. P., and Fuller, J. L. 1965. *Genetics and the social behavior of the dog.* Chicago: University of Chicago Press. Reprinted as *Dog behavior: The genetic basis.* Chicago: University of Chicago Press, 1974.

Segal, M. 1985. Mechanisms of action of noradrenaline in the brain. *Physiological Psychology* 13:172–78.

Snidman, N. 1984. Behavioral restraint and the central nervous system. Ph.D. diss., University of California, Los Angeles.

Stelmack, R. M.; Achorn, E.; and Michaud, A. 1977. Extraversion and individual differences in auditory evoked response. *Psychophysiology* 14:368–74.

Stelmack, R. M., and Campbell, K. B. 1974. Extraversion and auditory sensitivity to high and low frequencies. *Perceptual and Motor Skills* 38:875–79.

Stevenson-Hinde, J.; Stillwell-Barnes, R.; and Zunz, M. 1980. Subjective assessment of rhesus monkeys over four successive years. *Primates* 21:66–82.

Strelau, J. 1985. Temperament and personality: Pavlov and beyond. In *The biological bases of personality and behavior,* ed. J. Strelau, F. H. Farley, and A. Gale, 1:25–44. Washington, D.C.: Hemisphere.

Suomi, S. J. 1987. Genetic and maternal contributions to individual differences in rhesus monkey biobehavioral development. In *Perinatal development: A psychobiological perspective,* ed. N. A. Krasnegor, E. M. Blass, M. A. Hofer, and W. P. Smotherman, 397–420. New York: Academic Press.

Thomas, A., and Chess, S. 1977. *Temperament and development.* New York: Brunner/Mazel.

Thompson, R. F.; Donegan, N. H.; Clark, G. A.; Lavond, D. G.; Lincoln, J. S.; Madden, J.; Mamoulas, L. A.; Monk, M. D.; and McCormick, D. A. 1987. Neural substrates of discrete defensive conditioned reflexes, conditioned fear states and their interaction in the rabbit. In *Classical conditioning,* ed. I. Gormezano, W. F. Prokasy, and R. F. Thompson, 3rd ed., 371–99. Hillsdale, N.J.: Erlbaum.

Weinshilboum, R. M. 1979. Catecholamine biochemical genetics in human populations. In *Neurogenetics,* ed. X. O. Breakefield, 257–82. New York: Elsevier.

Williams, R. B. 1983. Neuroendocrine response patterns and stress: Bio-behavioral mechanisms of disease. In *Perspectives on behavioral medicine: Neuroendocrine control and behavior,* ed. R. B. Williams. New York: Academic Press.

2 Behavioral Inhibition in a Normative Sample

J. Steven Reznick, Jane L. Gibbons,
Maureen O. Johnson, and Paula M. McDonough

Introduction

Contributions to this volume by Kagan (chap. 1), Snidman (chap. 3), and Gersten (chap. 4) summarize the findings from two longitudinal cohorts followed from 2 to 7 years. These children were selected as extremely inhibited or uninhibited on the basis of their behavior in a laboratory and/or in a play setting with an unfamiliar peer. Inhibited children were slower to explore unfamiliar environments, objects, or people and more likely to withdraw from unfamiliarity and remain proximal to a parent. Uninhibited children showed the opposite profile, easily exploring unfamiliar situations and approaching unfamiliar people and objects. When retested longitudinally, the two groups showed strong stability of inhibited or uninhibited behavior over time and over widely varying contexts, including laboratory, school, and home.

The present study involves a third cohort that serves to replicate previous work and to offer several important clarifications and extensions. First, we have provided considerable detail concerning the quantification of variables and their combination into a composite index of behavioral inhibition. As is evident in the present volume, several laboratories are investigating behavioral inhibition. The clear specification of dependent variables and theoretical constructs is necessary to facilitate communication and scientific progress. Second, we have compared the extreme group strategy described above with a normative approach, attempting to replicate and extend previous findings. Our sample was not recruited to overrepresent extremes but was large enough to allow comparison of extreme groups and a normative sample. Finally, the current test battery included several popular parent-report temperament as-

This research was supported by a grant from the John D. and Catherine T. MacArthur Foundation Network on the Transition from Infancy to Childhood. We appreciate editorial assistance from Jerome Kagan, Helen Snively, and two anonymous reviewers. Mail reprint requests to J. Steven Reznick, Department of Psychology, P.O. Box 11A Yale Station, New Haven, CT, 06520-7447.

sessments and allowed us to explore the relation between behavioral inhibition and other dimensions of temperament and to compare the relative strength of predictions that are based on laboratory assessments and parent reports.

These data were gathered as part of the Individual Differences Project sponsored by the New England Node of the John D. and Catherine T. MacArthur Foundation's Network on the Transition from Infancy to Childhood. The collaboration included Edward Mueller, Catherine Snow, Malcolm Watson, and Dennis Wolf. The longitudinal research project focused on personality, cognitive development, and language, and the present report summarizes those parts of the corpus of data that are relevant to behavioral inhibition.

We will first describe the methodology of the study and then present the results on behavioral inhibition organized into three themes: (1) the operational definition of inhibition, (2) replication of previous work, and (3) extension beyond previous work.

Methodology

Subjects

The orginal sample consisted of 100 infants from the greater Boston area assessed within 2 weeks of their fourteenth month. Ninety-one children returned to the laboratory for a second assessment at 20 months, and 76 were retested at 32 months. The children who eventually dropped out of the study differed from the participants on two demographic characteristics: children from these families had lower birth weight, $t(75) = 2.40, p < .05$, and their fathers were younger, $t(58) = 2.10, p < .05$. In addition, they differed in inhibition classification as described below.

The sample was recruited through a mailing to parents of children born in Boston hospitals. This recruitment procedure produced predictable biases. The sample consisted of predominantly firstborn (66 percent), Caucasian (97 percent), full-term (91 percent) children of older and relatively well-educated parents with higher-status occupations (see table 1). While there was considerable range for each of these factors, the sample could hardly be considered "normative" in any demographic sense. However, because the children were not selected on any behavioral quality, our expectation was that the sample would be normally distributed for inhibition and other characteristics of temperament, as compared to the extreme groups recruited in our previous research.

Procedures at 14 and 20 Months

Each child participated in a 90-minute laboratory test battery at 14 months. This lengthy session was possible because the battery included a major change

Table 1: Demographic Characteristics of the Sample

	Mean	Standard Deviation	Range
Birth weight (pounds)	7.61	1.24	5.25–12.75
Age of mother	30.16	4.11	19.5–35
Age of father	31.46	4.85	20–49
Socioeconomic status (Hollingshead)	52.37	12.49	4–66
Day care (hours per week at 14 months)	6.06	11.19	0–40

of location every 20 minutes and a range of different contexts. The few children who became tired or upset completed the battery on a second session conducted within 1 week of the first. The 91 children who returned at 20 months participated in a similar battery with minor changes to age-appropriate materials. During and following both batteries, parents completed several interviews and forms, and additional data were collected at a visit to the child's home following both assessments.

Each of the collaborators was interested in a different aspect of behavior; this paper focuses on the six episodes relevant to inhibition.

1. *Warm-up.* On arrival in the laboratory, the parent and child were escorted into a small testing room. The experimenter urged the parent to "just play with your child and help him or her feel comfortable," and the ensuing behavior was videotaped for 5 minutes.

2. *Mask.* The experimenter allowed the child to play with a set of toys in the center of the room for a few minutes and then hung a large mask of a dog's face in the corner of the testing room. This procedure was used at 14 months only.

3. *Free Play.* The parent and child entered a large playroom. The parent was instructed to sit on the couch and respond to the child but to avoid initiating play. The room was equipped with a drum and drumsticks, two large balls, three large building blocks, a stuffed cloth horse, a train large enough to sit on, and a pop-up "Oscar the Grouch" toy. The procedure lasted 10 minutes.

4. *Interaction with Stranger.* At the end of free play, an unfamiliar female adult entered the room and sat quietly for 1 minute. She then began to play with an attractive truck containing small plastic dogs. If the child had not approached after a second minute, the stranger began to describe her own activity, but without addressing the child directly. If the child still had not approached after a third minute, the stranger offered the child an object without making eye contact and attempted to invite interaction by including some directives in her monologue.

5. *Alarm.* The experimenter reentered the room and allowed the child to play with a set of toys in the center of the room for a few minutes. While the child was playing, the experimenter turned on an alarm clock on the side of the testing room.

6. *Robot*. When the child had resumed playing, the experimenter revealed a large robot constructed from tin cans and light bulbs, which was stored in a cabinet in the corner of the room, and invited the child to touch it. This procedure was used at 20 months only.

Procedures at 32 Months

At 32 months, 76 of the children returned to the laboratory to participate in playgroups (for details, see McDonough 1986). Attrition was relatively high because assessments were conducted during the summer. The presence of young later-born siblings in the home also limited participation by some families.

A preliminary index of inhibition based on behavior at 14 and 20 months was used to divide the children into terciles, by gender. Each playgroup contained three children of the same gender, but each from a different tercile of the inhibition index. During the 30-minute play session, the three children were free to play with a variety of age-appropriate toys in the large laboratory room they had visited at 14 and 20 months. Parents were present but were asked to refrain from directing or playing with the children and spent the 30 minutes filling out forms.

Dependent Variables

Two easily coded behavioral domains in which 14- and 20-month-olds can express vulnerability to uncertainty are approach/withdrawal and emotional distress. All infants could change their location by crawling or walking and so regulate proximity to familiar or unfamiliar events. In the situations in which the child entered an unfamiliar place (Warm-up and Free Play), we coded three variables that captured their tendency to approach or withdraw: latency to leave the parent, latency to touch an object, and percentage of time within arm's reach of the parent. In the situations in which an unfamiliar event occurred after the child was settled in a room, we coded whether the child retreated to the parent, latency to interact with the event, and, if the episode was long enough, percentage of time within arm's reach of the parent. In each situation, infants could also display uncertainty emotionally: a more inhibited child is more likely to cry and fret, and presence of negative affect during each episode was coded on a present/absent basis. For theoretical clarity, we will keep the approach/withdrawal and emotional variables separate.

Videotapes of each 14- and 20-month laboratory session were coded for these behaviors. Table 2 lists the variables derived from each session. Censored data (e.g., when a child never left the parent or never touched the event or a toy) were replaced using the length of the particular episode as a substitute for the latency. Reliability of coding for each variable was determined by

Table 2: Episodes and Variables at 14 and 20 Months

| | Dependent Variable | | | | |
| | Approach/Withdrawal | | | | Emotion |
Episode	Leave Parent (Seconds)	Touch Toy or Event (Seconds)	Retreat (Yes or No)	Proximal Parent (%)	Negative Affect (Yes or No)
Warm-up	X	X		X	X
Mask (14-month only)		X	X		X
Free Play	X	X		X	X
Interaction with Stranger		X	X	X	X
Alarm		X	X		X
Robot (20-month only)		X	X		X

having a second person recode six of the sessions at 14 months and eight of the sessions at 20 months. Interrater correlations were extremely high at both ages. For latency to leave parent or touch toy or event, the correlations approached 1.00, with only one disagreement greater than 7 seconds at each age. For percentage of time proximal to parent, the correlations were somewhat lower, ranging from $r = .78$ to $r = .99$, but the disagreements were greater than 10 percent in only three cases. Correlations were generally lower owing to the attenuated range of this variable. Finally, negative affect and retreat were coded dichotomously as present or absent. Negative affect was coded at 14 and 20 months for four episodes, at 14 months for Mask, and at 20 months for Robot. For these 10 coding opportunities, both coders agreed on all cases for seven episode and had one disagreement on three episodes. Retreat was coded at 14 and 20 months for two episodes, at 14 months for Mask, and at 20 months for Robot. For these six coding opportunities, both coders agreed on all cases for four episodes, had one disagreement on one episode, and had two disagreements on two episodes.

The playgroup context at 32 months was also unfamiliar, but the increased sophistication of the children plus the presence of peers evoked additional forms of inhibited and uninhibited behavior. The children's behavior in the playgroups was coded live as well as from videotapes. The live coding, which allowed a flexibility of observation not possible with videotape, was done by three trained experimenters who used counter/timer boxes to code latency to leave the parent, touch a toy, approach another child, and enter the 6-foot-long plastic tunnel and duration of staring at another child and proximity to the parent while not playing with a toy. Videotapes were coded for frequency of approaches to another child, entering another child's territory (defined as the space within arm's length of a child), seizing an object from another child, and entering the tunnel. Additionally, the total time in social interaction with another child was quantified. We also coded for negative affect, but the peer play context did not evoke obvious negative affect from any child.

It was not possible to assess intercoder reliability for the seven live-coded variables. However, the videotapes were checked for accuracy of these latencies and durations. Previous studies using the same coding procedures suggest that the reliabilities for these variables can range from .66 to .99 (Garcia-Coll, Kagan, and Reznick 1984; Kagan et al. 1984; Reznick et al. 1986). Reliability for the variables coded from videotapes was assessed by having a second coder quantify data for 12 children. The average intercoder reliability correlation was .92.

Definition of Inhibition

" 'When *I* use a word,' Humpty Dumpty said in rather a scornful tone, 'it means just what I choose it to mean—neither more nor less' " (Carroll 1872). And so it should be with "inhibition." We chose this term to represent the construct of interest, and not "shyness," "fearfulness," or "timidity," because it seems to have fewer misleading evaluative connotations. Our theoretical definition of inhibition emphasizes vulnerability to the uncertainty caused by unfamiliar events that cannot be assimilated easily. We have operationally defined inhibition as specific behaviors in specific contexts. For example, in cohort 1, recruited at 21 months, we observed children in six episodes—Warm-up, Free Play, Interaction with a Stranger, Reaction to an Unfamiliar Event, Reaction to the Experimenter's Request to Perform a Task, and Separation from the Mother (for details, see Garcia-Coll et al. 1984). In each episode, we coded negative emotion, proximity to parent, latency to approach, and cessation of play and formed an inhibition index based on the cumulative frequency of these variables.

In cohort 2, recruited at 31 months, we observed children in a play setting with a peer and coded latency to play, proximity to parent, number of approaches to the peer, and reactions to approach as well as general negative affect. There was also an episode with a stranger that was coded as described above (for details, see Snidman 1984). As in cohort 1, the index of inhibition was based on the cumulative frequency of these behaviors.

Similar episodes and variables are available in the present study so we should be able to obtain a comparable index. However, the first question that arises is how to combine episodes and variables to obtain that index. Although this might seem like a simple mathematical question, it is actually an important conceptual issue because our analyses suggest that the equation used to calculate the index of inhibition can affect subsequent results and conclusions and hence is of theoretical significance. In addition, because several laboratories are currently investigating inhibition, it is important to specify an operational definition that clearly defines specific variables and describes how they are measured and combined to form a composite index of inhibition.

Aggregate across Situations or across Variables?

Given the list of variables that theory suggests should be relevant for behavioral inhibition (table 2), our goal is to combine these variables into a composite that reflects each child's level of inhibition and tracks the preservation of inhibition over time. Many episodes yield variables with the same name; hence, one option is to aggregate by combining these across the episodes and calculate an aggregate score for each. These "supervariables" are then averaged to form an inhibition composite. An alternative is to combine different variables within each episode to get a value for each episode and then combine episodes into an inhibition composite.

These two approaches are very similar, but each has different advantages. In the former case, the average score for each dependent variable should be more reliable than any single score because it reflects the occurrence of that variable in several contexts (episodes). In the second approach, each episode is regarded as unique, and so similarly named dependent variables from different episodes have different meanings. For example, "latency to approach" has a different meaning when the object being approached is a mask, a stranger, or an alarm clock. (Note that, for negative affect, we coded only one variable per episode; hence the two strategies are identical.)

To compare the utility of these approaches, we calculated the two composites. In the "variable" composite, an inhibited child was one who was inhibited on many variables; in the "episode" composite, an inhibited child was one who was inhibited in many episodes. There was an extremely high correlation between these two different composites at 14 months ($r = .89$) and 20 months ($r = .93$), suggesting that the choice of one approach over the other is not highly critical. However, the stability correlations reflecting preservation of inhibition across age were slightly higher for the episode composite: the average r was .31 for the variable composite and .40 for the episode composite. We suspect that this difference is due to the fact that the variable composite tends to weight dependent variables that occur in only a few situations as strongly as dependent variables that occur in all situations. Thus, for both theoretical and empirical reasons, we performed all subsequent analyses on composites that were based on the pooled dependent variables within each episode (i.e., the episode composite), except for the negative affect composite, which was based on the single variable aggregated across all episodes.

Including All or Some Variables

The next question concerns which variables should be included in the inhibition score for an episode. In some circumstances, all the theoretically relevant variables within an episode are highly intercorrelated, and their mean represents an obvious and compelling composite. For example, when a cohort contains children sampled to represent extreme groups, we expect that inhibited children will show some degree of each sign of inhibition and that uninhibited children will show none of these signs. However, with an unselected sample, children who are neither exremely inhibited nor extremely uninhibited (70–80 percent of the sample by our estimate) will probably show some degree of some signs. Correlations will be high across those signs that tend to co-occur, but co-occurrence is not a prerequisite for diagnosticity. For example, people report feeling sick when they have a fever or a sore throat and a cough. Sore throats and coughs tend to co-occur (i.e., are positively correlated), but they are not necessarily better predictors of feeling sick than is the presence of a fever. In other words, we have chosen to define inhibition as a disjunction of relevant signs, but not necessarily a conjunction of those signs, particularly for a normal population.

As expected, intercorrelations among the variable at 14 and 20 months were low for some episodes. However, when these variables were averaged across episodes, their intercorrelations were higher, bolstering our confidence in the disjunctive model and the possible relevance of each variable as a partial sign of inhibition. Children with long latencies to leave the parent also had longer latencies to touch the unfamiliar object (average $r = .25$), spent more time proximal to the parent (average $r = .27$), and were more likely to retreat from an unfamiliar event (average $r = .36$). Children with long latencies to touch an unfamiliar object had high scores for time proximal to the parent (average $r = .39$) and were more likely to retreat (average $r = .36$). Furthermore, inspection of the raw data revealed that lower correlations were observed for some specific episodes because the variables had little variance. For example, 91 percent of the children had a 0-second latency to leave the parent in the playroom; hence, correlations for that variable in that episode were low.

The playgroup sessions at 32 months were longer, and there were few variables with scores of 0 and many with approximately normal distributions. As might be expected, the resulting matrix had more highly correlated variables (average r across the 45 correlations was .43). A factor solution revealed a single factor with a signficiant loading on each variable. Thus, the decision to combine all theoretically relevant variables for the playgroup was straightforward.

Models for Combining Variables at 14 and 20 Months

Most of the dependent variables at 14 and 20 months had modal values near zero (representing lack of inhibition) but large ranges reflecting values indicating inhibition. For example, latency to touch a toy, to approach the stranger, or to touch the unfamiliar object were close to zero for most children, but they extended to many minutes for the very inhibited subjects. Percent of time proximal to the mother had a modal value of 0 percent, but a few inhibited children had very high values. Thus, any composite index that used the absolute value of each variable would produce an asymmetric distribution clustered at zero for lack of inhibition and skewed toward inhibition. One solution to this problem is to dichotomize variables so that inhibition is either present or absent for each variable. We accomplished this in two ways. In one analysis, we set a criterion for presence or absence of each sign of inhibition that was based on the frequency distribution for that variable. For example, a latency to leave the parent of greater than 1 minute was coded as "inhibited." In a second analysis, we used a logarithmic transformation of the original latencies and percentages. The resulting totals across episodes appear more normally distributed for both analyses, but the stability correlation across age was reduced. Clearly, the extremes of inhibition represented by skewed scores are informative and contribute to predictability.

To capture the information at the extreme, a second index was calculated on the basis of the single most extreme variable for the given child in each episode. But when we calculated an inhibition index on the basis of each child's most extreme value for any variable in each episode, we again found very low stability correlations across age. Inspection of each subject's data suggested that the correlations were low because the single extreme score approach was vulnerable to error. Thus, in order to capture the information represented by extreme scores, it is necesary to consider children as highly inhibited only if they have extreme scores on several variables.

Given the necessity of combining variables while preserving their distributional structure, a final problem is equating differences in scale. Because some variables are latencies (in seconds), some are proportions, and some are categorical (yes-no), a simple arithmetic mean of raw variables will be flawed owing to the influence of variables scaled to larger numbers. The solution we adopted was to calculate standard scores (z-scores) for each quantitative variable and to convert each categorical score to one and minus one, roughly in range with the distribution of standard scores. The arithmetic mean of these scores weights the variables equally, reflects the distributional structure of each dimension, and, as described below, suggests strong continuity over time. This index (based on the four approach/withdrawal variables listed in table 2) correlates moderately with each component dependent variable. The highest correlations were with latency to touch an unfamiliar object.

Replication of Previous Work

Distribution of Inhibition

In previous reports, we have estimated that our extreme groups represent the 10 percent most and 10 percent least inhibited children in a normal population at 20 months. The basis for that estimate was that the original screening for cohort 1 involved telephone calls to an initial sample of approximately 300 parents. Of these, we retained two groups of 30 children for the inhibited and uninhibited samples.

As figures 1 and 2 suggest, this estimate was realistic for the present sample of inhibited 14- and 20-month-old children but not for the uninhibited children. Inspection of the variables in table 2 suggests a reason for this asymmetry. As discussed above, inhibited children had longer latencies and spent more time proximal to a parent. While a ceiling on the inhibition index was possible, very few children failed to touch the unfamiliar object or remained proximal to the parent all the time, and no child behaved this way consistently across all episodes. However, there was a definite floor for lack of inhibition; many children consistently approached the unfamiliar event immediately and were never proximal to the parent. Thus, many uninhibited children received scores approaching zero, and there were no variables that reflected a "degree of uninhibited behavior" at 14 or 20 months.

Figure 3 illustrates that the distribution at 32 months was more normal and revealed the expected pattern of extremes to be roughly 10–20 percent of the sample. One reason for the difference between 20 and 32 months is that the 32-month play session had several variables more directly relevant to lack of inhibition (e.g., number of approaches to and time playing with the peer).

The distributions for 14, 20, and 32 months suggest that behavioral inhibition is not distributed categorically with a clear break point defining inhibited or uninhibited versus normal behavior. Thus, the definitions of extremely inhibited and particularly uninhibited groups are arbitrary, even with 100 subjects. Hence, it seems reasonable to adopt a procrustean criterion for the extremes, and we have chosen the top and bottom 15 percent. It is likely that these two groups are comparable to the subjects in cohorts 1 or 2, and, as we describe below, the data bolster our confidence in this conclusion.

Stability of Inhibition

The main question in this replication is whether behavioral inhibition was preserved from 14 to 20 and from 20 to 32 months. As shown in table 3, when only the data for the 15 percent extreme groups were included, the indexes of inhibition were positively correlated at 14 and 20 months ($r = .68$) and at 20 and 32 months ($r = .71$). The magnitude of the latter correlation was com-

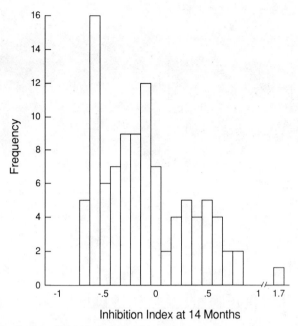

Fig. 1. Distribution of inhibition scores at 14 months.

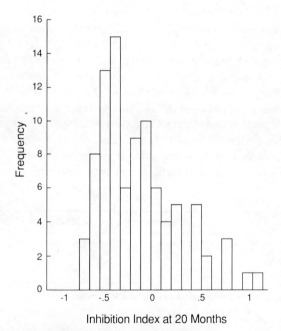

Inhibition Index at 20 Months

Fig. 2. Distribution of inhibition scores at 20 months.

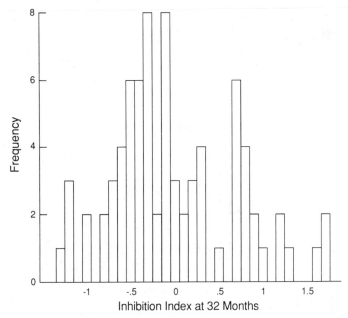

Fig. 3. Distribution of inhibition scores at 32 months

parable to cohort 1's correlation over the same time period ($r = .66$). This result is particularly impressive given that the sample size of the current extreme group was 14 in each group, half as large as cohort 1.

The occurrence of negative affect (crying and fretting) was correlated with inhibition at 14 months, $r = .19$, $p < .05$, and 20 months, $r = .30$, $p < .01$, but the 14-month negative affect scores predicted neither negative affect nor inhibited behavior at 20 months. A composite variable that contained both inhibition and negative affect predicted later behavior no more accurately than the inhibition index alone. Thus, although negative affect was one of the variables used to screen extreme groups for cohorts 1 and 2 (because of its contemporaneous correlation with other variables), its unique con-

Table 3: Stability of Inhibition

	14–20 Months	14–32 Months	20–32 Months
Entire sample	.51**	.44**	.25*
15 percent extremes	.68**	.66**	.72**
70 percent nonextremes	.16	.39**	.06

Note. Extremes are based on the index of inhibition at 20 months.
* $p < .05$.
** $p < .01$.

tribution to prediction of later inhibited behavior appears to be minimal. For theoretical clarity in subsequent analyses, we will define behavioral inhibition on the basis of approach/withdrawal only and exclude negative affect from the inhibition composite.

The design of the 32-month assessment also allowed a categorical analysis of the entire sample. Each triad was composed of three children: one child classified as inhibited, one as uninhibited, and one as neither. (Note that the term "inhibited" in this analysis refers to a division of the sample into equal thirds for each sex based on 14- and 20-month behavior combined.) An analysis of variance (ANOVA) conducted on the 32-month composite inhibition index revealed a main effect of the inhibition classification, $F(2,69) = 6.67$, $p < .002$. A planned contrast of the inhibited, neither, and uninhibited groups indicated a significant linear trend, $F(1,69) = 13.43$, $p < .001$, in the expected direction.

Each play session had its own unique character, ranging from quiet play to rough-and-tumble activity. In order to equate play sessions, each child of a triad was given a score of 1, 2, or 3, reflecting the rank of that child with respect to degree of inhibited behavior relative to the other two children in that triad. An ANOVA conducted on these ranks revealed a main effect of group, $F(2,69) = 11.3$, $p < .0001$. The children ranked as most inhibited in their triad had also been the most inhibited at 14 and 20 months.

Table 4 gives the inhibition classification at 20 and 32 months for children classified as extreme at 14 months. For the children classified as inhibited at 14 months, 50 percent remained in the extremely inhibited group at 20 months, and 93 percent were above the mean inhibition score. Only one inhibited child became uninhibited at a later age. Among the extremely uninhibited children, 25 percent remained extremely uninhibited at 20 months, and 83 percent were below the mean inhibition score. However, there was more change among the uninhibited than the inhibited children.

A comparable view emerges from table 5, which lists 14-month inhibition group classifications for children who became extremely inhibited at 20 or 32 months. That is, while table 4 describes the "outcomes" for extremely inhibited or uninhibited 14-month-olds, table 5 describes the "history" of extremely inhibited or uninhibited 20- or 32-month-olds. Children who are extremely inhibited at 20 or 32 months were more likely to have been classified as inhibited at 14 months, but the extremely uninhibited 20- and 32-month-olds were more variable in their 14-month classification.

This pattern of continuity does not match the finding from cohorts 1 and 2 that lack of inhibition is better preserved than inhibition and probably reflects the fact that lack of inhibition was not as well defined in the present study.

It is also important to note that families with extremely inhibited and uninhibited children were more likely to drop out of the study than were families

Table 4: Inhibition-Group Classification at 20 and 32 Months for Children Extremely Inhibited or Uninhibited at 14 Months

Inhibition Group	Extremely Inhibited at 14 Months	
	20-Month Inhibition Classification	32-Month Inhibition Classification
Most inhibited	7	4
Next most inhibited	4	2
Next most inhibited (Median)	2	2
Next most inhibited	0	0
Next most inhibited	0	0
Least inhibited	1	1
	Extremely Uninhibited at 14 Months	
Most inhibited	1	0
Next most inhibited	0	1
Next most inhibited (Median)	1	2
Next most inhibited	3	2
Next most inhibited	3	2
Least inhibited	4	2

with nonextreme children. At 20 months, seven of the nine missing subjects were extremes (four inhibited, three uninhibited), while none were from the 30 percent middle classification ($p < .008$, based on the binomial probability). At 32 months, 15 of the 24 missing subjects were extremes (seven inhibited, eight uninhibited), and only four were from the 30 percent middle classification ($p < .007$, based on the binomial probability). Our clinical impression was that many parents of extreme children discontinued participation because they found it difficult to manage their child in the laboratory session. The problems were due either to the child's extreme fear and resistance to participation or to the child's boldness and resistance to control. Because many of these missing extreme children may have retained their classification, the present data may underestimate stability.

Sex Differences

Cohorts 1 and 2 were sampled to obtain equal numbers of boys and girls in each extreme group, and the only sex differences were in the relation between inhibition and physiological variables. In the present sample, girls scored higher on the inhibition index than boys at 20 months, $t(89) = 2.86$, $p < .01$. For the extreme groups, girls constituted 10 of the 14 most inhibited but only three of the 14 most uninhibited children, $\chi^2 = 7.04$, $p < .01$. When the entire sample was divided into terciles, girls accounted for 67, 45,

Table 5: Inhibition-Group Classification at 14 Months for Children Extremely Inhibited or Uninhibited at 20 and 32 Months

Inhibition Group	Classification at 14 Months	
	Children Who Become Inhibited at 20 Months	Children Who Become Inhibited at 32 Months
Most inhibited	7	4
Next most inhibited	3	5
Next most inhibited (Median)	1	2
Next most inhibited	1	2
Next most inhibited	1	0
Least inhibited	1	0
	Children Who Become Uninhibited at 20 Months	Children Who Become Uninhibited at 32 Months
Most inhibited	1	1
Next most inhibited	1	0
Next most inhibited (Median)	3	4
Next most inhibited	2	3
Next most inhibited	3	3
Least inhibited	4	2

and 37 percent of the inhibited, neither, and uninhibited groups, respectively, $\chi^2 = 5.75$, $p < .05$. This difference is not surprising given the literature on sex-role stereotypes, and it replicates other research from our laboratory (Rosenberg 1987). Furthermore, it explains why we found it hard to recruit extremely inhibited boys in cohort 1. We had assumed that parental bias prevented parents from nominating their sons as inhibited, but the present data suggest that, at 20 months, extremely inhibited boys may in fact be less common than extremely inhibited girls.

The results were in the same direction at 14 months but did not reach statistical significance. Girls constituted 65 percent of the inhibited group at 14 months and 41 percent of the uninhibited group. Interestingly, at 32 months, girls appeared slightly less inhibited than boys, but the difference was not statistically significant: girls constituted 77 percent of the uninhibited and only 46 percent of the inhibited group. This tendency toward a reversal in direction of the sex difference highlights the importance of context of measurement. As noted above, the playgroups ranged from quiet play to rough and tumble. Triads of girls were more likely to play cooperatively as a group, thus generating more approaches, reciprocal play, and other signs of lack of inhibition among all three children. This resulted in lower inhibition scores. The rough-and-tumble atmosphere of the boys' sessions often completely intimidated one of the boys and caused him to receive a high inhibition score.

Birth Order

In both cohort 1 and cohort 2, we noted a tendency for later-born children to be inhibited (Kagan, Reznick, and Snidman 1987). The association was replicated in the present sample. Later-born children were more inhibited than firstborns at 14 months, $t(98) = 1.92$, $p < .058$, and at 20 months, $t(89) = 1.91$, $p < .059$. Although our recruitment procedures may underrepresent later borns (the present sample is 33 percent later born), the extremely inhibited 14-month-old children contained 53 percent later borns, while the unihibited extremes contained only 24 percent later borns, $\chi^2 = 3.11$, $p < .08$. At 20 months, the inhibited group was 50 percent later born and the uninhibited group only 21 percent later born, $\chi^2 = $ N.S. The evidence that later-born children are more inhibited is not unusually strong in the present study, but, if combined with the findings of cohorts 1 and 2, the association is more convincing.

It is unclear whether the source of the birth-order effect is the later born, the firstborn, or both and whether the causal path is based on experience or physiology. It is possible that the behavior of an older sibling can be a stressor causing a vulnerable later born to become more inhibited. It is also possible that the arrival of a sibling leads the firstborn to become more sociable and uninhibited (for a related discussion, see Arcus and McCartney, chap. 10, in this vol.). Finally, the differences may be attributed to fetal stress associated with later pregnancies.

A definitive study of birth-order effects would have to consider several other factors, including sex of child, sex of sibling, spacing between siblings, and firstborn versus only-child comparisons. In this study, when the entire 20-month population was considered, there was an interaction of sex and birth order. A sex × birth order ANOVA conducted on the composite index revealed a significant effect of sex, $F(1,87) = 4.04$, $p < .05$, and a marginal effect of birth order, $F(1,87) = 3.35$, $p < .07$, but a significant sex × birth order interaction, $F(1,87) = 4.30$, $p < .05$. The decomposition of the interaction was straightforward: firstborn boys were more uninhibited than the other three groups. At 14 months, the sex × birth order effect was marginal, $F(1,96) = 2.84$, $p < .09$, but again the pattern of means suggested that later-born boys were more inhibited than firstborn boys, while girls did not differ as a function of birth order. Thus, when the entire sample is examined, the tendency of later borns to be more inhibited holds best for boys. However, in cohorts 1 and 2, later borns of both sexes were more inhibited than firstborns, underscoring the complexity of this issue.

Eye Color

Rosenberg and Kagan (1987) have noted that inhibited children are more likely to be blue eyed than brown eyed. They support this claim with data from cohorts 1 and 2 as well as from studies of school-age children. The phenomenon is replicated in the present cohort. Inhibition scores were significantly higher for blue-eyed children at 14 months, $t(69) = 1.95, p < .05$, and in the same direction but not statistically significant at 20 months. The entire sample was 52 percent blue eyed, 36 percent brown eyed, and 12 percent other, comparable to the 47, 31, and 22 percent, respectively, reported by Kent (1956) for 1,292 Canadian schoolchildren. Among the extreme groups at 14 months, there were seven blue-eyed and eight brown-eyed uninhibited children but 10 blue-eyed and two brown-eyed inhibited children, $\chi^2 = 3.84, p < .05$. At 20 months, the distribution was comparable, with five blue-eyed and seven brown-eyed uninhibited children but eight blue-eyed and two brown-eyed inhibited children, $\chi^2 = 3.32, p < .06$. Finally, for children who were consistently uninhibited or inhibited across all three assessments (14, 20, and 32 months), the uninhibited group had seven blue-eyed and five brown-eyed children, while the consistently inhibited group had 11 blue-eyed children and only one brown-eyed child, $\chi^2 = 3.56, p < .059$. This relation between eye color and behavior replicates similar observations on cohorts 1 and 2 and can be added to the impressive array of studies associating inhibition, introversion, and social anxiety with iris pigmentation. (for details of the biological mechanisms that might support this relation, see Rosenberg and Kagan 1987).

Extension beyond Previous Work

Extremes versus Whole Group

The present study can help to resolve the question of whether inhibition is a quality that refers only to behavioral extremes or is a continuum on which any member of an unselected population can be placed. Stability of the individual differences in behavior observed in cohorts 1 and 2 may be true of all children or, alternatively, may represent a phenomenon that is true only for extremes. For example, it is reasonable to expect that weight and self-concept might be correlated for people who are overweight or underweight but independent for people of normal weight. As shown in table 3, the stability correlations were highest for the two extreme groups, lower for the entire population, and lowest for the children in the middle 70 percent of the distribution. For example, the stability correlation for inhibition from 20 to 32 months for the 15 percent extremes is .72; the comparable correlation for the entire population is only .25. For the 70 percent of the subjects who were not extremes, the correlation was only .06. While this pattern of correlations is consistent with the view that inhibition is preserved primarily by the extreme groups, it could also arise from changes in variability caused by isolating the extremes. The standard deviation of the inhibition index at 14 months is .45 for the entire sample, .69 for the 30 percent extreme groups, and .25 for the 70 percent who were not extremes. Other factors being equal, the greater the variability, the higher the expected correlation (Guilford and Fruchter 1973). The greater variation produced by combining scores from both tails of the distribution should (and does) result in a higher correlation, and the reduced variation when the extremes are eliminated should (and does) result in a lower correlation. In fact, Guilford and Fruchter suggest a formula that predicts the correlation for the whole sample from the correlation for a subsample when both variances are known. For the present data, the predicted value is .52, remarkably close to the observed correlation of .51. Thus, the higher correlations for the extreme groups are consistent with differences in variability that arise when extreme groups are selected.

A more forceful case for the significance of the extremes is based on the change data as a function of the 14-month inhibition classification. As indicated in table 4, 50 percent of the extremely inhibited children at 14 months remained in the extremely inhibited group at 20 months, and 93 percent were more inhibited than the average child. For the next most extreme 15 percent, the comparable percentages were 19 and 63 percent. For extremely uninhibited children, 25 percent remained extreme at 20 months, and 83 percent were more uninhibited than the average. For the next most uninhibited 15 percent, the comparable percentages were 19 and 50.

Clearly, the preservation of inhibition is due primarily to the behavior of the extreme children. They are most likely to retain their profile, particularly the tendency toward inhibition. Thus, the disproportionate loss of extremely inhibited and uninhibited subjects described above may have reduced the estimates of stability. While the lack of continuity for the 70 percent nonextreme group could reflect a lack of precision in measuring subtle differences in inhibition or the reduced variability that results when the extremes are eliminated, it seems prudent to suggest that some conclusions may apply only to extremely inhibited or uninhibited children and not to children in general. However, it is important to note that behavioral inhibition is also preserved in an unselected population containing extremes. The present results suggest that, if such a norml population is studied, it must be large enough to include an adequate number of extremes to generate robust effects and that efforts must be made to ensure that families with children classified as extreme do not drop out. Given the small effect sizes of most psychological variables, normative samples of at least 100 children may be necessary to support inferences about behavioral inhibition. The cost and inconvenience of recruiting and testing such large samples underscores the utility of the extreme-group approach used in our earlier work with cohorts 1 and 2.

Inhibition before 20 Months

A second major issue is whether one can measure the construct of inhibition before 20 months. Table 3 lists the correlations between 14 months and later ages for both the extreme group (selected at 20 months) and the entire sample. Both correlations were significant. Interestingly, for the entire sample, the correlation between inhibition scores at 14 and 32 months was somewhat higher than the comparable correlation for 20–32 months, $t(72) = 1.18$, $p < .07$. One possibility is that the difference is due to an artifact of our longitudinal strategy. To ensure comparability of the 14- and 20-month assessments, the two batteries were essentially identical, and the same examiner was used. But assessment of inhibition requires unfamiliar situations and events. Because the same events were repeated at 20 months, they were less novel and therefore may have been less valid. A second possibility is that because 20 months is a time of major psychological reorganization (Kagan 1981; McCall, Eichorn, and Hogarty 1977), behaviors at that time are more transient and thus poorer predictors of future development than are assessments of inhibition at 14 months. The present data do not allow us to choose between these two alternatives, but, because cohort 1 was selected at 20 months and their tendency toward inhibition showed moderate stability to 7½ years, the first explanation seems more likely.

Inhibition and Other Temperament Constructs

A third issue of interest is the relation between our index of behavioral inhibition and similar constructs used by other investigators to describe temperament related to inhibition (for a related discussion, see Plomin and Stocker, chap. 11, and Rothbart, chap. 7, both in this vol.). In order to compare behavioral inhibition with other popular constructs, we administered the Toddler Temperament Scale (Cary and McDevitt 1978; Fullard, McDevitt, and Carey 1978) at each age, the Infant Behavior Questionnaire (Rothbart 1981) and the Infant Characteristics Questionnaire (Bates, Freeland, and Lounsbury 1979) at 14 months, and the EAS (Emotionality, Activity, Sociability) Temperament Survey for Children (Buss and Plomin 1984) at 20 months. Additionally, we asked parents two questions relevant to behavioral inhibition during face-to-face home interviews at 14 and 20 months: "Would you describe your child as relatively outgoing or relatively shy?" and, "How does your child respond to new situations?" These Home Interview Questions were embedded in 21 others concerned with the family, the child's health, and other topics. Answers to the two questions were coded on a three-point scale

Table 6: Inhibition, Emotion, and Other Temperament Constructs

	Behavior in the Laboratory				
	14 Months		20 Months		32 Months
	Inhibition	Emotion	Inhibition	Emotion	Inhibition
14 months:					
TTS (N = 85):					
Approach	.41**	.00	.29**	.08	.30*
Mood	.16	.14	.12	.13	.04
Intensity	.11	.33*	.13	.19	− .06
IBQ (N = 79):					
Fear	.34**	.17	.29**	.21	.22
ICQ (N = 83):					
Unadaptable	.33**	− .01	.22	.09	.24
Unsocial	− .19	− .15	.01	− .12	− .09
HIQ (N = 92):					
Inhibition	.38**	− .07	.35**	.09	.40**
20 months:					
TTS (N = 47):					
Approach	.30*	.00	.33*	.18	.16
Mood	.21	.02	.25	.31*	.13
Intensity	.12	.19	.05	.29*	− .26
EAS (N = 67):					
Shyness	.38**	.04	.40**	.16	.33**
Emotional	.19	.03	.18	.34**	.26
Sociability	− .10	− .07	− .09	.00	.04
HIQ (N = 75):					
Inhibition	.23*	.14	.25*	− .02	.13
32 months:					
TTS (N = 73):					
Approach	.40**	− .05	.35**	− .03	.52**
Mood	.29*	− .01	.25*	.21	.09
Intensity	.02	.25*	.01	.29*	− .09

* $p < .05$.
** $p < .01$.

to reflect outgoing, medium, or shy temperaments. Table 6 lists the correlations between relevant variables from these scales and our index of behavioral inhibition at 14, 20, and 32 months and negative affect at 14 and 20 months.

The construct "approach/withdrawal" from the Toddler Temperament Scale (TTS), which represents one of Thomas and Chess's (1977) nine dimensions of temperament, correlated significantly with inhibition at each age ($r = .41$, .33, and .52, respectively). For the 15 percent extremes, the correlations were higher ($r = .57$, .51, and .56). This result is comparable to the data of cohort 1, for which the TTS approach/withdrawal score was also correlated with an observational index of behavioral inhibition ($r = .54$). This relation is not surprising given that the TTS questions about approach/withdrawal were used in cohort 1 in a telephone interview to screen for extremely inhibited and uninhibited children. The TTS questions ask about the child's response to new foods, toys, people, and places. The relation between the approach/with-drawal scale and behavioral inhibition in the laboratory suggests definite conceptual similarity. Both mood (defined as pleasant, joyful, and friendly vs. unpleasant, crying, or unfriendly behavior) and intensity (defined as highly energetic vs. less energetic response) correlated with negative emotion in the laboratory at 20 months, but the correlation was significant only for intensity at 14 months. Neither variable correlated with behavioral inhibition at any age, reinforcing our decision to keep inhibition and negative affect as separate variables.

It is interesting to note that correlations across age for TTS approach scores were large ($r = .79$ for 14–20 months, .63 for 14–32 months, and .81 for 20–32 months) and significantly larger than comparable correlations for behavior observed in the laboratory from 14 to 20 months, $z = 2.83, p < .01$, and from 20 to 32 months, $z = 4.57, p < .01$. Although this fact seems to imply that inhibition is more stable over time than we described, it is unclear whether this correlation reflects continuity of the child's behavior or of the parent's belief about the child.

The Infant Behavior Questionnaire (IBQ) fear scale also correlated with inhibited behavior at 14 months ($r = .34$). Rothbart (1981) defines this dimension as the child's distress at sudden changes in stimulation and distress at and latency of movement toward a novel social or physical object. Despite the inclusion of distress in Rothbart's measure, it did not correlate with negative affect in the laboratory. Additionally, when we redefined inhibition by combining the approach/withdrawal score with the negative affect component, the correlation did not increase in size.

The Infant Characteristics Questionnaire (ICQ) characteristic that Bates (1986) labels "unadaptable" correlated with behavioral inhibition at 14 months ($r = .33$). The ICQ items that contribute to this score concern the child's response (favorable vs. unfavorable) to new foods, people, places, and experiences. The ICQ also has an "unsociable" factor pertaining to the child's enjoyment of social interactions with the parent, but this factor does not appear to be related to behavioral inhibition.

In the EAS Temperament Survey for Children, administered at 20 months, shyness correlated with behavioral inhibition, emotion correlated with negative affect, and sociability correlated with neither variable. This pattern argues against Buss and Plomin's (1984) suggestion that behavioral inhibition is closely related to their construct of emotionality. Further, to the extent that the EAS can separate sociability (the tendency to affiliate with others vs. being alone) from shyness (behavior with people who are casual acquaintances or strangers), behavioral inhibition, at least at 20 months, is more closely related to shyness. The same general conclusion emerges from the ICQ at 14 months and argues against Bates's (1986) grouping of sociability and inhibition.

Surprisingly, the mean of the two Home Interview Questions (HIQ), with their meager three-point range, yielded correlations with inhibition at 14 months comparable in size to the TTS, IBQ, and ICQ measures. Additionally, the correlation from the 14-month interview to 32-month behavior appeared higher for the HIQ than for the other scales, but this difference was not statistically significant.

Multiple regression techniques were used to explore two questions regarding prediction of inhibited/uninhibited behavior. First, how do the interview techniques compare in their ability to predict inhibition? When the four parent-report measures at 14 months were used to predict behavior at 14 months, a comparison of R^2 for all models (four with one measure, six with two measures, four with three measures, and one with all four measures) suggested that the best subset was a single-measure model containing approach/withdrawal from the TTS. Further analysis with a stepwise model suggested that the HIQ variable improved prediction (R^2 increased from .16 to .18). In a hierarchical regression model, the TTS approach made a unique contribution to the model, $F(1,69) = 13.44, p < .01$, but HIQ entered subsequently did not. When the four parent-report measures at 14 months were used to predict behavior at 20 months, the HIQ was the only significant predictor, $F(1,64) = 8.37, p < .01$. Finally, when the four parent-report measures at 14 months were used to predict behavior at 32 months, the HIQ was again the only significant predictor, $F(1,53) = 16.03, p < .01$.

Using 20-month interview scores to predict behavior at 20 months, EAS shyness was the only significant predictor, $F(1,54) = 11.36, p < .01$. When the 20-month parental report was used to predict 32-month behavior, EAS shyness made the strongest contribution, but HIQ was also added to the model and raised R^2 from .08 to .10. Neither factor was statistically significant.

In general, these results suggest that the different questionnaires all reflect more or less the same parental insight about the child's behavioral inhibition. The TTS at 14 months and the EAS at 20 months provide the best contemporaneous descriptions of the child's degree of inhibition, although the other scales do relatively well. However, the HIQ appears to measure a quality more predictive of the preservation of inhibition; it predicted subsequent inhibited/uninhibited behavior better than any of the other measures. It is unclear whether this is because of question content or because of a special contemplative set evoked through direct questions in a face-to-face interview with an examiner. It is also unclear whether parents would be as accurate in their contemporaneous descriptions of other temperament or personality dimensions that have less salience for them. Timidity and shyness to the unfamiliar are distinctive qualities that concern many parents in American society.

A second question is whether parent-report measures improve the prediction of later behavior. Laboratory behavior accounted for the largest share of variance in predicting later laboratory behavior, and no additional variance in behavior at 20 months was explained by adding any additional interview information at 14 months. However, regression analysis indicated significant improvement in predicting 32-month inhibited behavior when the HIQ was added to the 14-month laboratory index, increasing R^2 from .24 to .34. In a hierarchical model, laboratory behavior was significant, $F(1,52) = 19.10$, $p < .01$, and the HIQ score entered after laboratory behavior was also significant, $F(1,52) = 8.55$, $p < .01$. These results suggest that the TTS, IBQ, ICQ, and EAS offer realistic contemporaneous descriptions of the child's inhibition but do not add significantly to the predictability of later behavior beyond predictions based on information from behavioral observation. However, parental knowledge of the child assessed through specific questions in an interview format does seem to improve long-term prediction of inhibited behavior.

Conclusions

We define the inhibited child as one who tends to be slower to explore an unfamiliar situation or object, spends more time proximal to the parent, and is more likely to retreat from unfamiliarity. The distribtion of inhibition scores in the present sample replicates the 10–20 percent skew toward inhibition at 20 months previously reported but fails to suggest a similar skew toward lack of inhibition, presumably owing to fewer behaviors that clearly differentiate the uninhibited child from the average child. But the variables at 32 months did yield 10–15 percent extremes at both ends of the dimension.

When extreme groups were defined at 15 percent cut points, inhibition was preserved from 14 to 20 to 32 months. Girls were more inhibited than boys at 14 and 20 months, and later-born boys were more inhibited than firstborns. As reported in previous work, the inhibited group had a higher proportion of blue-eyed children. There was also a disproportionately large dropout rate for families with extremely inhibited or uninhibited children, suggesting that extra effort is required to maintain a truly normal population.

The present results replicate many of the findings reported previously for extremely inhibited and uninhibited children, but these effects are clearly strongest at the extremes. This suggests that researchers wishing to study inhibition in relatively small normative samples may fail to find statistically significant effects because they do not have a sufficient number of inhibited and uninhibited children.

Finally, the present data help to anchor the construct "behavioral inhibition" with other well-established constructs describing temperament. Behavioral inhibition is related to the Thomas and Chess (1977) construct of "approach/ withdrawal" as measured by the TTS as well as to Rothbart's (1981) "fear," Bates's (1986) "unadaptable," and Buss and Plomin's (1984) "shyness." These standardized procedures for evaluating parental beliefs about the child's behavior offer reasonable descriptions of the child's contemporaneous behavioral inhibition but do not significantly improve prediction of later behavior beyond the prediction based on laboratory behavior alone. A second method of measuring parental perception using face-to-face interview questions about the child's shyness and reaction to new situations improves long-term prediction from 14 to 32 months.

References

Bates, J. E. 1986. The measurement of temperament. In *The study of temperament: Changes, continuities and challenges,* ed. R. Plomin and J. Dunn. Hillsdale, N.J.: Erlbaum.

Bates, J. E.; Freeland, C. A. B.; and Lounsbury, M. L. 1979. Measurement of infant difficultness. *Child Development* 50:794–803.

Buss, A. H., and Plomin, R. 1984. *Temperament: Early developing personality traits.* Hillsdale, N.J.: Erlbaum.

Carey, W. B., and McDevitt, S. C. 1978. Revision of the infant temperament questionnaire. *Pediatrics* 61:735–39.

Carroll, L. 1872. *Alice's adventures in Wonderland and Through the looking glass.* Middlesex: Penguin.

Fullard, W.; McDevitt, S. C.; and Carey, W. B. 1978. Toddler temperament scale. Philadelphia: Temple University, Department of Educational Psychology. Typescript.

Garcia-Coll, C.; Kagan, J.; and Reznick, J. S. 1984. Behavioral inhibition in young children. *Child Development* 55:1005–19.

Guilford, J. P., and Fruchter, B. 1973. *Fundamental statistics in psychology and education.* 4th ed. New York: McGraw-Hill.

Kagan, J. 1981. *The second year.* Cambridge, Mass.: Harvard University Press.

Kagan, J.; Reznick, J. S.; Clarke, C.; Snidman, N.; and Garcia-Coll, C. 1984. Behavioral inhibition to the unfamiliar. *Child Development* 55:2212–25.

Kagan, J.; Reznick, J. S.; and Snidman, N. 1987. The physiology and psychology of behavioral inhibition in children. *Child Development* 58:1459–73.

Kent, I. 1956. Human iris pigment: 2. Factors in schizophrenia. *Canadian Psychiatric Association Journal* 1:105–6.

McCall, R. B.; Eichorn, D. H.; and Hogarty, P. S. 1977. Transitions in early mental development. *Monographs of the Society for Research in Child Development,* vol. 42, serial no. 171.

McDonough, P. M. 1986. The stability of behavioral inhibition in an unselected population of children. B.S. honor's thesis, Harvard University, Department of Psychology.

Reznick, J. S.; Kagan, J.; Snidman, N.; Gersten, M.; Baak, K.; and Rosenberg, A. 1986. Inhibited and uninhibited children: A follow-up study. *Child Development* 57:660–80.

Rosenberg, A. 1987. Eye color and behavioral inhibition. Ph.D. diss., Harvard University.

Rosenberg, A., and Kagan, J. 1987. Iris pigmentation and behavioral inhibition. *Developmental Psychobiology* 20:377–92.

Rothbart, M. K. 1981. Measurement of temperament in infancy. *Child Development* 52:569–78.

Snidman, N. 1984. Behavioral restraint and the central nervous system. Ph.D. diss., University of California, Los Angeles.

Thomas. A., and Chess, S. 1977. *Temperament and development.* New York: Brunner/Mazel.

3 Behavioral Inhibition and Sympathetic Influence on the Cardiovascular System

NANCY SNIDMAN

Two mothers and their 30-month-old children, who have never met, enter a large room with toys scattered on the rug. One girl immediately leaves her mother, walks over to the toys in the middle of the room, and starts to play. The other girl sits close to her mother quietly watching the other child. The exploring child may talk to her mother or offer the quiet girl a toy and will spend little time next to her mother. The second girl will remain next to her mother for 10 or 15 minutes before moving to the toys and is unlikely to speak or to approach the other girl for the rest of the 30-minute play session.

This scenario captures the contrasting behaviors of the classic inhibited and uninhibited children my colleagues and I have been studying for almost 10 years, though not all children behave in as extreme a manner as the two just described. These differences are quantified easily and reliably. One child has longer latencies to approach a toy, spends more time within an arm's length of the mother, and makes fewer verbal approaches to the other child. Most observers of these two children would agree that they are different, even without knowing our coding system. Untrained observers often use words such as "shy," "fearful," or "tense" to describe our inhibited children and "outgoing," "bubbly," or "relaxed" to describe the uninhibited children. But would these children behave similarly in other unfamiliar situations? Would the quiet, withdrawn child be as shy at a party, or would she be one of the group's leaders? We would not want to characterize a child as inhibited unless the defining behavior were consistent over time and situations. Several longitudinal studies that my colleagues and I have conducted in our laboratory have found that 10–15 percent of the children demonstrate these two behavioral profiles in novel environments (Garcia-Coll, Kagan, and Reznick 1984; Kagan et al. 1984; Reznick et al. 1986). Therefore, my focus here is on two

This research was supported by grants from the John D. and Catherine T. MacArthur Foundation Network on the Transition from Infancy to Childhood. Mail reprint requests to Nancy Snidman, Department of Psychology, Harvard University, Cambridge, MA 02138.

related issues: (1) the underlying physiological systems that might participate in the expression of behavioral inhibition and (2) the quantification of one of these systems, the cardiovascular system, with noninvasive techniques.

Sources of Behavioral Inhibition

Understanding the etiology of behavioral inhibition and its complement is a more complex process than simply describing the two styles. Most researchers would agree that an explanation of the foundations of these differences probably includes a combination of experimental and biological factors. Much research has shown the importance of an organism's environment in shaping behavior. But research, some of which is reviewed in chapters in this volume by Kagan (chap. 1) and Adamec and Stark-Adamec (chap. 5) has also shown that, when confronted with an uncertain situation, a small percentage of individuals in many species display the withdrawal, immobility, and watchfulness characteristic of inhibited children. The biological predisposition to respond to unfamiliarity with inhibition will or will not be actualized depending on the life experiences of the infant. If stressors in the environment trigger an automatic physiological arousal that is perceived by an infant as "anxiety," that infant may become a 30-month-old who stays close to the mother in a playroom and is reluctant to approach unfamiliar children.

If physiological arousal participates in this class of behavior, we need to clarify the meaning of this term and determine valid ways to quantify it. I use the term "arousal" here to refer to the physiological responsivity of the limbic structures in the central nervous system (CNS) to a physical or psychological stressor. My colleagues and I believe several systems are activated, including the hypothalamic pituitary-adrenal axis, the reticular activating system, and the sympathetic branch of the autonomic nervous system (ANS). The responses of these systems are well documented (Guyton 1981).

Activation of these separate circuits may be perceived by a person as a tight throat, sweaty palms, tense muscles, or a heart that is "racing." These experiences usually occur only under conditions of extreme challenge. The intensity or duration of these responses will vary with individual characteristics, including physiological thresholds and psychological interpretation of the situation. For example, the immediate physiological response of a hiker and an animal behaviorist encountering a bear in the forest may be initially similar—activation of the limbic system—but their psychological responses differ. For the hiker, the physiological response, coupled with the knowledge that bears can be dangerous, may heighten the activity of the limbic area and stress circuits and produce a state so incapacitating that the person is not capable of rational decision. At this point, Walter B. Cannon's "flight or fight" mechanism (Cannon 1929) may become operative. By contrast, the animal behaviorist, prepared psychologically to control her aroused state, may feel a heightened tension and arousal that she channels into the productive behavior of retrieving a tranquilizer gun and picking the correct moment to fire.

When children initially enter our playroom, there is no bear, but some of the reactions may be similar. The two children may experience some physiological arousal. But the uninhibited child may interpret the sensation as excitement about a new place with new toys and a new playmate and respond by vocalizing and exploring the room. The inhibited child may interpret the sensation, which may be more intense, as uncertainty in a strange environment and display wariness and restraint.

Measuring Behavioral Inhibition

The theory my colleagues and I have developed assumes that inhibited and uninhibited children differ in the threshold of activation of limbic structures. Differences in the excitability of the limbic system could be due to quantity of various neurotransmitters, number of pre- or postsynaptic terminals, or functioning of uptake mechanisms. However, evaluating limbic activity in response to psychological challenge, in children, is difficult because of the lack of ways to assess and measure the system directly. This measurement problem, familiar to many psychologists, is similar to problems encountered during attempts to measure such psychological constructs as intelligence or superego. Physiologists have measured limbic activity directly, in animals. Recordings from the hypothalamus, amygdala, and hippocampus have specified the regions activated during stressful conditions (Fuchs, Edinger, and Siegel 1985). Administration of agonists and antagonists to the various catecholamines and glucocorticoids, in both animals and humans, has demonstrated that cortisol, epinephrine, dopamine, and/or norepinephrine are released when an animal or a human is exposed to a physical stress, such as water immersion (Weiss et al. 1980) or maternal separation (Suomi 1983).

Other less direct but reasonable measures of limbic activity include the activity of targets of the ANS, which reflects changes in CNS activity. Studies of animals employing lesions, drugs, ablation of pathways, or electrical stimulation have mapped the anatomic pathways and physiological functions that control the ANS and revealed the profile of peripheral responses produced by limbic activity (Guyton 1981). For example, the hypothalamic response to stress is release of corticotropin-releasing hormone, which in turn stimulates the pituitary to release adrenocorticotropic hormone (ACTH), which subsequently leads to an increased output of cortisol detectable in plasma, urine, or saliva. Activation of the sympathetic branch of the ANS, another of the circuits involved in the stress response, leads to increased norepinephrine production and changes in pupil dilation, muscle tone, and cardiovascular functions.

In the laboratory, my colleagues and I have utilized several peripheral measures to explore the physiological responses of children in varied situations. Here, I will consider how the response of the cardiovascular system to stress can help us understand the different behavioral responses to novel and challenging events.

Neural Control of the Cardiovascular System

The cardiovascular system is influenced by changes in CNS activity through both the parasympathetic and the sympathetic branches of the ANS. Stimulation of the vagus, the major parasympathetic nerve to the heart, releases the neurotransmitter acetylcholine, which results in a decrease in heart rate. Conversely, application of norepinephrine, a sympathetic neurotransmitter, to the appropriate beta receptors on the heart results in increased heart rate, contractility of the ventricles, and vascular resistance (Glick and Braunwald 1965). Many researchers have used these dimensions of cardiovascular response as indexes of ANS response to various stimuli.

One of the most common documented cardiovascular responses is a short-term change in heart rate in response to a wide array of psychological tasks. Investigators interested in immediate change in heart rate in response to a brief stimulus usually track beat-to-beat changes and observe a pattern of acceleration or deceleration over a 5–10-second period. The number and magnitude of heart-rate decelerations in habituation experiments with infants are often used as an index of a response to a warning tone or light in a signaled reaction-time task (Sroufe 1971) or as a sign that a new stimulus has been noticed (Berg 1972). Conversely, a rapid, short-term increase in heart rate, the result of either a withdrawal of parasympathetic activity or an increase in sympathetic activity, is a common reaction to a startling stimulus (Goodman and Gilman 1980).

Investigators interested in changes over a longer period of time often report mean heart rate, expressed as mean beats per minute, or mean interbeat interval (IBI) for a trial, an episode, or a condition. However, calculating the average heart rate or heart period does not use all the information contained in the sequence of heartbeats. The durations of IBIs are rarely constant, and they do not fluctuate only in response to a perturbation to the system. Reporting average heart rate implies that the cardiovascular control is designed as a steady-state system that seeks to maintain a homeostatic set point. But there are periodic fluctuations in heart rate that involve regular changes in the duration of successive beats—called heart-rate variability (HRV). These oscillations can be linked to changes in respiratory, vasomotor, or thermoregulatory factors (Akselrod et al. 1985; Katona and Jih 1975). When the heart rate is averaged over many seconds, these fluctuations will be masked. Yet this variability in rate may be a more useful indicator of some aspects of ANS function than an average heart rate. In recent decades, many investigators have reported changes, either increases or decreases, in HRV. For example, some studies have reported a decrease in HRV, or a more stable heart rate, under conditions of both physical (Ekelund and Holmgren 1967) and psychological stress (Coles 1972). Other studies have examined the suppression of HRV during such tasks as mental arithmetic or imagery requiring "cognitive effort" or "mental load" (Kalsbeek 1973).

Many theorists propose that an inhibition of parasympathetic activity, or vagal tone, during cognitive activity is the reason for the stabilization. But, because several biologic cycles influence HRV, it is not always clear whether the parasympathetic system, the sympathetic system, or both produced the change in total variability. It is possible that an increase or decrease in both the parasympathetic and the sympathetic system can result in a decrease in HRV. A single measure of HRV cannot distinguish the separate contributions of the parasympathetic and sympathetic systems. While a more sensitive measure than heart rate alone, HRV gives only a gross indication of the total effect of nervous-system activity on heart rate.

The fluctuations of the beat-to-beat variability in heart rate were first noted in the eighteenth century by Stephen Hales, who, while measuring arterial blood pressure, found a correlation among respiration, blood pressure, and heart rate. Subsequent research has shown that variation in either parasympathetic or sympathetic activity can alter the variability of heart rate (Axselrod et al. 1981).

Examination of an electrocardiogram (ECG) record reveals some of the heart-rate fluctuations. The variation most obvious to visual inspection is due to respiration and is called respiratory sinus arrhythmia (RSA). Heart rate increases slightly during inspiration but decreases slightly during expiration, producing a regular sinusoidal waveform in the heart-rate record. These changes associated with breathing are due to changes in parasympathetic activity. Parasympathetic antagonists attenuate or abolish this rhythmic respiratory variation in heart rate, while parasympathetic agonists increase the fluctuation.

Visual detection of other fluctuations that occur with less frequency than RSA is almost impossible. These slower fluctuations, which are due to both parasympathetic and sympathetic activity, can be detected with a mathematical procedure called spectral analysis.

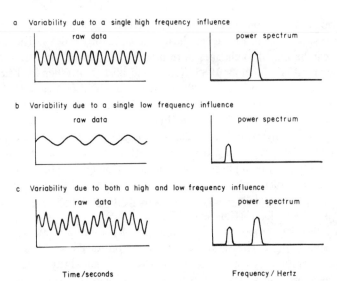

Fig. 1. Power-spectrum representation of periodic variability in physiological data. *a*, Variability due to a single high-frequency influence. *b*, Variability due to a single low-frequency influence. *c*, Variability due to both a high- and a low-frequency influence.

Spectral Analysis

Spectral analysis is a time-series statistical procedure that partitions the variance of any oscillation into its component frequencies. The variation in heart rate that is due to sympathetic activity can be dissociated from the variation due to parasympathetic activity because each produces characteristic, distinct cyclic fluctuations in heart rate. The spectral analysis distinguishes all the component cycles in a time series. For example, if spectral analysis is computed on a pure sine wave of .5 hertz, the power spectrum would show a peak at only .5 hertz and no power at any other frequency. If a more complex sine wave is spectrally analyzed, the two or more sine waves present would be revealed in the power-spectrum output as peaks at the appropriate frequencies (see fig. 1). Note that the individual sine waves that compose the complex wave cannot be separated in figure 1*c*. Only the power spectrum describes each source contributing to the total variability. The measurement units for the amplitude of the peak are in heart rate squared, and the combined area under all the peaks is equal to the variance of the total time series.

Spectral analysis of an ECG time series typically reveals several peaks. Of course, the presence and size of each peak provide useful information only if one understands the possible physiological functions responsible for each peak. Researchers have documented the various peaks in the heart-rate power spectrum as belonging to several physiological functions (Sayers 1973). As noted, RSA produces a characteristic peak in the heart-rate power spectrum at a frequency corresponding to the individual's respiration rate. For example, if a person is breathing 15 times a minute, a peak would be seen in the heart-rate power spectrum at .25 hertz (i.e., .25 of a respiratory cycle occurs in 1 second). Another known oscillation in heart rate, associated with blood pressure, occurs at a frequency of approximately .1 hertz. Manipulation of blood pressure affects this peak in the heart-rate power spectrum. Drugs that selectively block parasympathetic or sympathetic activity have shown that the respiratory peak is under parasympathetic control while the slower frequencies are controlled by both parasympathetic and sympathetic activity.

Recently, investigators have become interested in using spectral analysis to describe more clearly the influence of the ANS on the cardiovascular system (Mulder and Mulder 1981; Pomeranz et al. 1985; Porges et al. 1980). Because of its noninvasive quality (collect IBIs from a subject and run the data through the computer), it was hoped that this method might reveal the relation between sympathetic and parasympathetic action on the heart. But spectral analysis has limitations. As with all statistical procedures, if certain assumptions are not met, the validity of the results is questionable. Because the technique detects fluctuations of specific frequencies and amplitudes, two requirements for success are stationarity of the data (i.e., the cycles must be maintained with regularity throughout the time-series data) and an adequate temporal duration of the time series (i.e., the ECG record must contain enough heartbeats so that several repetitions of the slowest waveform of interest are included in the series).

Regularity of cycles in any dynamic biological system can be perturbed by large body movements. Hence, the first requirement is that a subject remain quiet during the recording period. The RSA cycle in heart rate is susceptible to disturbances in regularity even in a fairly quiet subject. If subjects alter their breathing pattern, by changing either the amplitude or the frequency of respiration, the amount of variability in heart rate will change (Hirsch and Bishop 1981). Even a single perturbance, such as a yawn, will cause a transitory increase followed by a decrease in heart rate. If the researcher is interested only in the amount of parasympathetic activity, singular perturbations in respiration can be accepted. One less regular breathing cycle will not change the power in the respiratory peak if the sample is of adequate duration. Several investigators interested only in vagal tone have used this technique successfully (Porges, McCabe, and Yongue 1982; Richards 1985).

But investigators using spectral analysis to evaluate sympathetic activity face more complex problems because the cycles reflecting sympathetic activity are at a lower frequency in the power spectrum and their analysis cannot tolerate large perturbations. A single irregularity in heart rate caused by a respiratory change can be described as a single slow sine wave that occurred once, at a low frequency. Thus, in a power spectrum, a yawn would appear as a solitary peak or would add inappropriate power to already existing low-frequency peaks. Therefore, to evaluate slow cycles in heart rate, respiration must remain stationary, with no change in breathing pattern during the entire time series to be analyzed. This issue is important in this chapter because my and my colleagues' hypothesis regarding the possible biological base for behavioral inhibition requires an evaluation of sympathetic activity through detection of the lower-frequency peaks in the power spectrum.

A second requirement is a heart-rate sample of sufficient duration. Of course, the amount of data required for spectral analysis depends on the question. The slower the cyclic fluctuations of interest, the longer the sample required in order to obtain sufficient repetitions of the cycle. For example, if the researcher is interested in the respiration cycle, which occurs between about 15 and 30 times a minute, a 30-second record yields enough repetitions of the cycle. By contrast, a cycle that occurs at .1 hertz, or once every 10 seconds, yields only three cycles in a 30-second sample, which is inadequate for reliable measurement of the cycles' exact amplitude and frequency band. All cycles that occur slightly above or below .1 hertz will overlap in the power spectrum, and biologically different cycles will be indistinguishable. However, if the investigator is not interested in the amount of power in a particular peak but wishes rather to compare the total amount of power in one band width with the power in another band width, it is not necessary that the peaks be so clearly defined.

In the present study, it was necessary to separate the power in the area of the respiratory peak (reflecting parasympathetic influence) from the power in the area below this peak (reflecting parasympathetic and sympathetic influence), but it was unnecessary to differentiate each of the individual cycles at the lower area of the spectrum. As a result, a 30-second duration of heart rate was adequate because it allowed discrimination of the respiratory peak from all the slower peaks. The equation that extracts this information will be described later. First, I present a description of the study in which children selected originally to be behaviorally inhibited or uninhibited were observed for signs of behavior and physiology reflecting differences in the tendency to become aroused to novel events.

Longitudinal Study

The description of the sample and the procedures is detailed so the reader will appreciate what behavioral qualities in what situations are related to variation in cardiovascular responses.

Subject Selection

The subjects were male and female children recruited from a volunteer subject file. All subjects were observed first within 1 month of 31 months of age and

Table 1: Sample Selection: Criteria for Selection of Inhibited and Uninhibited
Children at 31 Months

Variables	Inhibited	Uninhibited
Latency to touch the first toy	> 2 minutes	< 35 seconds
Latency to approach the other child for first time	> 13 minutes	< 9 minutes
Total time spent proximal to the mother	> 9 minutes	< 1 minute
Enter the toy cloth tunnel	No	Yes
Reaction to the first unfamiliar woman	No approach	Approach
Latency to approach the robot	> 2 minutes	< 1 minute

again within 1 month of 43 months of age. A total of 66 subjects, 32 males
and 34 females, were selected from a larger group of 175 children at 31
months. The children were observed during a 40-minute play session. Two
children of the same age and sex were randomly paired. The play session
occurred in a room containing a variety of age-appropriate toys and a one-way
mirror permitting observation from an adjoining room. The children were first
introduced outside the entrance of the playroom prior to the play session. The
mothers were given written instructions that described the session and instructed them to be seated on a couch, to limit interactions with the child, but
to intercede if problems developed. The 40-minute play session was divided
into two segments. During the first 35 minutes, the children were free to play
with each other and the toys in the room. Coders behind the mirror recorded
latencies to touch the first toy, to vocalize, to enter a cloth tunnel, and to
approach the other child and total time spent in proximity to the mother. During the last 5 minutes, two unexpected events occurred. First, an unfamiliar
woman wearing a plastic bag that covered her trunk and arms from neck to
waist entered, sat on the floor in the middle of the room, and did not speak.
After 30 seconds of quiet, she invited each child to play and, 30 seconds later,
regardless of the childrens' reactions, pulled from under the bag two amorphous cardboard objects and offered them to each child. She waited an additional 30 seconds and then left the room. Then a second unfamiliar woman
entered the room and placed on the floor a 3-foot-tall robot made of tin cans
and Christmas tree lights. The woman invited the children to turn the robot's
lights on and off. If either child approached and played with the light
switches, the robot "spoke" for 20 seconds (by means of an implanted micro-
phone), inviting the children to play with him. The behavioral criteria used
for classification of inhibited and uninhibited are shown in table 1.

Previous work has indicated that these behaviors differentiate 4-year-old
children who had been classified at 21 months as inhibited or uninhibited. In
the current study, a child was required to meet the criteria for time spent
proximal to the mother (greater than 9 minutes or less than 1 minute) in addition to meeting two of the other five criteria in order to be classified as either

inhibited or uninhibited. Fifty-five percent of the children met at least five of the six criteria. All children classified as either inhibited or uninhibited were then taken to another room in order to monitor their heart rate and respiration. A 2-minute quiet period was followed by the presentation of a filmed cartoon. An observer activated an event marker channel, which signaled the computer when the child was sitting quietly.

43-Month Assessment

A total of 54 of the original sample of 66 subjects were located and enlisted as subjects at 43 months. This cohort consisted of 27 inhibited children (14 females, 13 males) and 27 uninhibited children (14 females, 13 males). The purpose of the 43-month assessment was to evaluate the subject's behaviors across situations, gather physiological data during baseline periods and cognitive stress, and measure performance on cognitive tasks. The protocol included a peer-play session, a cognitive-testing session, a risk-room procedure, and a visit to the home.

The play session, which was similar to the one used at 31 months, occurred in the same room and had age-appropriate toys for the 36-minute session. Each child was paired with a child of the same sex but opposite behavioral classification (inhibited with uninhibited), a pairing based on the prior classification at 31 months. Two children of the same temperamental classification might have enhanced the behavior associated with that classification (number of approaches to other child, duration proximal to the mother). An uninhibited child, however, might be more likely to engage the inhibited child in play. Behaviors coded from the play session, either live or later from a videotape, included four of the behaviors recorded at 31 months: latency to touch the first toy, latency to first approach the other child, time spent in proximity to the mother (separated into playing and not playing), and latency to enter a cloth tunnel. Other variables included duration of looking at the other child and frequency of looking at the mother, entering the cloth tunnel, and approaching the other child.

In the risk room, the subject and mother were left alone in a small room containing several objects that could be interpreted as potentially risky if explored or manipulated: a balance beam, a hanging rope, a ladderlike apparatus, and a box with a hole and a handle. The mother was instructed to sit in a chair and interact as little as possible. The session was both observed and videotaped from behind a one-way mirror. Variables coded included latency to touch each toy, amount of total time playing with each toy, and amount of time proximal to the mother. After 5 minutes, an unfamiliar woman entered and asked the subject to imitate her as she played with each piece of apparatus. If the subject refused to imitate any behavior, the experimenter encouraged participation once and then, regardless of the subject's response, proceeded to the next behavior.

A 30-minute home visit was conducted by a female observer who was naive to the child's classification. The observer first emptied a bag of toys on the floor and then sat on a couch and recorded the child's behaviors: latency to touch first toy, to vocalize, and to approach within 1 foot of the observer; total time proximal to the mother, who was asked to stay in the room; and number of discrete interactions with the observer.

The cognitive battery included several difficult cognitive tasks that were designed to require "mental effort" and uncertainty and therefore were potentially stressful for children. Quiet baseline periods were included before and after the cognitive tasks. Heart rate and respiration were monitored throughout the session while the child sat at a small table across from the examiner. All heart-rate data were computer stored as IBIs, and the analog ECG and respiratory signal were also stored on frequency modulation (FM) tape.

Behavioral Stability

Each of the three behavioral settings (play situation at 31 months and the play and the home situation at 43 months) yielded a single standardized composite index of inhibition based on the variables in that situation that were significantly correlated. The standardized index from the play session at 31 months (Index31) included mean latency to touch a toy, enter the cloth tunnel, and approach the other child; number of approaches to the other child; and total duration proximal to the mother. Of course, Index31 significantly differentiated the inhibited and uninhibited children because the children were selected to differ on these behaviors. For the remainder of this chapter, description of a child as inhibited or uninhibited is based on that child's classification at 31 months.

The play session at 43 months yielded an index, Play43, that included variables similar to Index31: latency to touch a toy and to approach the other child, duration proximal to the mother while not playing, and total duration looking at the other child. Inhibited and uninhibited children differed significantly on Play43, $t = 14.95$, $p < .001$. Thus, the behavioral differences between the two groups were preserved.

The home visit was intended to capture the subjects' behavior in response to a stranger entering their homes. Inhibited children might be more timid in a laboratory, but the familiar home environment might reduce that inhibition. However, the inhibition did extend to the home in the presence of a stranger. There was a significant difference, $t = 13.1$, $p < .001$, between the two groups on a standardized index composed of mean latency to vocalize and to approach the observer and frequency of interactions with the observer (Home43).

Behavior in the risk room revealed a group × sex interaction. Inhibited girls spent more time proximal to the mother and less time playing with the toys than did the inhibited boys or the uninhibited boys and girls, all of whom were similar. However, both male and female inhibited children, more often than uninhibited children, refused to imitate the experimenter's acts, $\chi^2 = 5.09, p < .05$.

Index31 was related to behavior in each of the 43-month situations: Play43, $r = .59, p < .01$; Home43, $r = .34, p < .01$; and refusals in the risk room, $p < .05$. An aggregate behavioral index was created for each subject by computing the mean of the three separate standardized variables, Play43, Home43, and number of refusals in the risk room. The composite variable, called Index43, differentiated the inhibited and uninhibited children, $t = 4.63, p < .001$, and significantly correlated with Index31, $r = .57$, $p < .001$.

In sum, the children showed consistency in the tendency to respond with inhibition or lack of inhibition to unfamiliar events across time and situations. The children who remained close to the mother in the play session at 31 months also remained close to the mother in the 43-month play session. These inhibited children more often refused to imitate the experimenter in the risk room and made fewer approaches to the visitor during the home observation. The opposite profile was displayed by the uninhibited children.

This study affirms earlier work showing that the qualities of behavioral inhibition and lack of inhibition are stable. The following section deals with the cardiovascular correlates of these behaviors.

Cardiovascular Data

I suggested earlier that the inhibited children might have lower thresholds of activation of the stress circuits emanating from the limbic system and that the cardiovascular system might be a particular index of this state of limbic arousal. The cardiovascular data were exmamined in several ways.

The mean and standard deviation of the heart period at 31 months and the mean and standard deviation of the heart period during the baselines at 43 months were calculated for each child. The relation between heart rate and heart-rate standard deviation was significant at both ages: 31 months, $r = .70$; 43 months, $r = .56, p < .001$. The stability correlation for mean heart rate and for standard deviation of heart rate at 31 and 43 months was .62 and .50, respectively, both significant at $p < .001$. Heart rate and HRV are typically negatively correlated; a higher heart rate is usually associated with a less variable heart rate.

However, the two behavioral groups did not differ in either heart rate or heart-rate standard deviation during the baseline periods at 31 or 43 months. The inhibited group did show a higher mean heart rate in response to the laboratory tasks at 43 months, although the differences were not significant because of large variability within the groups. However, heart-rate change across the cognitive tasks did differentiate the two groups. A variable representing the change in mean heart rate from a pretask baseline to a posttask baseline was created for each child. Baselines were 1-minute periods during which the child listened to a neutral story. During the interval between the two baselines, the child was engaged in several different potentially stressful cognitive tasks. There were no group differences in task performance. However, the inhibited, but not the uninhibited, children showed a significant increase in heart rate across the cognitive tasks, $t = 3.34$, $p < .05$. My colleagues and I interpret this fact as indicating that the inhibited children became more aroused during the demanding cognitive battery. The increase in heart rate was independent of the initial heart-rate value on the pretask baseline. Even inhibited children with a relatively high heart rate as the laboratory session began showed an increase in heart rate over the course of the test session.

There is some evidence to suggest that some children have tonically higher heart rates, even under conditions of minimal stress. In the laboratory, my colleagues and I have been studying another longitudinal cohort of inhibited and uninhibited children for over 6 years. When these chiildren were 7½ years old, an all-night recording of heart rate and respiration was obtained using a Healthdyne Infant Monitor and Oxford Recorder. The recordings ranged from 6 to 12 hours in length, and the first and last hours were discarded to eliminate any heart-rate changes due to awareness of the monitor. Computer analysis of the quiet sleep periods revealed significant correlations between the child's sleeping heart rate at 7½ years and the heart rate in the laboratory at 21 months ($r = .37$), at 4 years ($r = .40$), at 5½ years ($r = .61$), and at 7½ years ($r = .49$). Children who entered the laboratory with relatively high heart rates tended to have a high heart rate in sleep, and these data, together with those of the present study, imply that more inhibited than uninhibited children are in a tonic state of higher limbic arousal.

In the present study, a measure of beat-to-beat HRV revealed that inhibited children also had a more stable heart rate across the baseline and task periods. These differences were not statistically significant because of high interindividual variability. Even though there was a significant difference between the two groups in heart rate from pretask baseline to posttask baseline, there was no group difference in HRV. An increase in sympathetic tone, a decrease in parasympathetic activity, or a combination of both conditions could have been responsible for the increased heart rate across tasks shown by inhibited children. To clarify the cardiovascular data at 43 months, an analysis of HRV was performed using spectral analysis.

Spectral Data

As noted earlier, spectral analysis can separate the amount of HRV associated with parasympathetic activity from that associated with sympathetic activity. This analysis required 30 continuous seconds of cardiovascular and respiratory data free of movement artifacts or transitory respiratory changes (yawns, sighs). All segments of cardiovascular data that met these criteria were considered suitable for analysis.

The FM tapes on which the heart-rate and respiration data had been recorded were analyzed in the following way. The ECG and impedance pneumograph output (used to measure respiration) were sampled by computer. A clock, triggered by the R wave of the ECG, recorded the length of each cardiovascular cycle. Simultaneously, the respiratory data were digitized by a 14-bit analog-to-digital converter at 8.53 hertz, yielding 256 sample points in the 30-second record. The respiratory data were first passed through a two-stage active filter with a cutoff frequency of 1 hertz. Instantaneous heart rate over the 30 seconds was determined from the series of R waves for the 256 time points in the respiration record. The instantaneous heart-rate values were calculated as the reciprocal of the IBI during the sample time point.

The power-spectrum density function of each of these two data sets was calculated using standard Fourier methods with appropriate windowing and smoothing techniques. The mean and any linear trend were first subtracted from the data by fitting a least-square linear equation to the data. A Fast Fourier Transform was then used to calculate the power-spectrum density function from 0 to 1 hertz.

The power spectrum for instantaneous heart rate was summarized by dividing the total power of the spectrum (total HRV over the 30 seconds) into only two regions. One region corresponded to the area associated with respiration, and the remaining region corresponded to the area from .05 hertz to the lower limit of the respiratory area (see fig. 2). These two regions essentially accounted for all the power in the spectrum, or the total variability of heart rate for that period.

A correlated respiratory area and total power area were also calculated and adjusted by a linear transformation to account for changes in tidal volume (reflected in variation in depth of respiration) within subjects across trials.[1]

A graph with three functions was plotted for each child, the three functions corresponding to the tasks at 43 months on which power spectra were available for that child. (For examples of these graphs, see fig. 3.) The three functions were the corrected total power (variability) in the heart rate, the amount

---

1. The correlation for changes in tidal volume across tasks was computed by adjusting the amount of power associated with the respiratory area in the power spectrum of heart rate by any change in the amount of power in the respiratory area in the power spectrum of respiration. Contact the author for more details.

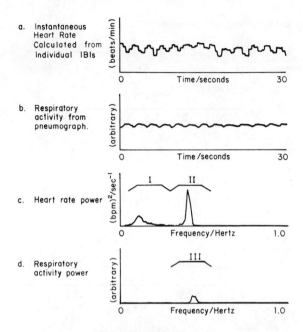

a. Instantaneous Heart Rate Calculated from Individual IBIs (beats/min)

0   Time/seconds   30

b. Respiratory activity from pneumograph. (arbitrary)

0   Time/seconds   30

c. Heart rate power (bpm)^2/sec^{-1}

I   II

0   Frequency/Hertz   1.0

d. Respiratory activity power (arbitrary)

III

0   Frequency/Hertz   1.0

Areas used to summarize spectra

. Total power   Area I + Area II
. Non-respiratory area (parasympathetic and sympathetic) of heart rates spectrum: Area I
. Respiratory area (parasympathetic) of heart rate spectrum: Area II
. Respiratory area of respiration spectrum: Area III

Fig. 2. An example of heart-rate and respiratory data and associated power spectra. *a,* Instantaneous heart rate calculated from individual IBIs. *b,* Respiratory activity from pneumograph. *c,* Heart-rate power. *d,* Respiratory activity power. Areas used to summarize spectra (see text): total area: area I + area II; nonrespiratory area of heart-rate spectrum: area I; respiratory area of heart-rate spectrum: area II; respiratory area of respiration spectrum: area III; corrected respiratory area: area I/area III; and corrected total area: area I + area II/area III.

of power contributed by the nonrespiratory area, and the amount of power contributed by the corrected respiratory area.

As noted earlier, the variability in heart rate at the respiratory frequency can be attributed completely to vagal (parasympathetic) activity. Unfortunately, the area below the respiratory peak reflects both parasympathetic and sympathetic activity (Pomeranz et al. 1985). This fact means that investigators must be creative in using spectral analysis if they wish to attribute some changes in heart rate to sympathetic activity. Without the aid of drug blockade or other invasive techniques, it is not possible to eliminate the amount of power that is due to parasympathetic activity in the lower cycles of the spectrum and to evaluate the power attributable to sympathetic activity. However, because the respiratory peak is controlled exclusively by parasympathetic ac-

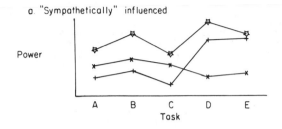

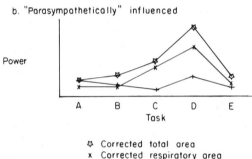

☼ Corrected total area
× Corrected respiratory area
+ Non-respiratory area

Fig. 3. Method of summarizing heart-rate power-spectrum changes across tasks to determine autonomic classification. *a*, Sympathetically influenced. *b*, Parasympathetically influenced. * = corrected total area; × = corrected respiratory area; and + = nonrespiratory area.

tivity, this fact can be used to estimate the relative contribution of parasympathetic and sympathetic activity to total HRV.

The influence of parasympathetic activity on the slower cycles below the respiratory peak is less than its influence at the respiratory peak. But, in order to be conservative, I shall assume that parasympathetic influence is distributed equally throughout the spectrum. It follows, therefore, that the magnitude of change in power at the respiratory peak between two points in time can be used to estimate the change in parasympathetic influence for all areas, including the low-frequency area. Thus, if the power at the respiratory peak decreased by x from time 1 to time 2, I will assume that it decreased by the same amount at the lower frequencies. Then any remaining amount of change in power must be due to a change in sympathetic activity.

Figure 3*a* reveals that the changes in corrected total power across tasks are more closely yoked to changes in the nonrespiratory area of the spectrum. Specifically, both the total amount of power and the power in the nonrespiratory area between task C and D increased while the amount of power in the respiratory area decreased. The decrease in the power at the respiratory peak is interpreted to mean that the influence of parasympathetic activity on the heart decreased between tasks C and D. Therefore, any increase in the power in the nonrespiratory area must be due to sympathetic activity. Conversely, in figure 3b, the total power and power in the respiratory area in the heart-rate spectrum increased from task C to task D, but the power in the nonrespiratory area showed only a very slight increase. In this case, the increased variability in heart rate should be attributed to increased parasympathetic activity.

I used each child's graphed power-spectrum data to assign each child to one of three autonomic categories. If changes in the corrected total variability of a child's spectra could be described best in terms of changes in sympathetic activity, that subject was classified as sympathetically influenced. If the changes in total variability could be described best in terms of parasympathetic changes, the subject was classified as parasympathetically influenced. The remaining children for whom classification was ambiguous were classified as sympathetic-parasympathetic. Interrater reliability between two raters for classification of the children was over 90 percent. This analysis revealed a significant difference between the two behavioral groups (Fisher's Exact Test, $p < .03$). Seventy percent of the inhibited children showed heart-rate changes across the tasks that were attributable to changes in sympathetic activity, while only 31 percent of the uninhibited children showed this profile (these figures are based on the 31-month index).

A second analysis was performed on the cardiovascular records for subjects who had power-spectrum data for both pre- and posttask baselines. These spectra were examined for shifts in autonomic activity from the pre- to the posttask period. A child received a classification of sympathetic if any of the following conditions were met: the nonparasympathetic area of the power spectrum increased from pre- to posttask period more than 10 percent, and the parasympathetic area remained the same or decreased; or the parasympathetic area decreased at least 10 percent, and the nonparasympathetic area remained the same or increased. A child received a classification of parasympathetic if the parasympathetic area increased by at least 10 percent and the nonparasympathetic decreased or remained the same or if the nonparasympathetic area decreased at least 10 percent and the parasympathetic remained the same or increased. Using this analysis, 80 percent of the inhibited children, while only 30 percent of the uninhibited children, showed a shift in the power spectra to increased sympathetic activity from pre- to posttask baseline (Fisher's Exact Text, $p < .05$).

These results differ from those based on a mean index of HRV. The patterns of parasympathetic and sympathetic activity in the power spectra suggest that stabilization of heart rate (i.e., less variability) is not only the consequence of a decrease in parasympathetic influence (or vagal tone) (Obrist 1982). A decrease in sympathetic activity can also result in a decrease in total variability. Conversely, increased HRV does not always mean an increase in parasympathetic activity because increased sympathetic activity can also increase the total variability. Spectral analysis of cardiovascular data, although stringent in its requirements, allows a clearer and more valid picture of the individual contributions of parasympathetic and sympathetic activity to HRV.

Summary

Psychologists have proposed different theories to explain dimensions of personality. Most of these personality characteristics have resisted sensitive measurement. A growing body of evidence, including the data of the present study, suggests that the tendency to approach or to withdraw from uncertain situations is stable over time and consistent across situations, especially in young children.

Further, the bases for this response may originate, in part, in different activities of stress circuits originating in the limbic system. Because the children in this study were young and not hospitalized, activation of limbic activity could be measured only peripherally, with noninvasive techniques. The cardiovascular system was chosen for a detailed analysis because changes in this system are easily measured and reflect alterations in both parasympathetic and sympathetic activity. Spectral analysis is able to distinguish the influence of each branch of the ANS on HRV. The results of this analysis suggest that changes in HRV over several cognitive tasks were more likely to be sympathetically influenced in inhibited than in uninhibited children. Among inhibited children, changes in HRV from a pre- to a posttask baseline were more often the result of increased sympathetic activity.

All individuals do not respond to stress with change in every physiological system. Biological systems are interconnected, and feedback mechanisms affect the responses. Thus, the results of these analyses are impressive. In future analyses of our cohorts, my colleagues and I will relate results of spectral analyses to other behavioral and physiological measures in order to explore the relation between sympathetic activity and behavioral inhibition further.

References

Akselrod, S.; Gordon, D.; Madwed, J. B.; Snidman, N.; Shannon, D. C.; and Cohen, R. J. 1985. Hemodynamic regulation: Investigation by spectral analysis. *American Journal of Physiology: Heart and Circulatory Physiology* 85:867–75.

Akselrod, S.; Gordon, D.; Ubel, F. A.; Shannon, D. C.; Barger, D. C.; and Cohen, R. J. 1981. Power spectrum analysis of heart rate fluctuation: A quantitative probe of beat-to-beat cardiovascular control. *Science* 213:220–22.

Berg, W. K. 1972. Habituation and dishabituation of cardiac responses in 4-month-old, alert infants. *Journal of Experimental Child Psychology* 14:92–107.

Cannon, W. B. 1929. *Bodily changes in pain, hunger, fear, and rage.* New York: Appleton.

Coles, M. G. H. 1972. Cardiac and respiratory activity during visual search. *Journal of Experimental Psychology* 96:371–79.

Ekelund, L. G., and Holmgren, A. 1967. Central hemodynamics during exercise. *Circulation Research* 10, no. 1, suppl.:I-33-I-43.

Fuchs, S. A.; Edinger, H. M.; and Siegel, A. 1985. The organization of the hypothalamic pathways mediating affective defense behavior in the cat. *Brain Research* 330:77–92.

Garcia-Coll, C.; Kagan, J.; and Reznick, J. S. 1984. Behavioral inhibition in young children. *Child Development* 55:1005–19.

Glick, G., and Braunwald, E. 1965. Relative roles of the sympathetic and parasympathetic nervous systems in the reflex control of heart-rate. *Circulation Research* 16:363–75.

Goodman, L. S., and Gilman, A., eds. 1980. *The pharmacological basis of theraputics.* New York: Macmillan.

Guyton, A. C. 1981. *Textbook of medical physiology.* Philadelphia: Saunders.

Hirsch, J. A., and Bishop, B. 1981. Respiratory sinus arrythmia in humans: How breathing pattern modulates heart rate. *American Journal of Physiology* 241:H620–H629.

Kagan, J.; Reznick, J. S.; Clarke, C.; Snidman, N.; and Garcia-Coll, C. 1984. Behavioral inhibition to the unfamiliar. *Child Development* 55:2212–25.

Kagan, J.; Reznick, J. S.; and Snidman, N. In press. The physiology and psychology of behavioral inhibition in children. *Child Development.*

Kalsbeek, J. W H. 1973. Do you believe in sinus arrythmia? *Ergonomics* 16:99–104.

Katona, P. G., and Jih, F. 1975. Respiratory sinus arrythmia: Non-invasive measure of parasympathetic cardiac control. *Journal of Applied Physiology* 39:801–5.

Mulder, G., and Mulder, L. J. M. 1981. Information and cardiovascular control. *Psychophysiology* 18:392–401.

Obrist, P. 1982. *Cardiovascular psychophysiology.* New York: Planum.

Pomeranz, B.; Macaulay, R. J. B.; Caudill, M. A.; Kutz, I.; Adam, D.; Gordon, D.; Kilborn, K. M.; Barger, A. C.; Shannon, D. C.; Cohen, R. J.; and Benson, H. 1985. Assessment of autonomic function in humans by heart rate spectral analysis. *American Journal of Physiology* 248:H151–H153.

Porges, S. W.; Bohrer, R.; Cheung, M. M.; Drasgrow, F.; McCabe, P. M.; and Keren, G. 1980. A new time-series statistic for detecting rhythmic co-occurrence in the frequency domain: The weighted coherence and its application to psychophysiological research. *Psychological Bulletin* 88:580–87.

Porges, S. W.; McCabe, P. M.; and Yongue, B. G. 1982. Respiratory–heart rate interactions: Psychophysiological implications for pathophysiology and behavior. In *Perspectives in cardiovascular psychophysiology,* ed. J. Cacioppo and Petty, R. 223–64. New York: Guilford.

Reznick, J. S.; Kagan, J.; Snidman, N.; Gersten, M.; Baak, K.; and Rosenberg, A. 1986. Inhibited and uninhibited children: A follow-up study. *Child Development* 57:660–80.

Richards, J. E. 1985. Respiratory sinus arrhythmia predicts heart rate and visual responses during visual attention in 14 and 20 week old infants. *Psychophysiology* 22:101–9.

Sayers, B. M. 1973. Analysis of heart rate variability. *Ergonomics* 16:17–32.

Sroufe, L. A. 1971. Age change in cardiac deceleration within a fixed foreperiod reaction-time task: An index of attention. *Developmental Psychology* 5:338–43.

Suomi, S. J. 1983. Social development in rhesus monkeys: Consideration of individual differences. In *The behavior of human infants*, ed. A. Oliverio and M. Zappella, 71–92. New York: Plenum.

Weiss, J. M.; Goodman, P. A.; Losito, B. G.; Corrigan, S.; Charry, J. M.; and Bailey, W. H. 1981. Behavioral depression produced by an uncontrollable stressor: Relationship to norepinephrine, dopamine, and serotonin levels in various regions of rat brain. *Brain Research Reviews* 3:167–205.

4 Behavioral Inhibition in the Classroom

MICHELLE GERSTEN

The origins and stability of temperamental characteristics have captured the attention of a growing number of investigators (Buss and Plomin 1984; Bronson and Pankey 1977; Carey and McDevitt 1978; Hinde, Stevenson-Hinde, and Tamplin 1985; Plomin and Rowe 1977; Garcia-Coll, Kagan, and Reznick 1984). One focus of this research has been individual differences in youngsters' customary style of responding to novelty or uncertainty. Conceptualized as sociability, introversion/extroversion, approach/withdrawal, inhibition, or social responsiveness, differences in initial reactions to unfamiliar people or events emerge in many studies. Although the terms used to describe these individual differences vary, the behaviors that define this temperamental dimension are less divergent. Following exposure to unfamiliar stimuli or events, children called "sociable," "uninhibited," "outgoing," "extroverted," or "fearless" typically exhibit no visible change in their ongoing behavior. Some may vocalize, smile, or spontaneously interact with or approach the unfamiliar. By contrast, children described as "shy," "inhibited," "vigilant," "withdrawn," "introverted," "timid," or "cautious" tend to show restraint when confronted with novelty. They typically stop their ongoing behavior, cease vocalizing, seek comfort from a familiar figure, or withdraw from the area in which the unfamiliar event occurred.

Kagan and his colleagues have reported on an extensive longitudinal investigation of inhibition to the unfamiliar (see Snidman, chap. 3, and Kagan, chap. 1, both in this vol.). This chapter reports on a component of that investigation, in which the unfamiliar setting was a kindergarten classroom.

The evidence gathered by Kagan and his colleagues in the 21-month, 48-month, and 5-year assessments suggests that individual differences in behavioral inhibition to the unfamiliar are relatively stable from infancy through the

I am grateful for the support and editorial assistance of Jerome Kagan and Steven Reznick at all stages in the preparation of this chapter.

preschool years. Moreover, the data suggest that patterns of heart rate are systematically related to facets of children's behavior in laboratory contexts.

Questions remain, however, concerning the extent to which the variations observed in laboratory contexts are related to differences in children's social behavior in naturalistic settings and the degree to which these differences will persist through the school years.

Most of the observational research on temperamental qualities to date has examined the relation between parental reports of temperament and behavior observed in classroom or home settings. However, interest in the consequences of temperamental traits such as approach-withdrawal for school behavior dates back to Chess and Thomas's (1977) New York Longitudinal Study (NYLS). They discuss how differences in a child's propensity to approach or withdraw from novelty play a major role in the nature of the child's adaptation to school because that propensity affects both approach to learning tasks and interactions with teachers and peers. The beginning of school places a number of new demands on the child, such as the mastery of complex tasks and the necessity of relating to peers, which are particularly stressful for the slow-to-warm-up child. Chess and Thomas cite parental report data from the NYLS indicating that infants who displayed a predominance of withdrawal responses to new stimuli (referred to as "slow-to-warm-up" children) were at risk for developing behavioral difficulties in the early school years.

Billman and McDevitt (1980) report that approach-withdrawal (as measured by the Behavioral Style Questionnaire and the Toddler Temperament Scale) was significantly related to observational ratings of peer interaction conducted in preschool. Specifically, preschoolers rated as "withdrawing" by their parents and teacher did more watching, more pushing away of others, and less talking and seized toys fewer times than did children rated as "approaching." Similarly, Kohn and Parnes (1974) report that the stylistic dimension of approach-withdrawal is a significant determinant of social behavior in the classroom. Withdrawn children were slow to approach and settle into new situations.

These studies imply that a predisposition to withdraw from novelty has adverse consequences for the child's social behavior in school. However, they rely on interview or questionnaire data to establish a connection between temperament and social adaptation.

The most extensive evidence suggesting a relation between inhibition and interpersonal behavior difficulties comes from research by Rubin and his colleagues (Rubin, Lemare, and Lollis, in press). The Waterloo Longitudinal Project has examined the concurrent and predictive correlates of observed social withdrawal in the early and middle years of childhood. The central goal of this investigation was to determine whether social withdrawal in early and middle childhood predicted a withdrawn interactive style and internalizing disorders in later childhood.

Preschool, kindergarten, and first-grade children were observed for six 10-second time samples each day, during free play, over a period of 6 weeks. When the children reached second and fourth grade, each subject was observed playing with 12 same-age, same-sex partners over four separate 15-minute free-play sessions. Social withdrawal indices derived from observations across grades revealed that social withdrawal from kindergarten to grade 5 was a moderately stable phenomenon. Isolate behavior in kindergarten correlated positively with isolate behavior in grade 2 and negatively with sociable behavior in kindergarten and grade 2.

This investigation also provided data bearing on the concomitants and consequences of social withdrawal. Observations of kindergarten children suggested that withdrawn preschoolers and kindergartners were less assertive, less successful in managing peer interactions, and more adult dependent than were more sociable children (Rubin 1982b). In addition, there was a relation between high rates of solitary, nonsocial behavior and teacher ratings of anxiety and fearfulness (Rubin and Clarke 1983).

The literature on peer relations also suggests that prototypically inhibited behavior is incompatible with behaviors that facilitate normal social interaction and development. McGrew (1972) and Putallaz and Gotteman (1981) have discussed the way in which fearful, restrained, and cautious behavior impedes the child's social development. More recently, Rubin, Lemare, and Lollis (in press) noted that the child's reticence to explore novel, out-of-home settings precludes the possibility of establishing peer relations and the development of social skills supposedly encouraged by these relations. Further, they envision the circular process of failure to develop social and cognitive skills leading to further withdrawal from the peer milieu.

If children continue to avoid interacting with peers, Rubin, Lemare, and Lollis (in press) hypothesize that these inhibited children may be at risk for manifesting clinical symptoms of social isolation or withdrawal. Indirect support for this hypothesis comes from sociometric and observational data (Hartup 1983) suggesting that peer acceptance is associated with friendliness, sociability, and outgoing behavior. Conversely, children rated low in peer acceptance were characterized by hovering cautious and apprehensive behavior (Gottman 1977).

The primary goal of the present investigation was to determine whether a predisposition toward inhibition to the unfamiliar in early childhood has implications for older children's behavior in both novel and familiar naturalistic settings and whether behavior displayed in the kindergarten classroom is similar to the behaviors exhibited by children in the laboratory. It was hypothesized that children classified as behaviorally inhibited at 21 months of age would exhibit more behavior characteristic of restraint on the first day of school than children originally classified as uninhibited, spending less time proximal to peers, interacting less with peers, and spending more time staring at peers than their uninhibited counterparts would. It was also hypothesized that children classifed as inhibited at 21 months would appear apprehensive and shy even after they had had 6 months to become accustomed to the classroom. Although it was anticipated that all the children would become more spontaneous with time, it was hypothesized that the children classified as inhibited at 21 months would continue to display apprehensive behaviors that distinguish them from the formerly uninhibited subjects.

Method

Subjects

The sample consisted of 39 of the 58 children who were participants in the ongoing longitudinal study conducted by Kagan and his colleagues (Garcia-Coll, Kagan, and Reznick 1984). The selection of subjects is described by them in detail and so will be discussed only briefly here.

The sample came from a group of over 300 Caucasian infants whose mothers participated in telephone interviews regarding the child's temperament. On the basis of these interviews, Garcia-Coll chose a sample of 117 children whose mothers described them as either consistently uninhibited or consistently cautious when confronted with unfamiliar events or people. These 117 21-month-olds were then assessed in a laboratory session that included initial meeting with an unfamiliar examiner, an encounter with an unfamiliar set of toys, a woman model displaying a trio of acts that were difficult to remember, an interaction with another female stranger, exposure to a large and odd-looking robot, and temporary separation from the mother. The major signs of inhibition were long latencies to interact with unfamiliar adults, retreat from unfamiliar objects, cessation of play and vocalization, and remaining proximal to the mother. Scores reflecting these behaviors were combined to form a continuous index of inhibited behavior ranging from 1 to 56. The children who displayed the relevant behaviors consistently across most of the incentive situations, on both occasions, as well as those who did not were selected to form groups of 28 inhibited and 30 uninhibited children. Each group represented about 10 percent of the original sample. Forty-three of these children participated in the 5-year assessment. We were able to obtain parental and principal's permission to observe 39 of these subjects in their kindergarten classrooms. Twenty-two of these had been classified as inhibited, and 17 had been classified as uninhibited. Twenty-four were female and 15 male, and the proportion of boys and girls in each of the two groups was similar. Mean age at the time of the fall school visit was 5 years, 2 months.

School Assessment

Procedure

The children were observed in their kindergarten classroom on two occasions: once during the first week of kindergarten and again in the spring of the same academic year. All the children also participated in two laboratory sessions at Harvard University. The initial school visit occurred before the first laboratory session; the second occurred while the laboratory assessments were underway. The vast majority of the children were visited on their first day of school. However, in a few cases, observers were not permitted school entry during the initial days of school, and these were seen during the first week of kindergarten.

Each child was visited by an observer who had no prior knowledge of the child's family or inhibition classification. Parents and teachers were asked not to notify the children of the impending visits. Observers assumed the stances of classroom visitors and quietly stood or sat at the room's periphery. Maximum distance permitting accurate observation was maintained between the subject and the observer. Throughout the study, no child displayed awareness of "being followed." As McGrew (1972) has noted, children conclude early that observers are dull prospects and ignore them in favor of other adults.

A total of 12 observers, including me, conducted the observations on the first day of school, while four different observers participated in the spring data-collection process. No observer visited the same school more than once.

Classroom observers employed a coding scheme devised by me and A. Rosenberg. The system was developed after an extensive review of ethological and observational studies of peer interaction (Billman and McDevitt 1980; McGrew 1972; Blurton-Jones 1972) and a review of the variables selected for analysis. A time-sampling procedure permitted a comparison of measures of behavior frequency objectively defined for different individuals in different classrooms. Each observer wore an earphone attached to a small audiocassette that issued a regular signal every 10–15 seconds (15 seconds for the fall observation, owing to the greater number of observers, and 10 seconds for the spring observation). At the signal, the observer looked up, took a mental snapshot of the child's location and behavior, and noted the occurrence of one or more predetermined variables on a coding sheet. Variables were included that differentiated among inhibited and uninhibited children in the laboratory and could be scored during live observations in the laboratory and school (see fig. 1). At every signal, the coder was to note the following.

1. The interpersonal setting was coded—that is, whether the child was physically isolated, proximal to peers, or proximal to the teacher.

2. The nature of the child's ongoing activity in relation to those around him

Subject _____ Context _____ Time _____ Coder _____ Pg _____

Setting	1			2			3		
Isolated									
Peer Group									
W/teacher only									

Activity	1			2			3		
Teacher Directed									
Inactive									
Wandering									
Interacting									
Solitary Task or Play									

Behavior (Not Obligatory)								
Offers help/object to peer								
Requests aid from teacher								
Touches peer, not hostile								
Seizes toy from peer								
Push, hit peer								
Laughing								
Crying								
Running, jumping								
Approaches Peer								
Approaches Adult								
Approaches Group								

Vocal Behavior				
Talks to Peer				
Talks to Adult				
Talks to Group				

Visual Fixation				
Look at Peer				
Look at Adult				
Look at Group				

Figure 1

was coded. The child could be coded as inactive, wandering, interacting, involved in solitary play, or participating in a teacher-directed activity. Though a "setting" variable might indicate that a child is in a group, it is the "activity" variable that indicates whether the child is actively involved with that group or is merely passive and proximal to other children.

The child's vocal and visual behaviors were categorized according to whom the look or utterance was directed. Unlike the measures of activity and interpersonal proximity, which were coded at each signal, visual and vocal behaviors were recorded when they occurred. Vocal behaviors were scored only in the spring because of the difficulty establishing reliability on the verbal behaviors from videotaped sessions in the fall training sessions.

3. The child's vocalizations were coded whenever the child appeared to be talking to others; self-directed speech was not coded. The child could be coded as talking to a peer, talking to a teacher, or talking to a group of two or more persons.

4. The child's visual behavior was coded only if the child was looking steadily (as opposed to merely glancing) and not simultaneously interacting. By excluding glances, which are natural concomitants of conversations or interactional exchange, the visual behavior category captured only those instances when the child was staring at others. The child could be scored as looking at the peer, looking at the teacher, or looking at a group of two or more.

5. In addition to verbal and visual behaviors, the coders also noted whenever the child engaged in one or more of the following behaviors: offers help to peer, requests aid, nonhostile touching, seizes toy, pushes, laughs, cries, runs, approaches peer, approaches group, or approaches adult.

Coders typically observed the children for an entire kindergarten session (typically, 1–3 hours in the fall and 3 hours in the spring). They were instructed to code for 15 continuous minutes before filling out a brief form indicating contextual information during teacher-directed activities, the nature of the settings, behavior of classmates, the degree to which the teacher guided the activities, and facets of the child's behavior. The observers also noted the nature of the class activity at continuous intervals so that the data could be divided into teacher-directed segments, seat work, or free play/unstructured activity.

Observers were encouraged to code as much free-play data as possible because pilot testing suggested that the time when children were allowed to play freely with minimal intervention on the part of the teacher yielded the greatest variability. At the completion of the visit, observers filled out a form asking for extensive detail about the physical setting of the classroom, the composition of the class, the extent of the teacher's directions, and the schedule of activities and for a brief description of the events of the day. Observers also ranked the child on a scale of inhibition relative to others in the class. Finally, observers summarized their clinical impressions of the children.

The children attended 38 kindergartens differing in setting, structure, teacher style, size, and the nature of the classroom activities. However, an examination of the relations among these setting variables and behavioral indices revealed that none were systematic or significant.

Interobserver reliability for the fall observations was determined by treating me as the criterion and having each of the other observers independently code videotapes of several different children in a classroom setting. Agreement between each of the 13 observers and the criterion coder ranged from 86 to 93 percent. The February visits to the school were made by four observers, two of whom had visited in the fall. However, these two coders observed different children on their spring visit. Interobserver reliabilities for the February visit were computed by having each observer code behavior in a natural school setting. Agreement between each of the three coders and me ranged from 93 to 99 percent. The denominator for computing percentage agreement did not include instances in which no behavior was coded by either observer.

Frequency measures within each category (e.g., interact) were summed across all the free-play and teacher-directed segments. Data from free-play segments were analyzed separately from those from teacher-directed segments because pilot testing revealed that structured activities had a dampening effect on the emergence of individual differences. Owing to the variation in the total duration of observational time for each subject, category totals were divided by the number of minutes of observation of each subject. This yielded a set of standard frequency scores that reflect "rate per 10 minutes." These normalized scores were used in all subsequent analyses.

Laboratory Assessment

The laboratory assessment at 5 years consisted of a testing situation with an examiner and a play situation with an unfamiliar child of the same age and sex. All children were tested by the same female examiner, who was unfamiliar with the child's prior classification. The child's behavior during the procedures was recorded on videotape, and the child's heart rate was monitored during the session.

On the first laboratory visit, the following challenging tasks were administered in an effort to increase task-related arousal: recognition memory for pictures, word recall, embedded figures, matching familiar figures, and haptic-visual matching procedure. The major variables coded were heart period and variability, response latency, and accuracy of responses. A parallel recognition-memory task was administered after the cognitive tasks to determine whether inhibited and uninhibited children differed in their memory performance following cognitive stress. The child was then asked to sit quietly while the examiner read a story to the child in order to record baseline heart rate. After a break for refreshments, the child was presented with a slide story, to determine whether inhibited or uninhibited children would display differential attentiveness to fearful and bold characters, and active-passive pictures, to assess whether children would attend preferentially to a passive or to a bold figure.

Coders unfamiliar with the child's prior classification coded the frequency of the following variables from a videotape of the child's behavior during the entire testing session: child glances up at the examiner, spontaneous comments to the examiner that were not elicited by the examiner's questions, and gross motor movements of the limbs and trunk.

The second laboratory session consisted of play in a "risk room," to determine if inhibited children would be more reluctant than uninhibited ones to play with novel objects and initiate novel activities, and peer play observation of a pair of children of the same sex, one inhibited and one uninhibited (judgments of inhibition were based on the child's 21-month classification). The variables coded from videotape of the peer play included latency to play with the first toy, latency to approach the other child, latency to first vocalization, total time looking at the other child, latency to first vocalization, total time looking at the other child while not in social interaction, and total time proximal to the mother while not playing. For a complete description of these laboratory procedures and measures, which were developed by other Harvard Infant Study investigators, see Reznick et al. (1986).

The major variables from the 5-year assessment that will be used in present analyses include the following: (1) a laboratory inhibition factor representing the mean standard score for two correlated variables: the number of spontaneous comments and the number of gross motor movements displayed during the testing session (both scores were reversed so that a high index indicated behavioral inhibition); (2) a peer-play factor derived from the mean correlated standard scores for latency to play, latency to first approach, time proximal to mother, and time staring at the other child during the peer-play session; (3) "look examiner," the number of times the child glanced up at the examiner during the testing procedure; (4) "risk avoidance," the mean standard score for latency to initiate play with any toy, number of novel acts not initiated, total time proximal to mother, and total time not playing while in the risk room; (5) "mean quiet heart period," the average duration between successive heart beats across those cognitive tasks during which a child did not have to talk or move; (6) "heart-rate variability," the standard deviation of the interbeat intervals during the above tasks; and (7) the aggregate index of inhibition, the average of the standard scores for peer-play inhibition, laboratory inhibition, school inhibition, risk avoidance, and look examiner.

Results

The presentation of results is divided into two sections. The first section describes the contemporaneous relations among the major variables presumed to assess behavioral inhibition and lack of inhibition in the school setting, on the one hand, and the major behavioral and physiological variables evaluated in the laboratory at 5½ years, on the other. The second section describes the predictive relations between behavioral and cardiac data gathered at 21 and 48 months and the major variables assessed in the school at 5½ years of age. Because there were no sex differences in the primary variables, the data were combined for the sexes.

Contemporaneous Relations at 5½ Years

Table 1 presents the mean scores on the variables assessed during free play for the children who had been classified originally as inhibited or uninhibited at 21 months of age.

An inspection of the correlations among variables assessed during free play for the episodes on the first day of school revealed several meaningful constellations of behavior. Staring at peers was highly correlated with the tendency to stare at adults, $r = .49, p < .01$, and groups, $r = .34, p < .001$, and with physical isolation, $r = .49, p < .05$. The relation between isolation from others and staring at others is not an artifact of the coding scheme because staring was not recorded while the child was proximal to a peer.

A network of associations also emerged for behaviors indicative of lack of inhibition. Children who were often proximal to peers were more apt to interact with them, $r = .49, p < .01$.

Table 1 also presents the mean scores for the two groups on the variables assessed during free-play episodes in the spring. An inspection of the correlations among variables derived from the free-play episodes revealed that the tendency to look at peers was strongly related to the inclination to be still or inactive, $r = .49, p < .01$. Staring at peers was also moderately correlated with the tendency to look at adults and to look at groups, $r = .29$ and $.30$, respectively, $p < .01$. There was also an association between the tendency to maintain distance from peers and the tendency to be inactive, $r = .37$, $p < .06$, or to wander, $r = .30, p < .06$.

A priori considerations led us to create an aggregate index of inhibition for the fall school visit by computing an average of the segments isolated from peers, staring at peers, and interacting (the value for interacting was reversed). The selection of these variables was based on prior research suggesting that these variables were sensitive in discriminating between the two groups.

Table 2 presents the mean scores on the major variables assessed during

Table 1: Play

	Fall				Spring			
	Inhibited[a]		Uninhibited[b]		Inhibited[a]		Uninhibited[b]	
	X	S.D.	X	S.D.	X	S.D.	X	S.D.
Isolated	.329	.187	.219	.174	.158	.119	.160	.215
With peer	.639	.186	.754	.171	.791	.152	.811	.237
With teacher	.035	.043	.028	.040	.052	.071	.029	.040
Teacher-directed activity	.021	.041	.017	.024	.164	.208	.143	.227
Inactive	.231	.110	.128	.104	.161	.101	.091	.074
Wanders	.063	.052	.046	.049	.038	.028	.017	.020
Interacts	.235	.206	.349	.245	.297	.245	.507	.161
Solitary Play	.431	.158	.453	.219	.341	.168	.245	.151
Offers toy	.127	.250	.525	.664	.111	.171	.391	.494
Requests	.340	.579	.366	.552	.327	.478	.369	.685
Touches peer	.123	.304	.810	1.451	.159	.445	.217	.292
Seizes toy	.070	.179	.165	.357	.000	.000	.117	.279
Pushes	.000	.000	.079	.211	.000	.000	.000	.000
Laugh	.197	.762	.642	1.766	.049	.182	.046	.102
Cries	.000	.000	.036	.136	.000	.000	.000	.000
Runs	.862	1.916	.716	1.552	.023	.086	.009	.034
Looks peer	6.360	4.256	2.251	2.196	3.079	2.354	2.357	1.236
Looks adult	1.768	1.565	.629	.639	1.848	1.406	.725	.742
Looks group	2.407	1.897	1.051	1.379	2.700	2.610	.893	.697
Talks peer	. . .	. . .	. . .	. . .	5.023	6.182	6.941	5.189
Talks adult	. . .	. . .	. . .	. . .	2.029	3.123	1.461	1.247
Talks group	. . .	. . .	. . .	. . .	.311	.272	.843	.802

[a] $N = 15$.
[b] $N = 14$.

teacher-directed episodes for the children who had been classified originally as inhibited or uninhibited at 21 months of age. Although behavior during teacher-directed episodes was less informative, a few meaningful correlations emerged among variable assessed in the fall. The tendency to stare at peers was positively correlated with the tendency to stare at adults, $r = .85$, $p < .0001$, and to spend time unoccupied during group activities such as singing or games, $r = .78$, $p < .0001$, and negatively related to working at a solitary task while classmates are engaged in teacher-guided activites, $r = .39$, $p < .05$. This correlation suggests that uninhibited children are more apt to disregard the teacher's instructions and engage in off-task behavior. Intercorrelations among variables assesed during teacher-directed episodes on the spring observation revealed fewer meaningful relations.

As anticipated, there were no significant relations between individual variables assessed during the fall and spring sessions. The lack of correlations

Table 2: Teacher Directed

	Fall				Spring			
	Inhibited[a]		Uninhibited[b]		Inhibited[a]		Uninhibited[b]	
	X	S.D.	X	S.D.	X	S.D.	X	S.D.
Isolated	.030	.021	.109	.212	.016	.037	.019	.037
With peer	.964	.024	.879	.219	.979	.045	.972	.058
With teacher	.005	.007	.012	.025	.005	.009	.010	.026
Teacher-directed activity	.298	.325	.369	.303	.827	.133	.847	.122
Inactive	.237	.291	.108	.131	.073	.128	.043	.030
Wanders	.012	.011	.010	.017	.005	.007	.032	.113
Interacts	.083	.090	.079	.077	.071	.057	.052	.045
Solitary play	.068	.075	.162	.171	.024	.037	.025	.038
Offers toy	.075	.135	.120	.381	.021	.080	.027	.103
Requests	.101	.343	.081	.152	.000	.000	.107	.241
Touches peer	.367	1.420	.139	.356	.000	.000	.321	.841
Seizes toy	.000	.000	.016	.061	.000	.000	.000	.000
Pushes	.000	.000	.000	.000	.000	.000	.000	.000
Laugh	.139	.319	.048	.189	.103	.303	.049	.145
Cries	.000	.000	.000	.000	.000	.000	.000	.000
Runs	.019	.075	.029	.107	.000	.000	.049	.191
Looks peer	5.156	4.945	2.539	2.067	.414	.653	1.371	1.637
Looks adult	5.071	6.505	1.184	1.755	.604	.758	.559	.841
Looks group	.949	1.115	.882	.979	.354	.710	.183	.317
Talks peer	...	...	...	...	1.146	1.457	.903	1.096
Talks adult	...	...	...	...	.520	.687	.940	1.592
Talks group	...	...	...	...	.114	.241	.566	.749

[a] $N = 15$.
[b] $N = 14$.

may reflect the fact that the first day of school and the spring visit provided different incentives for the display of inhibited and uninhibited behavior and captured different processes.

A composite variable called "spring inhibition" was derived by computing the average standard scores for physical isolation, staring at a peer, social interaction, and talking with a peer. (Because the latter two variables were negatively correlated with the former two, the values for talking to others and interacting with others were reversed.)

The "fall inhibition" factor was positively correlated with the spring inhibition factor, $r = .42$, $p < .01$, suggesting moderate stability for inhibited behavior in the classroom across a 6-month period. Hence, an average of the two factors was created and labeled "school inhibition."

Table 3: Intercorrelations among School Variables and Laboratory Indices of Behavior at 5½

School Variables	Laboratory Variables		
	Peer-Play Inhibition	Laboratory Inhibition	Composite Variable
Fall school inhibition	.11	.45*	.41*
Spring school inhibition	− .03	.34*	.37*
Combined school inhibition	.04	.45**	.35*

*$p < .05$.
**$p < .01$.

Contemporaneous Relations among Variables Assessed in the Laboratory and the School

Table 3 contains the intercorrelations between the major behavioral variables assessed in the laboratory and indexes of inhibited behavior in the school. Correlations between the peer-play inhibition factor and the school variables were low and insignificant. But the laboratory inhibition factor was moderately correlated with the fall school factor, $r = .45, p < .05$, the combined school factor, $r = .34$, $p < .001$, and the spring inhibition factor, $r = .34, p < .05$. There were no significant relations between heart rate and school inhibition, even though both heart period and heart-rate variability were associated with peer-play inhibition.

Predictive Relations

Table 4 presents the correlations between the major behavioral and heart-rate variables evaluated at 21 and 48 months and the major school variables. The predictor variables were the index of inhibition at 21 months, heart period at 21 months, heart-period variability at 21 months, the index of inhibited

Table 4: Prediction of School Behavior at 5½ Years from Earlier Data

	21 Months			4 Years			
	Index of Inhibition	Heart Period	Variability	Inhibited Index	Uninhibited Index	Heart Period	Variability
Fall school inhibition	.39*	.04	.13	.14	− .46**	− .23	− .16
Spring school inhibition	.20	.15	.07	.07	− .22	− .08	− .11
Aggregate school inhibition	.34*	.16	.008	.12	− .35*	− .19	− .17

*$p < .05$.
**$p < .01$.

behavior at 4 years, the index of uninhibited behavior at 4 years, heart period at 4 years, and heart-period variability at 4 years.

There was modest preservation of inhibited and uninhibited behavior from the earlier laboratory assessment to the assessment of school behavior 3½ years later. The correlations between the index of behavioral inhibition at 21 months and fall school inhibition and the aggregate index of school inhibition were .39 and .34, respectively, $p < .05$. Correlations between uninhibited behavior at 4 years and fall school inhibition and the aggregate index of inhibition were .46 and $- .35$, respectively, $p < .01$.

A rank ordering of the 39 subjects on the combined school inhibition index (from most to least inhibited) revealed that 19 of the 20 subjects with the highest scores on the inhibition factor were classified as inhibited at 21 months of age. Two of the three subjects with the lowest rankings on the school inhibition factor were classified as inhibted at 21 months of age, indicating a dramatic change in behavioral style for these two children.

Mean heart-rate variability and heart-rate period values obtained on these children at earlier ages were unrelated to school behavior at 5½ years of age.

Discussion

These results suggest moderate cross-situational and longitudinal consistency (average $r = .40$) for behavioral inhibition and lack of inhibition in unfamiliar settings. The preservation of these qualities is noteworthy in view of the 3½-year age span involved and the considerable differences between school and laboratory contexts.

Qualitative case material was also examined in order to evaluate within-group differences that are not revealed by the correlational analyses. The value of integrating qualitative and quantitative descriptions has been demonstrated in other longitudinal investigations (Kagan and Moss 1962; Thomas and Chess 1977, 1984). The approach adopted in this study is similar to that adopted by Kagan and Moss (1962) and Chess and Thomas (1977). Teacher and parent reports, interviews, laboratory assessments, home visitor's notes, and school observations on each subject were reviewed.

The case material on the eight subjects with the highest or lowest scores on the school inhibition factor illustrates the continuity between inhibition or lack of inhibition in infancy and shyness and timidity or its opposite, outgoing behavior in school. All four children who were extremely isolated and vigilant in school had been classified as behaviorally inhibited at 21 months of age. The four children who showed the fewest signs of behavioral inhibition in their kindergarten had been spontaneous and uninhibited in the laboratory at 21 months of age. These data highlight a number of themes worthy of subsequent empirical investigations. First, the social behavior of these children seems to be influenced more by enduring disposition than by local contextual conditions. Detailed examination of the information on the classroom settings indicated no association between the behaviors displayed by the subjects and variations in contextual conditions, such as classroom size, teacher's style, or classroom routine. This lack of association between social behavior and situational variables is illustrated by the fact that two subjects were both in very similar, large classrooms in suburban communities, with warm teachers who encouraged socialization. Yet these two boys showed very different behavioral styles. One was unusually active and aggressive, while the other was subdued and well behaved. On the other hand, two female subjects displayed similar profiles of uninhibited behavior. Yet one was in a permissive, very small classroom with a nurturant teacher, while the other was in a highly structured, large classroom with a directive teacher who discouraged social interaction.

Second, two of the four inhibited children had never shown the physiological signs associated with inhibition, while the other two had consistently shown high and stable heart rates and other signs of physiological arousal. The qualitative observations suggest that the former two displayed a slow-to-warm-up profile, while the latter two appeared to be more anxious and distressed.

There was also heterogeneity among the profiles of the four uninhibited children. Although all four exhibited high rates of social interaction and little behavior indicative of restraint, the two girls discussed above appear to be sociable but not aggressive, the third uninhibited child was aggressive, and the fourth had difficulty socializing with peers.

These longitudinal observations also reveal lack of preservation. A number of children who were inhibited during infancy shifted toward greater spontaneity when they reached school. Indeed, two children with exceptionally high scores on the behavioral index of inhibition at 21 months were outgoing and moderately sociable in school.

For some children, a shift from an inhibited posture to a less inhibited one appeared to stem largely from socialization factors. For example, a number of subjects came from families who valued autonomy and yet respected their child's tendecy to withdraw from uncertainty. Interviews with the mothers suggested that the parents encouraged the children to overcome their shyness by enrolling them in day care and by introducing peers into the home. Sensitive to their child's slow-to-warm-up style, they did not impose demands and expectations that were inappropriate and excessive for the child, and they made efforts to minimize the frequency and abruptness of transitions.

Temperament and Adaptation

This study suggests that a predisposition toward inhibition to the unfamiliar has implications for children's behavior in familiar naturalistic situations. The fact that some inhibited children continue to appear shy, cautious, and withdrawn in the kindergarten classroom, even after the novelty had worn off, suggests that behavioral inhibition has consequences for everyday behavior in familiar settings. Given that children continue to exhibit behavior characteristic of restraint even after they have had sufficient time to become acclimated to the classroom situation, one might speculate about the adverse influences that a temperamental tendency toward inhibition might have on a child's peer relations and the development of social skills.

Although the present study was not designed with an eye toward the clinical status of the children, the observational summaries provide information that bears indirectly on the purported relation between temperament and adaptation. A sizable number of inhibited children displayed adequate social skills, appeared to have friends, and were active participants in classroom activities. Other inhibited subjects preferred to remain distant from the peer group and appeared to be more task than person oriented. These children were constructive in their school activities and academically motivated. Although these children were quiet and noninteractive, they showed signs of anxiety in the school. In some cases, the withdrawal from peer contact seemed extreme and interfered with social functioning. These children were described by teachers and observers as anxious, insecure, submissive, or adult dependent.

Some behaviorally inhibited children appear to be at increased risk for manifesting signs of anxiety and social isolation. However, to date, the connection between behavioral inhibition and clinical symptomatology has not been subjected to empirical test. Conclusions regarding the connection mentioned above between behavioral inhibition and anxiety disorder must be regarded as speculative in the absence of blind diagnostic assessments of clinical functioning. However, there is some indirect evidence from other sources that bears on the relation between behavioral inhibition and maladjustment.

The increased incidence of interpersonal difficulties found in this sample of inhibited children is consistent with claims regarding the relation between social withdrawal and childhood behavior disturbances. The clinical literature is replete with hypotheses that socially isolated children are at risk for later disorder. On the basis of evidence that constitutional factors are a component of anxiety disorders, some have hypothesized that low sociability may be related to internalizing behavior problems (Bates, Maslin, and Frankel 1984; Rubin, Lemare, and Lollis, in press). Indeed, social withdrawal is currently implicated in three DSM-III categories of childhood psychiatric disturbance. Moreover, social withdrawal is included as a "symptom" of internalizing disorders in childhood on the grounds that it is often a concomitant of anxiety disorders and depression and appears often as a factor on other indices of childhood psychiatric disturbances (e.g., Achenbach and Edelbrock 1981).

Additionally, developmental theorists have pointed to the importance of peer interactive experiences for the development of social skills and mental health. Accordingly, developmental psychologists have hypothesized that children who do not interact with their peers and who withdraw from their social communities may be at risk for problems in the socioemotional, social-cognitive, and behavioral domains (Rubin, Lemare, and Lollis, in press). They posit that reticence to explore novel out-of-home settings may preclude establishing normal social relations and developing those social and cognitive skills presumably encouraged by these relations.

Directions for Future Research

The present investigation raises several questions that warrant further investigation. First, we do not know the extent to which differences between inhibited and uninhibited children wil persist over the school years. Other longitudinal studies report that a large number of children change during the period between 5 and 7 years of age. Kagan and Moss (1962) found that the continuity for social withdrawal in childhood and adulthood was most likely to become manifest during the early school years. Some of the poorer predictive power of behavior during the preschool years may be attributed in part to the important behavioral reorganiztion that occurs between the ages of 5 and 7. The 5–7-year-old period is marked by developmental reorganization and transition. Additionally, the advent of formal schooling exposes children to a host of potent influences such as the demands for socialization and routinization that are bound to affect the children's temperamental tendencies. For example, Hartup (1983) has pointed to the powerful role of peer experiences in modifying social development. Chess and Thomas (1977) discuss how the social adjustment of shy children may be markedly enhanced by the emergence of athletic, artistic, or cognitive skills.

Second, the relation between psychosocial factors and social withdrawal deserves further exploration. An examination of qualitative information on individual subjects in this study suggests that psychosocial factors may potentiate or mitigate children's temperamental disposition. Others (Rubin, Lemare, and Lollis, in press) emphasize the contribution of environmental factors to the likelihood of social withdrawal. They suggest that the developmental antecendents of social withdrawal observed in childhood may be found in the interaction between endogenous factors, socioecological setting conditions, and the social practices of the parents.

Citing evidence that links qualitative differences in the nature of children's early attachments to later variations in sociability with peers, Rubin emphasizes the critical role of an anxious, insecure attachment in the development of withdrawn behavior in early childhood and argues that social withdrawal may be preceded and, in part, caused by feelings of insecurity in one's primary attachment relationship. Rubin also suggests that parents' responses to their children's inhibited tendencies will play a significant role in the ultimate development of either positive or negative outcomes in these children. The interplay of temperamental socialization and socioecological factors in infancy and early childhood may set the stage for the experience of social anxiety and subsequent nonsocial activity with peers.

Rubin and his colleagues initiated their longitudinal investigation of social isolates when the children entered kindergartgen. Therefore, their hypotheses regarding the temperamental precursors and socialization histories of socially withdrawn children await empirical investigation. Studies that systematically assess temperamental characteristics, quality of attachment, caregiver perceptions and practices, and socioecological conditions are needed in order to gain an understanding of the interplay between endogenous and psychosocial factors. The findings from these studies are apt to be useful in designing preventative or intervention programs for severely withdrawn children.

Third, the relation between inhibition and anxiety merits further investigation. Despite some convergence of evidence from developmental, ethological, and clinical studies, a clear picture of the relation between behavioral inhibition in infancy and anxiety in childhood has not been fully sketched. Our understanding of the overlap between anxiety and inhibition is hampered by our inability to differentiate between anxious and shy behaviors.

Research must distinguish between social withdrawal that is a product of temperament and social withdrawal that stems from anxiety. Although the overt behavior characteristics of shy and anxious children may be highly similar, the underlying etiologies may be different. Research in our laboratory shows that it is possible for a child to display an inhibited behavioral profile that is the result of socialization experiences rather than a lower threshold of excitability in those limbic structures that serve the psychological states associated with uncertainty or anxiety (Kagan, Reznick, and Snidman, in press).

Measures that are sensitive to the more subtle aspects of behavior are sorely needed. Currently, physiological variables such as cortisol level, heart rate, and voice pertubation to mild cognitive stress appear to detect differences between temperamentally inhibited and anxious children.

Qualitative dimensions of inhibited children's solitary behavior should also be examined as not all nonsocial activity is associated with negative developmental prognosis (for a review, see Rubin 1982a). Measures of the affective quality of social interactions, postural tension, and facial expression are also likely to help distinguish among subtypes of behaviorally inhibited children.

Systematic investigation of the range of clinical difficulties and the sources affecting adjustment and maladjustment in inhibited children is needed. Before accepting the claim that inhibited children suffer from anxiety or social isolation, one would like to see multimethod assessments of multiple times with records of socialization experiences from teachers and parents. Measures of the children's self-concept using the triads procedure and sociometric peer rating would provide useful information. In the absence of objective multi-method assessments of clinical functioning, the conclusions regarding inhibition and anxiety in this sample must be regarded as speculative.

References

Achenbach, T. M., and Edelbrock, C. S. 1981. Behavioral problems and competencies reported by parents of normal and disturbed children aged four through sixteen. *Monographs of the Society for Research in Child Development,* vol. 46, serial no. 188.

Bates, J. E.; Maslin, C. A.; and Frankel, K. A. 1985. Attachment security, mother-child interaction, and temperament as predictors of behavior-problem ratings at age three years. In *Growing points of attachment theory and research,* ed. I. Bretherton and E. Waters, 167–93. *Monographs of the Society for Research in Child Development,* vol. 50, nos. 1–2, serial no. 209.

Billman, J., and McDevitt, S. C. 1980. Convergence of parent and observer ratings of temperament with observations of peer interaction in nursery school. *Child Development* 51:395–400.

Blurton-Jones, N. 1972. Categories of child-child interaction. In *Ethological studies of child behavior,* ed. N. Blurton-Jones. Cambridge: Cambridge University Press.

Bronson, G. W., and Pankey, W. B. 1977. On the distinction between fear and wariness. *Child Development* 48:1167–87.

Buss, A. H., and Plomin, R. 1984. *Temperament: Early developing personality traits.* Hillsdale, N.J.: Erlbaum.

Carey, W. B., and McDevitt, S. C. 1978. Stability and change in individual temperament diagnoses from infancy to early childhood. *Journal of the American Academy of Child Psychiatry* 17:331–37.

Chess, S., and Thomas, A. 1977. Temperamental individuality from childhood to adolescence. *Journal of the American Academy of Child Psychiatry* 16:218–26.

Chess, S., and Thomas, A. 1984. *Origins and evolution of behavior disorders.* New York: Brunner/Mazel.

Garcia-Coll, C.; Kagan, J.; and Reznick, J. S. 1984. Behavioral inhibition in young children. *Child Development* 55:1005–19.

Gottman, J. 1977. Toward a definition of social isolation in children. *Child Development* 48:513–17.

Hartup, W. W. 1983. The peer system. In *Handbook of child psychology,* ed. P. H. Mussen, 4th ed. Vol. 4, *Socialization, personality, and social development,* ed. E. M. Hetherington. New York: Wiley.

Hinde, R. A.; Stevenson-Hinde, J.; and Tamplin, A. 1985. Characteristics of three- to four-year-olds assessed at home and their interactions in preschool. *Developmental Psychology* 21:120–40.

Kagan, J., and Moss, H. A. 1962. *Birth to maturity.* New York: Wiley.

Kohn, M., and Parnes, S. 1974. Social interaction in the classroom: A comparison of apathetic, withdrawn, and angry-defiant children. *Journal of Genetic Psychology* 125:165–75.

McGrew, W. C. 1972. Aspects of social development in nursery school children with emphasis on introduction to the group. In *Ethological studies of child behavior,* ed. N. Blurton-Jones. Cambridge: Cambridge University Press.

Plomin, R., and Rowe, D. C. 1977. A twin study of temperament in young children. *Journal of Psychology* 97:107–13.

Putallaz, M., and Gottman, J. 1981. Social skills and group acceptance. In *The development of children's friendships,* ed. S. Asher and J. Gottman. Cambridge: Cambridge University Press.

Reznick, J. S.; Kagan, J.; Snidman, N.; Gersten, M.; Baak, K.; and Rosenberg, A. 1986. Inhibited and uninhibited children: A follow-up study. *Child Development* 57:660–80.

Rubin, K. H. 1982a. Non-social play in preschoolers: Necessary evil? *Child Development* 53:651–57.

Rubin, K. H. 1982b. Social and social-cognitive developmental characteristics of young isolate, normal, and sociable children. In *Peer relationships and social skills in childhood,* ed. K. H. Rubin and H. S. Ross. New York: Springer.

Rubin, K. H. In press. Socially withdrawn children: An "at risk" population? In *Peer relationships and social skills in childhood,* vol. 2, *Issues in assessment and training,* ed. B. Schneider, K. H. Rubin, and J. Ledingham. New York: Springer.

Rubin, K. H., and Clarke, M. L. 1983. Preschool teachers' ratings of behavioral problems: Observational, sociometric, and social-cognitive correlates. *Journal of Abnormal Child Psychology* 11:273–86.

Rubin, K.; Lemare, L.; and Lollis, S. In press. Social withdrawal in childhood: Assessment issues and social concomitants. In *Childrens' status in the peer group,* ed. S. R. Asher and J. D. Coie. New York: Cambridge University Press.

Thomas, A., and Chess, S. 1977. Temperament and development. New York: Brunner/Mazel.

5 Behavioral Inhibition and Anxiety: Dispositional, Developmental, and Neural Aspects of the Anxious Personality of the Domestic Cat

ROBERT E. ADAMEC AND CANNIE STARK-ADAMEC

Prologue

There is a growing body of evidence that individuals differ with respect to the degree to which prosocial and approach behaviors are inhibited by strange and threatening environments. Individual differences in behavioral inhibition have been reported in a variety of species, including rats (Gupta and Holland 1969), dogs (Murphree, DeLuca, and Angel 1974), primates (Suomi et al. 1981), and humans (Daniels and Plomin 1985; Kagan, Reznick, and Snidman 1987). The apparent cross-species universality of this phenomenon suggests that insights into the neural substrate of our own inhibitions should be gained from a study of the neural control of behavioral inhibition in animals.

In this chapter, we will review a series of studies investigating individual differences in behavioral inhibition in the domestic cat on a behavioral and neural level. For reasons described below, this species is particularly suitable for studying the neural substrate of behavioral inhibition. On a behavioral level, inhibited cats are more fearful in response to a variety of stimuli. This tendency is evident early in life and is stable in adult behavior, appearing as an "inhibited disposition." There is a striking parallel between our findings in the cat and those reported in human children by Kagan, Reznick, and Snidman (1987), who also describe an inhibited disposition in some children that is stable from 21 months of age to over 7 years of age. In the cat, as in human children, the inhibited disposition appears as long latencies to interact with, or a tendency to retreat from, unfamiliar and threatening stimuli.

The work reviewed in this chapter was supported by a grant to R. Adamec from the Medical Research Council of Canada (MRC MT-7022) and by a previous grant to R. Adamec from the National Institutes of Health, Bethesda, Maryland. The invaluable technical assistance of Raj Riar, Barbara Vari, Martin Graham, Naida Graham, and Ann Marie Madden is gratefully acknowledged.

93

Since the behavior of inhibited cats appears defensive in nature, we have also investigated how limbic neural circuits, which modulate defense in the cat, control the inhibited disposition. These systems are well documented in this species, and the prior research on these circuits provides a road map of where to look in the cat brain for mechanisms of behavioral inhibition. Our research on these systems may have uncovered principles of neural control of behavioral inhibition that apply to other species, including humans.

A case will be made that the pattern of behavioral inhibition seen in the cat is a manifestation of an "anxious personality" trait that is based on alterations of excitability of limbic circuits controlling emotional response to the environment. There is a conceptual parallel between our findings in the cat and studies of autonomic reactivity in inhibited children. Kagan, Reznick, and Snidman (1987) have proposed that the threshold of response of the limbic lobe and hypothalamic structures controlling autonomic reaction to unfamiliarity and challenge is tonically lower for inhibited children than for uninhibited children. Our data provide direct evidence in favor of this view in cats and furthermore, begin to define the neural processes involved.

As we detail our findings in the cat in this chapter, we will endeavor, where possible, to relate them to issues raised by studies of behavioral inhibition in children. While cats cannot model a human child, certain principles of determination of the inhibited disposition in cats may provide insights into the phenomenon in children and, possibly, new directions for research on our own species.

Introduction

Our investigation of behavioral inhibition in the cat has examined how exaggeration of defensive response to environmental threat (fearfulness) contributes to individual differences in inhibition of predatory aggression, social interaction, and free movement in strange and threatening environments. The role of fearfulness in behavioral inhibition has been studied in two time frames: repeated testing in the adult to assess stability of individual differences in behavioral inhibition and in development to determine the role of early experience in adult behavioral inhibition. We have used two approaches to study the neural basis of behavioral inhibition. First, we looked for individual differences in limbic excitability in inhibited (fearful) and uninhibited cats. Second, we determined how experimentally induced changes in limbic excitability alter inhibited behavior.

Four of the five sections of this chapter describe the theoretical background and findings of these four approaches to the phenomenon of behavioral inhibition. A final section is devoted to the implications of our findings.

Behavioral Inhibition in the Adult Cat:
A Defensive Disposition

Theoretical Background

Why are some domestic cats inhibited in their attacks on formidable prey (rats) while others are not? The key to answering this question comes from naturalistic evidence indicating that, in the wild, the species preyed on by feline predators are not passive witnesses to their own execution. Rather, the prey-predator relationship is better characterized as a battle between species, in which the predator is often the loser (Schaller 1967, 1972a, 1972b). Viewing the prey-predator interaction as a battle, Leyhausen (1956) first hypothesized, on the basis of his ethological observations, that cats may differ with respect to their level of "battle courage," that is, how readily they give up an attack in the face of a rat's attempts to defend itself. Adopting Leyhausen's view, we hypothesized that individual differences in "battle courage" reflected differences in sensitivity to the threat posed by the prey. A related question was, Do cats differ with respect to courage in battle with prey only, or do they differ with respect to sensitivity to environmental threat in general? The answer to this question may shed light on how generalized behavioral inhibition is in humans.

Laboratory Studies

We initially tested these ideas by examining the behavior of a population ($N = 44$) of aggressive (A, rat killing, $N = 18$) and nonaggressive (NA, non–rat killing, $N = 26$) cats in response to rats, mice, a novel environment, humans, and recorded threat howls of an aggressive cat threatening another cat. These stimuli were chosen because it was felt that they represented threats of differing degree to the cat.

Quantitative analysis of behavioral indices of withdrawal, approach, and attack (Adamec 1975) revealed four groupings of cats that differed individually in how threatened they were by a given stimulus (Adamec 1975, 1978). Cats most sensitive to threat (fig. 1, NA1 cats, $N = 6$, 13.6 percent of the total) showed generalized and increasing tendencies to withdraw from humans, novelty, rats, and recorded threat howls. These cats would not even approach, let alone attack, rats. This percentage of extremely inhibited cats is of interest since it has been reported that about 15 percent of human children in several samples are also extremely inhibited (Cranach et al. 1978; Kagan, Reznick, and Snidman, 1987). The correspondence of proportions is surprisingly close between the two species. A second group (fig. 1, NA2 cats, $N = 13$, 29.5 percent of the total) was equally defensive to the more severe

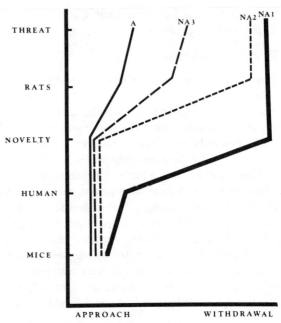

Fig. 1. A conceptual figure showing patterns of approach-oriented (including predatory aggression) and defensive (withdrawal-oriented) responses to several environmental stimuli by cats of differing defensive tendencies. Threat refers to conspecific threat vocalizations. "A" are uninhibited, aggressive, rat predators. NA1–3 are inhibited cats that do not kill rats. Though the approach-withdrawal dimension along the abscissa is conceptual, it is based on quantitative analysis. The figure is adapted from data described in Adamec (1975, 1978). For details of differences between the four groups of cats, see the text.

threats posed by cat howls and rats but was not intimidated by mice, humans, or the novel environment. A third group (fig. 1, NA3 cats, $N = 7$, 15.9 percent of the total) was less defensive toward rats and attempted to attack them with their paws and to bite them. Their attacks were ambivalent, however, being characterized by repeated attack-withdrawal sequences. Withdrawal from threat howls was also attenuated relative to the NA1 and NA2 cats, and, as were the NA2 cats, NA3 cats were not intimidated by mice, humans, or novelty. The least defensive and least inhibited of the cats were rat killers (fig. 1, A cats, $N = 26$, 41 percent of the total). These aggressive cats displayed little tendency to withdraw from any of the test stimuli.

It should be pointed out that the tendency to attack mice was equal across groups. The inhibition of attack on rats in the NA1–3 groups, then, cannot be attributed to lower predatory motivation in the inhibited cats. Rather, they are more intimidated by rats than are the uninhibited, aggressive cats.

Responses to all stimuli were retested at intervals of 6 months to 1 year.

The behavioral profiles of all cats were found to be stable over these lengthy test intervals.

Summary and Conclusions

These findings warrant a number of conclusions. First, the stability of inhibition of response to the various stimuli suggests that a disposition toward behavioral inhibition exists in the adult cat. Second, the most inhibited cats are also the most defensive, displaying the strongest withdrawal tendencies. Thus, the inhibited disposition is better called a defensive disposition. Third, the defensive disposition has the property of a personality trait because of its generality and stability. Fourth, behavioral expression of this trait is largely determined by the stimulus context and how threatening that context is to an individual organism. More severe expression of this trait appears as more behavioral inhibition in more contexts because a severely inhibited cat responds to more stimuli as potentially threatening or fear provoking. Thus, defensive sensitivity to threat determines severity of trait expression. Inhibited children have been called shy and fearful. It is possible that individual differences in behavioral inhibition in humans are mediated by individual differences in how threatening different contexts are perceived.

It is likely that inhibited (defensive) and uninhibited cats do not differ so much in kind as in the degree to which environmental stimuli activate the neural substrates of defense and approach-attack. Data will be presented later that support this conclusion. This view is at variance with that of Kagan, Reznick, and Snidman (1987), who suggest that inhibited children are qualitatively different from uninhibited children. They suggest that biological factors, such as genetic determinants of disposition, might mediate the differences seen between inhibited and uninhibited humans. They treat such factors as being better seen as differences in kind rather than degree of trait expression. Consideration of developmental factors and of the neural substrates of the inhibited disposition suggests that this disposition, in cats at least, may be determined by both continuous and qualitatively different mechanisms acting together.

The qualitatively different mechanisms are likely represented by at least two separate, antagonistic neural substrates in the cat brain. One facilitates aggressive reactions to prey and approach to environmental stimuli, while the other facilitates defensive reactions to prey and to the environment in general. Moreover, cats appear to differ in the degree to which antagonism of these two substrates controls their behavioral response to the environment.

One way to determine the separability of these posited substrates is to trace their development. With this purpose in mind, the next series of studies was designed to examine the ontogeny of the antagonism of aggression and defense in the adult cat.

The Development of Aggression and Defense in the Cat

Theoretical Background

Relatively little is known about developmental antecedents of defensiveness in cats. More is known about the factors that influence predatory aggression, however. There is considerable evidence that predatory attack among felines is not a rigid behavior pattern but is subject to modulation by factors including the size and response of the prey (Kuo 1933; Kreiskott 1969; Leyhausen 1956), hunger, which facilitates attack (Adamec 1976b; Leyhausen 1965), and early experience (Kuo 1930, 1933). Nevertheless, the fixed and nearly pan-specific nature and orientation of the killing neck bite (Hornocker 1969; Leyhausen 1956, 1965; Schaller 1972a, 1972b) suggests some common genetically based mechanisms. The neural mechanisms of predatory attacks are present even in cats that do not kill spontaneously. Attack may be elicited in cats by electrical stimulation of the hypothalamus (Flynn 1967), even after rearing in social isolation (Roberts and Berquist 1968). Brain lesions in cats (Bernston 1972) may also induce attack in nonaggressive animals. These data, in combination with those considered above, suggest that some aspects of attack behavior may be under the control of neural mechanisms that require little experience for their development but that may be under tonic suppressive control from brain areas involved in other behavioral functions. They further suggest that successful development of effective adult attack behavior depends, in part, on tipping the balance between defensive neurobehavioral mechanisms and attack mechanisms in favor of attack.

The literature on feline ontogeny supports this view. The optimal rearing condition for attack development seems to be one in which young cats are reared with an adult female and littermates (Hornocker 1969; Kruuk and Turner 1967; Kuo 1930; Leyhausen 1965; Schaller 1967; Schenkel 1966). The mother acts as a model for attack and provides partially injured prey whose self-defensive capabilities have been reduced. While the mother may model efficient predatory attack, studies of imitation in cats suggest that kittens' performance is most affected by observing responses already in their repertoire (Adler 1955; Berry 1908; Chesler 1969; Herbert and Harsh 1944). Predatory responses displayed for the young by the mother are components of play long before modeling by the mother begins (Hornocker 1969; Schenkel 1966), and very young kittens have been observed to kill on their first exposure to prey (Yerkes and Bloomfield 1910). Thus, the mother, as a model and provider of subdued prey, and perhaps littermate competition appear to function in early experience as excitors of latent attack tendencies, increasing the probability of attack on more "formidable" or threatening prey, rather than acting to teach the skill of hunting.

Taken together, the literature indicates a shaping rather than a determining function of early experience on attack. Attack mechanisms appear to be in place neurally at birth but may require certain early experiences in some cats to facilitate their behavioral expression. Our work suggests that one very important consequence of early experience is to attenuate a possibly inborn disposition to be defensive.

Laboratory Studies

Because of the paucity of data regarding the development of defensiveness in the cat, our studies were designed to trace the development of both defensive and aggressive behavior. Moreover, in view of the apparent conflict of defense and aggression in the adult, we sought to characterize the conflict of aggressive and defensive tendencies in growing kittens.

Twenty-six cats were reared from birth with littermates and periodically exposed to various combinations of conditions designed to mimic components of normal early feline experience (Adamec, Stark-Adamec, and Livingston 1980a, 1980b, 1980c). These included (1) no early experiences except cohabitation with mother and littermates until 4 months of age; (2) early, brief, and repeated exposure to rats and mice from 14 days of age to 11 months of age; (3) periodic hunger from 10 months of age to 11 months of age plus three exposures to totally subdued prey (killed rats) at 10 months of age; (4) competition from littermates for access to prey from 14 days of age to 11 months of age; and (5) observation of an adult cat (the father) attack rats from 14 days of age to 11 months of age. Adult behavior was assessed at 1 year of age and then 1 year later to determine the stability of the developmental outcome. A large number of behavioral measures of attack, defense, and play were taken, and these are detailed elsewhere (Adamec, Stark-Adamec, and Livingston, 1980a, 1980b, 1980c).

Effects of Early Experience on Adult Aggression and Defense

Hunger plus exposure to killed prey without early exposure to live prey was the most effective experience facilitating adult attack (biting) on rats. Eighty-three percent of cats in this condition were aggressive as adults. The next most effective attack-facilitating experience was the combination of early exposure to prey following observation of an adult attacking a rat plus hunger plus exposure to killed prey. Sixty-seven percent of cats in this condition were aggressive as adults. This percentage did not differ from the 83 percent mentioned above. The three least effective attack-facilitating experiences were (1) observation of an adult plus littermate competition plus early exposure to live prey (38 percent); (2) littermate competition plus early exposure to live prey plus hunger plus exposure to killed prey (0 percent); and (3) no early experiences of an attack-facilitating nature (0 percent). None of these percentages differed, but together they differed from the two most effective facilitating conditions, $\chi^2 = 7.90$, $p < .01$, 78 percent vs. 18 percent. Differences between cats in the various rearing conditions were stable over retest periods of 1 year.

All the cats were equally aggressive toward mice in development and as adults. Thus, attack-facilitating factors appear to be working to promote onset of predatory attack against large prey (rats).

It appears that observation of adult attack does not add much to attack development. Nor does group competition. The reason for this latter finding is that competition has two effects, facilitating attack in some cats and inhibiting attack in others. As will be discussed later, competition adversely effects only those kittens who display early evidence of a defensive disposition, and this finding has implications for human development.

The one aspect of adult behavior that accounted for differences in aggressiveness toward rats was withdrawal tendency. Withdrawal tendency was measured as the average time spent withdrawn from the prey. Regardless of rearing condition, inhibited (nonaggressive) cats, as adults, withdrew more from rats than did uninhibited (aggressive) cats. Both groups, however, withdrew equally little from mice (fig. 2d). The objective behavioral threat posed by rats and mice to the two groups of cats was equal since prey self-defense in response to inhibited and uninhibited cats was equal. These findings suggest that the same stimulus input provided by the rat was in fact more threatening to inhibited cats. Moreover, there appears to be a continuum of control of defensive response over attack in these cats. Withdrawal from rats correlates negatively with biting across cats, $r = -.83$ and $.75$, $p < .01$, duration and latency. On the other hand, there is no correlation between withdrawal from mice and biting. These data suggest that degree of defensive sensitivity to rat self-defense modulates the degree of inhibition of attack in a linear fashion. Response to mice, on the other hand, likely reflects the operation of the attack neural substrate unfettered by action of opposing defensive response systems. If this is true, then the attack neural substrates in both inhibited and uninhibited cats were equally developed and active, whereas the primary difference must lie in sensitization of the defensive substrate to environmental threat in inhibited cats.

This interpretation requires that the substrates of attack and defense are separate but interacting. Careful examination of the development of attack and defense in ontogeny provides evidence that this is so (Adamec, Stark-Adamec, and Livingston, 1980b).

Development of Attack and Defense

Clear and separable stages of onset of approach to prey (at 20 days of age), followed by withdrawal from prey (at 27 days of age), followed by attack on prey (at 52 days of age), were observed (table 1). Attack behavior emerged

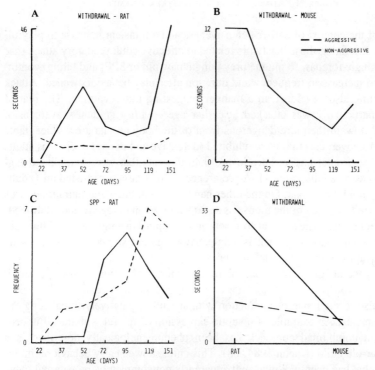

Fig. 2. *a*, Mean withdrawal times (in seconds) from rats are plotted against age in days for kittens that became inhibited (defensive or nonaggressive) and uninhibited (aggressive) as adults. *b*, Mean withdrawal times (in seconds) from mice are plotted against age in days for all kittens combined, including those that became inhibited (defensive or nonaggressive) and uninhibited (aggressive) as adults. *c*, Mean SPP frequencies over all targets on the rat (front, middle, and rear combined) are plotted against age in days for kittens that became inhibited (nonaggressive) or uninhibited (aggressive) as adults. *d*, Mean withdrawal times (in seconds) from rats and mice are plotted for aggressive (uninhibited) and defensive (inhibited and nonaggressive) cats at 1 year of age. These data are from the same kittens whose data appear in 2*a*, *b*, and *c*. For details, see Adamec, Stark-Adamec, and Livingston (1980a, 1980c).

Table 1: Table of Mean Kitten Age (in Days) of Onset of Responses to Rats

Response	Mean Age	Response	Mean Age
Approach	20	Prey defense	52
Withdraw	27	Bite	71
Attack	52		

Mean Kitten Age (in Days) of Onset of Attack By Target

	SPP Attack			Biting Attack		
	Front	Middle	Rear	Front	Middle	Rear
Uninhibited cats	119	51	53	118	76	75
Inhibited cats	184	51	52	140	122	67

out of the context of earlier defensiveness and a transient increase in playful-ness. Primarily, those behaviors related to effective adult predatory attack (use of a single forepaw to pin the prey [single paw pin or SPP] and biting) contin-ued to increase in frequency and duration after play behaviors waned. Attack targeting also developed in a manner suggesting initial caution. The rear of rats particularly was attacked at earlier ages, with a gradual movement of attack toward the more dangerous front of the body as cats grew older (table 1). Moreover, cats that were inhibited (defensive and nonaggressive) as adults attacked frontal targets later in life than did cats that were uninhibited (ag-gressive) as adults (table 1). A preference for rear targets persisted into adult-hood in inhibited cats. On the other hand, both inhibited and uninhibited cats preferred the body of the mouse as an attack target in ontogeny and adulthood, this being the easiest target to reach on the rapidly fleeing mouse. Thus, de-fensive inhibition of attack is subtle. Attack is not stopped entirely, but its topography is shaped by defensiveness.

In general, then, when describing behavioral inhibition in any species, it may be worthwhile to attend not only to suppression of particular behaviors but also to the mode of interaction with stimuli in putatively threatening en-vironments. An example of a subtle expression of fearful withdrawal imbed-ded in uninhibited approach has been phenomenologically described in a 4-year-old child (Kagan 1984, 68). This child showed early behavioral inhib-ition that had been modified, but apparently not completely, by parental inter-vention. It is obvious from this example, and the cat data, that it would be worthwhile to develop formal behavioral measures of subtle expression of fearfulness in future studies of the human child.

The cat data indicate that development of attack and defense are separate but interacting. The early development of defense interacts with later attack development to produce initial attacks that are cautious. Moreover, the differ-ences in degree of caution in attack shown by inhibited and uninhibited cats in development and adulthood are primarily accounted for by differences in defensive response in the first 2 months of life. Inhibited (nonaggressive) cats show an early increase in withdrawal from rats at 37 days of age (fig. 2a), which grows when attack and prey reactions begin at 52 days of age (table 1) and remains elevated throughout development. Withdrawals of uninhibited (aggressive) animals do not increase with age, remaining at a low level, which is less than that of inhibited cats. Inhibited cats appear more defensive than uninhibited cats to the same threat very early in life since the prey do not react differently to inhibited and uninhibited cats during this phase of development. Nor have the rats done anything to overtly frighten the cats since they do not defend themselves from cat approaches prior to 52 days of age. Finally, the defensive responsiveness of these cats seems to be quite stable since there is a high correlation among defensive cats between withdrawal from rats at 37 days of age and at 1 year of age, $r = .89, p < .05$.

The 37–52 days of age when strong defensive responses to prey emerge in kittens parallels findings in primates and humans. Fear reactions to faces appear at 4 months of age in socially isolated rhesus monkeys (Kenney, Mason, and Hills 1979). Kagan (1984) suggests that, given the fourfold faster growth of brain and body of monkeys in comparison to children, the comparable age in infants for the development of fearfulness should be 7–15 months if analogous developmental processes were occurring in humans. This is the precise age period in which fear of strangers and separation anxiety emerge in humans. A similar principle seems to apply in the cat. Assuming cat growth is sevenfold faster than that of infants (cats have one-seventh the human life span), the 1–2 month period of emergence of early defensiveness translates into 7–14 months for the human. Since fear of faces appears in socially isolated primates and fear of rats appears after very little experience in some kittens, it is likely that neural maturational processes requiring little specific experience to develop mediate the onset of fearfulness in primates and cats. The close parallel of timing of emergence of fearfulness in the three species suggests that similar processes may exist in humans (Kagan 1984).

Fearfulness does not dominate the early behavior of inhibited kittens, however, in that there is a conflict between attack and defense. This conflict is evident in the development of inhibited (nonaggressive) cats in that the dip in withdrawal from rats between 72 and 119 days is paralleled by a mirror-image transient rise in SPP attacks against rats (fig. 2c). In contrast, this conflict is not evident in the uninhibited, aggressive cats, who show a simple linear rise in SPP behavior. These data suggest two possibilities. First, attack mechanisms can suppress defensive withdrawal, at least temporarily, in the development of inhibited cats. Second, it is possible that development of defensiveness is biphasic. The first view seems more likely since defensiveness at 37 days of age correlates so highly with defensiveness at 1 year of age.

The confict between attack and defense is not an inevitable event in development but occurs only in animals who develop exaggerated defensive responses early in life. Moreover, even inhibited cats show no conflict when the stimulus is a nonthreatening mouse. Withdrawal responses to mice are low and equal in inhibited and uninhibited cats and show a decreasing linear trend as the cats grow older (fig. 2b). Except that inhibited cats begin their attacks on mice at a later age, inhibited and uninhibited cats do not differ with respect to their attacks on mice.

Specificity of Early Defensiveness

Taken together, the data clearly indicate that development of approach-attack is powerfully modulated by an early emergent defensive sensitivity to some threats in a subpopulation of cats. How specific is this defensive sensitivity? Other studies of these cats as adults indicate that cats that are defensive toward rats early in development are also defensive as adults in response to novel environments and to cat threat howls, whereas cats who were uninhibited as kittens are not (Adamec, Stark-Adamec, and Livingston 1983). Moreover, defensive response to novel environments and to threat howls correlates with withdrawal from rats, suggesting that a common substrate mediates these responses. The social responses of inhibited cats toward humans, however, are not suppressed and are equal to those of uninhibited cats. This deviation from the pattern seen in a random sample of adult cats who are cautious in novel environments may be due to the fact that cats reared in the laboratory were very familiar with the experimenter who served as the test person.

These data suggest that defensive disposition is characterized not by a continuous state of fearfulness but rather by a reactive state produced by and selective for particular kinds of complex stimulus situations. They also suggest that positive experiences with particular stimuli can override the inherent cautiousness of defensive cats. This conclusion is consistent with the evidence presented above that approach-attack mechanisms can interfere with defensive response. In the example above, however, it is apparent that insufficient positive experiences associated with attack were supplied to the inhibited kittens to override their initial defensive responses to rats permanently.

There is a parallel to this finding of selectivity of defensive response in cats in human children. Inhibited children are also selective in their responses to the environment. Familiar sources of rewarding experiences, such as their mothers, are certainly not avoided; rather, they are approached more when unfamiliar stimuli are present. It is not unreasonable, then, to propose that the inhibited disposition in human children may be due to an enhanced, reactive, and selective state of fearfulness as it appears to be in the cat.

Summary and Conclusions

The early age of onset of defensiveness and its generality in adult behavior in cats suggests that some animals may be born with a predisposition to respond defensively. Defensive disposition appears to be unmodifiable by experiences that facilitate attack-approach when kittens are exposed at an early age to threatening stimuli. Moreover, early defensiveness overrides later attack-facilitating experiences. On the other hand, the defensive disposition may be overridden if kittens do not interact with live prey during their early sensitive period. The cats in our study that were not exposed to prey early in life and then were exposed only to "safe" subdued (killed) prey at 10 months of age while hungry were not defensive as adults. Complete lack of exposure to threatening prey, however, may enhance development of defensive dispositions since 100 percent of the animals reared this way were defensive as adults.

Parallel observations have been made in children. Evidence of the inhibited disposition has been found as early as 21 months of age, and it has been suggested that this disposition may be part of the genetic makeup of the child (Kagan, Reznick, and Snidman, 1987). While the inhibited disposition in children is stable in development in many children followed to 7 years of age, it is not invariant. Some children with early emergent inhibition tendencies do become less inhibited over time, suggesting that something in their later experience alters the inhibited disposition. For example, North American mothers of inhibited children who later become less inhibited self-consciously helped their children to overcome their inhibitions by introducing peers into the home and teaching coping strategies to deal with stress (Kagan, Reznick, and Snidman, 1987). Cat mothers seem to perform a similar service for their young by bringing subdued prey to them and encouraging them to attack by example. In our study, exposure to subdued prey was the most effective experience in overcoming defensive inhibition of attack and of the defensive disposition in general.

If the parallel may be explored further, our data would suggest that exposing an inhibited child to potentially threatening stimuli too early in life, especially in a competitive behavioral context, without coping support would likely exacerbate inhibition in a child predisposed to inhibition from birth. This suggestion arises from two sources. First, as described above, exposure to threatening stimuli at a time when defensiveness is just beginning to emerge powerfully suppresses approach-attack despite later experiences that normally facilitate approach-attack. Second, competition for prey access is a two-edged sword in development. Competition was found to facilitate attack in cats that were not defensive early in development. Cats in the same litter showing early defensive responses to prey, on the other hand, were inhibited by competition, often attempting to escape from the testing situation. Inhibited cats reared in groups that contained aggressive animals were nearly as defensive as animals given no special early experiences, suggesting that competition exacerbated defensiveness in these cats. This finding parallels a suggestion made by Kagan, Reznick, and Snidman (1987) to explain why more inhibited children are later born rather than firstborn. They propose that infants born with a biological disposition to be inhibited respond to competition from older siblings for toys or mild rivalry with exaggerated withdrawal that enhances subsequent withdrawal to the unfamiliar. While their suggestion is speculative for humans, our findings provide evidence that competition does have such a selective effect on defensively predisposed kittens.

The data reviewed also support the view that approach-attack and defense are controlled by separate but interacting neural mechanisms. The findings indicate, further, that it is differences in early development of the defensive mechanisms and not in approach-attack mechanisms that determine adult expression of the defensive (inhibited) disposition. Thus, qualitatively different substrates interact to produce the observed behavioral inhibition. Though the substrates are separable, their interaction is continuous in that degree of defensive response to threat largely determines the degree and topography of attack inhibition in a linear fashion. If some cats are born with a predisposition to respond defensively, as the data suggest, then the findings illustrate that it is possible for a genetically determined disposition to express itself, in part, as a continuous process.

We know of no human parallel to this conclusion, partly because studies in the human have not examined behavioral inhibition from the viewpoint of two separate but interacting mechanisms governing approach and withdrawal. Nor have there been attempts to devise independent behavioral measures of these processes. The questions raised by the study of cat behavior are worth exploring in the human case, however. For example, it would be important to know to what extent inhibition in human children is determined by shyness or fearfulness and by a lack of motivation to approach and interact with novelty per se. Answers to a question like this would have consequences both for efforts to help children overcome behavioral inhibition and for theories regarding the nature of biologic mechanisms determining behavioral inhibition.

Physiological Basis of the Defensive Disposition

Prologue

Kagan (1984) believes that the primate and human data on development of fearfulness point to the existence of a relatively experientially independent set of neural maturational processes. Our data in the cat suggest that analogous processes exist in a third species. Moreover, our physiological investigations have begun to define the nature of these processes. These investigations are the third topic of this chapter. Our studies have examined the role of limbic modulators of predatory attack and defensive behavior in the inhibited (defensive) disposition.

The behavioral data suggest that two separate but interacting and antagonistic neural substrates mediate behavioral expression of the defensive disposition. Evidence will be reviewed that supports the view that the substrates of attack and defense are anatomically separate in the feline brain.

The behavioral data also indicate that biases toward defensive or aggressive responses to the same stimulus account for behavioral differences between inhibited and uninhibited cats. These behavioral biases are stable, indicating that a tonic or lasting bias must also exist in the neural substrates mediating attack and defense. The neural substrates of attack and defense can be divided functionally into circuits that produce an overt behavioral response and circuits that modify or modulate the excitability of circuits producing attack or defense. Moreover, some of these modulating circuits appear to exert a lasting or tonic effect on the excitability of circuits responsible for expression of aggression or defense. These tonic modulators will be described. Then studies from our laboratory will be reviewed that indicate that the excitability of the tonic modulatory circuits differs between inhibited (defensive) and uninhibited (aggressive) cats. These studies are relevant to humans since it has been suggested that the threshold of response of limbic lobe and hypothalamic structures to unfamiliarity is tonically lower for inhibited than for uninhibited children (Kagan, Reznick, and Snidman, 1987). Our data indicates that limbic lobe structures do indeed differ between inhibited and uninhibited cats. However, the difference is expressed not only in threshold of response but also as a difference in degree of expression and distribution of neural excitatory and neural inhibitory processes in particular limbic circuits.

Theoretical Background

Our investigation of limbic involvement in the inhibited disposition has been guided by a mapping of brain circuits involved in predatory aggression and defense by Flynn, Bandler, Siegel, and their colleagues (for a review, see Flynn, Vanegas, Foote, and Edwards 1970). Their work, begun in the early 1960s, revealed a variety of networks involving thalamic, hypothalamic, and brain stem systems controlling the neural and behavioral response to complex species-relevant stimuli that evoke predatory aggression and defense in the cat. Circuits that produce predatory attack involve the lateral hypothalamus, its ascending projections through the thalamus, and its descending projections to the lateral portions of the midbrain. Circuits that produce defensive behavior involve structures that are separated anatomically and occupy a position predominantly medial to the attack circuits. Defense-producing circuits involve the ventromedial hypothalamus (VMH), the anterior hypothalamus, and their projections to the midbrain periaqueductal gray.

Surrounding these behavior-producing circuits is a system of structures that send neural projections to them that modify their excitability. The limbic system is one major source of modifying or modulating input to the attack- and defense-producing circuits. These limbic areas do not in themselves produce overt behavior when activated; rather, they influence or modulate behavior produced by activation of other brain areas. This modulation is expressed tonically by some but not all limbic structures. For example, it is possible to evoke directed predatory attack against rodents by electrically stimulating the feline lateral hypothalamus (LH). If the stimulus parameters are held constant, and if the stimulation is alternated between the LH and a tonic attack modulator that facilitates attack, attacks are faster than with LH stimulation alone. Modulators are stimulated electrically at intensities that do not provoke any behavior when the modulator is stimulated alone. If one destroys part of the tonic facilitator and then stimulates the LH again, attack is permanently slowed. This effect suggests that the tonic modulator is applying a lasting, or tonic, facilitatory influence on attack mediated by activation of the LH (Siegel and Flynn 1968). Using the same paradigm, it can be demonstrated that other limbic areas exert tonic inhibitory influences on attack (Egger and Flynn 1967) and tonically facilitate defense (Adamec 1978; Maeda and Hirata 1978; Stokman and Glusman 1970).

The tonic facilitators of attack are the lateral amygdala and the ventral hippocampus (VHP). The basomedial amygdala (BM) tonically inhibits attack and tonically facilitates defensive behavior (Adamec and Stark-Adamec 1983a). The BM has been implicated in mediating fear states in a variety of species of animals, including humans (Adamec and Stark-Adamec 1983a; Ervin, Mark, and Stevens 1969; Kaada 1972; and Gloor 1986). Because of the intimate connections of the BM with temporal neocortical areas involved in complex perceptual processes, the cells in the amygdala have complex sensory properties, responding to species-relevant stimuli, such as rats, in cats (O'Keefe and Bouma 1969) and facial emotional expression in primates (Leonard et al. 1985; and Rolls 1984). The amygdala thus stands in a unique position to integrate complex information about the external world and emotional states. Moreover, in humans, this integration may have been extended to include integration of internal representations of the external world in the form of memory images with emotional experiences associated with those memories (Gloor 1986).

Given these considerations, it seemed to us that the most likely places in the nervous system to look for evidence of neural biases underlying the inhibited disposition would be in tonic modulators of attack and defense. Since the defensive disposition appears as a stimulus-selective, heightened defensive responsiveness, the BM seemed a likely candidate structure in which to find a neural correlate of this heightened responsiveness. In view of the apparent conflict of attack and defense, it also seemed important to consider the excitability of tonic attack facilitators. So we chose to investigate the VHP.

Laboratory Studies

Our investigations have concentrated on the BM, the VHP, and the circuits in which they are imbedded. Using cats reared in the studies just described, we have found that defensive disposition varies directly with several indices of excitability of these limbic structures. One that we feel to be the most important will be discussed here: the strength of transsynaptically conducted neural activity assessed by evoked potential techniques.

Studies of the Amygdala

The first circuit we investigated is the excitatory pathway joining the BM to the VMH. This pathway is of considerable interest for several reasons. First, defensive behavior can be elicited by electrical activation of the VMH (e.g., Adamec 1976a; Maeda 1976). Second, the BM facilitates defensive behavior elicited by stimulating the VMH when this facilitation is induced either by direct electrical stimulation of the amygdala (Stokman and Glusman 1970) or by environmental threat (Maeda and Maki 1987). Third, it is very interesting that the period of growth of defensive response in development (37–52 days) corresponds to the period in which Kling and Coustan (1964) observed that the amygdala begins to modulate the hypothalamic substrate of defense in cats. It may be, then, that early differences in defensive responses are the behavioral signature of differences in this neural-developmental process. Moreover, this process may be reflected in the way that excitatory information is conducted over the pathway from the amygdala to the VMH.

What we found is consistent with this latter view. The more defensive the cat, the larger the excitatory synaptic potentials evoked in the VMH substrate of defense by pulsed stimulation of the BM (fig. 3). The peak height of potentials from defensive cats exceeded those of aggressive cats over the range of intensities of BM stimulation from 100 to 175 percent of threshold intensity to evoke a potential in the VMH. Moreover, there were no differences between groups of cats in cellular response to stimulation in the amygdala or the VMH over the intensity range examined (Adamec and Stark-Adamec 1984). Finally, the threshold for evocation of a VMH potential did not differ between groups of cats. Taken together, these data imply that the larger excitatory potential in inhibited (defensive) cats is due to an increased strength of synaptic drive into the VMH from the BM as the intensity of that drive is increased.

There are several implications of this finding. First, the excitability of neither BM nor VMH cells differs between groups of cats, only the strength of excitatory synaptic communication between them. Thus, one component of the defensive disposition appears neurally as a strengthening of excitatory synaptic transmission in a circuit that modulates defensive response to complex stimulus input. Second, cats differ with respect to an excitatory modulatory influence of the BM on VMH cells. The data suggest that firing the amygdala cells, which occurs normally in response to complex threatening stimuli, would not cause VMH cells to fire but would render them more excitable to subsequent excitatory input. This has the effect of lowering the firing threshold of VMH cells by reducing the degree of excitatory input to the VMH necessary to fire cells and produce a defensive response. The difference in this modulatory influence between inhibited and uninhibited cats would appear behaviorally as an enhanced defensive responsiveness to the same stimulus in inhibited (defensive) cats relative to uninhibited cats.

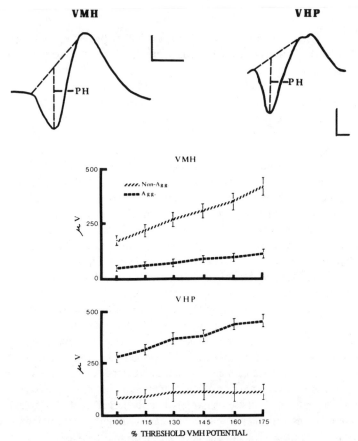

Fig. 3. Plotted in the upper part of the figure are two typical computer averages of field potentials evoked simultaneously in the VMH and the VHP by single pulsed stimulation of the basomedial amygdala in the cat. Calibrations are 120 microvolts (vertical) and 5 milliseconds (horizontal) for the VMH and 100 microvolts and 10 milliseconds for the VHP. Lines drawn on the potentials illustrate how the size of the potentials (peak height, PH) was found by computer. The lower part of the figure displays changes in peak heights of these potentials as the intensity of amygdala stimulation was raised from 100 to 175 percent of threshold for evoking a VMH potential. Mean peak height (in microvolts) and standard errors of the means for 20 potentials at each intensity are plotted against percent of threshold. Data are from uninhibited (aggressive, Agg.) and inhibited (nonaggressive, Non-Agg.) cats and are plotted separately. For further details, see Adamec and Stark-Adamec (1984).

Finally, the difference in response over intensity of BM stimulation suggests that stimuli that have a weaker effect on firing of amygdala cells would nevertheless have a stronger modulatory effect on VMH cells in defensive cats. Behaviorally, this could appear as a more generalized defensive response to a wider range of stimuli, some of which normally fire amygdala cells only weakly. Individual variation in the slope of rise of VMH potential size over intensity of BM stimulation could provide a mechanism whereby stimulus generalization of defensive response to qualitatively different stimuli translates neurally to differences in degree of excitatory modulation of VMH cells.

Support for this view comes from our findings that population cellular responses of BM and VMH to complex stimuli differ between inhibited and uninhibited cats. The response of cells in the BM and the VMH when inhibited cats view rats is larger than when uninhibited cats view rats. Moreover, the ratio of VMH/BM response to rats is larger in defensive cats, suggesting that the VMH response is exaggerated by the potentiated synaptic input from the BM demonstrated in the evoked potential studies (Adamec and Stark-Adamec 1988). This pattern of cellular response is not seen when the cats view mice.

All these considerations illustrate how both threshold of limbic lobe response and degree of limbic lobe response to environmental input may together contribute to the inhibited (defensive) disposition. It is likely that threshold in behavioral response circuits is tonically modulated in a graded fashion by synaptic inputs from tonic modulators. The tonicity of that input, however, is not expressed continuously but appears only when strengthened synapses are activated by complex stimulus input. This mechanism of action is consistent with the behavioral impression that defensive disposition is reactive to threatening stimuli rather than a continuous state of fearfulness.

Studies of the VHP

The amygdala not only projects to the VMH but also has excitatory projections to the VHP, a tonic attack facilitator. Thus, complex sensory information received by the amygdala is relayed both to defensive circuits (the VMH) and to aggression circuits (the VHP). Unlike the BM input to the VMH, the relay from the BM to the VHP is indirect. Amygdala cells first excite the entorhinal cortex, and then the entorhinal cortical cells excite VHP cells (Adamec and Stark-Adamec 1986; Krettek and Price 1977, 1978). One can detect the influence of the amygdala on VHP cells as a negative field potential that is evoked simultaneously with VMH potentials when the BM is stimulated. We have found that these VHP potentials change over intensity of BM stimulation in a manner opposite to VMH potentials (fig. 3). In uninhibited (aggressive) cats, VHP potentials increased with intensity of BM stimulation, but, in inhibited (defensive) cats, they did not change over intensity. Furthermore, VHP potentials from uninhibited (aggressive) cats were larger over all intensities than those recorded from inhibited (defensive) cats. Unlike VMH cells, VHP cells were fired in response to BM stimulation, and more so in uninhibited cats (Adamec and Stark-Adamec 1984). The greater cellular response to VHP in uninhibited cats is due to an enhanced synaptic input to the entorhinal cortex from BM because the excitability of the entorhinal cortical projection to the VHP does not differ between uninhibited and inhibited cats (Adamec and Stark-Adamec 1984). Finally, the VHP cells are not more excitable in aggressive cats; that is, they do not have lower activation thresholds because output/input ratios of cell firing to size of VHP potentials are constant and equal over intensity of BM stimulation in uninhibited and inhibited cats (Adamec and Stark-Adamec 1984).

Many of the conclusions for the BM-VMH pathway for defensive cats may, therefore, apply for the BM-VHP pathway for aggressive cats. Once again, differences in behavioral disposition are reflected in an enhancement of excitatory synaptic communication between limbic structures. These findings also suggest that a qualitative functional difference exists between the brains of uninhibited and inhibited cats. Not only does the same stimulus input to the BM of both types of cats modulate the excitability of the VMH differently, but it also excites different populations of cells in circuits having opposing behavioral functions. Stimuli reaching the BM in uninhibited (aggressive) cats preferentially excite cells in the VHP, a tonic attack facilitator, whereas little excitation of the VHP occurs in inhibited (nonaggressive and defensive) cats. Thus, the inhibited (defensive) disposition is due not only to enhanced excitation of the substrate of defense (VMH) but also to an attenuation of a perhaps normal flow of excitation from the BM to the VHP. Effective predatory stimuli, which normally excite amygdala cells strongly, cannot drive VHP cells and facilitate attack in defensive cats. Rather, these stimuli facilitate defensive circuits. The opposite occurs in uninhibited (aggressive) cats.

The reduction of flow of information from the BM to the VHP in defensive cats seems to be due to a weakening or lack of development of synaptic connections from amygdala to the entorhinal cortical input to VHP. This is not the only factor at work, however, in attenuating VHP responsiveness. Inhibited (defensive) cats also show greater local recurrent neural inhibition in the VHP (Adamec and Stark-Adamec 1984). Increased recurrent inhibition has the effect of reducing the ability of the VHP to follow high-frequency input, acting to attenuate its output, which would likely attenaute VHP modulation of behavior via VHP output to the lateral septum (Watson, Edinger, and Siegel 1983). The lateral septal projection is of particular interest since Gray et al. (1981) have implicated it in a system that suppresses behavioral inhibition in anxiety-provoking situations. One might then view the VHP-septal projections as participating in preventing behavioral inhibition in situations that might otherwise evoke it. The logic of this argument also requires that the VHP functions to facilitate approach-attack only in those situations that are more likely to evoke a defensive response since inhibited cats are just as likely as uninhibited cats to attack mice.

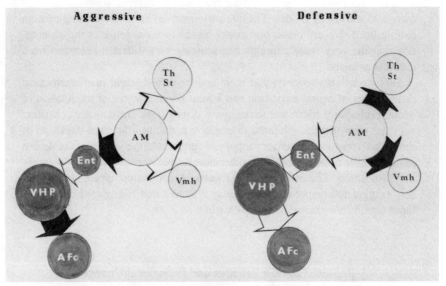

Fig. 4. The figure portrays the proposed differences in flow of neural information between limbic structures in naturally uninhibited (aggressive) and naturally inhibited (defensive) cats. Darkened arrows indicate enhanced flow of excitatory neural activity. Light arrows indicate reduced flow of excitatory neural activity. AM refers to the basomedial amygdala; VMH refers to the ventromedial hypothalamus; Ent refers to the entorhinal cortex, a major source of excitatory input to the ventral hippocampus; VHP refers to the ventral hippocampus; Th and St refer to the thalamus and subthalamus, respectively; and AFc refers to attack-facilitating circuitry, including the lateral septum. A proposed input to the AM from secondary cortical sensory areas is not shown. For details, see the text and Adamec (1978) and Adamec and Stark-Adamec (1984, 1986).

Summary and Conclusions

Taken together, the data suggest the following functional model of limbic determination of the inhibited (defensive) disposition. In uninhibited (aggressive) cats, neurosensory activity from temporal cortical secondary sensory areas (Prelevic, Burnham, and Gloor 1976; O'Keefe and Bouma 1969) is preferentially routed from the BM to the VHP (a tonic attack facilitator; fig. 4). Reduced recurrent inhibition in the VHP amplifies VHP output to the septum (AFc in fig. 4), facilitating predatory aggression. In inhibited (defensive) cats, neural information is routed away from the VHP because of weakened excitatory connections with it and because of greater inhibition within the VHP. This attenuates any effect the VHP might have on response inhibition and predatory attack via its connections with the septum. At the same time, neural information is routed into the defensive circuitry (including the VMH) (Adamec 1978; Adamec and Stark-Adamec 1984, 1986), ensuring a defensive response to the stimulus. This is, of course, only a first approximation to a working model. The circuitry involved is far more complex than that outlined. Nevertheless, this model begins to make sense of the observation that the very same stimulus can provoke very different reactions from different animals.

This model also suggests that both qualitatively different neuroanatomical distributions of neural excitation and inhibition and degree of modulation of neural excitability contribute to defensive disposition. The data are consistent with the view that the inhibited disposition is due to a lowered threshold of limbic lobe response to sensory input and further add the view that the degree of limbic lobe response may also determine degree of expression of the inhibited disposition. The mechanism of threshold modulation appears to be a latent exaggerated response of particular synapses that is engaged only when those circuits are excited by complex stimulus input.

Repeated Limbic Seizures and Behavioral Change

Theoretical Background

In the fourth section of this chapter, we review laboratory studies designed to test whether the physiological patterns correlated with differences in the inhibited (defensive) disposition are causal determinants of that disposition. One way to determine the role that these differences in neural excitability patterns play in behavior is to change those patterns directly and see what happens to the behavior. One way to do this is to elicit local, electrographic seizure discharges in the limbic system with high-frequency electrical stimulation. If one does this repeatedly, a number of changes in limbic excitability occur and last for long periods of time (weeks or months) in the absence of further discharges. Lasting change in excitability has been called kindling and has been well documented in a variety of species (for a review, see Racine 1978).

Laboratory Studies

Repeated electrographic limbic seizures (not motor seizures) or afterdischarges (ADs) were induced by electrical stimulation of the BM or the VHP of cats reared in the developmental studies as well as in a randomly selected adult cat population. When this is done, a number of lasting interictal (between-seizure) behavioral and neurophysiological changes were observed. These changes lasted as long as the cats were kept (60–120 days [Adamec 1978; Adamec and Stark-Adamec 1983b, 1983c]). Moreover, behavioral changes do not depend on continued seizures for their maintenance. It should be emphasized that behavioral changes are not a postictal (post-seizure) consequence of a single limbic AD in that they require 7–19 ADs to occur. Thus, some cumulative effect of repeated limbic AD is necessary for behavioral change.

Two types of behavioral change have been observed. The first is a lasting increase in defensive response to environmental threat (i.e., to rats, threat howls, and mice in some cases, but no change in social response to familiar humans). The second is an increase in predatory aggressiveness, accompanied by a decrease in defensiveness (Adamec 1978; Adamec and Stark-Adamec 1983a).

Increases in defensiveness may be observed in both naturally aggressive and naturally defensive cats. When seizures are triggered in the BM, aggressive cats cease attacking rats and display a generalized increase in defensive response to several environmental threats (Adamec 1978). A similar pattern of behavioral change is observed if seizures are triggered in the VHP of naturally defensive cats, likely due to the spread of seizures to the BM (Adamec and Stark-Adamec 1983c). Increased defensiveness interictally is accompanied by lasting increases in transsynaptic communication in BM projections to the substrate of defense including the VMH. In addition, there is an increase in recurrent inhibition in the VHP. Thus, the pattern of distribution of local excitabilities correlated with the defensive disposition is recreated by limbic seizures and leads to an increase in defensiveness.

Of particular interest is the finding that the degree of increase in defensiveness following VHP stimulation appears to depend on how seizures alter transsynaptic communication in the BM-VHP pathway (fig. 5). Half the cats show increases in BM-VHP evoked potentials, whereas half do not (Adamec and Stark-Adamec 1986). Those that do display less of an increase in defensive response than those that do not. These cats do not differ with respect to postictal changes in transsynaptic communication in other limbic circuits. These data suggest that increases in BM-VHP communication antagonize the behavioral effect of increases in transsynaptic communication in defensive neural circuits (BM-VMH). This antagonism is consistent with the model proposed earlier of how limbic communication contributes to aggressive and defensive disposition. The data also suggest another way in which degree of expression of defensive disposition may be modulated by degree of potentiation of synaptic communication between limbic structures.

Eliciting ADs in the VHP of naturally aggressive cats, on the other hand, increases their aggressiveness and attenuates defensive response to prey. In this case, there is no evidence of increased transsynaptic communication from the BM to the VMH (Adamec 1978). It is likely that other parts of the attack-facilitating system were changed in these cats, but this circuitry has yet to be investigated. Nevertheless, these data suggest that increases of transsynaptic communication within the defensive circuits are at least necessary for an increase in defensiveness.

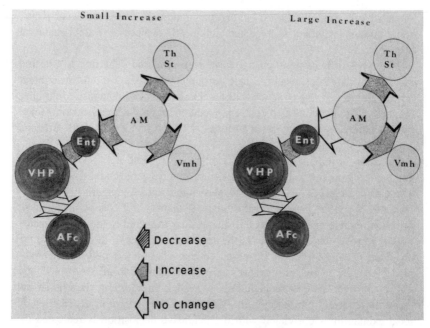

Fig. 5. The figure illustrates the changes in flow of neural information between limbic structures in cats made more defensive by repeated limbic afterdischarges. The proposed decrease in
flow of information from the VHP to the AFc is based on the observed increase in recurrent
neural inhibition in the VHP. The figure on the left illustrates the fact that cats showing a small
increase in defensive response to rats display an increase in flow of excitatory information from
the AM to the Ent, whereas cats showing a large increase in defensive response to rats (right
figure) do not. Labels of anatomical areas are the same as in figure 4. For details, see the text
and Adamec (1978) and Adamec and Stark-Adamec (1983b, 1983c, 1986).

Summary and Conclusions

Taken together, the data strongly suggest that the naturally occurring patterns of differences in transsynaptic communication between limbic structures
found to distinguish inhibited (defensive) from uninhibited (aggressive) cats
are causally determining the behavioral differences observed. Thus, the naturally occurring early developing differences in defensive disposition are represented neurally as stable differences in neuronal function at neural excitatory and inhibitory synaptic junctions. Moreover, the pattern of distribution
of these differences appears to be important. Our current model is that these
differences in local excitabilities determine how complex sensory information
is routed within limbic circuits that modulate hypothalamic and brain stem
circuits that control behavioral response to such stimuli. This model begins to
make sense of the behavioral observations that the same stimulus evokes very
stably different responses from different animals.

Since it is possible to recreate the physiological patterns associated with naturally occurring differences in the inhibited (defensive) disposition, it is likely that an understanding of the mechanism of that recreation will reveal how the naturally occurring patterns are produced in nature. These mechanisms are currently poorly understood, though there are some leads. The seizure-induced changes in transsynaptic communication resemble long-term potentiation (LTP) of synaptic transmission. Long-term potentiation is currently being intensely investigated in the hippocampus of rodents, and several candidate molecular mechanisms have been advanced (Baudry and Lynch 1982; Routenberg and Lovinger 1985). The most exciting recent work suggests that activation of a particular protein channel, called the NMDA (N-methyl-D-aspartate) receptor, which passes calcium into cells, is essential for initiation, but not maintenance, of LTP produced in a number of ways, including kindling (Collingridge and Bliss 1987; Stelzer et al. 1986). Of even greater interest is the evidence that NMDA receptors participate in some forms of learning (Collingridge and Bliss 1987). It is possible that a genetically determined trait relies on molecular mechanisms for its expression that are also employed by the brain for storing new information during the establishment of memories. Seizure-induced increases in hippocampal inhibition are dependent on a different mechanism, which may involve an increase in the number of benzodiazepine receptors, which facilitate the functioning of GABA receptors that produce recurrent inhibition (Tuff, Racine, and Adamec 1983; Tuff, Racine, and Mishra 1983). Thus, more than one molecular mechanism may be involved in establishing the neural pattern associated with the inhibited disposition.

General Conclusions and Implications

The term "anxious personality" may be an appropriate label for the pattern of behavioral inhibitions observed in the cat. Current definitions of anxiety used for the purpose of modeling the phenomenon in animals define animal "anxiety" as a reflection of activation of the neural substrates controlling behavioral, somatic, and endocrine response to natural threats (Skolnick et al. 1984). The limbic areas involved in defensive behavior are closely intertwined with hypothalamic, medullary, and brain stem areas mediating autonomic activation associated with anxiety (Smith and DeVito 1985). For example, VMH stimulation in the cat produces defensive behavior or defensive attack (Adamec 1976a; Maeda and Maki 1987) associated with increases in plasma catecholamines (Stoddard-Apter, Siegel, and Levin 1983), part of the autonomic "anxiety" pattern in animals and humans. These changes in catecholamines also occur during spontaneous defensive behavior elicited by environmental threats (Stoddard et al., in press). It is of interest in this regard that increased norepinephrine turnover has been correlated with behavioral inhibition in children (Kagan, Reznick, and Snidman 1987). Moreover, Smith and DeVito (1985) describe a hypothalamic area involving the perifornical region and most of the medial portion of the LH, which they designate as the hypothalamic area controlling emotional response (HACER) since it seems to be the site of hypothalamic control of patterned autonomic activation in response to threat. The HACER system may be a separate but interacting system that forms an interface between the neural substrate of behavioral emotional response and associated autonomic activation. The HACER receives widespread inputs from other brain areas involved in defensive behavior (such as the medial hypothalamus and periaqueductal gray [see Bandler 1984]) and may feed back to them (Smith and DeVito 1985). Thus, assessment of autonomic reactivity could reflect degree of activation of circuits mediating defensive behavior, and possibly modulators of those circuits, such as the amygdala. This implication deserves further investigation since studies in humans have relied in part on measures of autonomic reactivity to study anxiety-prone children (Kagan, Reznick, and Snidman 1987). Moreover, enhanced autonomic reactivity to the unfamiliar has been associated with the inhibited disposition in children, suggesting the possibility that the function of limbic modulators of fearfulness in humans may be enhanced, as it seems to be in cats.

The limbic system has been implicated in anxiety because of a substantial body of evidence indicating that the action of benzodiazepine anxiolytics may be mediated by the benzodiazepine receptor (BZR). These receptors are prevalent in the limbic systems of animals and humans (Braestrup, Albrechtsen, and Squires 1977; Young and Kuhar 1980). Moreover, Gray et al. (1981) have implicated the hippocampal-septal system in behavioral inhibition associated with anxiety and in the action of anxiolytics. The work reported here similarly implicates this system in defensive response differences in cats. Moreover, Maeda (1978) has shown that lateral septal destruction lowers the threshold for a particular type of defensive behavior elicited by electrical stimulation of the VMH of the cat. Maeda distinguishes two types of VMH-elicited defense, one that is in vacuo, without provocation, and one that is in response to environmental provocation (provoked). Lateral septal destruction lowers thresholds for provoked but not for in vacuo defense. Since the amygdala mediates the effect of the environment on provoked VMH defense (Maeda and Hirata 1978; Maeda and Maki 1987), these data suggest that sensory information routed through the amygdala reaches the lateral septum and modifies excitability of the defensive circuits. These data are also consistent with the model presented in this chapter.

Finally, several lines of evidence suggest that benzodiazepine agonists and antagonists alter defensiveness in cats and anxiety in humans. Agonists such as diazepam, an effective anxiolytic in humans, raise the threshold for in vacuo and provoked VMH-elicited defense (Maeda 1976), reduce withdrawals from mice in kittens (Wolgin and Servidio 1979), and, when injected into the amygdala, block carbachol-induced defensive behavior (Nagy and Decsi 1973). Inverse agonists such as FG-7142, which induce panicked anxiety in humans (Dorrow et al. 1983), increase fearful behavior in cats (Ongini, Banzaghi, and Marzanatti 1983). More recently, FG-7142 has been found lastingly to increase defensiveness in cats as measured in the studies reported in this chapter (Adamec 1988). The acute behavioral effects of FG-7142 are blocked by the specific BZR blocker RO-15-1788, strongly suggesting that the BZR mediates some aspects of cat anxiety. Moreover, the lasting increases in cat anxiety induced by FG-7142 appear to be mediated by two mechanisms, one involving the BZR and a second mechanism that does not. It has been proposed that the BZR independent mechanism involves the NMDA receptor discussed above as a candidate mechanism for the LTP of limbic communication underlying the inhibited disposition (Adamec 1988). Thus, an interaction between the molecular mechanisms that create anxiety and molecular mechanisms that create lasting memories may interact to produce an anxious disposition.

Taken together, all these data suggest a BZR involvement in the mechanisms underlying amygdala, VMH, and septal contributions to modulation of defense. In addition, a wealth of data indicate BZR modulation of hippocampal inhibition (for an example, see Adamec et al. 1981).

All these considerations support the use of the term "anxiety proneness" in cats. If the cats studied are, indeed, anxious, it is likely a form of self-protective anticipatory anxiety that is reactive to particular environmental threats. Though the proneness to defensive response appears chronic, it does not totally dominate the cats' behavior since defensive cats show uninhibited social interactions with familiar humans and are willing to attack mice. Even when cats are made more defensive by limbic seizures, their "friendly" social responses to familiar humans do not change (Adamec and Stark-Adamec 1983b). Thus, prior experiences of a nonthreatening nature with a situation alter defensive responsiveness to that situation.

Our studies in the cat also suggest that what appear as qualitative differences in behavior may be determined by neural processes that vary both in quality (neuroanatomical pattern) and in degree. It may be that a choice between qualitative or continuum differences is not necessary to explain behavioral inhibition in cats or in humans. It is possible, in principle, that both are operating in human children, as they seem to be in cats.

In conclusion, the data add to an emerging consensus that organisms differ with respect to a possibly genetically based proneness to defensive response to environmental threat. Enhanced defensiveness in young organisms may be adaptive, but extreme defensiveness and its persistence into adulthood could be maladaptive. The defensive personality trait may be dependent, in part, on a neural bias in limbic-system structures that carry complex sensory information to neural circuits mediating behavioral, somatic, and endocrine responses to sensory input. Though defensive bias is chronic in that neural bias is continually present, it is not always manifested in behavior but must be elicited by threatening events. Moreover, defensive response to the environment appears modifiable by experiences of a nonthreatening nature, but perhaps under very special conditions during development.

There are a number of striking parallels between our studies in cats and studies of behavioral inhibition in children, and we have endeavored to point them out in this chapter. In several cases, the principles governing development and shaping of expression of the inhibited disposition appear analogous in the two species. While facile generalizations across species are to be avoided, the analogies suggest that answers to questions asked of the cat brain may point to physiological principles of importance to understanding the sources of our own species inhibitions. Some of those principles may be emerging in recent and continuing advances in understanding of the molecular bases of learning, LTP, and anxiety.

References

Adamec, R. 1975. The behavioral bases of prolonged suppression of predatory attack in cats. *Aggressive Behavior* 1:297–314.

Adamec, R. 1976a. Hypothalamic and extrahypothalamic substrates of predatory attack suppression and the influence of hunger. *Brain Research* 106:57–69.

Adamec, R. 1976b. The interaction of hunger and preying in the domestic cat (*Felis catus*): An adaptive hierarchy? *Behavioral Biology* 18:263–72.

Adamec, R. 1978. Normal and abnormal limbic system mechanisms of emotive biasing. In *Limbic mechanisms*, ed. K. E. Livingston and O. Hornykiewicz, 405–55. New York: Plenum.

Adamec, R. 1988. FG-7142 and "anxiety" in the cat: Acute and lasting after effects on defensive behavior—Implications for epilepsy and anxiety. St. John's: Memorial University. Typescript.

Adamec, R.; McNaughton, B.; Racine, R.; and Livingston, K. E. 1981. Effects of diazepam in hippocampal excitability in the rat: Action in the dentate area. *Epilepsia* 22:205–15.

Adamec, R., and Stark-Adamec, C. 1983a. Limbic kindling and animal behavior—Implications for human psychopathology associated with complex partial seizures. *Biological Psychiatry* 18(2): 269–93.

Adamec, R., and Stark-Adamec, C. 1983b. Partial kindling and emotional bias in the cat: Lasting after-effects of partial kindling of ventral hippocampus: 1. Behavioral changes. *Behavioral and Neural Biology* 38:205–22.

Adamec, R., and Stark-Adamec, C. 1983c. Partial kindling and emotional bias in the cat: Lasting after-effects of partial kindling of ventral hippocampus: 2. Physiological changes. *Behavioral and Neural Biology* 38:223–39.

Adamec, R., and Stark-Adamec, C. 1984. Contribution of limbic connectivity to stable behavioral characteristics of aggressive and defensive cats. In *Modulation of sensorimotor activity during altered behavioral states,* ed. R. Randler, 341–49. New York: Liss.

Adamec, R. E., and Stark-Adamec, C. 1986. Partial kindling and behavioral change—Some rules governing the behavioral outcome of repeated limbic seizures. In *"Kindling 3,"* ed. J. Wada, 195–212. New York: Raven.

Adamec, R., and Stark-Adamec, C. 1988. Population cellular responses to species-characteristic stimuli in the limbic systems of aggressive and defensive cats raised from birth. St. John's: Memorial University. Typescript.

Adamec, R. E.; Stark-Adamec, C.; and Livingston, K. E. 1980a. The development of predatory aggression and defense in the domestic cat *(Felis catus)*: 1. Effects of early experience on adult patterns of aggression and defense. *Behavioral and Neural Biology* 30:389–409.

Adamec, R. E.; Stark-Adamec, C.; and Livingston, K. E. 1980b. The development of predatory aggression and defense in the domestic cat *(Felis catus)*: 2. Development of aggression and defense in the first 164 days of life. *Behavioral and Neural Biology* 30:410–34.

Adamec, R. E.; Stark-Adamec, C.; and Livingston, K. E. 1980c. The development of predatory aggression and defense in the domestic cat *(Felis catus)*: 3. Effects on development of hunger between 180 and 365 days of age. *Behavioral and Neural Biology* 30:435–47.

Adamec, R.; Stark-Adamec, C.; and Livingston, K. E. 1983. The expression of an early developmentally emergent defensive bias in the adult domestic cat *(Felis catus)* in non-predatory situations. *Journal of Applied Animal Ethology* 10:89–108.

Adler, H. E. 1955. Some factors of observational learning in cats. *Journal of Genetic Psychology* 86:159–69.

Bandler, R. 1984. Identification of hypothalamic and midbrain periaqueductal grey neurones mediating aggressive and defensive behavior by intracerebral micro injections of excitatory amino acids. In *Modulation of sensorimotor activity during alterations in behavioral states,* ed. R. Randler, 369–91. New York: Liss.

Baudry, M., and Lynch, G. 1982. Possible mechanisms of LTP: Role of glutamate receptors. In *Neurosciences research program bulletin—Hippocampal long term potentiation: Mechanisms and implications for memory,* vol. 20, no. 5, ed. L. Swanson, T. J. Taylor, and R. F. Thompson, 663–71. Cambridge, Mass.: MIT Press.

Bernston, G. G. 1972. Blockade and release of hypo-thalamically and naturally elicited aggressive behaviors in cats following midbrain lesions. *Journal of Comparative and Physiological Psychology* 81:541–54.

Berry, C. C. 1908. An experimental study of imitation in cats. *Journal of Comparative Neurology and Psychology* 18:1–10.

Braestrup, C.; Albrechtsen, R.; and Squires, F. R. 1977. High densities of benzodiazepine receptors in human cortical areas. *Nature* 269:702–4.

Chesler, P. 1969. Maternal influence in learning by observation in kittens. *Science* 166:901–3.

Collingridge, G. L., and Bliss, T. V. P. 1987. NMDA receptors—Their role in long-term potentiation. *Trends in Neuroscience* 10(7): 288–93.

Cranach, B. V.; Grote-Dham, R.; Huffner, V.; Marte, F.; Reisbeck, G.; and Mitelstadt, M. 1978. *Das social Gehemmte Kind im Kindergarten, Praxis der Kinderpsychologie und Kinderpsychiatrie* 27:167–79.

Daniels, D., and Plomin, R. 1985. Origins of individual differences in infant shyness. *Developmental Psychology* 21(1): 118–21.

Dorrow, R.; Horowski, R.; Paschelke, G.; Amin, M.; and Braestrup, C. 1983. Severe anxiety induced by FG-7142, a B-carboline ligand for benzodiazepine receptors. *Lancet* 2:98.

Egger, D. M., and Flynn, J. P. 1967. Further studies on the effects of amygdaloid stimulation and ablation of hypothalamically elicited attack behavior in cats. In *Progress in brain research,* vol. 27, Structure and function of the limbic system, ed. W. R. Adey and T. Tokizane. Amsterdam: Elsevier.

Ervin, F. R.; Mark, V. H.; and Stevens, J. 1969. Behavioral and affective responses to brain stimulation in man. In *Neurobiological aspects of psychopathology,* ed. J. Zubin and C. Shagass. 54–65. New York: Grune & Stratton.

Flynn, J. P. 1967. The neural basis of aggression in cats. In *Neurophysiology and emotion,* ed. D. C. Glass, 40–60. New York: Rockefeller University Press.

Flynn, J. P.; Vanegas, H.; Foote, W.; and Edwards, S. 1970. Neural mechanisms involved in a cat's attack on a rat. In *The neural control of behavior,* ed. R. E. Whalen, R. F. Thompson, M. Verzeano, and N. M. Weinberger, 135–73. New York: Academic Press.

Gloor, P. 1986. Role of the human limbic system in perception, memory and affect: Lessons from temporal lobe epilepsy. In *The limbic system: Functional organization and clinical disorders,* ed. B. K. Doane and K. E. Livingston, 159–69. New York: Raven.

Gray, J. A.; Davis, M.; Feldon, J.; Nicholas, T.; Rawlins, P.; and Owen, S. R. 1981. Animal models of anxiety. *Progress in Neuropsychopharmacology* 5:143–57.

Gupta, B. D., and Holland, H. C. 1969. An examination of the effects of stimulant and depressant drugs on escape/avoidance conditioning in strains of rats selectively bred for emotional/non-emotionality. *Psychopharmacologia* (Berlin) 14:95–105.

Herbert, M. J., and Harsh, C. M. 1944. Observational learning by cats. *Journal of Comparative Psychology* 37:1–95.

Hornocker, M. G. 1969. Winter territoriality in mountain lions. *Journal of Wildlife Management* 33(3): 457–64.

Kaada, B. R. 1972. Stimulation and regional ablation of the amygdaloid complex with reference to functional representations. In *The neurobiology of the amygdala,* ed. B. E. Eleftheriou, 205–82. New York: Plenum.

Kagan, J. 1984. *The nature of the child.* New York: Basic.

Kagan, J.; Reznick, S.; and Snidman, N. 1987. The biology and psychology of behavioral inhibition in young children. *Child Development.* 58:1459–73.

Kenney, M.; Mason, W. A.; and Hills, S. 1979. Effects of age, objects and visual experience on affective responses of rhesus monkeys to strangers. *Developmental Psychology* 15:176–84.

Kling, A., and Coustan, D. 1964. Electrical stimulation of the amygdala and hypothalamus in the kitten. *Experimental Neurology* 10:81–89.

Kreiskott, H. 1969. Some comments on the killing response behavior of the rat. In *Aggressive behavior,* ed. S. Garattini and E. R. Sigg, 200. New York: Wiley.

Krettek, J., and Price, J. 1977. Projections from the amygdaloid complex and adjacent olfactory structures to the entorhinal cortex and to the subiculum in the rat and cat. *Journal of Comparative Neurology* 172:723–52.

Krettek, J., and Price, J. 1978. A description of the amygdaloid complex in the rat and cat with observations of intra-amygdaloid axonal connections. *Journal of Comparative Neurology* 178:225–54.

Kruuk, H., and Turner, M. 1967. Comparative notes on predation by lion, leopard, cheetah and wild dog in the Serengeti area, East Africa. *Mammalia* 31:1–27.

Kuo, Z. Y. 1930. The genesis of the cat's response to the rat. *Journal of Comparative Psychology* 11:1–35.

Kuo, Z. Y. 1933. Further study on the behavior of the cat toward the rat. *Journal of Comparative Psychology* 25:1–8.

Leonard, C. M.; Rolls, E. T.; Willson, F. A. W.; and Baylis, G. C. 1985. Neurons in the amygdala of the monkey with responses selective for faces. *Behavioral Brain Research* 15:159–86.

Leyhausen, P. 1956. Verhaltensstudien an Katzen. *Zeitschrift fur Tierpsychologie Beiheft* 2:1–120.

Leyhausen, P. 1965. Uber die funktion der relativen stimmungeshierarchie. *Zeitschrift fur Tierpsychologie* 22:412–95.

Maeda, H. 1976. Effects of psychotropic drugs upon the hypothalamic rage response in cats. *Folia Psychiatrica et Neurologica Japonica* 30(4): 539–46.

Maeda, H. 1978. Effects of septal lesions on electrically elicited hypothalamic rage in cats. *Physiology and Behavior* 21:339–43.

Maeda, H., and Hirata, K. 1978. Two-stage amygdaloid lesions and hypothalamic rage: A method useful for detecting functional localization. *Physiology and Behavior* 21:529–30.

Maeda, H., and Maki, S. 1987. Dopamine agonists produce functional recovery from septal lesions which affect hypothalamic defensive attack in cats. *Brain Research* 407:381–85.

Murphree, O. D.; DeLuca, D. C.; and Angel, C. 1974. Psychopharmacologic facilitation of operant conditioning of genetically nervous Catahoula and Pointer dogs. *Pavlovian Journal of Biological Science* (January–March): 17:24.

Nagy, J., and Decsi, L. 1973. Location of the site of the tranquillizing action of diazepam by intralimbic application. *Neuropharmacology* 12:757–68.

O'Keefe, J., and Bouma, H. 1969. Complex sensory properties of certain amygdala units in the freely moving cat. *Experimental Neurology* 23:384–94.

Ongini, E.; Banzaghi, C.; and Marzanatti, G. 1983. Intrinsic and antagonistic effects of B-carboline FG-7142 on pentobarbital in cats. *European Journal of Pharmacology* 95:125–29.

Prelevic, S.; Burnham, W. M.; and Gloor, P. 1976. A microelectrode study of amygdaloid afferents: Temporal neocortical inputs. *Brain Research* 105:437–57.

Racine, R. 1978. Kindling: The first decade. *Neurosurgery* 3(2): 234–52.

Roberts, W. W., and Berquist, E. H. 1968. Attack elicited by hypothalamic stimulation in cats raised in social isolation. *Journal of Comparative and Physiological Psychology* 66:590–95.

Rolls, E. T. 1984. Neurons in the cortex of the temporal lobe and in the amygdala of the monkey with responses selective for faces. *Human Neurobiology* 3:209–22.

Routenberg, A., and Lovinger, D. M. 1985. Selective increase in phosphorylation of a 47-KDa protein (F1) directly related to long-term potentiation. *Behavioral and Neural Biology* 43:3–11.

Schaller, C. B. 1967. *The Deer and the Tiger.* Chicago: University of Chicago Press.

Schaller, G. B. 1972a. Predators of the Serengeti: 1. The social carnivore. *Natural History* 81(2): 38–49.

Schaller, G. B. 1972b. Predators of the Serengeti: 2. Are you running with me Hominid? *Natural History* 81(3): 60–68.

Schenkel, R. 1966. Play exploration and territoriality in the wild lion. In *Play, exploration and territoriality in mammals,* ed. P. A. Jewell and C. Loizos, 1–10. New York: Academic Press.

Siegel, A., and Flynn, J. P. 1968. Differential effects of electrical stimulation and lesions of the hippocampus and adjacent regions upon atack behavior in cats. *Brain Research* 7:252–60.

Skolnick, P.; Ninan, P.; Insel, T.; Crawley, J.; and Paul, S. 1984. A novel chemically induced animal model of human anxiety. *Psychopathology* 17 (suppl. 1): 25–36.

Smith, O., and DeVito, J. L. 1985. Central neural integration for the control of autonomic responses associated with emotion. *Annual Review of Neuroscience* 7:43–65.

Stelzer, A.; Slater, N. J.; Galvan, M.; and ten Bruggencate, G. 1986. N-methyl-D-Aspartate receptors and hippocampal kindling. In *Excitatory amino acid transmission,* ed. T. P. Hicks, D. Lodge, and H. McLennan, 71–74.

Stoddard-Apter, S.; Siegel, A.; and Levin, B. E. 1983. Plasma catecholamine and cardiovascular responses following hypothalamic stimulation in the awake cat. *Journal of the Autonomic Nervous System* 8:343–60.

Stokman, C. L. J., and Glusman, M. 1970. Amygdala modulation of hypothalamic flight in cats. *Journal of Comparative and Physiological Psychology* 71:365–75.

Stoddard, S. L.; Bergdall, B. K.; Conn, P. S.; and Levin, B. E. In press. Increases in plasma catecholamines during naturally elicited defensive behavior in the cat. *Brain Research.*

Suomi, S. J.; Kraemer, G. W.; Baysinger, C. M.; and DeLizio, R. D. 1981. Inherited and experimental factors associated with individual differences in anxious behavior displayed by rhesus monkeys. In *Anxiety: New research and changing concepts,* ed. D. F. Klein and J. Rabkin, 179–97. New York: Raven.

Tuff, L. P.; Racine, R. J.; and Adamec, R. 1983. The effects of kindling on GABA-mediated inhibition in the dentate gyrus of the rat: 1. Paried pulse depression, *Brain Research* 277:70–90.

Tuff, L. P.; Racine, R. J.; and Mishra, R. K. 1983. The effects of kindling on GABA-mediated inhibition in the dentate gyrus of the rat: 2. Receptor binding. *Brain Research* 277:91–98.

Watson, R. E.; Edinger, H. M.; and Siegel, A. 1983. An analysis of the mechanisms underlying hippocampal control of hypothalamically-elicited aggression in the cat. *Brain Research* 269:327–45.

Wolgin, D. L., and Servidio, S. 1979. Disinhibition of predatory attack in kittens by oxazepam. *Society for Neuroscience Abstracts* 5:667 (abstract no. 2282).

Yerkes, R. M., and Bloomfield, D. 1910. Do kittens instinctively kill mice? *Psychological Bulletin* 7(8): 253–63.

Young, W. S., and Kuhar, M. J. 1980. Radiohistochemical localization of benzodiazepine receptors in rat brain. *Journal of Pharmacology and Experimental Therapeutics* 212(2): 337–46.

6

Behavioral Inhibition: Issues of Context

JOAN STEVENSON-HINDE

Introduction

Inhibition and the related concepts of fear, wariness, and shyness may span several levels, ranging from subjective experience through actual behavior to underlying physiological and biochemical mechanisms. It is likely that, the more levels analyzed, the richer the research (e.g., Kagan, chap. 1, and Reznick et al., chap. 2, both in this vol.). While level of analysis, which involves the actual variables being measured, is necessarily in the foreground, issues of context are too often left in the background. It then becomes unclear whether a concept is being applied over many contexts or restricted to a specific one, to what extent indices of a construct are or should be consistent across different contexts, or whether a construct may influence and be influenced by context. It is hoped that discussion of these issues will clarify our thinking and improve communication between differing approaches. I shall be concerned primarily with a behavioral level of analysis and shall begin by ordering concepts according to the range of contexts covered, from broad to narrow.

Context and terminology

1. *Behavioral inhibition* (e.g., Kagan, Reznick, and Snidman 1985) has been used over a wide range of contexts, including cognitive tasks. Behavioral inhibition refers to "the child's initial behavioral reactions to unfamiliar people, objects, and contexts or challenging situations" (53). It involves not only discrete measures such as latency to approach but also behavioral style— "restrained, watchful, gentle" (54). For example, "when the inhibited child

I would like to thank R. A. Hinde and M. K. Rothbart for their helpful comments.

125

throws a ball, knocks down a tower of blocks, or hits a large toy clown, the act is monitored, restrained, almost soft" (54). Thus, behavioral inhibition refers to responding in both familiar and unfamiliar settings.

2. *Fear of the unfamiliar,* analyzed by Bronson (1968, 1972), excludes behavior in many of the contexts used in the above research on behavioral inhibition, such as difficult cognitive tasks, stories with pictures of fearful or fearless children, or a "risk room." Bronson and Pankey (1977) distinguished between "an inherent 'wariness of the unfamiliar' " and learned fears, "ascribed to an association with some previous distressing experience" (1167). There is a possible resemblance here between "inherent versus learned" or "unfamiliar versus familiar" and the "innate versus learned" dichotomy, attacked years ago as being "not only false but sterile" (Hinde 1970a, 425–34; see also Schneirla 1952; Hebb 1953; Lehrman 1953; Beach 1955). Indeed, it is unlikely that anything is truly unfamiliar. Even from very early on, stimulus generalization and active comparison with past experiences must operate in "unfamiliar" settings. An artificial dichotomy may be avoided by postulating a continuum of contexts, ranging from unfamiliar to familiar.

3. *Fear of strangers* (e.g., Bretherton and Ainsworth 1974) or *wariness of strangers* (e.g., Sroufe 1977) applies only to social contexts. In addition to age of the child, the nature of the situation (e.g., presence vs. absence of mother, home or lab setting), aspects of the stranger (e.g., peers, female or male adults, adults in white coats, or even midgets [Brooks and Lewis 1976]), and the stranger's behavior (e.g., sensitive vs. intrusive approach) will influence the reaction (see also Harmon, Morgan, and Klein 1977).

A related concept is *shyness:* "Inhibition, withdrawal, and fear displayed by infants in reaction to novel social situations is generally known as stranger fearfulness or wariness, but it can also be conceptualized as infant shyness" (Daniels and Plomin 1985, 118). Buss (1986) uses the term "fearful shyness," again restricted only to social contexts and distinct from what he calls "self-conscious shyness." For Buss, immediate causes of "fearful shyness" are social novelty, intrusiveness, and social evaluation. The latter is a worry only to adults and children who have been socialized sufficiently to be aware of appropriate standards and consequences of failure. Thus, shyness may become more complex from infancy to adulthood. Jones, Briggs, and Smith (1986) define shyness as "a tendency to respond with heightened anxiety, self-consciousness, and reticence in a variety of social contexts; a person high in the trait of shyness will experience greater arousal than a person low in shyness independent of the level of interpersonal threat in the situation" (630). They go on to confirm, with their own results from the Social Reticence Scale, the view that shyness should be seen as a separate and distinct construct, related to but different from constructs such as introversion or sociability (for further discussion of this point, see below).

Context as a "Setting"

Consistency across contexts: Temperament

The above consideration of the range of contexts covered by a construct is separate from that of whether the construct reflects consistent individual differences. On the one hand, a construct may be viewed simply in a normative sense, such as seeing fear of strangers as a developmental milestone, reached by most children by about 9 months of age (e.g., Schaffer 1966). On the other hand, a construct may be viewed as an individual characteristic or trait (as in the above definition of shyness), distinguishing one individual from another. Within the framework of temperament theory, a trait must be relatively stable across contexts and time, present early in life, and (for Buss and Plomin) "genetic in origin" (see Goldsmith et al. 1987). This implies some degree of consistency across different contexts and raises the important but neglected question of how much consistency, across how wide a range of contexts, should be required in establishing a "trait."

Changes in responsiveness: Behavior systems

While a temperament approach focuses on individual consistency across contexts, a behavior systems approach focuses on *changes* in responsiveness. A behavior system is "distinguished on the basis of common causation . . . [and is] usually found to subserve a particular biological function. . . . Differences in responsiveness of one individual at different times can be understood on the basis of variations in the balance between different motivational systems" (Baerends 1976, 731, 733). For example, when given a choice of two egg models on the rim of its nest, an incubating herring gull normally retrieved the larger one first. However, when the smaller egg was retrieved first, accompanying behavior suggested a relative increase in the tendency to escape (escape system) compared with the tendency to incubate (incubation system [Baerends and Kruijt 1973]). While the precision of Baerends's experiments is unlikely to be obtained with human subjects (see Bischof 1975), the concept of a behavioral system is nevertheless useful as a way of organizing behavioral data.

Implications

Correlations within a particular context

Even within one context, measures of a particular construct will have far from perfect intercorrelations. Yet we may have reasons for postulating that the different measures are related to a common behavior system. For example, in our present study with 2.5-year-olds, fear of stranger was assessed by latency to approach a female stranger when asked to come and see what she had in her hand as well as by ratings of fear expressed. Each rating was based on facial expression, body posture, and avoidant behavior to stranger. These measures were taken from videotapes of the Ainsworth Strange Situation with mother present (episode 2) immediately after mother and child had been in the strange room on their own for 3 minutes (episode 1). Ratings on a four-point scale were made when the stranger (1) entered the room, (2) sat down, (3) invited the child to approach her and see what she had in her hand, and (4) sat on the floor to play with the child. The four ratings were then averaged to obtain a fear of stranger score. The correlation between the fear rating and latency to approach was .44 (Pearson r, $p < .001$, two tailed, $N = 82$ [Stevenson-Hinde and Shouldice, in preparation]). On the one hand, this is highly significant; on the other hand, knowing one variable explains only 19 percent of the variance in the other. Nevertheless, both relate to "fear of strangers."

Of course, low agreement may be attributed partly to measurement error. However, low correlations between measures of fear in a given context occur even in highly controlled situations. For example, chaffinches (*Fringilla coelebs*) and many other songbirds emit a predictable and stereotyped "mobbing" display to a stationary novel object or potential predator (for further description, see Marler and Hamilton [1966, 248–49]). One component of this display is a discrete alarm call, which sounds like a "chink" (see sound spectrograms in Marler and Hamilton [1966, 464–67]). This response may be studied in the laboratory by presenting an isolated chaffinch with a stationary stimulus for varying amounts of time and with varying interstimulus intervals. The preparation has provided an excellent means of studying behavioral habituation (e.g., Hinde 1970b). Of interest here is that the alarm call may be taken as an index of "fear." Thus, the stronger the stimulus (e.g., stuffed owl > toy dog), the shorter the latency to the first alarm call, the higher the rate of occurrence over the first 6 minutes of the stimulus presentation, and the higher the rate during the second 6 minutes relative to the first 6 minutes (i.e., the response wanes more slowly with a stronger stimulus). Turning to intercorrelations, the correlation between rate of responding in the first 6 minutes and latency to the first response was $-.59$ ($N = 100$) for an owl stimulus and $-.33$ for a toy dog, and the correlation between rate of responding in the first 6 minutes and relative rate in the second 6 minutes was .38 for an owl and .42 for a dog. "The correlations, however, are not very high, and indicate considerable independent individual variation in these response characteristics" (Hinde 1960, 404). Thus, even with this relatively simple response, assessed in a controlled, nonsocial situation, correlations between what might be called measures of fear are low, and it is unlikely that the low values can be written off as due primarily to measurement error. One interpretation of low intercorrelations is that not all possible relevant responses are equally activated when a particular system is activated. If different responses are activated differently for each individual, then intercorrelations between measures of fear will not be high.

Correlations across different contexts

If context is important, and if other systems interact with a fear system, then one would not expect individuals to be completely consistent in the degree of fear shown across contexts. While supporting a behavior systems approach, Sroufe (1977) also views "stranger reactions as reflecting the infant's context-based evaluation of the event" (735). Thus, what an individual brings to a situation that activates a particular behavior system such as fear will determine the nature and degree of the fearful behavior expressed.

At a less restricted level than fear of strangers, fear of the unfamiliar involves the following contextual variables: the nature of the setting (e.g., home or lab), presence or absence of the mother or other supportive figures, characteristics of the unfamiliar person, animal or object (e.g., male or female stranger, degree of intrusiveness [see Skarin 1977]), and so on. In our current longitudinal study, one measure of fear of strangers was based on mothers' ratings of behavior to unfamiliar adults and children in naturally occurring situations (three items from the McDevitt and Carey [1978] scale and three similar items that we constructed). After a mother rated her child at 2.5 years, fear was then assessed in a laboratory procedure (the Ainsworth Strange Situation—see above), followed by a test involving strange animals (Mongolian gerbils; for further details, see Stevenson-Hinde and Shouldice [in preparation]). The correlation between fear of strangers outside the lab and fear of a female stranger in the lab was .44 (Pearson r, $p < .001$, two tailed, $N = 82$). Within the lab, the correlation between ratings of fear of stranger (episode 2) and fear of strange room (episode 1) was .39 ($p < .001$, two tailed) and that between fear of stranger and fear of strange animals (Mongolian gerbils) .24 ($p < .05$, two tailed). Thus, individuals were significantly consistent across contexts, but they were also inconsistent, in that less than 20 percent of the variance from one context to another was explained. A temperament approach combined with a behavior systems approach would predict both consistency and inconsistency, over and above any measurement error. For example, a particular child's past experience of strange animals may have been more or less frightening than meeting a stranger. The same fear system would be activated, but activated to a different degree, in each situation.

Over a still broader range of contexts, Reznick et al. (1986) found intercorrelations ranging from .45 to near zero (.04) to −.31 between peerplay inhibition, laboratory inhibition, school inhibition, risk avoidance, and frequency of looking at an examiner. Yet, because of their theoretical framework, these were all viewed as "major behavioral indexes of inhibition" (666). Their approach is compatible with the view that such a range of contexts may imply different degrees of "threat" for any particular child, thereby activating a fear behavior system differently across contexts. Furthermore, if another system, such as affiliation during peer play, was activated more for some individuals than others, and if this interacted with a fear system, then individual consistency in inhibition across contexts would be lowered further.

Fear and Affiliative Behavior as Separate Traits or Systems

Most temperament and attachment theorists would agree that fear of the unfamiliar should be kept distinct from affiliative behavior or sociability. With a behavior systems approach, a postulated affiliative system is distinct from a fear/wary system, although the two may influence each other. Indeed, interest lies in the balance between interdependent but separate systems, such as fear, affiliation, exploration, and attachment (e.g., Greenberg and Marvin 1982; Sroufe 1977). At the empirical level, studies of wariness of strangers have produced conflicting results for various reasons, including the combination of positive (affiliative) and negative (fearful) responses to a stranger, which obscured the percentage of infants showing wariness (reviewed in Sroufe [1977]). The point is that, when confronted with a stranger, infants may show affiliative behavior (e.g., look, smile) in alternation with wariness (e.g., look away) or even both at once (e.g., smile while turning away). If they do approach the stranger, this is often followed by an immediate return to the mother. This could be described as activation of the following systems in succession: affiliative to fear to attachment (Bretherton and Ainsworth 1974).

Long-term developmental changes may be explained similarly in terms of a changing balance between behavior systems. Greenberg and Marvin (1982) used a behavior systems approach for understanding reactions to a stranger in children aged 2–4 years. They found that whereas 2-year-olds combined wariness with approach and proximity to the mother, 3- and 4-year-olds "displayed lengthy combinations of wary and sociable behavior, for example, withdrawal from the stranger and displaying extended coy expressions, while at the same time conversing in a sociable way with her" (488–89). Such changes with age were described in terms of "the decreased developmental coupling of the wary and attachment systems, and the increased developmental coupling of the wary and sociable systems" (489). Greenberg and Marvin conclude that, throughout life, most animals are wary of strange conspecifics; what changes is the organization of behavioral systems.

Theories of temperament make a similar distinction between fearfulness and sociability. For example, Buss and Plomin (1984) separate sociability and shyness (see also Daniels and Plomin 1985), and Thomas and Chess (1977) have a dimension of "initial approach/withdrawal" but not one of sociability (see also Jones, Briggs, and Smith, 1986).

At the empirical level, Reznick et al. (1986) found that, with 5.5-year-olds, "a high and stable heart rate was more closely related to the responses that reflect initial restraint rather than lack of social spontaneity" (667). Since the latter measure was based on frequency of social interactions in school and talking to the examiner (as well as gross motor movement during testing), it may be viewed as primarily a sociability measure, with properties different from those of the initial restraint measure. Thus, there seem to be good theoretical reasons for distinguishing affiliative/sociability constructs from those relating to fearfulness, though in practice interactions between behavioral systems mean that our behavioral measures are rarely pure reflections of one particular construct (see also Kagan, chap. 1, and Rothbart, chap. 7, both in this vol.).

The Context of Early Relationships

As we have seen, within the framework of attachment theory, activation of a fear behavior system may lead to activation of an attachment behavior system (e.g., Bowlby 1982; Bretherton and Ainsworth 1974; Greenberg and Marvin 1982; Sroufe 1977) in all infants or young children. However, individuals differ in the ways in which they are able to use the mother as a secure base. How a child uses an attachment figure as a secure base is better seen under higher stress than meeting a stranger, such as, on reuniting with the mother (or the father) after a period of separation (Ainsworth et al. 1978).

The child's reunion behavior is taken to index an aspect of the relationship with the attachment figure (e.g., Bretherton 1985; Hinde 1982; Sroufe 1985). This does not imply that temperament is unimportant in the development of attachment (e.g., Egeland and Farber 1984; Grossmann and Grossmann, in press) or in the expression of behavior on reunion in the Strange Situation (e.g., Belsky and Rovine 1987). However, viewing the attachment classification as primarily relational does imply a basis in antecedent parent/child interactions as well as reunion behavior that may differ according to which attachment figure is present. Supporting the fundamental work of Ainsworth (summarized in Ainsworth et al. [1978]), the Grossmanns' longitudinal studies have related maternal sensitivity—reflected in affectionate holding, appropriate reactions to crying, and frequent responses to vocalizations, often with a tender-warm voice quality—to a secure classification with the mother in the Strange Situation (Grossmann et al. 1985; Grossmann, Friedl, and Grossmann 1987). Just as sensitive responsiveness fosters the development of a secure pattern of attachment, insecure patterns are viewed as strategies developed by the child in the course of interacting with an attachment figure who

Table 1: Relations between *Fear of Stranger* and How 2.5-Year-Olds Use Mothers as a *Secure Base* in the Ainsworth Strange Situation.

	Correlations: Secure Base Ratings vs. Fear of Stranger Ratings	Mean Secure Base Ratings According to Subgroups With:				
		Low Fear		Medium Fear		High Fear
Boys (N = 41):						
Reunion 1	−.29	3.6	<	3.7	>*	2.9
Reunion 2	−.26	3.3	>	3.1	>	2.6
Girls (N = 41):						
Reunion 1	−.64***	3.6	>	3.2	>*	2.2
		3.6		>***		2.2
Reunion 2	−.53***	3.3	>	2.8	>	2.0
		3.3		>**		2.0

* $p < .05$, two tailed (t test).
** $p < .01$, two tailed (t test).
*** $p < .001$, two tailed (Pearson r or t test).

does not show the above sensitivity (e.g., Main and Weston 1982; Main and Hesse, in press). Thus, the pattern of attachment shown on reunion with one parent does not predict the pattern shown with the other (e.g., Grossmann et al. 1981; Main and Weston 1981), and must be seen as an aspect of the relationship with the attachment figure in question.

In our current study, 2.5-year-olds were assessed in the Ainsworth Strange Situation. When the mother entered the room after a brief separation (episodes 4 and 7), reunion behavior of the child to the mother was examined for hesitation, avoidance, and/or resistance (a security rating of 1) as opposed to the use of the mother as a secure base in a free, direct, and straightforward way (a security rating of 4). Fear of a stranger was independently rated with the mother present and prior to any separation (episode 2) as described above. The boys and girls were then divided into three subgroups of approximately equal size, according to low, medium, or high fear of stranger ratings, and their security ratings were compared across subgroups. Children with low or medium fear had significantly higher security ratings on reunion than did children with high fear, especially if they were girls (see table 1). As this implies, correlations between fear and security were negative, although not always significant, since the medium fear group sometimes had the highest security ratings. Here, the nonsignificant correlations indicated only nonlinearity rather than absence of a relation between variables (see also Hinde and Dennis 1986).

This relation between fear of strangers, a characteristic of a child that was significantly consistent across situations, and an aspect of the mother/child relationship indicates that one may make a prediction from an individual to a relationship or vice versa. The direction of effect, of whether the child's characteristic drove the relationship or whether the relationship influenced the characteristic, is an issue that requires a precise formulation, in terms of differences between the participants at one particular time or changes in the participants across time (see Hinde 1979, chap. 19).

From a theoretical view, the importance of early relationships for development of the individual is a key assumption of attachment theory (Bowlby 1982). The above finding, that the most positive secure base behavior went with low or moderate fear, fits the prediction that a secure relationship should produce a less fearful, more confident child than an insecure relationship. The importance of any relational influence on fear, and indeed some other individual characteristics, probably increases initially. That is, over the first 6 months, a relational influence may not be as important as it is over the second 6 months, when clear-cut attachment relationships are formed, or later, as the child develops "working models" of relationships (e.g., Bowlby 1982; Bretherton 1985; Main, Kaplan, and Cassidy 1985) and becomes more susceptible to family expectations and social pressures (Huston 1983; Maccoby and Jacklin 1975, 303–48). Following Kagan's intriguing suggestion that by about 7 years of age inhibition becomes relatively fixed, as if connections were "soldered in" (Kagan, chap. 1, in this vol.), relational influences on a fear system may be greatest from 1 to 7 years.

Evidence in the other direction, for the child driving the relationship, is suggested by studies that identify an individual characteristic early on and that demonstrate some consistency and heritability. In particular, behavioral inhibition (e.g., Rothbart, chap. 7, in this vol.) and then fear of strangers (e.g., Schaffer 1966) appear during the first year of life; consistency of behavioral inhibition and its physiological correlates have been shown in a variety of contexts (Kagan, Reznick, and Snidman 1985; Reznick et al. 1986); and behavioral genetic studies "suggest that shyness in both infancy and adulthood is heritable and that genetic variance in infancy continues to affect individual differences in adulthood" (Daniels and Plomin 1985, 121), with possible changes in heritability across age (Rose and Ditto 1983).

Thus, the predominant direction of effects between a trait and relationships may change with age. An example comes from an earlier study of 42- and 50-month-old children. With shyness rated from maternal interview questions about initial approach/withdrawal to strange people and places (Garside et al. 1975), consistency from 42 to 50 months was .61 (Spearman r, $N = 41$, $p < .001$, two tailed). For girls, shyness was significantly positively correlated with mother sensitive to child, mother enjoys child, joint activities with mother and with father, a positive relationship with the older sibling, and conversational questions to mother and negatively correlated with child actively hostile to mother, child passive (i.e., not engaged) with mother, mother/child activity changes (implying that they did not do one thing for long), child reactively hostile to peers in nursery school, and both peers and adults disconfirming the child. The opposite held for 50-month-old boys (for details, see Hinde, Stevenson-Hinde, and Tamplin [1985], Hinde and Tamplin [1983], and Simpson and Stevenson-Hinde [1985]).

Similar associations have been found by Radke-Yarrow and her colleagues in their research on families with and without a history of psychiatric disorder. They report, "Mothers seemed not to be pleased with shyness in boys. Boys' shyness was associated with less joyfulness in their mothers. Mothers' interactions with shy girls, in contrast, were characterized by tenderness, affection, and sadness" (Radke-Yarrow, Richters, and Wilson 1988, 58). They also found that the children themselves differed, with shyness in boys associated with tension and negative mood and shyness in girls "associated with a more complex set of personal qualities, including tension, sadness, lower levels of anger and social competence, and higher levels of affection and compliance" (58).

Returning to our own study, whereas only four correlations between shyness and measures at home and school differed greatly (i.e., by more than 70 points) between boys and girls at 42 months; at 50 months, 12 correlations differed greatly (Stevenson-Hinde and Hinde 1986). Mothers' comments during interviews suggested why such differences were more common at the later age. Some mothers complained that their sons should have grown out of their shyness, having been in nursery school for a year, while others commented with pleasure that their daughters still preferred being at home with them. Similarly, E. Maccoby and H. K. A. Sants (personal communication, February 1984) found that mothers, when asked to label adjectives as masculine or feminine, tended to label "shy" as a feminine characteristic but "assertive" as masculine. Thus, mothers (and fathers) may have different attitudes toward shyness in boys and in girls, with shyness in boys becoming less acceptable as they get older. This suggests that shyness may be driving social interactions one way for girls and another way for boys. However, no sex differences in the absolute levels of shyness had appeared at either 42 or 50 months. If interactions were driving the shyness, one would expect, from a reinforcement model, that girls in the sample should become more shy than boys. We are testing this prediction in our present longitudinal study, which follows children from 2.5 to 7.0 years (for further discussion of sex differences, see Reznick et al. [chap. 2, in this vol.] and Rothbart [chap. 7, in this vol.]).

In brief, a fear system may have different levels of activation for different individuals. The threshold may be affected by the quality of close relationships (e.g., raised by secure relationships). By the time a child is about to start primary school, fearfulness for a girl may have different correlates from and be more socially acceptable than it is for a boy. If social reinforcement operates, girls should eventually be more fearful than boys. Finally, following

Kagan's suggestion, any setting of a fear behavior system may become more difficult to alter by about 7 years of age.

Conclusion

This chapter has focused on the need to make context explicit. In the first instance, this is important if we are to build a science based on agreed terminology. It involves explicit recognition that some of the concepts we use may not have unlimited generality. In the case of fear, at least three levels, ranging from general to specific, are suggested. Second, the utility of a temperamental trait depends critically on its cross-situational consistency. Too often, however, this issue is glossed over or significant correlations are accepted with scant attention to the low proportion of variance explained. In practice, even within a particular context, changes in responsiveness may occur, and correlations between theoretically related measures may be low. It has been suggested here that such moderate degrees of consistency can be accommodated by integrating behavior systems and temperament approaches. Third, the social context, and especially early relationships, may influence the development and expression of a trait. This has been discussed in terms of a particular example—the empirically found relation between secure attachment and low to moderate fear of strangers. Emphasis is placed on the continuous interplay between traits and relationships in order to underline the general principle that an understanding of development demands not just one approach but an integration of approaches.

References

Ainsworth, M. D.; Blehar, M. C.; Waters, E.; and Wall, S. 1978. *Patterns of attachment*. Hillsdale, N.J.: Erlbaum.

Baerends, G. P. 1976. The functional organization of behaviour. *Animal Behaviour* 24:726–38.

Baerends, G. P., and Kruijt, J. P. 1973. Stimulus selection. *In Constraints on learning*, ed. R. A. Hinde and J. Stevenson-Hinde, 23–50. New York: Academic Press.

Beach, F. A. 1955. The descent of instinct. *Psychological Review* 62:401–10.

Belsky, J., and Rovine, M. 1987. Temperament and attachment security in the Strange Situation: An empirical rapprochement. *Child Development* 58:787–95.

Bischof, N. 1975. A systems approach toward the functional connections of fear and attachment. *Child Development* 46:801–17.

Bowlby, J. 1982. *Attachment and loss*. Vol. 1, *Attachment*. London: Hogarth.

Bretherton, I. 1985. Attachment theory: Retrospect and prospect. In *Growing points of attachment theory and research*, ed. I. Bretherton and E. Waters, 3–35. *Mono-*

graphs of the Society for Research in Child Development, vol. 50, nos. 1–2, serial no. 209.

Bretherton, I., and Ainsworth, M. D. S. 1974. Responses of one-year-olds to a stranger in a strange situation. In *The origins of fear,* ed. M. Lewis and L. A. Rosenblum, 131–64. New York: Wiley.

Bronson, G. W. 1968. The fear of novelty. *Psychological Bulletin* 69:350–58.

Bronson, G. W. 1972. Infants' reactions to unfamiliar persons and novel objects. *Monographs of the Society for Research in Child Development,* vol. 37, no. 3, serial no. 148.

Bronson, G. W., and Pankey, W. B. 1977. On the distinction between fear and wariness. *Child Development* 48:1167–83.

Brooks, J., and Lewis, M. 1976. Infants' responses to strangers: Midget, adult, and child. *Child Development* 47:323–32.

Buss, A. H. 1986. A theory of shyness. In *Shyness: Perspectives on research and treatment,* ed. W. H. Jones, J. M. Cheek, and S. R. Briggs, 39–46. New York: Plenum.

Buss, A. H., and Plomin, R. 1984. *Temperament: Early developing personality traits.* Hillsdale, N.J.: Erlbaum.

Daniels, D., and Plomin, R. 1985. Origins of individual differences in infant shyness. *Developmental Psychology* 21:118–21.

Egeland, B., and Farber, E. A. 1984. Infant-mother attachment: Factors related to its development and changes over time. *Child Development* 55:753–71.

Garside, R. F.; Birch, H.; Scott, D.; Chambers, S.; Kolvin, I.; Tweddle, E. G.; and Barber, L. M. 1975. Dimensions of temperament in infant school children. *Journal of Child Psychology and Psychiatry* 16:219–31.

Goldsmith, H.; Buss, A. H.; Plomin, R.; Rothbart, M. K.; Thomas, A.; Chess, S.; Hinde, R. A.; and McCall, R. B. 1987. What is temperament? Four approaches. *Child Development* 58:505–29.

Greenberg, M. T., and Marvin, R. S. 1982. Reactions of preschool children to an adult stranger. A behavioral systems approach. *Child Development* 53:481–90.

Grossmann, K., Friedl, A.; and Grossmann, K. E. 1987. Preverbal infant-mother vocal interaction patterns and their relation to attachment quality. Paper presented at the second international symposium "Prevention and Intervention in Childhood and Youth: Conceptual and Methodological Issues," Bielefeld, Federal Republic of Germany, September 28–30.

Grossmann, K., and Grossmann, K. E. In press. Newborn behavior, early parenting quality and later toddler-parent relationships in a group of German infants. In *The cultural context of infancy,* vol. 2, ed. J. K. Nugent, B. M. Lester, and T. B. Brazelton. Norwood, N.J.: Ablex.

Grossmann, K.; Grossmann, K. E.; Spangler, G.; Suess, G.; and Unzner, L. 1985. Maternal sensitivity and newborns' orientation responses as related to quality of attachment in northern Germany. In *Growing points of attachment theory and research,* ed. I. Bretherton and E. Waters, 233–56. *Monographs of the Society for Research in Child Development,* vol. 50, nos. 1–2, serial no. 209.

Grossmann, K. E.; Grossmann, K.; Huber, F.; and Wartner, U. 1981. German children's behavior towards their mothers at 12 months and their fathers at 18 months in Ainsworth's Strange Situation. *International Journal of Behavioral Development* 4:157–81.

Harmon, R. J.; Morgan, G. A.; and Klein, R. P. 1977. Determinants of normal variation in infants' negative reactions to unfamiliar adults. *Journal of Child Psychiatry* 16:670–83.

Hebb, D. O. 1953. Heredity and environment in mammalian behaviour. *British Journal of Animal Behaviour* 1:43–47.

Hinde, R. A. 1960. Factors governing the changes in strength of a partially inborn response, as shown by the mobbing behaviour of the chaffinch (*Fringilla coelebs*): 3. The interaction of short-term and long-term incremental and decremental effects. *Proceedings of the Royal Society*, B, 153:398–420.

Hinde, R. A. 1970a. *Animal behaviour: A synthesis of ethology and comparative psychology.* 2d ed. New York: McGraw-Hill.

Hinde, R. A. 1970b. Behavioural habituation. In *Short-term changes in neural activity and behaviour,* ed. G. Horn and R. A. Hinde, 3–40. Cambridge: Cambridge University Press.

Hinde, R. A. 1979. *Towards understanding relationships.* London: Academic Press.

Hinde, R. A. 1982. Attachment: Some conceptual and biological issues. In *The place of attachment in human behavior,* ed. C. M. Parkes and J. Stevenson-Hinde, 60–76. New York: Basic.

Hinde, R. A., and Dennis, A. 1986. Categorizing individuals: An alternative to linear analysis. *International Journal of Behavioral Development* 9:105–19.

Hinde, R. A.; Stevenson-Hinde, J.; and Tamplin, A. 1985. Characteristics of 3–4 year olds assessed at home and interactions in preschool. *Developmental Psychology* 21:130–40.

Hinde, R. A., and Tamplin, A. 1983. Relations between mother-child interactions and behaviour in preschool. *British Journal of Developmental Psychology* 1:231–57.

Huston, A. 1983. Sex-typing. In *Handbook of child psychology,* ed. P. H. Mussen, 4th ed. Vol. 4, *Socialization, personality and social development,* ed. E. M. Hetherington, 387–467. New York: Wiley.

Jones, W. H.; Briggs, S. R.; and Smith, T. G. 1986. Shyness: Conceptualization and measurement. *Journal of Personality and Social Psychology* 51:629–39.

Kagan, J.; Reznick, J. S.; and Snidman, N. 1985. Temperamental inhibition in early childhood. In *The study of temperament: Changes, continuities and challenges,* ed. R. Plomin and J. Dunn, 53–65. Hillsdale, N.J.: Erlbaum.

Lehrman, D. S. 1953. A critique of Konrad Lorenz's theory of instinctive behaviour. *Quarterly Review of Biology* 28:337–63.

Maccoby, E. E., and Jacklin, C. N. 1975. *The psychology of sex differences.* Stanford, Calif.: Stanford University Press; London: Oxford University Press.

McDevitt, S. C., and Carey, W. B. 1978. The measurement of temperament in 3–7 year old children. *Journal of Child Psychology and Psychiatry* 19:245–53.

Main, M., and Hesse, E. In press. Lack of resolution of mourning in adulthood and its relationship to infant disorganization: Some speculations regarding causal mechanisms. In *Attachment in the preschool years: Theory, research, and intervention,* ed. M. Greenberg, D. Cicchetti, and M. Cummings. Chicago: University of Chicago Press.

Main, M.; Kaplan, N.; and Cassidy, J. 1985. Security in infancy, childhood, and adulthood: A move to the level of representation. In *Growing points of attachment theory and research*, ed. I. Bretherton and E. Waters, 66–104. *Monographs of the Society for Research in Child Development*, vol. 50, nos. 1–2, serial no. 209.

Main, M., and Weston, D. 1981. The quality of the toddler's relationship to mother and to father: Related to conflict behavior and the readiness to establish new relationships. *Child Development* 52:932–40.

Main, M., and Weston, D. 1982. Avoidance of the attachment figure in infancy: Descriptions and interpretations. In *The place of attachment in human behavior*, ed. C. M. Parkes and J. Stevenson-Hinde, 31–59. New York: Basic.

Marler, P., and Hamilton, W. J. 1966. *Mechanisms of animal behavior.* New York: Wiley.

Radke-Yarrow, M.; Richters, J.; and Wilson, W. E. 1988. Child development in a network of relationships. In *Relationships within families: Mutual influences*, ed. R. A. Hinde and J. Stevenson-Hinde, 48–67. Oxford: Clarendon Press.

Reznick, J. S.; Kagan, J.; Snidman, N.; Gersten, M.; Baak, K.; and Rosenberg, A. 1986. Inhibited and uninhibited children: A follow-up study. *Child Development* 57:660–80.

Rose, R. J., and Ditto, W. B. 1983. A developmental-genetic analysis of common fears from early adolescence to early adulthood. *Child Development* 54:361–68.

Schaffer, H. 1966. The onset of fear of strangers and the incongruity hypothesis. *Journal of Child Psychology and Psychiatry* 7:95–106.

Schneirla, T. C. 1952. A consideration of some conceptual trends in comparative psychology. *Psychological Bulletin* 49:559–97.

Simpson, A. E., and Stevenson-Hinde, J. 1985. Temperamental characteristics of three- to four-year-old boys and girls and child-family interactions. *Journal of Child Psychology and Psychiatry* 26:43–53.

Skarin, K. 1977. Cognitive and contextual determinants of stranger fear in six- and eleven-month-old infants. *Child Development* 48:537–44.

Sroufe, L. A. 1977. Wariness of strangers and the study of infant development. *Child Development* 48:731–46.

Sroufe, L. A. 1985. Attachment classification from the perspective of infant-caregiver relationships and infant temperament. *Child Development* 56:1–14.

Stevenson-Hinde, J., and Hinde, R. A. 1986. Changes in associations between characteristics and interactions. In *The study of temperament: Changes, continuities and challenges*, ed. R. Plomin and J. Dunn, 115–29. Hillsdale, N.J.: Erlbaum.

Stevenson-Hinde, J.; and Shouldice, A. In preparation. Fear and attachment in 2.5-year-olds. Cambridge: Cambridge University.

Thomas, A., and Chess, S. 1977. *Temperament and development.* New York: Brunner/Mazel.

7 Behavioral Approach and Inhibition

MARY KLEVJORD ROTHBART

With behavioral inhibition defined as the child's vulnerability to uncertainty toward the unfamiliar (Garcia-Coll, Kagan, and Reznick 1984) and to challenge (Kagan, Reznick, and Snidman 1987), we might have reason to believe that behavioral inhibition would not be present in the newborn but would develop with the onset of fearfulness in the last half of the first year of life (Sroufe 1979). Nevertheless, most studies of behavioral inhibition have observed children aged 14 months or older (Garcia-Coll, Kagan, and Reznick 1984; Reznick et al., chap. 2, in this vol.).

In this chapter, I review several developmental studies of infants' responsiveness to unfamiliarity and challenge during the first year of life. This research suggests that we may wish to consider temperamental individual differences in approach or motor activation as well as later-developing individual differences in behavioral inhibition to novelty or challenge. I also decribe our observations of across-age stability and instability in infants' approach and inhibition of reaching (Rothbart 1988). This research indicates that approach tendencies show stability from 6.5 to 13.5 months of age, whereas behavioral inhibition as assessed via reaching does not show stability over this period. Finally, research on the development of approach and inhibition is related to models of temperament in adults and to developmental models in animals.

Early Development of Behavioral Inhibition

In considering the early development of infants' inhibition of motor approach, the research of Schaffer and his colleagues on the development of wariness (Schaffer 1974; Schaffer, Greenwood, and Parry 1972) is very important.

Research reported in this chapter was supported in part by National Institute of Mental Health grant 2674 and by a grant from the Center for the Study of Women in Society, University of Oregon. Critical comments by Susan Green, Michael Posner, and Myron Rothbart on an earlier version of this chapter are greatly appreciated.

139

Schaffer operationalized wariness as "a relative increase in the time taken before contact is made on first exposure to an unfamiliar object" (Schaffer, Greenwood, and Parry 1972, 173). Schaffer argues that the important change occurring in the third quarter of the first year of life is not so much the onset of avoidance responses as it is the onset of the child's initial inhibition of approach responses.

Schaffer, Greenwood, and Parry (1972) carried out a longitudinal study in which 20 infants' responses to unfamiliar stimuli were observed monthly from 6 to 12 months of age. While infants at the earliest age revealed from their increased looking time that they were sensitive to the unfamiliarity of objects (and more recent research has indicated that unfamiliarity also affects manipulation time [see Rubenstein 1974, 1976; Ruff 1976]), they approached unfamiliar objects "impulsively and immediately" (Schaffer, Greenwood, and Parry 1972, 14). Only at 8 months and beyond was reaching and grasping influenced by familiarity. At this age, infants demonstrated hesitation in their approach, sometimes but not always accompanied by distress and/or avoidance. When contact was finally made with the object, it tended to be abbreviated and cautious. Schaffer (1974) suggests that, during this hesitation, the children were subjecting the stimulus "to intense and uninterrupted visual inspection—as though appraising it before selecting a resonse deemed suitable in terms of the individual's past experience of that stimulus. Impulsiveness thus gave way to wariness, and the response that emerged after the period of immobility could take the form of approach or avoidance (i.e., cautious exploration or a fear reaction)" (Schaffer 1974, 15).

An interesting aspect of the approach responses of 6-month-old infants observed in our laboratory is that they can lead to distress if an object grasped is a highly exciting one. The reaching and grasping of the 6-month-old may be seen as having a compulsory quality, and, just as the early looking behavior of the infant has been described as obligatory attention (Stechler and Latz 1966), so the reaching of most 6-month-olds may be described as obligatory reaching.[1] As Schaffer observed, by the time infants are 8 months of age and older, however, they will be reaching and grasping unfamiliar objects more slowly and cautiously. Thus, if we were to apply a construct used to describe temperament in adults, 6-month-olds would be seen as generally more novelty seeking or extraverted in their behavior than 8- or 10-month-olds.

Are there relatively stable individual differences in infants' rate of approach and in their wariness tendencies during the first year of life? We have investigated the latency of approach responses (latency to reach and grasp objects) in a longitudinal sample of infants seen at 6.5, 10, and 13.5 months of age (Rothbart 1988). For these infants, the speed of approaching a set of low-intensity, relatively familiar toys (e.g., a rattle, bell, or cup) varied from child

---

1. I am grateful to Holly Ruff for suggesting this expression.

to child, with some children reaching the grasping rapidly and others more slowly. There were also consistencies in speed of approach across objects reflected in positive correlations across these stimuli. Latency to grasp these toys also showed moderate stability from one age to another. In addition, the children who reached faster tended generally to demonstrate more positive affect, that is, more smiling and laughter.

At each age, the infants were also presented with high-intensity novel toys (mechanical duck, dog, and bear). We expected these toys to be both relatively unfamiliar and challenging, in that they moved in an unpredictable manner and were sound producing. We found that the children who reached for and grasped the low-intensity toys more rapidly also tended to reach for and grasp the high-intensity toys more rapidly. That is, it was possible to identify a general approach component to the children's response that generalized across conditions of both low and high novelty and challenge. However, there were also important differences in the children's reaction to toys that differed in novelty/intensity. At all ages, the high-intensity toys were grasped more slowly than were the low-intensity toys. In addition, older infants grasped the intense toys more slowly and showed more hesitations in approach (inhibition of movement toward the toy for .5 seconds or longer) than they did when they were younger. Finally, individual differences in speed of reaching and grasping the novel, high-intensity toys were not stable across age, unlike the reaching for low-intensity, relatively familiar toys, suggesting that inhibition of approach to novel/high-intensity toys may have been developing at different rates over this period for some children than for others.

These developmental findings suggest that both approach tendencies and behavioral inhibition may be involved in children's reactions to challenging and novel stimuli during this early period. Developmentally, individual differences in speed of approach can be observed before children begin to show extended periods of nonapproach and hesitations in approaching novel, high-intensity toys. These individual differences are maintained over the period when behavioral inhibition appears to be developing. They must be assessed under conditions of relative familiarity and low challenge, however, because, by 10 months, some children will be greatly inhibiting their approaches under conditions of novelty and challenge. Another important aspect of children's approach to novelty and challenge is that some children will continue to approach very rapidly under conditions of unfamiliarity and may do so even more rapidly than under familiar conditions. In the 4-year follow-up of Garcia-Coll, Kagan, and Reznick's (1984) inhibited children by Kagan et al. (1984), uninhibited behavior was also assessed, using indices of the number of spontaneous approaches and frequency of running across the room, and this uninhibited behavior may reflect increased motor activation to novelty.

Thus, not only may novelty increase inhibition, but it may also increase approach. To explore this possibility, we can consider some of the literature on the development of "fear" of strangers during the first year of life. The emphasis on negative affect, withdrawal, and inhibition in the study of fear has meant that possible positive activation or approach reactions (e.g., rapid approach to a stranger coupled with smiling) tend to be neglected. Nevertheless, positive, approaching responses have often been found. To quote Rheingold and Eckerman (1973, 205), "Washburn (1929), it should be noted, used an unfamiliar examiner playing games with infants *in order to* study smiling and laughing. Shirley (1933) characterized 60% of her subjects as friendly during the first two years of life: they smiled at the examiners, touched them, played with their bodies or clothing, went to them, held out toys to them, and showed delight in their presence. And positive responses to a stranger were more characteristic than negative ones in the two recent studies making this comparison (Brody & Axelrad, 1971; Morgan & Ricciuti, 1969)."

Rheingold and Eckerman thus note that chldren may respond to novelty and intensity in two ways: with approach and/or positive affect or with avoidance or nonapproach and/or negative affect. In a review of the literature on children's laughter (Rothbart 1973), I have also concluded that situations likely to elicit smiling and laughter are also situations likely to elicit fear. In order to determine whether more of these positive reactions are found under unfamiliar conditions, however, a familiar control condition would be needed.

One study, by Morgan and Ricciuti (1969), suggests that increased challenge may lead to increased positive reactions. In their longitudinal study of stranger fear in 64 infants, Morgan and Ricciuti reported high levels of positive reactions to the stranger at 4.5 and 6.5 months, with a decline of positive reactions over age to 12.5 months. As the stranger moved across the room and touched the infant, over half the infants at 4.5 and exactly half the infants at 6.5 months became more positive (in this case, the extent of challenge might be seen as the distance of the stranger from the infant); this figure declined to 20 percent at 12.5 months, but it still constituted a sizable proportion of the sample. Increases in negative reactions as the stranger approached were increasingly found with development, with less than 1 percent of the infants at 4.5 months and 40 percent at 12.5 months showing increasing negative reactions. This research emphasizes the influence of the novel social stimulus on both kinds of reactions, positive and negative. Finally, in our research on 2-year-olds' reactions to a novel, surprising, and intense toy (a jack-in-the-box), we have found evidence of both positive and negative reactions, approach and avoidance, in the same children (Pien and Rothbart 1980).

In their 1986 paper, Kagan, Reznick, and Snidman also give the following example of 2-year-olds' behavioral inhibition to an unfamiliar peer, which suggests that both approach and inhibitory tendencies may be operating: "One small group of children becomes extremely quiet and stares at the unfamiliar peer while remaining close to the caregiver for a period of 5 to 15 min. But even after the initial period of obvious inhibition has passed, these children rarely approach the unfamiliar peer. A second, somewhat larger, group of children shows no signs of timidity, begins to play immediately, and usually makes the first social overture to the other child. The former group seems to be a young version of the prototypic introvert; the latter appears to be an early representative of the extravert" (Kagan, Reznick, and Snidman 1986, 54). This distinction suggests that some children rapidly become activated in an unfamiliar situation. The question raised by the possibility of both approach and inhibition processes operating is whether the prototypical extraverts are, in addition to being less inhibited, also more activated than most children. In further discussion of this question, I now consider the relation between the construct of behavioral inhibition and other constructs within the temperament literature, including Thomas and Chess's (1977) approach-withdrawal, Eysenck's (1967) introversion-extraversion, and Gray's (1971) behavioral activation (approach) and behavioral inhibition.

Behavioral Inhibition and Other Temperament Constructs

There are strong conceptual similarities between Kagan, Reznick, and Snidman's (1986) construct of behavioral inhibition and Thomas and Chess's (1977) construct of approach-withdrawal. Thomas and Chess define approach-withdrawal as "the nature of the initial response to a new stimulus" (Thomas and Chess 1977, 21). Approach for Thomas and Chess includes the expression of positive affect and motor approach; withdrawal includes the expression of negative affect and motor withdrawal or rejection of an object. As with the behavioral inhibition construct, approach-withdrawal represents a single dimension of variability, with approach accompanied by positive affect at one pole and withdrawal accompanied by negative affect at the other.

There are two major differences between the constructs of behavioral inhibition and approach-withdrawal, however. One is that the Thomas and Chess (1977) construct appears to refer to more active withdrawal, whereas Kagan, Reznick, and Snidman (1986) refer to both active withdrawal and passive nonapproach in their behavioral inhibition construct. The second is that Kagan et al. (1984) argue that behavioral inhibition refers chiefly to extreme responses to novelty, while Thomas and Chess would see approach-withdrawal as a continuous dimension. Kagan, Reznick, and Snidman (1986) stress the importance of considering only the 10 percent extremes of reactions to the unfamiliar as being representative of behavioral inhibition in American children; Thomas and Chess alternatively would consider these behaviors to represent the extremes of a continuous distribution (see the discussion of this issue in Reznick et al. [chap. 2, in this vol.]).

Although the construct of behavioral inhibition was introduced to the developmental literature by Garcia-Coll, Kagan, and Reznick and Kagan et al. in 1984, closely related temperamental constructs have also been present in the literature on adult temperament for some time. A good place to begin is in considering possible relations between behavioral inhibition and Eysenck's introversion-extraversion construct, as suggested by Kagan, Reznick, and Snidman's (1986) example of the prototypical introverts and extraverts. In his account of introversion-extraversion, Eysenck (1967, 1976, 1981) posits that individuals differ in their degree of reticular activating system arousability and therefore in their optimal level of stimulation, that is, in the level of stimulation that gives the greatest amount of pleasure before becoming overstimulating and unpleasant. In Eysenck's model, the higher arousability posited for introverts is seen to lead to optimal levels of cortical arousal at lower levels of environmental stimulus intensity than are necessary for extraverts. As a result of their low optimal arousal levels, introverts are seen to enjoy and approach mild stimulation and to avoid more intense and novel forms of stimulation. Extraverts, on the other hand, seen as having relatively unreactive reticular systems, show relatively high optimal levels of stimulation and are expected to approach and enjoy intense and novel forms of stimulation more often.

In exploring the individual differences in susceptibility to distress or negative affect that Thomas and Chess (1977) include as part of the approach-withdrawal construct, we must consider a second form of arousability from Eysenck's theory, limbic in origin, which is seen to influence behavior along a "neuroticism-stability" dimension. On this dimension, more reactive individuals (neurotics) are seen as prone to more intense autonomic (chiefly sympathetic) discharges than stable individuals are. In Eysenck's view, neuroticism is orthogonal to introversion-extraversion. However, initial scales measuring introversion-extraversion and neuroticism showed correlations of the magnitude of .2–.3, with more introverted individuals tending to be more neurotic (Gray 1981). These correlations have been increasingly removed from Eysenck's measures by altering the balance of sociability items (sociability tends to be negatively correlated with neuroticism) to impulsivity items (impulsivity tends to be positively correlated with neuroticism) in the extraversion measure (Gray 1981).

As Kagan and Reznick (Kagan, Reznick, and Snidman 1986; Kagan et al. 1984) have suggested, we would expect behavioral inhibition to be correlated with introversion. In addition, however, since Kagan et al. (1984) have identified autonomic, chiefly sympathetic reactivity as a likely physiological basis for inhibition, we would also expect it to be related to Eysenck's neuroticism dimension. In order to allow for a positive relation between negative affect and behavioral inhibition within the same theoretical construct, we turn to Gray's (1981, 1982) revision of Eysenck's theory of introversion-extraversion.

Gray (1971, 1981, 1982) has proposed a theory of temperament that involves a 45-degree rotation of Eysenck's introversion-extraversion and neuroticism dimensions, identifying two orthogonal temperamental dimensions of behavioral inhibition (anxiety) and behavioral activation (impulsivity). Increasing levels of anxiety proneness (identified at a physiological level with the action of the septal-hippicampal system) are seen as reflecting individuals' increasing sensitivity to novelty, signals of nonreward and punishment, and innate fear stimuli. Higher levels of impulsivity, on the other hand, are seen to reflect higher susceptibility to signals of reward and nonpunishment.

In Gray's theory, introversion-extraversion and neuroticism are seen as secondary results of the activity of behavioral inhibition and activation, with individuals whose inhibition system is stronger than their activation system identified as introverts and those whose activation system is stronger than their inhibition system as extraverts. Neuroticism (which can be described as a measure of degree of negative affect, given its very high correlations with measures of anxiety and depression [cf. Watson and Clark 1984]) is seen to reflect the joint strength of both systems. In Gray's model, individuals with both high activation and high inhibition systems would be expected to show the most negative affect. In addition, individuals susceptible to high behavioral inhibition would be seen as demonstrating behavioral inhibition (anxiety) that is relatively stronger than behavioral activation (impulsivity). Negative affect or distress would be a product of both inhibitory and activational tendencies.

It can be seen that Gray's constructs of behavioral inhibition and activation are quite similar to the approach and behavioral inhibition systems suggested by our (Rothbart 1988) and Schaffer's (1974) observations of the early development of reaching for objects. Recently, Cloninger (1986, 1987a, 1987b) has developed a tripartite model for personality that is based on underlying brain systems and neuromodulator functioning and that is closely related to two of Gray's dimensions. Cloninger's model specifies the following personality characteristics: (1) *harm avoidance*, ranging from the individual who is relaxed, confident, uninhibited, optimistic, and energetic to the individual who is cautious, inhibited, apprehensive, shy, pessimistic, and subject to fatigue; (2) *novelty seeking*, ranging from being rigid, reflective, orderly, and attentive to details to being impulsive, exploratory, excitable, distractible and disorderly; and (3) *reward dependence*, ranging from being socially detached, cool, tough minded, and independently self-willed to being emotionally dependent, sentimental, warmly sympathetic, persistent, and sensitive to social cues (Cloninger 1987a).

These characteristics are in turn linked to the action of neuromodulators, with novelty seeking (which Cloninger sees as similar to Gray's behavioral activation) related to dopamine functioning, harm avoidance (seen as similar to Gray's behavioral inhibition) to the functioning of serotonin and the septo-hippocampal system, and reward dependence (leading to behavioral mainte-nance) to norepinephrine functioning. Both Gray (1981) and Cloninger (1987a, 1987b) argue for their choice of temperamental dimensions as being based on biologic evidence, including the effects of drugs on behavior and evidence from behavioral genetics

Behavioral Inhibition and Uninhibited Behavior (Disinhibition)

Thinking about two general dimensions (activation and inhibition) as under-lying reactions to novelty and challenge allows us to explore a second kind of reaction to the unfamiliar or to challenging signals of punishment (note that, within Gray's model, these two reactions are a function of the same system), that is, the relatively uninhibited behavioral tendencies of extraverts. Goren-stein and Newman (1980) argue that the effects of septal lesions on rats (im-plicating, as did Gray's behavioral inhibition construct, the septal-hippocampal system) provide a model for the construct of impulsivity, as exhibited in human subjects in psychopathic, antisocial, alcoholic, hyperac-tive, and extraverted tendencies. Gorenstein and Newman (1980) stress the tendency of extraverts and psychopaths to continue to emit dominant re-sponses in spite of punishment, extinction, or the reversal of contingencies (these characterisic deficits of animals with septal lesions having been origi-nally pointed out by McCleary [1966]). It should be clear that this work in-volves a broadening of the construct of behavioral inhibition beyond Kagan, Reznick, and Snidman's (1986) view to that of Gray's, suggesting that chil-dren who are more susceptible to fear will also be more susceptible to the inhibiting effects of punishment.

Research from Newman's (1986) laboratory is, I think, particularly relevant for enlarging our understanding of behavioral inhibition and activation. New-man and his collaborators have assessed impulsive subjects' (extraverts' and psychopaths') use of cues for punishment to withhold inappropriate approach-driven behavior. The basic experimental paradigm for investigating these questions is a "go–no go" or passive avoidance procedure, in which the sub-ject must inhibit responses associated with punishment. In an adaptation of a procedure from Chesno and Kilmann (1975), Newman, Widom, and Nathan (1985) gave adult subjects a series of two-digit numbers, asking them to learn by trial and error to respond to some of the numbers but not to others. Extra-verts make more errors of commission in this procedure than do introverts (Newman, Widom, and Nathan 1985). This finding would be in agreement with Gray's interpretation of the introvert as being more sensitive to punish-ment than the extravert. However, extraverts do not show this tendency when they are given either punishment-only or reward-only feedback (Newman 1986).

To investigate this phenomenon further, Nichols and Newman (1986) developed a paradigm in which subjects are asked to view a pattern on a monitor and then match it against a subsequent pattern in a same-different judgment. Administration of rewards and punishments in this paradigm is preprogrammed and noncontingent to the subject's actual response. Nichols and Newman (1986) found that introverts responded more slowly to the trials following punishment, as expected. However, extraverts responded more quickly on trials following punishment. Again, the effect was found only when both reward and punishment were administered. In addition, extraverts were found to respond more quickly in a reward-only than in a punishment-only condition. Finally, Patterson, Kosson, and Newman (1987) found that the interruption of a reward-response set, that is, the subjects' tendency to slow down after a punished item, was significantly related to the subjects' performance on a go–no go task and again significantly related to introversion.

Newman, Widom, and Nathan's (1985) results suggest that introverts and extraverts may both be influenced by negative feedback, but in different directions: for introverts punishment moderates goal-directed responses, but for extraverts punishment increasingly activates goal-directed responses. Given these findings in adults, it is possible that, in the context of previously rewarded behavior, the effect of punishment on relatively uninhibited children may actually be to increase approach. Further research might thus usefully employ an approach in which both inhibited and disinhibited behavior of children is observed (e.g., Kagan et al. 1984).

Some research on children's behavior problems is relevant to this point. In Patterson's (1980) studies of aggressive problem behavior, he has found that parents of nonproblem children are effective in stopping their children's aversive behavior on three out of every four occasions when they punish. However, when parents of problem children used similar punishment, the likelihood that the problem child would continue the punished behavior actually increased rather than decreased (Patterson 1976, 1980). This result has been replicated by Snyder (1977). Thus, punishment of problem behavior in some children increases problem behavior in a manner similar to Newman's extraverts' decreasd latency to perform a previously punished act.

In families where aversive acts are a way of life, the modeling and direct instigation of aggression by family members may lead to aggressive interactions involving escalation rather than retreat by the problem child, and Patterson has noted that the child is rewarded for aggression by getting what he or she wants when the other family member "gives up." This reward then serves as the background for the child's future performance of uninhibited aversive acts (Patterson 1976).

I have previously argued (Rothbart 1984) that one of the eventual consequences of the study of temperament will be to specify some of the constraints
that temperamental individual differences place on processes of social learning. We are currently developing an adaptation of Nichols and Newman's
(1986) paradigm to use with young children whose inhibited and uninhibited
behavior has been observed during infancy, and this kind of research may
allow us to specify some of those constraints.

Sex Differences in Inhibition

During the second half of the first year of life, we have observed sex differences in one of our measures of inhibited approach, that is, the number of
motor hesitations infants demonstrated during reaches (Rothbart 1988). Sex
differences have also been found in parent report on the approach-withdrawal
dimension of temperament in several cross-cultural samples (Carey and
McDevitt 1978; Hsu et al. 1981; Maziade et al. 1984), with males showing
greater approach than females. If we subscribe to a two-element model of
approach and inhibition, we would not know without further research, however, whether these differences are due to variability in approach or in inhibition.

Sex differences in behavioral inhibition have also been reported. In their
study of behavioral inhibition in unselected infants at 14 and 21 months of
age, Reznick et al. (chap. 2, in this vol.) report sex differences at both 14 and
21 months (significant only at the later age) in the direction of greater inhibition for girls. In Garcia-Coll's original study of behavioral inhibition in 21-
month-olds, extreme groups were selected for laboratory study. In this research, the cell that required so much time to fill that it delayed the study was
the cell with inhibited boys (C. T. Garcia-Coll, personal communication,
1986).

In examining the observational fear literature for possible sex differences,
it is interesting to note that probably the classic study on the development of
fear (Jersild and Holmes 1935) utilized a latency-to-approach measure. In this
study, 105 children between the ages of 24 and 71 months were observed in
the laboratory. Latency-to-approach episodes included a dark room (the child
was asked to retrieve a ball thrown 18 feet down a dark corridor), strange
person (the child was asked to obtain toys placed next to a woman dressed in
a long gray coat, large black hat, and veil), high place (the child was asked to
walk across a board at varying heights), loud noise (the child was asked to go
behind a screen to see what happened), snake (the child was asked to obtain a
toy from a box containing the snake), and large dog (the child was asked to
pat the dog).

Jersild and Holmes (1935) gave the child a score for each episode on the following scale: 0, performs without hesitation; 1, performs alone but after a delay; 2, performs alone but after some intervening behavior such as clinging to the observer, 3, performs but only when accompanied or aided by the experimenter, and 4, complete refusal to participate. They reported that the percentage of girls showing extended latencies to approach was higher on almost every episode than was that of boys. In addition, for a subsample of boys and girls matched on other variables, higher aggregated fear scores were found for the girls.

Sex differences in other behavioral dimensions that could be related either to the development of behavioral inhibition or to the development of inhibitory control (the ability to delay an action given verbal instructions) can also be observed. Maccoby and Jacklin (1974) conclude that greater activity level for boys does not emerge until after the first year, a period that follows the developmental onset of behavioral inhibition. Eaton and Enns (1986) have more recently reported overall activity-level differences, with greater activity for boys, but there is also an indication that these differences may be less evident in early infancy.

Inhibitory controls on activity level could include behavioral inhibition in response to novelty or conditioned cues for punishment. Inhibitory controls related to the ability to delay and plan would also moderate approach, however, and we have called this more active form of control "effort" (Rothbart and Posner 1985; Rothbart, in press). In Keogh, Pullis, and Caldwell's (1982) Teacher Temperament Questionnaire, tests of 3–6-year-olds found boys scoring lower than girls on persistence and higher on activity, intensity, and distractibility. These findings suggest possible early sex differences in inhibitory control that may be related to either active goal-directed behavior or to more passive behavioral inhibition.

If sex differences in the development of one or the other of these inhibitory controls were established, they could prove to be quite important for social development. If verbally controlled inhibition is built on the capacity to inhibit behavior, and if girls demonstrated both earlier capacity to inhibit and earlier development of language (Schachter et al. 1978), then they may be more susceptible to early socialization efforts than boys, on the average. The results of several studies do indicate that young girls are more likely than boys to comply with their mothers' prohibitions and commands (Minton, Kagan, and Levine 1971; Pederson and Bell 1970; Smith and Dagliesh 1977). An additional review paper suggests that girls may be more strongly inhibited by cues of potential punishment. In Caplan's (1979) meta-analysis of observational studies of aggression in preschool children, she notes that sex differences are usually not found when the children do not think they are being observed (and presumably could not then be punished for aggression); sex differences are more likely to be found if there is a supervising or observing adult present. These results could clearly have been influenced by differential care-giver socialization of control in boys and girls, but individual differences in the capacity to inhibit reward-related responses may also be implicated.

Both forms of inhibitory control may also be seen to oppose other species-typical behavior patterns involving approach, such as aggression. We would expect on the basis of this argument that girls would be less susceptible to aggressive and acting-out problems and more susceptible to problems involving inhibition of action (e.g., timidity), and this appears to be the case (Achenbach 1982). If there are sex differences in behavioral inhibition, we would also expect young girls to be less easily stimulated to activity in novel and challenging social situations, and this is observed in Jacklin and Maccoby's (1978) research, in which, at 33 months, girls paired with boys were more likely to stand watching or withdraw to their mothers than were boys in any pairing or girls paired with girls.

Sex differences in control could also be related to findings of a greater effect of home-environment variables on the development of behavior problems in males than in females (Rutter and Garmezy 1983). If, in the relative absence of self-regulatory controls for behavior of the child, the function of the family in providing these controls assumes primary importance (cf. Snow, Jacklin, and Maccoby's [1983] argument that 12-month-old boys may "need" more parental control), then a familys' failure to provide control as a result of internal discord and disorganization will be more likely to result in behavior problems for the less internally controlled children. The data, reviewed by Rutter and Garmezy (1983), indeed suggest that family variables are generally related to aggression and conduct problems and that maleness is a major risk factor for such problems. Discussions of possible sex differences in inhibitory control are at this point highly speculative. Nevertheless, the study of early sex differences in self-regulation may prove to be a topic that brings together temperament and socialization literatures in an important way.

Theoretical questions about behavioral inhibition and approach are of special interest because there is reason to believe that the tendency toward behavioral inhibition versus approach is a relatively stable characteristic from early life to adulthood. In addition to the findings of early stability from Garcia-Coll, Kagan, Reznick, and their colleagues, Honzik (1965) has noted that Fels Longitudinal Study subjects' scores on "spontaneity" versus "social interaction anxiety" were stable and predictive for males from the first 3 years to adulthood and for females from 6–10 years to adulthood (Kagan and Moss 1962). She reported in addition that three other major longitudinal studies have found long-term stability on similar dimensions. Thus, Schaeffer and Bayley (1963) found their most stable and persistent category of behavior between birth and age 18 to be "active, extraverted" versus "inactive, introverted" behavior. Honzik (1965) and Bronson (1972) also found the two most stable dimensions of personality in the Berkeley Guidance Study to be "introversion" and "excessive reserve" versus "spontaneity." Finally, Tuddenham (1959) reported stability from 14 to 33 years in the Oakland Growth Study on scales indexing "spontaneity" versus "inhibition."

Biological Accounts of Inhibition

Another level at which the development of behavioral inhibition has been considered can be found in animal studies of biological maturation. These studies are likely to reflect aspects of response to novelty and punishment that are shared across species (see also Suomi 1984, 1986). Amsel (1986) relates developmental changes in effects of novelty (and punishment) on the inhibition of behavior in the rat to development of the septohippocampal system: approximately 90 percent of the development of the granule cells of the dentate gyrus in the hippocampal formation of the rat occurs after the birth of the animal, with the greatest differentiation occurring between days 12 and 14 and with near-adult levels reached by days 25–30. Amsel points out that the theta rhythm of the hippocampal electroencephalogram (EEG) is not demonstrated until around 11–12 days and that the granule cells of the hippocampal dentate gyrus are theta producing. In addition, he notes that theta rhythm is linked temporally not only to the effects of frustrative nonreward (punishment) but also to the effects of novel or disruptive stimulation.

Previous researchers have also linked hippocampal development to the development of inhibitory capacities. Douglas (1975) noted that rats with hippocampal lesions show decreases in signs of Pavlovian internal inhibition such as susceptibility to extinction and passive avoidance learning as well as the tendency to alternate trials to two different locations when neither of them is rewarded (spontaneous alternation). Douglas observed that juvenile rats showed similar performance to hippocampal-lesioned adult rats but changed to more adult behavior by 35 days of age. He noted that these changes occur at a time when major differentiation of granule cells in the hippocampal dentate gyrus had occurred (Altman, Brunner, and Bayer 1973).

An additional location related to tasks involving inhibition is the lateral convexity of the prefrontal cortex (Rosenkilde 1979), which is connected to the dentate gyrus via the entorhinal cortex. Frontal systems in the infant have also been found to show functional development across the period of 8–9 months in a study of glucose utilization by Chugani and Phelps (1986). Recently, it has also been argued that serotonin activity is involved in behavioral inhibition to cues of punishment (Soubrie 1986). Serotonin functioning has been linked to the inhibition of activity (Soubrie 1986) and to the inhibition of emotional responding (Panskepp 1982). Work with animals also suggests that serotonin functioning is a later-developing system (Mabry and Campbell 1974).

On the other hand, dopamine functioning, which in rats can be observed very early in postnatal development (Phelps, Koranyi, and Tamasy 1982), has been related to approach responses. Wise's (1980, 1982) model for the role of dopamine in reward identifies dopamine cells in the ventral tegmental area as receiving input from multiple sources of reward, including the administration of opiates and hypothalamic stimulation. Stellar and Stellar (1985) note that this model suggests that dopamine-depleted rats are not active because environmental stimuli are not rewarding enough to induce approach. A second view relating dopamine systems to approach suggests that dopamine influences general motor activity through activation of the nucleus accumbens (Kelly and Stinus 1984; Kelly, Stinus, and Iverson 1980). Dopamine depletion in these areas reduces speed and probability of response without affecting its accuracy.

It is of interest that a later-developing motor-inhibiting effect associated with dopamine functioning in the ventral tegmental area–prefrontal cortex pathway has also been reported (Heffner et al. 1983; Shaywitz, Yager, and Klopper 1976). Although we cannot directly translate these effects to humans, it is important to recognize that research on animals has identified neurophysiological regulatory processes developing over time that are related to behavioral activity and inhibition of activity.

Summary

In reviewing theoretical positions about behavioral inhibition, we find several models that make predictions about temperamental self-regulation (approach vs. withdrawal) along a single dimension. These include Eysenck's (1967, 1976, 1981) introversion-extraversion construct, Thomas and Chess's (1977) approach-withdrawal dimension, and Garcia-Coll, Kagan, and Reznick's (1984) and Kagan et al.'s (1984) definition of behavioral inhibition. On the other hand, Gray's (1971, 1982) and Cloninger's (1986) models include both approach and inhibition systems, and elsewhere I have attempted to develop a developmental model that incorporates both systems (Rothbart, in press). In this chapter, I have put forward developmental data suggesting that individual differences in approach can be seen at an age *before* the onset of behavioral inhibition.

If two dimensions are involved, they have implications for social development. Such a model suggests that some individuals, who would otherwise actively seek rewards, can become inhibited in unfamiliar, potentially punishing, or highly challenging conditions. These persons may be especially variable in their behavior, depending on whether situations and task demands are threatening. Creating environments that are supportive and secure may be especially helpful to these persons. Individuals who lack inhibitory controls resulting from behavioral inhibition may, on the other hand, be able to control their behavior by using alternative means of self-control, such as verbal self-regulation. Learning more about the development of individual differences in approach and inhibition not only gives us a psychological account of these relatively stable response tendencies but also allows us to consider changes in the social world and the individual that might facilitate the development of a wide range of persons.

References

Achenback, T. M. 1982. *Developmental psychopathology*. 2d ed. New York: Wiley.

Altman, J.; Brunner, R. L.; and Bayer, S. A. 1973. The hippocampus and behavioral maturation. *Behavioral Biology* 8:557–96.

Amsel, A. 1986. Daniel Berlyne Memorial Lecture: Developmental psychobiology and behavior theory: Reciprocating influences. *Canadian Journal of Psychology* 40:311–42.

Brody, S., and Axelrad, S. 1971. Maternal stimulation and social responsiveness of infants. In *The origins of human social relations*, ed. H. R. Schaffer, 195–209. New York: Academic.

Bronson, W. C. 1972. The role of enduring orientations to the environment in personality development. *Genetic Psychology Monographs* 86:3–80.

Caplan, P. J. 1979. Beyond the box score: A boundary condition for sex differences in aggression and achievement striving. In *Progress in experimental personality research*, vol. 9, ed. B. A. Maher, 41–87. New York: Academic.

Carey, W. B., and McDevitt, S. C. 1978. Revision of the Infant Temperament Questionnaire. *Pediatrics* 61:735–39.

Chesno, F. A., and Kilmann, P. R. 1975. Effects of stimulation intensity on sociopathic avoidance learning. *Journal of Abnormal Psychology* 84:144–50.

Chugani, H. T., and Phelps, M. E. 1986. Maturational changes in cerebral function in infants determined by [18]FDG positron emission tomography. *Science* 231:840–43.

Cloninger, C. R. 1986. A unified biosocial theory of personality and its role in the development of anxiety states. *Psychiatric Development* 3:167–226.

Cloninger, C. R. 1987a. Neurogenetic adaptive mechanisms in alcoholism. *Science* 236:410–16.

Cloninger, C. R. 1987b. A systematic method for clinical description and classification of personality variants. *Archives of General Psychiatry* 44:573–88.

Douglas, R. J. 1975. The development of hippocampal function: Implications for theory and for therapy. In *The hippocampus*. Vol. 2, *Neurophysiology and behavior*, ed. R. L. Isaacson and K. H. Pribram. New York: Plenum.

Eaton, W. A., and Enns, L. R. 1986. Sex differences in human motor activity level. *Psychological Bulletin* 100:19–28.

Eysenck, H. J. 1967. *The biological basis of personality.* Springfield, Ill.: Thomas.

Eysenck, H. J., ed. 1976. *The measurement of personality.* Baltimore, Md.: University Park Press.

Eysenck, H. J., ed. 1981. *A model for personality.* New York: Springer.

Garcia-Coll, C. T.; Kagan, J.; and Reznick, J. S. 1984. Behavioral inhibition in young children. *Child Development* 55:1005–19.

Gorenstein, E. E., and Newman, J. P. 1980. Disinhibitory psychopathology: A new perspective and a model for research. *Psychological Review* 87:301–15.

Gray, J. A. 1971. *The psychology of fear and stress.* New York: McGraw-Hill.

Gray, J. A. 1981. A critique of Eysenck's theory of personality. In *A model for personality,* ed. H. J. Eysenck, 246–76. New York: Springer.

Gray, J. A. 1982. *The neuropsychology of anxiety.* Oxford: Oxford University Press.

Heffner, T. G.; Heller, A.; Miller, F. E.; Kotake, C.; and Seiden, L. S. 1983. Loco motor hyperactivity in neonatal rats following electrolytic lesions of mesocortical dopamine neurons. *Developmental Brain Research* 285:29–38.

Honzik, M. P. 1965. Prediction of behavior from birth to maturity. *Merrill-Palmer Quarterly* 11:77–88.

Hsu, C. C.; Soong, W. T Stigler, J. W.; Hong, C. C.; and Liang, C. C. 1981. The temperamental characteristics of Chinese babies. *Child Development* 52:1337–40.

Jacklin, C. N., and Maccoby, E. E. 1978. Social behavior at 33 months in same-sex and mixed sex dyads. *Child Development* 49:557–69.

Jersild, A. T.; and Holmes, F. B. 1935. Children's fears. *Child Development Monographs,* vol. 20. New York: Teachers' College, Columbia University.

Kagan, J., and Moss, H. A. 1962. *Birth to maturity.* New York: Wiley.

Kagan, J.; Reznick, J. S.; and Snidman, N. 1986. Temperamental inhibition in early childhood. In *The study of temperament: Changes, continuities and challengs,* ed. R. Plomin and J. Dunn, 53–67. Hillsdale, N.J.: Erlbaum.

Kagan, J.; Reznick, J. S.; Clarke, C.; Snidman, N.; and Garcia-Coll, C. 1984. Behavioral inhibition to the unfamiliar. *Child Development* 55:2212–25.

Kagan, J.; Reznick, J. S.; and Snidman, N. 1987. The physiology and psychology of behavioral inhibition in young children. *Child Development* 58:1459–73.

Kelly, A., and Stinus, L. 1984. Neuroanatomical and neurochemical substrates of affective behavior. In *Affective development: A psychobiological perspective,* ed. N. A. Fox and R. J. Davidson. Hillsdale, N.J.: Erlbaum.

Kelly, A.; Stinus, L.; and Iverson, S. D. 1980. Interactions between d-ala-metenkephalen, A 10 dopaminergic neurons, and spontaneous behavior in the rat. *Behavioral Brain Research* 1:3–24.

Keogh, B. K.; Pullis, M. E.; and Caldwell, J. 1982. A short form of the Teacher Temperament Questionnaire. *Journal of Educational Measurement* 19:323–29.

Mabry, P., and Campbell, B. A. 1974. Ontogeny of serotonergic inhibition of behavioral arousal in the rat. *Journal of Comparative and Physiological Psychology* 86:193–206.

McCleary, R. A. 1966. Response-modulating function of the limbic system: Initiation and suppression. In *Progress in physiological psychology,* ed. E. Stellar and J. M. Sprague. New York: Academic.

Maccoby, E. E., and Jacklin, C. N. 1974. *The psychology of sex differences.* Stanford, Calif.: Stanford University Press.

Maziade, M.; Boudreault, M.; Thivierge, J.; Caperaa, P.; and Cote, R. 1984. Infant temperament: SES and gender differences and reliability of measurement in a large Quebec sample. *Merrill-Palmer Quarterly* 30:213–16.

Minton, C.; Kagan, J.; and Levine, J. 1971. Maternal control and obedience in the two-year-old. *Child Development* 42:1873–94.

Morgan, G. A., and Ricciuti, H. N. 1969. Infants' responses to strangers during the first year. In *Determinants of infant behavior,* vol. 4, ed. B. M. Foss. London: Methuen.

Newman, J. P. 1986. Reaction to punishment in extraverts and psychopaths: Implications for the impulsive behavior of disinhibited individuals. Paper presented at the meeting of the American Psychological Society, Washington, D.C., August.

Newman, J. P.; Widom, C. S.; and Nathan, S. 1985. Passive-avoidance in syndromes of disinhibition: Psychopathy and extraversion. *Journal of Personality and Social Psychology* 48:1316–27.

Nichols, S., and Newman, J. P. 1986. Effects of punishment on response latency in extraverts. *Journal of Personality and Social Psychology* 50:624–30.

Panksepp, J. 1982. Toward a general psychobiological theory of emotions. *Behavioral and Brain Sciences* 5:407–67.

Patterson, C. M.; Kosson, D. S.; and Newman, J. P. 1987. Reaction to punishment, reflectivity and passive avoidance learning in extraverts. *Journal of Personality and Social Psychology* 52:565–75.

Patterson, G. R. 1976. The aggressive child: Victim and architect of a coercive system. In *Behavior modification and families,* ed. L. A. Hamerlynck, E. J. Mash, and L. C. Handy. Pt. 1, *Theory and research.* Pt. 2, *Applications and development,* 267–316. New York: Bruner/Mazel.

Patterson, G. R. 1980. Mothers: The unacknowledged victims. *Monographs of the Society for Research in Child Development,* vol. 45, serial no. 186.

Pederson, F., and Bell, R. Q. 1970. Sex differences in preschool children without histories of complications of pregnancy and delivery. *Developmental Psychology* 3:10–15.

Phelps, C. P.; Koranyi, L.; and Tamasy, V. 1982. Brain catecholamine concentration during the first week of development of rats. *Developmental Neuroscience* 5:503–7.

Pien, D., and Rothbart, M. K. 1980. Incongruity, humor, play and self-regulation of arousal in young children. In *Children's humour,* ed. A. Chapman and P. McGhee. New York: Wiley.

Rheingold, H. L., and Eckerman, C. O. 1973. Fear of the stranger: A critical examination. In *Advances in child development and behavior,* ed. H. W. Reese, vol. 8, 185–222. New York: Academic.

Rosenkilde, C. E. 1979. Functional heterogeneity of the prefrontal cortex in the monkey: A review. *Behavioral and Neural Biology* 25:301–45.

Rothbart, M. K. 1973. Laughter in young children. *Psychological Bulletin* 80:247–56.

Rothbart, M. K. 1984. Social development. In *Atypical infant development,* ed. M. J. Hanson. Baltimore, Md.: University Park Press.

Rothbart, M. K. 1988. Temperament and the development of inhibited approach. *Child Development* 59:1241–50.

Rothbart, M. K. In press. Temperament in childhood: A framework. In *Handbook of temperament in childhood,* ed. G. Kohnstam, J. Bates, and M. K. Rothbart. London: Wiley.

Rothbart, M. K., and Posner, M. I. 1985. Temperament and the development of self regulation. In *The neuropsychology of individual differences: A developmental perspective,* ed. L. C. Hartlage and C. F. Telzrow, 93–123. New York: Plenum.

Rubenstein, J. 1974. A concordance of visual and manipulative responsiveness to novel and familiar stimuli in six-month-old infants. *Child Development* 45:194–95.

Rubenstein, J. 1976. Concordance of visual and manipulative responsiveness to novel and familiar stimuli: A function of test procedures or of prior experience? *Child Development* 47:1197–99.

Ruff, H. 1976. The coordination of manipulation and visual fixation: A response to Schaffer (1975). *Child Development* 47:868–71.

Rutter, M., and Garmezy, A. 1983. Developmental psychopathology. In *Handbook of child psychology,* ed. P. H. Mussen. Vol. 4, *Socialization, personality, and social development,* ed. E. M. Hetherington. 4th ed. New York: Wiley.

Schachter, F. F.; Shore, E.; Hodap, R.; Chalfin, S.; and Bundy, C. 1978. Do girls talk earlier? Mean length of utterance in toddlers. *Developmental Psychology* 14:388–92.

Schaeffer, E. S., and Bayley, N. 1963. Maternal behavior, child behavior and their intercorrelations from infancy through adolescence. *Monographs of the Society for Research in Child Development,* vol. 28, no. 3, serial no. 87.

Schaffer, H. R. 1974. Cognitive components of the infant's response to strangeness. In *The origins of fear,* ed. M. Lewis and L. A. Rosenblum. New York: Wiley.

Schaffer, H. R.; Greenwood, A.; and Parry, M. H. 1972. The onset of wariness. *Child Development* 43:165–75.

Shaywitz, R. A.; Yager, R. D; and Klopper, J. H. 1976. Selective brain dopamine depletion in developing rats: An experimental model of minimal brain dysfunction. *Science* 191:305–8.

Shirley, M. 1933. *The first two years: A study of 25 babies.* Minneapolis: University of Minnesota Press.

Smith, P., and Dagliesh, L. 1977. Sex differences in parent and infant behavior in the home. *Child Development* 48:1250–54.

Snow, M. E.; Jacklin, C. N.; and Maccoby, E. E. 1983. Sex-of-child differences in father-child interaction at one year of age. *Child Development* 54:227–32.

Snyder, J. A. 1977. A reinforcement analysis of interaction in problem and nonproblem children. *Journal of Abnormal Psychology* 86:528–35.

Soubrie, P. 1986. Reconciling the role of central serotonin neurons in human and animal behavior. *Behavioral and Brain Sciences* 9:319–64.

Sroufe, L. A. 1979. Socioemotional development. In *Handbook of infant development,* ed. J. D. Osofsky. New York: Wiley.

Stechler, G., and Latz, E. 1966. Some observations on attention and arousal in the human infant. *Journal of the American Academy of Child Psychiatry* 5:517–25.

Stellar, J. R., and Stellar, E. 1985. *The neurobiology of motivation and reward.* New York: Springer.

Suomi, S. J. 1984. The development of affect in rhesus monkeys. In *The psychobiol-*

ogy of affective development, ed. N. A. Fox and R. J. Davison, 119–59. Hillsdale, N.J.: Erlbaum.

Suomi, S. J. 1986. Anxiety-like disorders in young nonhuman primates. In *Anxiety disorders of childhood,* ed. R. Gittelman, 1–23. New York: Guilford.

Thomas, A., and Chess, S. 1977. *Temperament and development.* New York: Bruner/ Mazel.

Tuddenham, R. D. 1959. The constancy of personality ratings over two decades. *Genetic Psychology Monographs* 60:3–29.

Washburn, R. W. 1929. A study of the smiling and laughing of infants in the first year of life. *Genetic Psychology Monographs* 6:397–537.

Watson, D., and Clark, L. A. 1984. Negative affectivity: The disposition to experience aversive emotional states. *Psychological Bulletin* 96:465–90.

Wise, R. A. 1980. Action of drugs of abuse on brain reward systems. *Pharmacology, Biochemistry and Behavior* 13:213–33.

Wise, R. A. 1982. Neuroleptics and operant behavior: The anhedonic hypothesis. *Behavioral and Brain Science* 5:39–87.

8 The Infantile Expression of Avidity in Relation to Later Assessments of Inhibition and Attachment

L. L. LaGasse, C. P. Gruber, and L. P. Lipsitt

Introduction

Much has been written recently on the phenomenon of inhibition in children, the multiplicity of its definitions, and the diverse ways in which the attribute or trait of the inhibited child may be observed and measured (Kagan 1984). Current research, particularly from the Harvard group of researchers led by Kagan, has helped determine the reliability and significance of individual differences in this trait through the early childhood years and has documented the stability of the condition of "shyness" over a protracted period of time (Garcia-Coll, Kagan, and Reznick 1984; Kagan et al. 1984; Reznick et al. 1986).

The question of whether discernible psychological attributes such as temperamental qualities have stability over a fairly wide age range, particularly from birth onward, has been a perplexing issue since the first studies of child development. There has been no satisfying resolution, although the history of scientific concern and many attempts at empirical documentation have been well described (for an excellent treatment, see Brim and Kagan [1980, esp. chaps. 1 and 2]). Our special interest here is to explore the possibility that some infantile proclivities, or conditions of very early behavior, may constitute a "congenital core" of a particular set of temperamental qualities that will be manifested months later. Specifically, we examine the relation between a characteristic of neonatal behavior that we call "avidity" and the later expression (at 18 months of age) of inhibition, shyness, or wariness.

This research program has been supported by funds from the John D. and Catherine T. MacArthur Foundation, the March of Dimes Birth Defects Foundation, the Harris Foundation, and Hasbro, Inc. The authors are indebted to Cara Regan, Bernice Reilly, and Marsha Schiller for their extensive role in data collection and reduction and to Margaret Forrest and Helen Haeseler for contributing to the efficient management of the longitudinal project. We also wish to thank others with whom we have interacted, and who contributed constructively, during various phases of the project: Sarah Friedman, Cynthia Garcia-Coll, Jerome Kagan, Leon Kuczynski, Marion Radke-Yarrow, Steven Reznick, and Tracy Sherman.

We will begin with suggested reasons to suspect links between this aspect of neonatal behavior and eventual expressions of inhibition and follow this with a report of data that seem, at least preliminarily, to substantiate the relation. We make no claim that such precursor conditions as avidity are the sole or even principal causes of children's later inclinations toward shyness. The best of psychological causal analyses suggest that the origins of childhood, adolescent, and adulthood traits are multifactorial and involve important contributions from both congenital dispositions and experiential events. However, we do propose, following Sameroff and Chandler (1975), that infants have some stable characteristics from the earliest moments after birth, that avidity is one such aspect of neonatal behavior (Lipsitt 1975; Lipsitt et al. 1976), that these infantile attributes generate reciprocating and response-modifying behaviors in the child's caretakers, and that relations between the early manifested characteristics and the later may be bridged by qualities of affective arousal and specific responses to environmental stimulation. We suggest, moreover, that the relation between the earlier and the later characteristics may imply a mediational process involving heightened limbic sensitivity.

The present chapter constitutes a progress report on one aspect of a series of ongoing studies examining avidity, measured by assessing how the newborn human infant's contingent sucking behavior changes with increases in the sweetness of the fluid presented through a nipple. Those babies who show specific kinds of response change to increasingly sweet fluids (e.g., emit more sucks, have reduced latencies between sucks as well as shorter intervals between bursts of sucks, and show an increased heart rate) are said to be more avid (Lipsitt 1975; Crook and Lipsitt 1976; Lipsitt et al. 1976). We present evidence here that individual differences in avidity relate to inhibited behavior at later ages.

The Relation of Avidity to Inhibited Behavior

At the outset, let us be clear that we see avidity and inhibition as distinct constructs. Assessment of avidity involves the recording of responses that yield self-administered pleasurable stimulation in the very young. Assessment of inhibition involves the stimulation of what are, to the inhibited child, aversive reactions. We will return to these considerations later. First, however, consider three ways in which the behavioral systems involved in avid and inhibited responses may be thought to overlap.

Avidity and inhibition both reflect individual differences in perceptual and affective reactivity to changes in the environment.[1] Lipsitt and his colleagues

1. That the baby "behaves" more in the presence of the sweet taste is also part of the story, of course, and avidity may be related more to behavioral change than to sensory receptivity. But we need not be concerned with this issue now; sweet-induced variations in other measures suggest

found, for example, that neonates vary in their responsivity to small changes in taste stimulation (Lipsitt et al. 1976). Parallel to this, Reznick (1982) found that children judged to be vigilant or wary, on the basis of behavioral and cardiovascular criteria, were more sensitive to small differences in stimulation. We suspect that the affective component of these reactions serves as a mediating link between the avidity and the inhibitory behavioral systems. In pursuing this, we follow recent proposals that affective components may serve a powerful organizing function linking a variety of temperamental characteristics (Goldsmith and Campos 1982).

A second commonality between avidity and inhibition stems from the fact that both constellations of behavior are accompanied by physiological changes indicative of sympathetic arousal. Inhibited children show higher and more stable heart rates when confronted with unfamiliar or unexpected stimuli (Garcia-Coll, Kagan, and Reznick 1984; Kagan et al. 1984). Avidity studies conducted by Lipsitt have demonstrated that infants show higher and more stable heart rates as the sweetness of the taste stimulus is intensified (Crook and Lipsitt 1976; Lipsitt 1975).

The third area of overlap is that both avidity and inhibition involve behavior that serves to regulate stimulation. Avidity researchers have shown that infants characteristically alter their own behavior in the direction of optimizing contact with pleasurable tastes (Crook and Lipsitt 1976; Lipsitt et al. 1976). Studies of children's inhibited behavior in the presence of novel stimuli have documented how inhibited children sensitively withdraw and thus reduce contact with unfamiliar events (Garcia-Coll, Kagan, and Reznick 1984; Kagan et al. 1984; Reznick et al. 1986). Self-adjusting behavior of these kinds may, as Brazelton and his colleagues have suggested, support the individual's tendency to seek equilibrium or become organized when challenged (Brazelton, Koslowski, and Main 1974). Moreover, as Lipsitt (1977) has pointed out, infantile responsivity to perturbations imposed by the environment may help assure the infant's survival. For example, avid sucking behavior may reflect well-organized responses that can help protect against respiratory occlusion and other related annoyances (Lipsitt 1979). The presence of avid and inhibited behavior implies that individuals are competent in implementing self-regulatory behaviors effecting an equilibrium between endogenous and exogenous factors.

Let us now return to the readily apparent differences between the overt expression of avidity and inhibition. Most obviously, the emotions aroused in each case are of opposite valence: avidity involves the evocation of pleasurable sensation, while inhibition involves the activation of fear. Less obvious,

---

that the reciprocating relation between sensory sensitivity and behavioral outputs will turn out to be a complex one.

but more important, there is a striking difference in the directness with which these two response systems appear to be evoked.

For avidity, there is a direct link between the external stimulation and the positive response. A long line of research on contingency theory stemming from the work of Watson (1966) explicates this link. Watson (1966, 1972) demonstrated responsiveness to contingencies prior to 3 months of age. Lipsitt and his associates used operant procedures successfully in neonates, with sucking and other oral behaviors as the dependent measures (Lipsitt 1963, 1977; Siqueland and Lipsitt 1966). DeCasper and Carstens (1981) have now extended the essentially behavioral paradigm into the affective domain by contrasting infants' responsivity in contingent and noncontingent conditions. Using activity levels, grimacing, head movements, and crying as indicators of affect, they found that contingent stimulation resulted in positive affect, that noncontingent stimulation resulted in neutral affect, and that both conditions together resulted in negative affect.

The assessment of avidity ties directly with these results. The use of contingent stimulation appears to extend the link to pleasurable arousal through the use of varied levels of sweetened solution. In a series of studies, infants have demonstrated higher sucking rates and fewer pauses between sucking bursts to increasing levels of sweetness (Desor, Maller, and Turner 1973; Lipsitt et al. 1976). The results of this report will include additional evidence of the infant's preference for sweet tastes.

For inhibition, in contrast, the link between the external event and the emotional response appears much less direct. For inhibited behavior to be evoked, there must be, first, a "recognition" of an event as novel and, second, an "anticipation" of consequent difficulty. Recognition of novel (and, by implication, unfamiliar) events requires reference to a prior discriminative history. Anticipation of events implies the existence of past experiences that form the basis of the expectation. Kagan (1981) suggests that children in the second year have the capability to make inferences about the causes of events as well as their significance. Inability to predict the consequences of an unfamiliar person or event may generate uncertainty in the child (Kagan 1984). Inhibited responses seem to necessitate this kind of interpretive context in the individual. When failing to assimilate novel events or to predict their consequences, the child shows wariness and withdrawing behaviors.

Beyond these theoretical issues, there is also research evidence that the link between external events and behavioral responses must be indirect in the case of inhibition. Various studies have looked at the responses of the very young to "novel" visual stimuli (for reviews, see Cohen and Gelber 1975; and Fantz, Fagan, and Miranda 1975; and see also Friedman, Nagy, and Carpenter 1970; Friedman and Carpenter 1971; and Friedman 1972a, 1972b). Findings differ somewhat with the kinds of stimuli used and the kinds of criterion behavior observed, but only after about the second month do infants seem able to detect novel aspects of stimuli, and only after about the third month do they begin to show the kind of consistent preference for novelty that is the norm for most (i.e., noninhibited) individuals. These findings tend to support the notion that inhibited responses require not only experience but also some minimum threshold of cognitive comprehension on which to base a stable reaction to novel events.

There are two ways, then, in which avidity and inhibition diverge. First, although both involve affective arousal, the valence of the arousal is opposite. Second, while both appear to involve self-regulatory behavior, these two constructs arise at different levels of organization. Avidity is indexed more or less directly by changes in responses to contingent reinforcement and pleasant sensory events; inhibition is mediated through a more cognitively organized system of reactive internal responses and external withdrawal behaviors.

We propose, however, that a unique congenital status may predispose children to show more avid responses in their earliest days of life and to form a more organized system of behavior in later years that serves to ward off exposure to the unfamiliar. That is, avid behavior in the neonate may presage the development of inhibited behavior in the early childhood years. The results available to date, however, cannot give a fully satisfying account of the course of this transition. We have presently drawn out evidence for only the two critical end points: measures of neonatal avidity and early childhood inhibition. We test the tendency for those neonates who are most avid (i.e., highly reactive to sweet tastes) to be those children who later show tendencies toward withdrawal from the unfamiliar or toward being most inhibited.

The Brown Study

We are currently conducting a longitudinal study extending from birth through 4.5 years. Our first measure is of neonatal avidity, earlier described by Lipsitt and associates (Lipsitt 1975; Lipsitt et al. 1976). Previous success in documenting this phenomenon led us to perform an extended series of follow-up assessments in an effort to discern its developmental significance. At the time of the analyses for this report, we have obtained neonatal records on 230 infants and a variety of cognitive and social measures at later ages. Fifty-one children have reached 30 months of age, the oldest assessment period undertaken to that time. The results reported here pertain to avidity in the neonate and inhibition at ages 4, 18, and 30 months.

Subjects were first tested, with maternal permission, at a metropolitan teaching hospital associated with Brown University, the Women and Infants Hospital of Rhode Island. Mothers were contacted by a nurse research associate on the day of delivery to invite participation in the study. All the children were full term (two had a gestational age of 37 weeks) with no traumatic prenatal or perinatal difficulties. At the time of neonatal assessment, all subjects were in their first or second day of life and were seen in a laboratory on the hospital premises. At later assessments, subjects were seen within 2 weeks of their assessment age (4, 18, and 30 months) at the Child Study Center follow-up unit. Our longitudinal analyses pertain to the 51 subjects who had been seen at 30 months, although we will occasionally refer to larger numbers of subjects when results apply to measures at only the younger age.

Procedures for Assessing Avidity

During the first day or two of life, the infant was placed in a special crib in the laboratory, where electrodes were placed on the chest and leg to monitor heart rate, a pneumo-belt encircled the abdomen to record respiration, and activity level was monitored by a strain-gauge stabilimeter. A Grass polygraph recorded these functions on separate channels. Sucking behavior was measured through the use of a pressure transducer, within a commercial rubber nipple, which converted suction (negative pressure) into an electrical signal that was amplified and recorded continuously on a separate channel of the polygraph. The amplifier was adjusted at the start of testing for each child and remained at that setting for the duration of the 10-minute session so that the potentials reaching a preset criterion amplitude could activate the delivery of fluid. A polyethylene tube in the nipple was connected to three identical pumps, each of which delivered .02 milliliters of fluid for each criterion suck made by the infant (Lipsitt et al. 1976).

The procedure comprised five 2-minute periods, each involving contrasting trials of contingent reinforcement. During the first and last periods, the infant was allowed simply to suck with no fluid delivery. In the second through the fourth periods, one of the three pumps delivered a .02 milliliter drop of solution contingent on each criterion suck. In period 2, a pump transferred water. In period 3, a pump provided 5 percent solution of sucrose in water. In period 4, 15 percent sucrose solution was delivered by the third pump.

For each period, five parameters of sucking behavior were recorded: total sucks, mean sucks per burst, mean intersuck interval, number of pauses between bursts, and duration of pauses between bursts. In addition, heart rate and heart-rate variability were recorded for the same intervals. Although each of the sucking and heart-rate parameters contributed distinct information about the neonate's response to sweet taste (e.g., sucking rate, heart rate, number and duration of pauses, and heart-rate variability), we focused on a single parameter, total number of sucks. This was the most straightforward aspect of infant behavior during this set of treatments and met the motivational and perceptual assumptions of the avidity paradigm (described below). The basal nonnutritive number-of-sucks measure was shown by Lipsitt et al. (1976) to bear a 24-hour test-retest stability coefficient of .62 ($p < .001$). The number-of-sucks parameter during each 2-minute period showed some positive skew (a common characteristic of counts) and was thus corrected to a better approximation of a normal distribution through a square-root reexpression.

Procedures for Assessing Inhibition

Inhibition has proved a difficult phenomenon to measure and analyze, largely because its effects are subtle. Single instruments such as maternal questionnaires provide reliable evidence when sample sizes are large. With results commonly showing correlations in the area of .20 in normal populations, 100 or more subjects appear to be needed to obtain significance (Kagan et al. 1984; Worobey 1986). For the present analyses, we used procedures for multivariate estimation to deal with this difficulty. We focused primarily on observational evidence of inhibited behaviors, following the approach of Garcia-Coll, Kagan, and Reznick (1984). Using a multivariate aggregation, ratings were combined to assess the occurrence of inhibited responses across a variety of contexts. By combining these measures into a single variable, a final inhibition index was obtained with the property of reduced error and enhanced sensitivity.

We restricted our behavioral observations to the 18-month level, as it has been noted that response to novelty stabilizes late in the first year. Kagan (1984) has indicated that behavioral withdrawal in the face of unfamiliar events becomes observable during the second year, and our protocol at 18 months included extensive videotapes of children's interactive behaviors that bear a close resemblance to the protocol used by Garcia-Coll, Kagan, and Reznick (1984) to elicit inhibition during the second year.

Ratings of direct observations

At 18 months, each mother and child participated in two standardized interaction sequences. In the Strange Situation (Ainsworth et al. 1978), the child is exposed to mildly distressful separations from the mother in conjunction with the presence of a strange adult. The so-called Doctor Situation (Radke-Yarrow 1982) simulates a visit to the pediatrician. Although the mother is present throughout the doctor sequence, it is an experience also likely to be somewhat stressful for young children. Both these standard sequences provided changing or challenging circumstances, from which can be assessed specific tendencies toward inhibited responses.

From the Strange Situation, we rated the child's proximity seeking of the mother under several conditions: mother and child alone (episode 2 by Ainsworth's designation), stranger with mother and child (episode 3), and two reunions in which mother returns to the child after separation (episodes 5 and 8). We also rated the child's avoidance of the stranger under three conditions: stranger with mother and child (episode 3), stranger with child after mother leaves (episode 4), and stranger with child after child has been alone (episode 7). Ratings from the Strange Situation were on a seven-point scale following the behavioral definitions for these interactive behaviors by Ainsworth et al. (1978). Ratings were summed across the three relevant conditions for the avoidance-of-stranger variable. Ratings for proximity seeking of the mother were combined across the four relevant conditions. High scores indicated greater proximity seeking of the mother and greater avoidance of the stranger, respectively.

From the Doctor Situation, a trained observer rated two behavioral patterns: proximity seeking of the mother and exploration of the doctor or equipment. However, so few children "explored" that this latter variable had to be eliminated from consideration. The overall score for proximity seeking of the mother was determined by averaging the ratings assigned to each consecutive 15-second interval throughout the sequence (5 minutes). A behaviorally anchored five-point scale was used to rate each interval: (1) no contact (physical or across a distance) with the mother; (2) thumb sucking, glances, or verbalization to the mother; (3) some movements toward the mother (i.e., reaching) but no steps toward her; (4) contact by the mother's initiative, approach of the child ends in touch by the mother, leans on the mother, and stays in close proximity to the mother; and (5) full approach, clamber leading to full contact with the mother, and hiding behind the mother. A higher score indicated increased contact with the mother.

The ratings from both situations showed a mild positive skew and were corrected through a square-root reexpression before analyses were conducted. The construction of the final behavioral index for inhibition from these data will be described below.

Maternal questionnaires

We also included two maternal report questionnaires to provide some validation for our behavioral index. At 4 months, the mother was asked to complete the Infant Temperament Questionnaire (Carey and McDevitt 1978). For this study, we used the child's score on the approach/withdrawal dimension of that questionnaire as an early index of inhibition. At 30 months, a maternal questionnaire asked the mother to rate her child's tendency to show shy and withdrawing behavior in response to new people and places (e.g., "Is your child shy or fearful with strangers at first?"). A four-point rating scale was

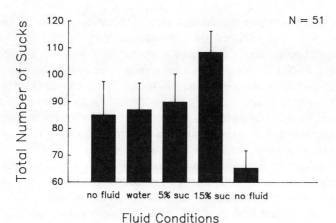

Fig. 1. Total number of sucks across fluid conditions.

used for each question. The ratings were summed, with high scores indicating tendencies toward shy and withdrawing behavior.

Results from Newborn Avidity Measures

A central assumption of the avidity paradigm is that neonates find sucrose solutions rewarding and are motivated to alter their sucking behavior in order to prolong contact with the sweet taste (Ashmead, Reilly, and Lipsitt 1980; Burke 1977; Lipsitt 1975). The motoric capability to do so has been explored elsewhere (Wolff 1968; Lipsitt 1977). An increase in total number of sucking responses within a 2-minute period yields more fluid, hence greater contact with the taste. To test whether sucking levels increased with increasing sweetness in the present study as in previous studies, a univariate repeated measures F-test was performed on the sucking counts, with the 2-minute periods as the within-group factor. The resulting $F = 26.52$, $df = 4$, $p < .001$, indicated that the response varied significantly across fluid conditions. As a curvilinear pattern is expected across the five periods (no fluid, water, 5 percent, 15 percent, no fluid), a quadratic polynomial contrast test was used to examine the predicted pattern of means across the five periods. The result was significant, $F = 40.537$, $df = 1$, $p < .001$. As indicated in figure 1, the means showed steady increases from period 1 to period 4, decreasing sharply during period 5. These findings suggested that the sucking-count measure reflected the clear reward value of sweet tastes for neonates.

As with other response characteristics of newborns, reliable individual differences occur among neonates with respect to avidity. To test this supposition in the present study, sucking frequencies from the baseline fluid condition (water) to the 5 percent sucrose condition were correlated with the difference from the baseline (water) condition to 15 percent sucrose. Across the 230 children for whom we had avidity data, the correlation coefficient was $r = .61, p < .001$. Within the smaller sample ($N = 44$) on whom we had 18-month inhibition data, the correlation was $r = .27, p < .05$. The analysis of variance (ANOVA) indicates that the infants responded to the intensity of the sweet taste by increasing the number of sucks relative to the concentration of the sucrose solution, and the correlation coefficients demonstrate that a condition of internal consistency is present in the newborns; that is, those who tend to increase their sucking frequencies most to 5 percent sucrose are those who tend to increase most to 15 percent sucrose as well.

Since we measured responses to increasing sucrose in a temporal sequence, the possibility arose that children who appeared to show heightened response to sucrose were simply reflecting an increasing state of arousal. The large drop in sucking rates from the fourth period (15 percent sucrose) to the final period (no fluid) argues against that supposition. However, to rule out this possibility, we used the infant's sucking change from the first to the fifth period (both no fluid periods) as an index of simple arousal. Using this as a covariate did not alter the significance of the relation between the two sucrose-difference scores. Thus, it appeared our measure was of response to sweetness distinct from overall arousal.

Inhibition Results at 18 Months

To guide the combination of variables into an overall index of behavioral inhibition, we performed a principal components analysis on the behavioral ratings taken from the Strange Situation and the Doctor Situation. With a varimax rotation, the first component showed loadings exclusively for approaching the mother within the Strange Situation. We took this to be an index of the child's relationship to the mother rather than inhibition, especially since this scale involves two reunion episodes between the mother and the child. The second component showed strong loadings for proximity seeking of the mother during the Doctor Situation and avoidance of the stranger during the Strange Situation. We viewed this component as reflecting the child's response to unfamiliarity and challenge. To construct our final index of behavioral inhibition, we took a simple linear sum of the standardized scores of avoidance of the stranger during the Strange Situation and proximity seeking of the mother during the Doctor Situation.

To provide validation for our inhibition index, we correlated the index with scores from the two mother-report questionnaires. The approach/withdrawal score (Carey Infant Temperament Scale completed when the infants were 4 months old) had only 20 cases because of delayed implementation of the scale in our protocol. However, the resulting correlation, $r = .40, p < .05$, suggested that approach/withdrawal tendencies of 4-month-old infants, as reported by their mothers, were related to our behavioral index of inhibition at

18 months. A correlation between the inhibition index and mothers' reports of their children's shy, withdrawing behavior at 30 months showed a similar result, $r = .36$, $p < .01$, $N = 51$. Thus, besides validating our inhibition index, these results replicated the findings of Kagan and his associates in favor of temporal stability of inhibited behavior through developmental periods (Kagan et al. 1984; Reznick et al. 1986).

The Resulting Relation between Avidity and Inhibition

The critical hypothesis of this report predicted a positive relation between neonatal avidity and 18-month-old inhibition. The result of a regression test on the inhibition index using the avidity index was $r = .40$, $p < .003$, $N = 44$. High levels of avidity at 2 days old were related to high levels of inhibition at 18 months.

Discussion

A primary goal of this study was to gain greater knowledge about the relation between avidity and inhibition. A large portion of this report therefore described the rationale and empirical steps taken in the construction of the avidity and inhibition indices. In proceeding in this way, we found it necessary to evaluate some of the central features of each construct. Testing our index of avidity provided evidence for neonatal preferences for sweet tastes and for stability in individual differences in response to the sweetness of the fluid for which the babies sucked. Testing our inhibition index provided evidence for continuity of this attribute ("shyness") across widely spaced ages, including a viable expression of withdrawal tendencies in 4-month-old infants. Each construct appears to be a source of important individual differences that may have a palpable influence on developmental progress.

Our central concern was in documenting the relation between neonatal avidity and inhibition observed 18 months later. The findings suggest that avidity and inhibition share some common underlying processes, possibly involving perceptual and affective reactivity, limbic-system sensitivity, and regulation of environmental stimulation. It is reasonable to expect that some genetic predispositions are expressed in different behavioral systems at different ages. This supposition follows from long-held psychobiological views that much of early child development involves the gradually accruing, largely learned, capacity of the child to gain control, mediated by the cortex, over congenital unlearned, subcortically mediated behaviors (Lipsitt and Werner 1981; Rovee-Collier and Lipsitt 1982).

We further hypothesize that, developmentally, avidity may be a real progenitor of inhibition, in the sense that inhibitory processes depend for their development on the capacity of infants to experience the pleasures and annoyances of sensation and to have opportunities to self-regulate these. We suggest that the avid/to-be-inhibited newborn enters the world with greater sensitivity (a lower threshold of response) to external events and the potential for a higher state of affective arousal in his or her early interactions with the environment. In early experience with such pleasing events as are involved in the avidity paradigm used here (contingent reinforcement and sweet tastes), the result is heightened rates of behavioral arousal and responsiveness. In subsequent real world experience with more equivocal and even aversive events (e.g., non-contingent or mixed reinforcement), the child comes to experience similarly high levels of far less pleasing states of affective arousal. Ultimately, in this account, an organized system of behavior develops that helps buffer the child from such experiences. For a child with heightened sensitivity, this system may afford protection against overstimulation—a competent and adaptive implementation of self-regulatory behaviors effecting an equilibrium between endogenous and exogenous factors. Yet it is also a system that adult observers may judge to be "inhibited" and deviant from the cultural norm.

Implications for Attachment Classification

The Strange Situation served the central purpose in our study of challenging the child with environmental changes and novelty, allowing the opportunity to assess inhibition. The procedure also provided a means to evaluate the mother-child relationship as it creates a complex social context in which several behavioral systems interact (Ainsworth et al. 1978).

The dyadic interaction during the events of the Strange Situation has been the focus of alternative interpretations. Ainsworth (1983) has argued that the child's behavior in the Strange Situation reflects the mother's responsivity and availability to the child during the first year and indexes the history of the relationship, primarily directed by maternal behavior.

Others have argued that the child's temperament (e.g., susceptibility to fear) may directly influence Strange Situation behavior or, more subtly, may have determined the pattern of interaction established with the mother (Campos et al. 1983; Goldsmith, Bradshaw, and Rieser-Danner 1986; Thompson 1986). Sensitivity to the contingencies in the environment may also affect the child's reactions within a specific social context such as the Strange Situation or, in a more general sense, have played a role in the ontogeny of the mother-child relationship (Plomin, DeFries, and Loehlin 1977; Scarr and McCartney 1983). We used the Strange Situation to explore the relation among attachment, avidity, and inhibition.

Analyses of avidity, inhibition, and attachment

There are three major classifications derived from the Strange Situation: "A" indicates an avoidant-insecure attachment to the mother, "B" indicates a secure relationship, and "C" indicates an ambivalent-insecure attachment.[2] We first considered whether our measures of inhibition or avidity were significantly different as a function of Ainsworth's three main classifications (A, B, and C). It is important to note that the reunion episodes of the Strange Situation (specifically, the child's responses to the mother) so critical to attachment classification were not included in the construction of our inhibition index, preserving independence between these constructs. An ANOVA comparing inhibition scores among the three attachment classifications was not significant. In contrast, an ANOVA comparing the avidity index by attachment classification was significant, $F(2,41) = 6.045$, $p < .005$. Evaluation of the means indicated that avidity level was higher for the A and C groups than for the B classification. High avidity was related to insecure attachments. Inhibition did not vary significantly among the Ainsworth groupings.

Ainsworth further partitioned the three main classifications into subgroups that accounted for variations in the child's behaviors that preserved the same outcome (e.g., avoidance of intimacy, A; use of the mother as a secure base, B; and dependency, C). Prior research has suggested that the Ainsworth subclassifications are sensitive to the child's temperament (Easterbrooks and Lamb 1979; Thompson and Lamb 1983; Sroufe 1985). With eight possible subgroups, and the normative tendency for B or secure classification to predominate, our subgroup sample sizes were too small for definitive analysis. For exploratory purposes, however, table 1 presents the means of the avidity and inhibition indices by subgroup classifications. For avidity, it is clear that results are consistent: group differences in avidity are strongly related to major classifications and show little variation by subgroup. For inhibition, however, results vary as much between subgroups as among major classifications. It is nevertheless noteworthy that both avidity and inhibition reach their highest levels among the children with the C classification.

Discussion of Avidity and Inhibition in Relation to Attachment to the Mother

Attachment classifications result from a careful coding and evaluation of the child's behavior throughout the Strange Situation, with a particular focus on the child's responses to the mother during the reunion episodes. The insecure C children show ambivalent patterns of behavior with the mother. They

---

2. Recent work by Main and Solomon (1986) has identified a fourth classification known as "D" or disorganized. The category description includes a constellation of child behaviors during reunion with the mother such as freezing, confusion, disorientation, crying at the stranger's departure, depression, or fear. We have not coded our sample with the D classification as an alternative. However, none of the subjects was found to be difficult to classify using Ainsworth's original definitions or to exhibit the defining behaviors of the D classification.

Table 1: Means of Avidity and Inhibition Indices by Ainsworth Subgroups

Subgroup		Avidity[a]	Inhibition[b]	Typical Behaviors during Reunion
Group A, Insecure-Avoidant:				
A1	(N = 5)	44.75	−.565	Avoids/ignores the mother while playing
A2	(N = 7)	39.17	.439	Some approach, but mostly avoids the mother
Group B, Secure:				
B1	(N = 13)	4.27	−1.100	Greets the mother, but continues play
B2	(N = 6)	18.67	.380	Some contact with the mother, then returns to play
B3	(N = 14)	17.64	.416	Full contact with the mother, then returns to play
Group C, Insecure-Ambivalent:				
C1	(N = 6)	50.17	.994	Approaches/avoids the mother, distressed, clingy

[a] Results of an ANOVA on the avidity index by group classification (A, B, C) were $F(2,41) = 6.045$, $p < .005$.
[b] An ANOVA on the inhibition index by group classification (A, B, C) was not significant.

may show anger, avoidance, clinging, or excessive passivity. These children appear to be preoccupied by the mother, but they are not satisfied by her responses to their distress and often show little interest in play. In contrast, insecure A children typically avoid contact with the mother when she returns. They may appear totally engrossed in play or may seem equally friendly to the stranger and the mother. Those children classified as B or secure show a clear preference for the mother's presence. They welcome her return (sometimes with tears and long embraces) and, if distressed by her leaving, are consoled by her efforts to comfort, returning to play within a short time. (For a complete description of Ainsworth's coding and classification system and validation studies, see Ainsworth et al. [1978].)

Despite their tentative nature, the pattern of data from table 1 suggests a possible integration of organismic and environmental factors. One basis for the highly avid/insecure child's discomfort with intimacy may relate to the adaptation styles we discussed earlier. Inconsistent mothers may not provide as much buffering from aversive stimulation as these sensitive children require. Over time, these children may react to and become less dependent on, or less trusting of, maternal assistance. Moreover, to the extent that they are nonresponsive, these mothers may offer comparatively little positive contingent reinforcement or, as DeCasper and Carstens (1981) characterize the situation, may generate little positive affect within their dyadic interactions. The child thus does not learn, following this view, to associate security or pleasure with the parent. In these ways, inconsistent mothers may come to engender withdrawn or angry reactions in their highly avid children, who cannot make sense of their mothers' random response patterns. These two forms of adaptation might help to explain the avoidance or ambivalence these children demonstrate regarding close contact with the mother.

Concluding Comments

Our primary purpose was to determine if some aspects of neonatal behavior may represent precursor conditions for inhibited behavior at 18 months. We used individual differences in avidity to sweet taste as our neonatal measure because that measure bears some theoretical and empirical similarities to inhibition expressed in the second year. Both constructs reflect the child's perceptual and affective reactivity to the environment. While avidity connotes behavior that prolongs contact with pleasurable tastes, and inhibition involves actions that presumably minimize aversive events, both can be seen as part of the child's capacity to regulate stimulation. In addition, physiological changes relating to sympathetic arousal and limbic sensitivity accompany both avidity and inhibited behaviors.

Confirming our hypothesis, we found a positive relation between avidity and inhibition. Those infants who as newborns showed greater reactivity in our avidity paradigm tended to be the children who were wary and withdrawing in the face of unfamiliarity 18 months later.

Although the major focus in this report has been on the measurement and interrelatedness of avidity and inhibition, we have tried to explore some implications for these organismic factors within a social context important to young children. We considered the possibility that individual differences in neonatal reactivity to stimulation might be reflected in the child's relationship with the mother. We found that highly avid neonates were more likely to be classified as A or C (insecurely attached to the mother by Ainsworth's interpretation) at 18 months while less avid infants tended to be classified as B or securely attached children. The child's tendency to be wary and inhibited at 18 months did not clearly discriminate these contemporaneous attachment groups. Highly inhibited children were found primarily in the ambivalent-insecure C group or those secure B groups involving close contact with the mother.

We contend that avidity and inhibition have common roots in the sensory sensitivity and responsivity of the infants and that these early characteristics influence the mother-child relationship. The confluence of these attributes may themselves be affected, however, by the contingencies within the history of the dyad and within the specific context. Further research should elucidate the interactional dialogue that contributes to the progression from individual differences in reactivity to hedonic stimulation to observed patterns of socially adaptive, self-regulatory behavior.

References

Ainsworth, M. D. S. 1983. Patterns of infant-mother attachment as related to maternal care. In *Human development: An interaction perspective*, ed. D. Magnusson and V. Allen. New York: Academic.

Ainsworth, M. D. S.; Blehar, M.; Waters, E.; and Wall, S. 1978. *Patterns of attachment*. Hillsdale, N.J.: Erlbaum.

Ashmead, D. H.; Reilly, B. M.; and Lipsitt, L. P. 1980. Neonates' heart rate, sucking rhythm, and sucking amplitude as a function of the sweet taste. *Journal of Experimental Child Psychology* 29:264–81.

Brazelton, T. B.; Koslowski, B.; and Main, M. 1974. The origins of reciprocity: The early mother-infant interaction. In *The effect of the infant on its caretaker, ed. M. Lewis and L. Rosenblum*. Vol. 1, *The origins of behavior*. New York: Wiley.

Brim, O. G., Jr., and Kagan, J., eds. 1980. *Constancy and change in human development*. Cambridge, Mass.: Harvard University Press.

Burke, P. M. 1977. Swallowing and the organization of sucking in the human newborn. *Child Development* 48:523–31.

Campos, J. J.; Barrett, K. S.; Lamb, M. E.; Goldsmith, H. H.; and Stenberg, C. 1983. Socioemotional development. In *Handbook of child psychology*, ed. P. H. Mussen. Vol. 2, *Infancy and developmental psychobiology*, ed. M. M. Haith and J. J. Campos. New York: Wiley.

Carey, W. B., and McDevitt, S. C. 1978. Revision of the Infant Temperament Questionnaire. *Pediatrics* 61:735–39.

Cohen, L. B., and Gelber, E. R. 1975. Infant visual memory. In *Infant perception: From sensation to cognition*, ed. L. B. Cohen and P. Salapatek. New York: Academic.

Crook, C. K., and Lipsitt, L. P. 1976. Neonatal nutritive sucking: Effects of taste stimulation upon sucking rhythm and heart rate. *Child Development* 47:518–22.

DeCasper, A. J., and Carstens, A. A. 1981. Contingencies of stimulation: Effects on learning and emotion in neonates. *Infant Behavior and Development* 4:19–35.

Desor, J.; Maller, O.; and Turner, R. 1973. Taste in acceptance of sugars by human infants. *Journal of Comparative and Physiological Psychology* 84:496–501.

Easterbrooks, M. A., and Lamb, M. E. 1979. The relationship between quality of infant-mother attachment and infant competence in initial encounters with peers. *Child Development* 50:380–87.

Fantz, R. L.; Fagan, J. F.; and Miranda, S. B. 1975. Early visual selectivity. In *Infant perception: From sensation to cognition,* ed. L. B. Cohen and P. Salapatek. New York: Academic.

Friedman, S. 1972a. Habituation and recovery of visual response in the alert human newborn. *Journal of Experimental Child Psychology* 13:339–49.

Friedman, S. 1972b. Newborn visual attention to repeated exposure of redundant vs. "novel" targets. *Perception and Psychophysics* 12:291–94.

Friedman, S., and Carpenter, G. C. 1971. Visual response decrement as a function of age in human newborn. *Child Development* 42:1967–73.

Friedman, S.; Nagy, A. N.; and Carpenter, G. C. 1970. Newborn attention: Differential response decrement to visual stimuli. *Journal of Experimental Child Psychology* 10:44–51.

Garcia-Coll, C.; Kagan, J.; and Reznick, S. 1984. Behavioral inhibition in young children. *Child Development* 55:1005–19.

Goldsmith, H. H.; Bradshaw, D. L.; and Rieser-Danner, L. A. 1986. Temperament as a potential developmental influence on attachment. In *Temperament and social interaction in infancy and childhood,* ed. J. V. Lerner and R. M. Lerner. San Francisco: Jossey-Bass.

Goldsmith, H. H., and Campos, J. J. 1982. Toward a theory of infant temperament. In *The development of attachment and affiliative systems,* ed. R. N. Emde and R. J. Harmon. New York: Plenum.

Kagan, J. 1981. *The second year.* Cambridge, Mass.: Harvard University Press.

Kagan, J. 1984. *Nature of the child.* New York: Basic.

Kagan, J.; Reznick, S.; Clarke, C.; Snidman, N.; and Garcia-Coll, C. 1984. Behavioral inhibition to the unfamiliar. *Child Development* 55:2212–25.

Lipsitt, L. P. 1963. Learning in the first year of life. In *Advances in child development and behavior,* vol. 1, ed. L. P. Lipsitt and C. C. Spiker. New York: Academic.

Lipsitt, L. P. 1975. The synchrony of respiration, heart rate, and sucking behavior in the newborn. Paper presented to the session Biologic and clinical aspects of brain development, Mead Johnson Symposium on Perinatal and Developmental Medicine, Marco Island, Fla.

Lipsitt, L. P. 1977. The study of sensory and learning processes of the newborn. *Clinics in Perinatology* 4:305–10.

Lipsitt, L. P. 1979. Critical conditions in infancy. *American Psychologist* 34:371–76.

Lipsitt, L. P.; Reilly, B. M.; Butcher, M. J.; and Greenwood, M. M. 1976. The stability and interrelationship of newborn sucking and heart rate. *Developmental Psychobiology* 9:305–10.

Lipsitt, L. P., and Werner, J. S. 1981. The infancy of human learning processes. In *Developmental plasticity,* ed. E. S. Gollin. New York: Academic.

Main, M., and Solomon, J. 1986. Discovery of an insecure-disorganized/disoriented attachment pattern. In *Affective development in infancy,* ed. T. B. Brazelton and M. Yogman. Norwood, N. J.: Ablex.

Plomin, R.; DeFries, J. C.; and Loehlin, J. C. 1977. Genotype-environment interaction and correlation in the analysis of human development. *Psychological Bulletin* 84:309–22.

Radke-Yarrow, M. 1982. *Affective disorders and affective development: A study of child rearing and child development in normal families and families with affective disorders*. National Institution of Mental Health Protocol 79-M-123. Washington, D.C.: U.S. Government Printing Office.

Reznick, S. 1982. The development of perceptual and lexical categories in the human infant. Ph.D. diss., University of Colorado, Boulder.

Reznick. S.; Kagan, J.; Snidman, N.; Gersten, M.; Baak, K.; and Rosenberg, A. 1986. Inhibited and uninhibited children: A follow-up study. *Child Development* 57:660–80.

Rovee-Collier, C. K., and Lipsitt, L. P. 1982. Learning, adaptation, and memory in the newborn. In *Psychobiology of the human newborn*, ed. P. Stratton. New York: Wiley.

Sameroff, A. J., and Chandler, M. J. 1975. Reproductive risk and the continuum of caretaking casualty. In *Review of child development research*, vol. 4, ed. F. D. Horowitz, M. Hetherington, S. Scarr-Salapatek, and G. Siegel. Chicago: University of Chicago Press.

Scarr, S., and McCartney, K. 1983. How people make their own environments: A theory of genotype-environment effects. *Child Development* 54:424–35.

Siqueland, E. R., and Lipsitt, L. P. 1966. Conditioned head turning in human newborns. *Journal of Experimental Child Psychology* 3:356.

Sroufe, L. A. 1985. Attachment classification from the perspective of infant-caregiver relationships and infant temperament. *Child Development* 56:1–14.

Thompson, R. A. 1986. Temperament, emotionality, and infant social cognition. In *Temperament and social interaction in infancy and childhood*, ed. J. V. Lerner and R. M. Lerner. San Francisco: Jossey-Bass.

Thompson, R. A., and Lamb, M. E. 1983. Security of attachment and stranger sociability in infancy. *Developmental Psychology* 19:184–91.

Watson, J. S. 1966. The development and generalization of contingency awareness in early infancy: Some hypotheses. *Merrill-Palmer Quarterly* 17:139–52.

Watson, J. S. 1972. Smiling, cooing, and "the game." *Merrill-Palmer Quarterly* 18:321–39.

Wolff, P. H. 1968. The serial organization of sucking in the young infant. *Pediatrics* 42:943–55.

Worobey, J. 1986. Convergence among assessments of temperament in the first month. *Child Development* 57:47–55.

9 Heart-Rate Variability and Behavioral Reactivity: Individual Differences in Autonomic Patterning and Their Relation to Infant and Child Temperament

NATHAN A. FOX

Recent work by Kagan and his colleagues (Garcia-Coll, Kagan, and Reznick 1984; Kagan 1982; Kagan et al. 1984; Reznick et al. 1986) has indicated that there is a stable and predictive relation between the pattern of heart rate observed in young children during the performance of cognitive tasks and certain aspects of their social behavior. Specifically, children with high and stable heart rates are more likely to display behaviors in social situations that lead them to be described as being shy, fearful, or introverted. These children appear to be more anxious and more distressed by mildly stressful events; they also tend not to engage their age peers in spontaneous social interaction. Kagan and his coworkers have called these children "behaviorally inhibited" (Kagan et al. 1984). They have argued that the high and stable heart rate found among these inhibited children reflects greater sympathetic activation. This activation, they believe, occurs when a child fails to understand or assimilate discrepant or uncertain events.

Theoretical Background

The search for relations between autonomic patterning and individual differences in behavior has a long and varied tradition in the psychological literature. Eppinger and Hess (1915) first pointed out that individuals might differ in the degree to which their autonomic nervous system dominated or regulated behavior. Individuals with low resting levels of heat rate and greater heart-rate variability—both of which reflect parasympathetic dominance—were consid-

Partial support for the research presented in this chapter is from a grant from the National Institutes of Health (HD 17899).

ered vagotonic. These individuals were described as being depressed and list-less and lacking energy. Individuals with high resting levels of heart rate and low heart-rate variability were considered to be more sympathetically domi-nant (sympatheticotonia) and were described as being high strung and anx-ious. Subsequently, Wenger (1941) considered the relation between the two types of the autonomic nervous system and proposed a model of autonomic balance. Wenger described five different types of autonomic nervous system response patterns that would be reflected in different patterns of behavior. These were relative sympathetic dominance, parasympathetic dominance, balance, beta pattern, and tubercular pattern.

Some years later, Lacey and Lacey (1958) reported finding, quite by acci-dent, different patterns of autonomic nervous system activity among adult women who were to be subjects in their laboratory for a reaction-time study. Some women displayed patterns of frequent oscillations in resting heart rate and skin conductance, while others displayed a relatively stable pattern across measures. The Laceys analyzed the two groups of subject's experimental data with respect to their resting baseline patterns and found that individuals with a high frequency of oscillatory patterns were slower in their reaction time but more accurate while individuals with stable nonoscillatory patterns displayed more impulsive behavior and were less accurate. More recently, Porges (1976) has speculated that individual variations in parasympathetic influence may be associated with different manifestations of psychopathology. He gave partic-ular emphasis to those disorders that might involve deficits in attention. In this model, individuals with problems in attention or those who could not make use of strategies to regulate behavioral activity are characterized as being low in parasympathetic influence, and individuals with an inability to shift attention are placed at the opposite end of the continuum.

The issue of attention as a strategy for self-regulation is an important one in several models of infant temperament. Thomas, Chess, and Birch (1968) included attention span as one of their nine primary dimensions of tempera-ment. Rothbart (Posner and Rothbart 1986; Rothbart and Posner 1985) has characterized strategies involving attention as serving an important function in the individual's self-regulatory behavior. Rothbart (Rothbart and Derry-berry 1981) highlights two dimensions of individual differences that she be-lieves constitute early temperament. They are reactivity and self-regulation. Reactivity involves specific parameters of the organism's response to different levels of stimulation. Thus, factors such as threshold and intensity are of concern. Self-regulation involves the organism's attempt to deal with stimu-lation and the modulation of the reactive response. Rothbart states that the basis for individual variation in both dimensions involves differences in ma-turation of autonomic and central nervous system processes. In her model, emotion or affect-motivational systems are intimately involved in the expres-sion of reactivity to stimulation and in the organism's attempt to modulate response (Derryberry and Rothbart 1984). She places great emphasis on the development of attention. Rothbart argues (Posner and Rothbart 1986) that the infant's ability to selectively attend to stimuli in the environment allows it strategies for dealing with its own physiological arousal. Early in life, that arousal is a function of the intensity of the stimulus, later on it is a function of the appraisal process (with reduction of arousal accompanying successful assimilation of novelty and continued arousal associated with unsuccessful assimilation). In other words, given stimuli of moderate uncertainty or novelty, there will be individual differences in infant reaction to the stimulus and individual differences in modulation of that reaction. The latter differences are in part a function of regulatory strategies available to the child.

The data to be presented in this chapter will focus on the relation between the patterning of the electrocardiogram (ECG) and individual behaviors reflecting behavioral reactivity and emotion regulation. The general strategy of my research program has been to examine the relations between measures of heart-rate variability, brain electrical activity, and social behavior. The data in this chapter describe the results only with reference to heart rate and vagal tone. For an overview of the research on affect and EEG, see Fox and Davidson (1987, 1988). Heart-rate variability was chosen on theoretical grounds as a measure that might tap constitutional differences in reactivity and self-regulation. Research has demonstrated an association between heart-rate variability and sustained attention to auditory and visual stimuli. Individuals with high heart-rate variability exhibit greater sustained attention than do individuals with low heart-rate variability. In addition, certain measures of heart-rate variability may reflect central cholinergic activity, which is involved in the modulation of attention (Porges 1983). A number of papers indicate a relation between heart-rate variability and attention in adults and infants. For example, Porges (Porges, Arnold, and Forbes 1973; Porges 1974) found that subjects with greater baseline heart-rate variability had faster reaction times and were better able to focus attention in a perceptual task than were subjects with low baseline heart-rate variability. Richards (1987) found that infants with high respiratory sinus arrhythmia (derived from the variability of the heart-period pattern) displayed greater sustained attention and were less easily distracted by peripheral visual stimuli than were infants with low respiratory sinus arrhythmia. Fox and Porges (1985) found that infants with high resting levels of vagal tone had positive cognitive outcomes at 8 and 12 months of age. High-risk infants with resting vagal tone at or above the mean of healthy newborns did not display Bayley mental scores below the norm.

It is widely known that one can extract from the pattern of heart rate the variance contributed by respiratory sinus arrhythmia (RSA). A number of researchers (for a review, see Grossman [1983]) have studied RSA as a marker of individual differences in susceptibility to stress and emotional regulation. Individuals with high RSA cope more successfully with moderate stress than those with low RSA do. Porges and his associates (Porges, McCabe, and Yongue 1982) have demonstrated that the amplitude of RSA is primarily the result of parasympathetic or vagal influence to the heart. Stimulation of the aortic depressor nerve in the rabbit reflexively increased vagal tone and increased the amplitude of RSA (McCabe, Yongue, Porges, and Ackles 1984). The administration of pharmacological agents that are known to increase (phenylephrine) or decrease (atropine) vagal tone result in parallel effects on RSA in unanesthetized moving rats (Yongue et al. 1982). Thus, choice of heart-rate variability as a physiological index of individual differences in self-regulation is based on two dimensions: its conceptual underpinnings as reflecting the degree of RSA influence or parasympathetic influence on heart rate and the empirical work that has demonstrated that the RSA influence on heart-rate variability is associated with more efficient strategies of attention to the environment and regulatory responses to stress.

The choice of measurement of the respiratory component in heart-rate variability is itself important. Researchers studying differences in RSA have sometimes used the peak-to-trough height of respiration (Grossman and Wientjes 1986) rather than examining the heart-period process. This measure, while adequate for certain studies of adult populations in which movement is kept to a minimum, may not be adequate for studies with infants and young children. Workers studying infant and child populations have traditionally used different measures of the variance in heart period to approximate the contribution of RSA in the heart-period process. Included among these measures are the variance of the process or the range (e.g., Garcia-Coll, Kagan, and Reznick 1984) and the mean of the absolute value of the successive differences (Fox 1983). Each of these measures indirectly taps a portion of the variance in the heart period attributable to respiration. A number of more recent techniques have employed spectral analysis (Richards 1986) or digital filtering (Porges 1985) to extract the variance due to RSA. Richards (1987) focuses on a measure called the extent of RSA, while Porges calls his measure $\hat{V}$ (an estimate of vagal tone).

In the research presented here, both Porges' $\hat{V}$-measure and additional measures of heart-rate variability (e.g., mean successive difference) are presented. In general, heart-period variance and the range of heart period are similar in statistical and inferential characteristics and present a similar pattern of associations with the behavioral data. The successive difference measure and Porges's $\hat{V}$ are both inferential of the physiological process underlying the influence of respiration on heart rate; both display a similar pattern of associations with behavioral data. The intercorrelations between some of the variability measures are, in fact, quite high. Table 1 presents the intercorrelations between heart period, heart-period variance, successive differences, and $\hat{V}$ for seven data sets from our laboratory. I performed a meta-analysis on these data, weighting and transforming each of the correlations and then comparing the

Table 1: Intercorrelations between Measures of Heart-Period Variability across Seven Independent Samples

Study	HP-HPV	HP-V	HP-SD	HPV-V	SD-V	HPV-SD
Stifter (1987) (neonates, $N = 74$)	.60	.56	.54	.85	.92	.82
Stifter (1987) (5 months, $N = 62$)	.73	.66	.70	.80	.92	.69
Stifter, Fox, and Porges (in press) (5 months, $N = 20$)	.53	.51	.52	.82	.95	.74
Stifter, Fox, and Porges (1987) (10 months, $N = 14$)	.79	.82	.82	.96	.94	.92
Healy (1986) ($N = 72$)	.72	.71	.77	.75	.87	.80
Fox and Field (in press) (October, $N = 28$)	.71	.68	.65	.87	.84	.93
Fox and Field (in press) (March, $N = 21$)	.72	.77	.68	.92	.93	.90

Note. HP = heart period; HPV = heart period variance; SD = successive differences; and $\hat{V}$ = vagal tone.

weighted z-scores. The results of this analysis revealed that the correlation between successive differences and Porges's $\hat{V}$ was significantly greater than each of the other pairs, $z = 3.49$, $p = .002$. This indicates that these two measures of heart-rate variability are more highly related to each other than to any of the other heart-rate variability measures. One possible reason for this high degree of association is that successive differencing acts as a high-pass filter, filtering out the slow frequency components that may confound the estimate of RSA. Porges's filtering technique acts similarly on the heart-period data, filtering out the aperiodic slow-frequency components. Of course, simply because two measures are highly correlated with each other does not mean that they will be equally related to an investigated behavior (Porges 1987).

For clarity here, I will present and contrast the measures of heart-period variance and Porges's $\hat{V}$ (when it was computed). In cases in which the results using $\hat{V}$ and the successive difference measure differ, this too will be noted.

The studies in this chapter represent a program of research on the relations between heart-rate variability and individual differences during the first years of life. The data will be presented in three sections. The first set of studies deals with the relations between heart-rate variability and emotional expressivity, in particular, facial expressivity. The second set specifically examines self-regulatory behaviors in early infancy. The third set examines the relations of heart-rate variability to social behavior and temperament in older infants and young children.

Studies on Facial Expressivity

Facial behavior is an important vehicle for the communication of state or mood, particularly during the first year of life (Izard 1977). Recent research has demonstrated that the young infant is capable of exhibiting different facial expressions during the first year and that these expressions are read by care givers as meaningful representations of emotional state (Izard et al. 1980). Indeed, very early on, parents reinforce different facial expressions in their infants (Malatesta and Haviland 1982). Facial expressions may also reflect the infant's underlying motivational response to the environment. For example, Izard (1977) has written that the infant's facial expression during periods of attention (the expression of interest) reflects the infant's underlying processing of nonsocial stimuli. Sroufe (Sroufe and Wunsch 1972), Rothbart (1973), and Kagan (1971) have discussed the meaning of the infant's smile immediately after assimilation of moderately discrepant events. Sroufe and Rothbart view the smile as accompanying reduction in arousal or tension, which is itself the result of the novel event. Kagan views the smile as indicating mastery at assimilation of moderate discrepancy. In all three cases, interest and smile expressions may be viewed as having a dual purpose: they represent manifestations of the infant's self-regulatory process and may act as regulators in social interaction. Thus, an interest expression or smile subsequent to presentation of a novel event might indicate the infant's regulation of the tension caused by the initial discrepancy. The same smiles and interest expressions during social interaction might be effective behaviors in regulating interaction with a care giver (Tronick 1982). For example, young infants will smile in response to adult faces, particularly their mother's face (Stern 1977), and will turn away or change expression when the level of arousal of the interaction increases (Tronick et al. 1978). Ten-month-old infants display different types of smiles to the approach of unfamiliar and familiar adults (Fox and Davidson 1988) and, under certain conditions, display wary expressions and gaze aversion to unfamiliar persons (Sroufe, Waters, and Matas 1974). Thus, facial expressivity may be viewed as an important behavior reflecting the child's attempt at regulating his or her emotional response.

I have investigated the relation between heart-rate variability and facial expressivity in a number of studies and with a number of different age children. In the first study (Fox and Gelles 1984), we observed 3-month-old children and their mothers in a face-to-face situation in which the mother was asked to respond to her child as she would at home. Three minutes of resting EKG had been recorded from the infant prior to the onset of the interaction. Measures of heart period, range, and mean successive difference were computed from the heart-period data. The videotaped interaction was scored by having a coder trained on Izard's (1979) MAX system score the infant's facial expression during the 2-minute interaction. A second, independent, coder scored a set of maternal behaviors. Two findings from this research are of interest. First, mothers responded contingently with positive affective behavior (touch, kiss, present toy) to positive infant facial expressions such as interest or smiling. Second, there was a positive association between heart-rate variability (the mean successive difference measure) and duration of interest expressions. Infants with higher resting heart-rate variability displayed a longer duration of interest expressions. Interestingly, these infants also had mothers who turned toward them and displayed positive affection more often than infants with low resting heart-rate variability. Thus, infants with higher heart-rate variability who displayed facial expressions of interest had more responsive mothers in this situation.

In a second study (Stifter, Fox, and Porges, in press), we observed 34 infants (20 5-month-olds and 14 10-month-olds) in a standardized stranger approach/mother approach paradigm. There were eight possible conditions: mother could approach either first or second and with either a smiling face or a neutral face and the stranger could approach either first or second and with either a smiling face or a neutral face. Each infant viewed four conditions, one stranger (happy/neutral) and one mother (happy/neutral) approach. Prior to the onset of the experiment, 5 minutes of EKG were recorded while the infant sat quietly in his or her mother's lap. Infant facial behavior was coded using Izard's MAX system. In addition, infant gaze aversion, fret, and cry were also coded. Measures of mean heart period, $\hat{V}$, and heart-period variance were derived from the 5-minute recording.

Of interest here are the data relating measures of heart-rate variability and facial expressivity. Because of significant differences between the 5- and 10-month-olds in measures of heart-rate variability, data were calculated separately for each group. Pearson correlations were computed to determine the relations between positive expressions of interest and heart-rate variability. Group differences in resting heart-rate variability between infants that did and did not express each of the emotions of sadness and anger were analyzed as well. We found a significant relation between expressivity and heart-rate variability for 5-month-old infants. Infants with greater baseline heart-rate variability displayed a greater number of positive emotional expressions, especially in response to the approach of the stranger, r $(n = 20) = .48$, $p < .05$. That relation, however, was not present for the 10-month-olds. In addition, we found that 10-month-old infants who expressed negative affects such as sadness were also those who displayed higher heart-rate variability at rest.

The five-month data replicate our earlier finding of a relation between interest expression and heart-rate variability. Five-month-olds displaying interest had higher resting heart-rate variability levels than did those with fewer interest expressions. Izard (1977), in his description of differential emotions theory, has conceptualized interest as an expression seen during active attention. The fact that infants in our study displayed greater interest expressions to the stranger than to the mother may indicate that they are actively attending to and processing the approach of this unfamiliar person. The expression of interest during stranger approach may function to regulate the child's emotional response to the discrepant event. The association between heart-rate variability and facial expressions denoting attention confirms the relation between attention and heart rate found by others (Kagan and Lewis 1965; Porges 1974). It is interesting to note that, in a study of interest expressions and attention, Izard (Langsdorf et al. 1983) found a positive relation between heart-rate deceleration and interest expressions. Because heart-rate deceleration is vagally mediated (Porges 1976), it is no surprise that those infants with greater resting variability are also the ones who display greater attentiveness and interest to novel events.

The lack of a relation between heart-rate variability and the facial expression of interest in the 10-month-old group is troublesome. It may be that these infants used strategies other than visual attention and interest to regulate their response to the stranger's approach. Other emotional responses to this situation (such as wariness) reflect a more complex response. Strategies for emotional regulation may change with age and in response to different stimulus situations. Five-month-olds may regulate their level of arousal to novel events such as stranger approach via visual attention, while 10-month-olds respond with facial signs of wariness and negative affect.

Studies on Self-Regulation

The infant's ability to regulate its reaction to different stimuli is viewed by some theorists as of primary importance in understanding individual differences in temperamental style. Rothbart (Rothbart and Derryberry 1981; Rothbart and Posner 1985) views the development of temperament as involving increasing regulatory control over initial patterns of reactivity. Regulation in this model is the result of the development of mechanisms involved with attention, particularly selective attention (Posner and Rothbart 1986), that provide strategies for dealing with novel or moderately stressful events. Regulatory processes may be seen in the infant's behavior in interaction with nonsocial stimuli (sustained or selective attention) as well as in interaction with social stimuli (the sustaining of interaction between mother and infant). Tronick (1980, 1982; Gianino and Tronick 1985) has articulated a similar model on the development of regulation within the mother-infant dyadic interaction in which specific behaviors (many of which can be viewed as attention-getting and attention-holding behaviors) are seen as playing an important role in the infant's ability to regulate "conversation" or interaction.

In an effort to investigate the development of self-regulatory abilities and their relation to differences in heart-rate variability, Stifter and Fox (in press) undertook a longitudinal study in which they observed 80 infants at 1–2 days of age and again at 5 months of age. In the newborn period, infant EKG was recorded for 5 minutes of quiet sleep. While infants were in a quiet alert state, they were presented with a pacifier withdrawal task (Bell, Weller, and Waldrop 1971). At 5 months of age, infant and mother came to our lab for an assessment that included a visual attention task, a peek-a-boo play session, and a moderate restraint task in which the mother was asked to hold her infant's arms down gently for 2 minutes. The purpose of the tasks at both ages was to observe infants' reactivity to mild stress as well as their ability to regulate their arousal.

The newborn data revealed that, among those infants who responded to the pacifier withdrawal (approximately half the sample), there was a significant relation between heart-rate variability and infant response. Infants with high heart-rate variability took longer to begin to cry and took longer to soothe than infants with low resting levels of heart-rate variability, $r(n = 26) = .45, p < .01$.

At 5 months, one of the important dimensions investigated was self-regulatory behavior, particularly during the arm-restraint procedure. Self-regulatory behaviors that were coded during this procedure included look to mother, look to mirror (infants were videotaped through a one-way mirror, and the window in which the infant could see itself was exposed during the procedure), number of arm and leg thrusts, and number of vocalizations. A summary measure was computed that included each of these individual measures as well as the latency to look measure derived from the visual attention task. Analysis of the relation between neonatal $\hat{V}$ and 5-month self-regulatory behavior revealed a significant positive relation: infants with high resting levels of heart-rate variability displayed more self-regulatory abilities at 5 months, $r = .48, p < .01$, for $\hat{V}$ and self-regulation.

These data seem to indicate that individual differences in the parasympathetic tone present at birth are associated with the young infant's ability to regulate its own distress and that these same individual differences predict variations in self-regulatory behavior at 5 months of age. It is interesting that the measure of regulatory behavior at 5 months was a composite score of individually coded behaviors, most of which were associated with the infant's attention strategies in dealing with the mild stress (look at mirror, look at mother) or in dealing with a moderately complex visual stimulus (latency to look). One important aspect, it seems, of the regulatory process is the ability selectively to attend to stimuli in the environment. In response to the moderate restraint situation, infants who were successful in regulating their distress (they either did not cry or were able to soothe and quiet themselves) used attention-like behaviors to accomplish this goal. Individual differences in the use of these behaviors was associated with newborn heart-rate variability.

Table 2: Pearson correlations for autonomic measures recorded at 2 days of age (newborn) and again at 5 months of age ($N = 63$)

	5 Months			
Newborn	HP	HPV	SD	$\hat{V}$
Heart period (HP)	.01			
Heart-period variance (HPV)		.15		
Successive Differences (SD)			−.05	
Vagal tone ($\hat{V}$)				−.07

An important caveat to these findings is the absence of a relation between measures of heart-rate variability computed from EKG recorded at 5 months and 5-month laboratory behavior. There was little relation between heart-rate variability at 5 months and either positive or negative reactivity; nor did heart-rate variability correlate clearly with infant self-regulation. However, there was also little stability in heart-rate variability across the 5-month period of time. Table 2 presents the correlations between age for the 63 infants seen at both the neonatal and the 5-month period. In a subsequent section, the issue of stability will be more fully addressed.

Heart-Rate Variability and Temperament

As part of our interest in the relations between vagal activity and infant temperament, we followed the infants described in the previous study to 14 months of age. At that point in time, 64 infants returned to our lab for an assessment of their responses to novel objects and mildly discrepant social events. For example, after a brief free-play period with the mother in the room, an unfamiliar person entered holding an attractive toy. This person sat down in a corner of the room, head bowed and still for 2 minutes. After 2 minutes, she began to play with the new toy, and shortly after that she tried to engage the child in interaction. We coded duration proximity to the mother and latency to approach the stranger during this episode. Children were also presented with a novel object. The experimenter presented a small talking and moving robot. We coded latency to approach and touch the novel toy. Finally, we observed each of the children in the Ainsworth and Wittig Strange Situation. Prior to these stimulus situations, the 14-month-olds sat in a high chair while we recorded the EKG. The EKG was recorded under seven different conditions: baseline; watching 2 minutes of "Sesame Street"; baseline; manipulating a novel toy; baseline; manipulating a number of different novel toys; baseline. We derived measures of heart period and vagal tone from the EKG. Those children with a z-score for $\hat{V}$ above the mean on each of the seven separate heart-rate recordings were placed in one group, while those with a vagal tone score below the mean on each of the recordings were placed in a

Table 3: Mean 14-Month Behavioral Measures for Two Groups of Infants (Those with High and Stable Heart Rate and Those with Low and Variable Heart Rate at 14 Months), with Standard Deviations in Parentheses

	Low Vagal Tone at 14 Months (N = 16)	High Vagal Tone at 14 Months (N = 16)
Latency to approach stranger	305.56 (128.95)	133.60* (175.81)
Latency to approach robot	61.44 (18.73)	42.47 (20.11)
Latency to cry to maternal separation	129.31 (79.46)	111.0 (82.11)

*$p < .01$.

second group. Sixteen children were in the high vagal tone group and 15 in the low vagal tone group. We then examined the social behavior of these children at 14 months. Table 3 presents the data on infant latency to approach the stranger, latency to approach robot, and latency to cry at maternal separation (the first separation of the Strange Situation). The latency to approach the stranger is significantly different between groups, with infants in the high vagal tone group displaying a shorter latency than those with low vagal tone do. Table 4 presents the distribution of children by vagal tone group and when they approached the stranger. As can be seen, fewer children in the low vagal tone group approached during the initial time period than did those with high vagal tone. There was also a tendency for the high vagal tone children to approach the robot more quickly than those with low vagal tone did.

We also examined these children's 5-month laboratory behavior. We had, as previously mentioned, seen these children at 5 months and had observed them interacting with their mothers and an unfamiliar adult in a peek-a-boo game and with their mothers in moderate restraint of the hands. Table 5 presents the 5-month data for the two groups of infants. As can be seen, infants at 14 months with low vagal tone were less likely to cry to moderate restraint and displayed less negative affect during the testing session. Infants with high vagal tone at 14 months, on the other hand, were more likely to cry to moderate restraint and to be reactive during the testing session. Finally, as can be seen in table 5, there was a good deal of stability between 5 and 14 months for these two groups in heart period and vagal tone. Infants at 14 months with

Table 4: Distribution of Children by Vagal Tone Group and Type of Approach to Stranger at 14 Months

	First 3 Minutes	3–7 Minutes	No Approach
Low vagal tone	2	10	4
High vagal tone	11	1	3

Table 5: Mean 5-Month Behavioral Measures for Two Groups of Infants (Those with High and Stable Heart Rate and Those with Low and Variable Heart Rate at 14 Months), with Standard Deviations in Parentheses

	Low Vagal Tone at 14 Months ($N = 16$)	High Vagal Tone at 14 Months ($N = 16$)
Positive reactivity (5 Months)	24.78	26.18
	(15.24)	(13.97)
Negative reactivity (5 Months)	25.87	61.73*
	(44.56)	(47.32)
Heart period (5 Months)	410.38	429.76*
	(23.76)	(22.83)
Heart-period variance (5 Months)	19.62	26.51
	(6.64)	(10.78)
Variance (5 Months)	2.40	3.45*
	(.69)	(.79)

*$p < .05$.

low vagal tone had significantly lower vagal tone at 5 months than did infants with high vagal tone at both ages.

We interpret these data to indicate that, during the first year of life, higher vagal tone may reflect a tendency toward greater behavioral reactivity and that low vagal tone may be associated with passive responses toward mildly discrepant or novel events. Arm restraint may be seen as an example of this hypothesis. The task was designed and used to produce anger and frustration in infants. Indeed, the modal facial response of infants was anger. Infants with high vagal tone were more likely to express anger and frustration at having their hands restrained than were infants with low vagal tone. Nine months later, these same infants displayed quite different patterns of social behavior in the lab. The infants with high vagal tone who reacted with anger and frustration at 5 months were more sociable and responsive at 14 months, while the infants who responded passively at 5 months were more shy and restrained in their social behavior. Thus, vagal tone may be an important physiological correlate of reactivity in the first year. This particular type of behavioral reactivity (response to frustration) may be associated with subsequent outgoing versus introverted responses during the second year.

We performed another study, with somewhat older children, in order to observe their behavioral response to a mildly stressful event in a nonlaboratory natural environment (Fox and Field, in press). The study examined children's behavior in response to their first exposure to nursery school. Previous research (Field and Reite 1984) had found distinct behavioral changes in children in response to entry into preschool. Field and Reite (1984), for example, found that children moving into a new preschool classroom exhibited more aggressive and less socially interactive play and were reported to exhibit, at home, more toileting, feeding, and sleep problems. Field and Reite likened these children's responses to those seen in primates in response to prolonged maternal separation. We were interested in examining a similar situation for nursery school children and observing entry and play behaviors. Our goal was to relate individual differences in resting heart-rate variability to maternal perception of child temperament and to the children's response to their first experience in preschool.

Thirty children who had never been to nursery school served as subjects for this study. One week prior to entry into the nursery school, the parent and child visited our lab. Five minutes of resting EKG were recorded from the child, and the mother completed the DOTS temperament questionnaire (Lerner et al. 1982). Each child was observed for 1 hour weekly (with the day of the week randomly assigned over the course of the study) for the 6 weeks of the study. We specifically coded the frequency of behaviors that, on the basis of previous data, seemed to be affected by exposure to this new environment. For example, we observed a number of different entry behaviors (e.g., solitary play, proximity to teacher, aimless wandering) as well as general play behavior (parallel, associative, constructive). A change score was then computed for both categories of behavior (entry and play). The change score for entry behavior consisted of the mean score for the first 2 weeks minus the mean score for the last 2 weeks of the behaviors listed above. The change play score consisted of the mean of the last 2 weeks minus the mean of the first 2 weeks of the frequency of behaviors listed in that category. We also computed a summary score from the individual DOTS dimensions (activity level, mood, etc.) in accordance with previous research to derive a scale score that went from easy to difficult temperament.

Six months later, the parents were again asked to fill out the DOTS questionnaire. In addition, each child was brought to our lab, and, again, 5 minutes of EKG were recorded. With these data, we were able to answer, among others, the following questions. What is the relation between the child's change in entry-related and play-related behaviors over the 6-week period and their initial level of heart-rate variability and mother-reported temperament? What is the intraindividual stability of measures of heart-rate variability and mother-reported temperament over a 6-month period of time.

Table 6 presents the correlations between the easy-difficult scale, the change entry and change play scores, and the autonomic measures recorded 1 week prior to school (heart period, heart-period variance, and $\hat{V}$). There is a significant negative correlation between mother-reported temperament and $\hat{V}$, indicating that children rated by their mothers as difficult had lower levels of RSA-influenced resting heart-rate variability. There was also a negative correlation between the change play score and $\hat{V}$, indicating that children displaying a larger change in play over the 6 weeks had higher resting levels of RSA-influenced heart-rate variability prior to school entry. The relation be-

Table 6: Intercorrelations among Temperament and Autonomic Measures Recorded 1 Week prior to School Entry ($N = 28$)

	DOTS	HP	HPV	V	CP	CE
DOTS	. . .	−.07	−.31	−.40*	.08	.07
Heart period (HP)		. . .	.71**	.68**	−.10	.33
Heart-period Variance (HPV)			. . .	.87**	−.34	.32
Vagal tone (V̂)				. . .	−.36*	.21
Change play (CP)					. . .	.24
Change entry (CE)						. . .

* $p < .05$.
** $p < .01$.

tween V̂ and the change entry score was not significant. The correlations between heart-period variance and these measures were similar to those of V̂, though they were not as strong. The correlation between heart period and the change entry score was nearly significant, indicating that children with high heart period (slow heart rate) displayed a greater change in entry behavior over the 6-week period. Thus, children who over their first 6 weeks of nursery school exhibit an increase in interactive play display higher resting levels of RSA-mediated heart rate than do the children displaying less change. In addition, mothers rated children with higher resting levels of heart-rate variability as temperamentally easier.

These data indicate that resting levels of heart-rate variability, particularly vagal tone, are associated with maternal perception of child temperament. Children rated by mothers as more difficult had higher, more stable heart rates. Vagal tone was also associated with the change in play behavior over the first 6 weeks of school. Children who played more during the latter third of that period compared to the first third had higher resting levels of vagal tone. The differences in behavior across the first 6 weeks in play may reflect the child's adaptation to the novel school environment. Entry to preschool has been viewed as mildly stressful for some children. A child's ability to cope successfully with this stress may be associated with certain temperamental differences in reactivity and regulation.

An examination of the correlations between the temperament and autonomic measures recorded 6 months later revealed a pattern similar to that found prior to the beginning of school. Children rated by their mothers as more difficult displayed lower levels of V̂ and heart-period variance, $r = −.49$ and $−.54$, $p < .05$ for both.

Pearson product-moment correlation coefficients were also computed on heart period and vagal tone between the two measurement periods (October and March). Vagal tone displayed a test-retest correlation of .85, while the test-retest for heart period was .69 (for 26 subjects). Parent report of child temperament exhibited a .59 correlation coefficient between the two time periods.

The stability of the relation between vagal tone and the mother's temperament rating should also be noted. Mothers showed a good deal of consistency in rating their children across the two time periods, and the similar, significant relation at both points in time underscores the conceptual relation between temperament and vagal tone. Finally, the 6-month stability of the autonomic measures (ranging from .69 to .85) underscores the consistency of this marker of individual differences. Kagan and his colleagues (Kagan et al. 1984) have found similar stability of their measures of heart-rate variability over a longer time span. The lack of stability reported in the neonatal study above (Stifter and Fox in press) can be addressed at this point.

There are few longitudinal studies of the development of heart-rate variability across the first year of life. Those studies that report longitudinal data have found a significant shift in the level of variability around 2–4 months of age (Harper et al. 1976; Lewis et al. 1970). This shift may reflect a general physiological reorganization of the central nervous system shifting from dominant subcortical to cortical control for many aspects of sensory processing and attention. In this vein, others (McGuire and Turkewitz 1979) have noted a shift in infant response to sensory and perceptual stimuli around this age, with a change from stimulus dominance to the child's active processing of sensory events. This reorganization may underscore the lack of stability between newborn and 5-month behaviors found in the data reported earlier. On the other hand, it does not directly explain why neonatal patterning of heart rate is a better predictor of regulation at 5 months than heart-rate variability at 5 months. One can speculate that heart-rate variability at or around birth reflects the general physiological status of the infant, including differences in the potential influence of RSA on behavior. Over the first year, the infant undergoes substantive physiological organization in the control over heart rate and the interaction of respiratory and cardio-regulatory centers. This process may not be complete until early childhood, at which time individual differences in the influence of vagal control will be more stable within individuals.

Summary and Conclusions

The purpose of this chapter was to review a program of empirical studies aimed at exploring the relation between heart-rate variability and self-regulatory behavior in infants and young children. Heart-rate variability was chosen as an independent marker of interest since neurally mediated variance in the heart-period process is the result of RSA and variations in RSA are a direct result of parasympathetic influences. Variations in parasympathetic tone or RSA have been found to be associated with certain behavioral styles, in particular, the subject's response to stress; individuals displaying high levels of resting RSA are apparently better able to modulate their response to mild stressors.

Data from three areas of research were reviewed. Studies of facial expressivity and heart-rate variability seem to indicate that individual differences in RSA-mediated heart-rate variability are associated with the expression of positive emotions such as interest and that such facial displays are often associated with states of attention. It is argued that these facial expressions serve as regulators for the young infant in its ongoing interaction with novel objects and social interaction. Research specifically examining regulatory behaviors in the first 6 months of life revealed a relation between individual differences in heart-rate variability and regulation. Neonatal levels of heart-rate variability predicted infant regulatory behaviors at 5 months in a mildly stressful situation. Note that these regulatory behaviors involved attention-like strategies, with infants who were able to focus attention on objects or persons in the environment better able to regulate their distress. Finally, data on young children who entered nursery school for the first time indicated a relation between resting levels of heart-rate variability and adaptation to preschool. Children with high levels of RSA-mediated heart rate displayed a greater change in play behavior over the first 6 weeks of school than did children with low resting levels. In addition, children whose mothers rated them as having easy temperaments displayed low and variable heart rates, while children rated as difficult displayed high and stable heart rates. This relation appeared consistent over a 6-month period.

Heart-rate variability or vagal tone may be an important indirect measure of individual differences in level of parasympathetic tone. These differences in level may be associated with the child's ability selectively to attend to stimuli in its environment. If selective attention is indeed an important strategy in the child's self-regulatory abilities, heart-rate variability may tap this important temperament factor.

References

Bell, R. Q.; Weller, G. M.; and Waldrop, M. F. 1971. Newborn and preschool: Organization of behavior and relations between periods. *Monographs of the Society for Research in Child Development,* vol. 36, no. 2, serial no. 142.

Derryberry, D., and Rothbart, M. 1984. Emotion, attention and temperament. In *Emotion, Cognition and Behavior,* ed. C. E. Izard, J. Kagan, and R. Zajonc. Cambridge: Cambridge University Press.

Eppinger, H., and Hess, L. 1915. Vagotonia: A clinical study in vegetative neurology. *Journal of Nervous and Mental Disease* 20:1–93.

Field, T., and Reite, M. 1984. Children's responses to separation from mother during the birth of another child. *Child Development* 55:1308–17.

Fox, N. A. 1983. Maturation of autonomic control in preterm infants. *Developmental Psychobiology* 16:495–504.

Fox, N. A., & Davidson, R. J. 1987. EEG asymmetry in ten month old infants in response to approach of a stranger and maternal separation. *Developmental Psychology* 23:233–40.

Fox, N. A., and Davidson, R. J. 1988. Patterns of brain electrical activity during facial signs of emotion in ten month old infants. *Developmental Psychology* 24:230–36.

Fox, N. A., and Field, T. In press. Individual differences in preschool entry behavior. *Journal of Applied Developmental Psychology.*

Fox, N. A., and Gelles, M. 1984. Face-to-face interaction in term and preterm infants. *Infant Mental Health Journal* 5:192–205.

Fox, N. A., and Porges, S. W. 1985. The relation between neonatal heart period patterns and developmental outcome. *Child Development* 56:28–37.

Garcia-Coll, C.; Kagan, J.; and Reznick, J. S. 1984. Behavioral inhibition in young children. *Child Development* 55:1005–19.

Gianino, A., and Tronick, E. 1985. The mutual-regulation model: Infant self and interactive regulative coping and defense. In *Stress and coping,* ed. T. Field, P. McCabe, and N. Schneiderman. Hillside, N.J.: Erlbaum.

Grossman, P. 1983. Respiration, stress, and cardiovascular function. *Psychophysiology* 20:284–300.

Grossman, P., and Wientjes, K. 1986. Respiratory sinus arrthymia and parasympathetic cardiac control: Some basic issues concerning quantification, applications and implications. In *Cardiorespiratory and cardiosomatic psychophysiology,* ed. R. Grossman, K. H. L. Janssen, and D. Vital. 117–38. New York: Plenum.

Harper, R. M.; Hoppenbrouwers, T.; Sterman, M. B.; McGinty, D. J.; and Hodgman, J. 1976. Polygraphic studies of normal infants during the first rate and variability as a function of state. *Pediatric Research* 10:945–51.

Healy, B. E. 1986. The heritability of autonomic patterning and social behavior in young children. Ph.D. dissertation, University of Maryland, College Park.

Izard, C. E. 1977. *Human emotions.* New York: Plenum.

Izard, C. E. 1979. *The maximally discriminative facial movement coding system (MAX).* Newark, Del.: Instructional Resources Center.

Izard, C. E.; Heubner, R. R.; Risser, D.; McGinnes, G. C.; and Dougherty, L. M. 1980. The young infant's ability to produce discrete emotional expressions. *Developmental Psychology* 16:132–40.

Kagan, J. 1971. *Change and continuity in infancy.* New York: Wiley.

Kagan, J. 1982. Heart rate and heart rate variability as signs of temperamental dimensions in infants. In *Measuring emotions in infants and children,* ed. C. E. Izard, 38–66. Cambridge: Cambridge University Press.

Kagan, J., and Lewis, M. 1965. Studies of attention in the human infant. *Merrill-Palmer Quarterly* 11:95–127.

Kagan, J.; Reznick, J. S.; Clarke, C.; Snidman, N.; and Garcia-Coll, C. 1984. Behavioral inhibition to the unfamiliar. *Child Development* 55:2212–25.

Lacey, J. K., and Lacey, B. C. 1958. The relationship of resting autonomic activity to motor impulsivity. *Research Publications and Association for Research in Nervous and Mental Disease* 36:144–209.

Langsdorf, P.; Izard, C. E.; Rayias, M.; and Hembree, E. A. 1983. Interest expression, visual fixation and heart rate change in 2- to 8-month old infants. *Developmental Psychology* 19:375–86.

Lerner, R. M.; Palermo, M.; Spiro, A.; and Nesselroade, J. R. 1982. Assessing the dimensions of temperamental individuality across the life span. The Dimensions of Temperament Survey (DOTS). *Child Development* 53:149–59.

Lewis, M.; Wilson, C. D.; Ban, P.; and Baumel, M. H. 1970. An exploratory study of resting cardiac rate and variability from the trimester of prenatal life through the first year of postnatal life. *Child Development* 41:799–812.

McCabe, P. M.; Yongue, B. G.; Porges, S. W.; and Ackles, P. K. 1984. Changes in heart period variability and spectral analysis estimate of respiratory sinus arrhythmia during aortic nerve stimulation in rabbits. *Psychophysiology* 21:149–58.

McGuire, I., and Turkewitz, G. 1979. Approach-withdrawal theory and the study of infant development. In *Cognitive growth and development*, ed. M. Bortner New York: Brunner/Mazel.

Malatesta, C. Z., and Haviland, J. 1982. Learning display rules: The socialization of emotional expression in infancy. *Child Development* 53:991–1003.

Porges, S. W. 1974. Heart rate indices of newborn attentional responsivity. *Merrill-Palmer Quarterly* 20:131–54.

Porges, S. W. 1976. Peripheral and neurochemical parallels of psychopathology: A psychophysiological model relating autonomic imbalance to hyperactivity, psychopathy, and autism. In *Advances in child development and behavior*, vol. 2, ed. H. W. Reese. New York: Academic Press.

Porges, S. W. 1983. Heart rate patterns in neonates: A potential diagnostic window to the brain. In *Infants born at risk: Physiological and perceptual processes*, ed. T. Field and A. Sostek, 3–22. New York: Grune & Stratton.

Porges, S. W. 1985. Spontaneous oscillations in heart rate: Potential index of stress. In *Animal stress: New directions in defining and evaluating the effects of stress*, ed. P. G. Moberg, 97–111. Bethesda, Md.: American Physiological Society.

Porges, S. W. 1987. Heart rate variability and individual differences in behavior. The metaphor, the model and the measure. Paper presented at the meeting of the Society for Research in Child Development, Baltimore, Md., April.

Porges, S. W.; Arnold, W. R.; and Forbes, E. J. 1973. Heart rate variability: An index of attentional responsivity in human newborns. *Developmental Psychology* 8:85–92.

Porges, S. W.; McCabe, P. M.; and Yongue, B. G. 1982. Respiratory–heart rate interactions: Physiological implications for pathophysiology and behavior. In *Perspectives in cardiovascular psychophysiology*, ed. J. Cacioppo and R. Petty, 233–64. New York: Guilford.

Posner, M. I., and Rothbart, M. K. 1986. *The concept of energy in psychological theory.* Eugene: Cognitive Science Program, University of Oregon.

Reznick, J. S.; Kagan, J.; Snidman, N.; Gersen, M.; Baak, K.; and Rosenberg, A. 1986. Inhibited and uninhibited children: A follow-up study. *Child Development* 57:660–88.

Richards, J. E. 1986. Power spectral analysis quantification of respiratory sinus arrhythmia. *Psychophysiology* 23:412.

Richards, J. E. 1987. Infant visual sustained attention and respiratory sinus arrhythmia. *Child Development* 58:488–96.

Rothbart, M. K. 1973. Laughter in young children. *Psychological Bulletin* 80:247–56.

Rothbart, M. K., and Derryberry, D. 1981. Development of individual differences in temperament. In *Advances in developmental psychology,* ed. M. E. Lamb and A. L. Brown, 1:37–86. Hillsdale, N.J.: Erlbaum.

Rothbart, M. K., and Posner, M. I. 1985. Temperament and the development of self-regulation. In *The neuropsychology of individual differences: A developmental perspective,* ed. L. C. Hartledge and C. Telzrow. New York: Plenum.

Sroufe, L. A.; Waters, E.; and Matas, L. 1974. Contextual determinants of infant affective response. In *The origins of fear,* ed. M. Lewis and L. Rosenblum, 49–72. New York: Wiley.

Sroufe, L. A., and Wunsch, J. 1972. The development of laughter in the first year of life. *Child Development* 43: 1326–44.

Stern, D. N. 1977. *The first relationship: Infant and mother.* Cambridge, Mass.: Harvard University Press.

Stifter, C. A. 1987. A study of the causal relationship between physiological functioning and later temperament from birth to five months of age. Ph.D. dissertation, University of Maryland, College Park.

Stifter, C. A., and Fox, N. A. In press. Infant reactivity and regulation: Physiological correlates of newborn and five month temperament. *Developmental Psychology.*

Stifter, C. A.; Fox, N. A.; and Porges, S. W. In press, The relationship between emotional expressivity and autonomic activity in 5 and 10-month-old infants. *Infant Behavior and Development.*

Thomas, A.; Chess, S.; and Birch, H. G. 1968. *Temperament and behavior disorders in children.* New York: New York University Press.

Tronick, E. Z. 1980. The primacy of social skills in infancy. In *The exceptional infant,* vol. 4, ed. D. Sauvin, R. Hawkins, L. O. Walker, and J. Panticull. New York: Brunner/Mazel.

Tronick, E. Z. 1982. *Social interchange in infancy: Affect cognition, and communication.* Baltimore: University Park Press.

Tronick, E.; Als, H.; Adamson, L.; Wise, S.; and Brazelton, T. B. 1978. The infant's response to entrapment between contradictory messages in face-to-face interaction. *Journal of the American Academy of Child Psychiatry* 17:1–13.

Wenger, M. A. 1941. The measurement of individual differences in autonomic balance. *Psychosomatic Medicine* 3:427–34.

Yongue, B. G.; McCabe, P. M.; Porges, S. W.; Rivera, M.; Kelley, S. L.; and Ackels, P. K. 1982. The effects of pharmacological manipulations that influence vagal control of the heart on heart period, heart-period variability and respiration in rats. *Psychophysiology* 9:426–32.

10 When Baby Makes Four: Family Influences in the Stability of Behavioral Inhibition

Doreen Arcus and Kathleen McCartney

As investigators strive to understand temperamental sources of continuity in development, they must also attend to sources of change. Studies of behavioral inhibition have uniformly documented moderate levels of stability in randomly selected samples (e.g., Reznick et. al., chap. 2, in this vol.; Stevenson-Hinde, chap. 6, in this vol.), but they have also uncovered change even when extreme groups have been studied (Garcia-Coll, Kagan, and Reznick 1984). Thus, while temperamental factors may guide the trajectory, there are probably important environmental influences on its path. Viewing the child as inextricably linked to ecological systems (Bronfenbrenner 1979) is likely to facilitate the identification of such experiential contributions to change and stability.

For most young children, the system of interest is the family and, within the family, the sibship constellation. A change in the sibship that is due to the arrival of a new baby places the elder child in what Bronfenbrenner has termed an "ecological transition," a period during which change may occur when one would otherwise expect stability. In the complexity of the modern American family, these transitions may be associated with changes in other family systems, such as maternal employment. Approximately half of mothers with children under 3 years of age were employed outside the home in 1983, and demographic trends indicate that this proportion is growing (Waldman 1983). This implies that, in addition to the sibship, substitute care is an important component of the ecological system of large numbers of young children. Furthermore, there are indications that this component is not necessarily stable. Clarke-Stewart (1984) found that 75 percent of her sample changed day-care settings—61 percent across type of setting—during a 1-

This research was supported by grants from Harvard University, the Spencer Foundation, and the National Institutes of Mental Health (1 R01 MH41807–01A1) to Kathleen McCartney. We wish to thank Roger Brown, Daniel Chambers, Jerome Kagan, and J. Steven Reznick for their comments and suggestions. We also thank a dedicated staff, especially Katherine Dobroth and Maura Kerrigan, for their assistance in data collection and coding.

year longitudinal study of 2–4-year-old children. Although many of these changes appeared to reflect age-appropriate shifts for the child, for example, from home care to group or center-based care, it is easy to imagine how a second child's arrival might precipitate day-care change. The mother who returned to work while her firstborn was young may reevaluate that decision with another child doubling the cost of day care and diminishing her financial return. Thus, transitions in two spheres of influence, sibship constellation and day-care experience, may occur in tandem. Whether these transitions are associated with change in behavioral styles that might otherwise remain stable becomes an interesting question.

It is difficult, however, to interpret the literature concerning the relation between ordinal position within the sibship constellation and behavioral style or personality, largely because many studies do not distinguish between only-born and firstborn children (as we will in this paper) and do not consider sibship spacing and sex (see Wagner, Shubert, and Shubert 1979, 1984). With regard to behavioral inhibition, studies of extreme groups have found later borns overrepresented among inhibited children and firstborns—including singletons—predominant among the uninhibited (Kagan, Reznick, and Snidman 1987; Reznick et al., chap. 2, in this vol.). Additionally, an effect of birth order for peer sociability in a randomly selected sample of 33-month-old children has been reported (Snow, Jacklin, and Macoby 1981), establishing significant differences between only borns and all others but not between firstborns and later borns. While Snow and her colleagues concluded that these effects followed from differences in interpersonal experience rather than inherent biological differences, they did not suggest mechanisms by which these effects were realized, perhaps because they did not consider potentially significant variables such as sex of the sibling or sibship spacing.

Given that the firstborn children in the Snow, Jacklin, and Maccoby (1981) study were once singletons and, presumably, more sociable at that time, the birth of a second child appears to be a source of change in the firstborn's social behavior. This may be a function of the tendency to inhibit activity in domains in which others in the environment are far more competent, for, although infants may be far less competent than their older siblings in all other areas of functioning, they are immeasurably better at securing the attention of adults. Thus, the new experience of the mother's relative unavailability may compel firstborn children to reassess their established manner of interacting with parents and other adults. In addition, firstborns who concurrently experience change in day care are also exposed to changes in peer-group and care-giver interaction, possibly requiring some reevaluation and readjustment.

The effects of such disruptions during these periods of transition can be considered in terms of social comparison theory (Festinger 1954), that is, the tendency for individuals to prefer to evaluate themselves in comparison to others who are similar. This theory provides a framework for conceptualizing the process of reassessment and change in the firstborn child as well as for explaining why all children are not immobilized by constant comparison to the superior competence of their parents. Thus, the more similar the comparison child to the evaluating child, the more severe the reassessment, a situation with further implications for firstborns when the younger sibling is of the same sex. In other words, because children as young as 2 years have been shown to understand aspects of gender differences (Kuhn, Nash, and Brucken 1978), it may be that sex of the sibling is a salient dimension for comparisons by firstborns.

This change via social comparison is consistent with the observations of many investigators who, though seldom employing a control group, have documented adverse reactions of the eldest child to the birth of a sibling (Dunn and Kendrick 1983; Field and Reite 1984; Legg, Sherrick, and Wadland 1975; McCall 1984; Trause et al. 1981). For example, marked increases in the firstborn's acts of "deliberate naughtiness" while the mother fed, diapered, or otherwise tended to the second-born infant were observed by Dunn and Kendrick (1983). These instances provide many illustrations of the firstborn child's reaction to his or her sibling's ability to engage the mother's attention, as in the following anecdote: "One child, whose mother and baby sister were gazing at each other in a long absorbed exchange, picked up his cup, which had a lid with holes in the top, and looking across to the baby and his ecstatic cooing mother, started to sprinkle his milk all over the sofa" (Dunn and Kendrick 1983, 42).

The traditional clinical position (Legg, Sherrick, and Wadland 1975; Spock 1969) has been that these acts of deliberate naughtiness are symptoms of emotional upset—acts of rage or jealousy on the part of the firstborn designed to punish either the infant or the mother by disrupting the closeness of their interaction—rather than misguided attempts to regain the mother's attention. However, this argument is incompatible with the observation that firstborns of mothers who breast-fed the new infant displayed significantly fewer of these disruptive behaviors than did children whose mother bottle-fed the new baby (Dunn and Kendrick 1983). With one hand free and without bottles or formula to prepare beforehand, nursing mothers are apparently better able to distract and engage the firstborn, resulting in less disruption from the older child and, at the same time, more joint play. It is therefore reasonable to conclude that, because it is adult attention that dampens them, the older child's new, unconventional overtures are attempts to win that attention.

There is a much smaller body of literature suggesting that similar changes in children's social behavior may be associated with changes in day-care environment. For example, 6-year-old children with more than two changes in care setting prior to the age of 5 display more insecure, fearful, and "clingy" behavior than peers with relatively stable child-care arrangements (Moore 1969). It has also been observed that children in day care increase positive affect and proximity seeking to more stable care givers (Cummings 1980). Modifications in child-care arrangements are likely to require the child to adjust to a new peer group and a new care giver with established patterns of social interaction. Instability in day care may therefore disrupt stability in the child's behavioral style with adults.

To test the hypotheses that instability in the social domain would follow the birth of a sibling and changes in day care, we have focused on the interaction of behavioral inhibition with environmental events in a randomly selected sample of 21–35-month-old children. By observing children after the birth of their first sibling, comparing them to others who did not experience the birth of a younger sibling, and examining differences in child-care experiences, we have sought to identify family influences on the relative change or stability of behavioral inhibition during this time period.

Methods

Subjects

Subjects were selected on the basis of birth-order status from a larger pool of children who had participated in a longitudinal study of mother-child inter-action and language development, described in detail elsewhere (McCartney 1986). The original 40 mother-child dyads were recruited from the Cam-bridge, Massachusetts, area by consulting local birth records, through a com-munity health maintenance organization, and from canvassing a local shop-ping center in an effort to ensure as random a sample as possible from both working- and middle-class families. Half the children were male and half female; all were Caucasian, native speakers of standard English, and, by their mothers' reports, free of any medical problems.

All children were observed twice in their homes, once at 21 months and again at 35 months. Because we were interested in examining the effects of the birth of a sibling, we selected subjects who were singletons at the first visit and firstborn at the second visit for our sibling group and subjects who were singletons at both visits for our no-sibling group. This led to a loss of nine subjects from the original pool: three because of attrition following the first visit (two families moved, leaving no forwarding address, and another declined further participation because of time constraints), two because of technical failures during videotaping, and four because they already had younger siblings at the first visit. The remaining 31 subjects were all single-tons at the first observation, which took place within 2 weeks of their 21-month birth date. In the 14-month interval between this initial visit and the visit at 35 months, 12 of the families had a second child (the sibling group), while the only-born status of the remaining 19 (the no-sibling group) was left unchanged.

The two groups did not differ by sex, maternal level of education, or verbal intelligence as assessed by the Peabody Picture Vocabulary Test (PPVT; Dunn 1979) at 35 months. There were, however, significant differences between the groups on day-care experience. The sibling group spent fewer hours per week in substitute care at 21 months (sibling group, mean = 9.67; no-sibling group, mean = 19.53, t = 1.68, p ≤ .10) and at 35 months (sibling group, mean = 5.83; no-sibling group, mean = 19.79, t = 2.79, p ≤ .01), and the groups differed significantly on the stability of number of hours spent in daycare from 21 to 35 months (sibling group, r = − .02; no-sibling group, r = .70, Z = − 2.13, p ≤ .05).

The 12 children in the sibling group ranged in age from 24 to 33 months at their sibling's arrival (median age = 30 months). A majority of these new siblings were female (10 out of 12), thus producing five same-sex (female in all cases) and seven different-sex dyads.

Procedure

Two female research assistants conducted the 21- and 35-month home observations, one serving as the interviewer and session coordinator, the other serving as the videocamera operator. While the camera operator set up the equipment, the session coordinator explained that the purpose of this developmental study was to gather information about how mothers and children play together.

Mothers first completed a short demographic questionnaire asking about parents' age, education, and occupation as well as about the child's substitute care and medical histories. Mothers and children were then asked to play together with a standard set of toys for about 25 minutes and were encouraged to do so as normally as possible despite the presence of researchers in the room. Next, mothers were given the Toddler Temperament Scale (TTS; Fullard, McDevitt, and Carey 1978; for a review, see Hubert et al. 1982) to begin while children played alone with a new toy for 10 minutes. Finally, mothers and children were asked to put the toys away; this typically lasted for 5 minutes.

At this point, the gift-giving task, designed to elicit individual differences in behavioral inhibition, was introduced. The session coordinator explained that the purpose of this episode was to see how the child reacted to another adult. Each mother was asked to refrain from initiating interaction with her child and to respond to any overtures by encouraging the child to return to the experimenter. The session coordinator then told the child, "You did a really good job today. Now [the camera operator] has something for you."

It is important to note that the camera operator had not yet interacted with either the child or the mother. All conversation between the experimenters and subjects had been through the session coordinator, minimizing the likelihood that the child would have adapted, either directly or vicariously (see Feiring, Lewis, and Starr 1984), to the second experimenter prior to her stepping from behind the camera and offering the child a gift. It should also be noted that, although the same experimenter served as the camera operator for all but two of the 35-month visits, six different experimenters performed that function for the 21-month visit.

The ensuing gift-giving episode followed a standardized procedure in which the experimenter stood approximately 6 feet from the child, held out a brightly wrapped gift (a book), and said, "[Name], look what I have for you." This statement was repeated every 15 seconds until either the child approached the experimenter or 60 seconds had passed, at which time the experimenter approached the child. After the child had taken the gift, the experimenter followed a five-line script, each time awaiting the child's response or reaction to, "Let me help you open your present," "Oh! What is it?" "Can you turn the pages?" "What do you see?" and, finally, "Let's look at the book together." A 5-minute period of unstructured story reading followed. Thus, gift giving comprised three distinct phases: the approach, which terminated with, "Let me help you open your present"; the questions that followed; and the story, beginning with, "Let's look at the book together."

Videotaping was terminated at the end of this 5-minute interval, ending the 21-month visit. Administration of the revised PPVT followed gift giving to conclude the visit at 35 months.

Coding

Videotapes of gift giving were coded for the child's approach and withdrawal behaviors. The approach phase was coded for latencies to take the first step, to approach within arm's reach, to touch the gift, and to vocalize. Verbal or nonverbal response to standardized questions was scored for presence or absence. Initial affect and overall engagement were judged to be positive, negative, or neutral. Finally, six behaviors were scored as present or absent in each of the three phases of the task: retreats from the experimenter, needs proximity of mother, makes overtures toward the experimenter, positive returns to mother (e.g., for communicative purposes), returns to mother in distress, and clings to mother. The final score for each of these six variables became the number of phases in which the behavior occurred. Median interjudge agreement for both visits was 90 percent at 21 months and 85 percent at 35 months (range, .60–1.00 for both); consensus became the basis for final judgment in cases of discrepancy.

In scoring the TTS, several of the six-point Likert scales were reordered to provide consistency in the direction of the correlations. Thus, positive numeric values correspond to positive values of the construct being measured for all the TTS scales.

Data Reduction

Separate principal components analyses using varimax rotation were conducted for the 21- and 35-month observations to serve as a guide in the construction of composite variables. Two theoretically related composite variables emerged at both ages. The first, *approach to experimenter,* comprised overlapping, though not identical, items at 21 and 35 months: latencies to take the first step, to approach within arm's length, and to touch the gift at 21 months (Cronbach's alpha = .95) and the above latencies plus latency to vocalize, overtures toward the experimenter (loading negatively), and retreats from the experimenter at 35 months (Cronbach's alpha = .88). The second, *proximity to mother,* included clings to mother, returns in distress to mother, and needs proximity of mother at both 21 (Cronbach's alpha = .83) and 35 (Cronbach's alpha = .53) months.

The approach to experimenter composite variable was constructed by individually standardizing each of the component variables, adding them, and reversing the signs, when necessary, so that positive values reflected increased approach. However, in the course of reviewing videotapes, we began to suspect that the proximity to mother composites, which were based on component variables that had been coded only as present or absent, might not have completely captured the variability among children. Under the original scoring system, for example, a child who clung to the mother once and a child who clung 10 times during a given phase of the observation would have received identical scores. Therefore, we collapsed over the component variables (clings, returns, and needs proximity) and counted the total number of occurrences over the entire gift-giving task. These numbers, computed separately for the 21- and 35-month visit, became the final proximity to mother composite scores. Recomputing the principle components analysis using the final proximity to mother composite resulted in replication of factors for 21 months, but 35-month results approximated only approach to experimenter. Thus, it should be noted that these proximity variables, while grounded in the results of principle components analyses, are not strictly defined factor-based scores.

In order to account for the effect of day-care differences by using partial correlation procedures, two composite variables were constructed. The first, *day-care change,* was a sum of standard scores of components that reflected the magnitude (but not the direction) of change from 21 to 35 months. These components were change in setting (coded as follows: 0 = no change;

1 = change across type of day care, e.g., from family day care to a day-care center; and 2 = starting or stopping day care) and change in total hours per week spent in day care (scored as the absolute value of hours at 35 months minus hours at 21). The second, *overall day care,* reflected the change variables above, setting and hours, as well as number of hours spent in substitute care at 21 and at 35 months. Measures of internal consistency, Cronbach's alpha, were .89 and .63, respectively. Plots of each of these day-care variables against inhibition variables were examined to rule out any obvious nonlinear trends—trends for which partial correlation procedures would not control. Although Jacobson and Willie (1984) found a U-shaped relation between the number of hours spent in substitute care and the amount of distress displayed in the Strange Situation, no such relation was found in these data.

We then reclassified the groups on day-care measures. The first, *day-care change* versus *day-care stable,* was created by assigning those with zero values for both components of the composite day-care change variable to the day-care stable group and those with nonzero scores to the day-care change group. These groups did not differ by sex, level of maternal education, hours per week in day care at 21 or 35 months, PPVT verbal intelligence at 35 months, or birth-order change. The second, *day care* versus *no day care,* was created by assigning the 14 children receiving substitute care at both 21 and 35 months to the day-care group and the 10 receiving none at either time to the no day care group. These groups also did not differ by sex, 35-month PPVT, or birth-order change. Level of maternal education, $t = 1.91$, $p \leq .05$, did differ significantly: mothers of children in day care, on the average, holding 4-year college degrees and mothers of children at home, on the average, holding 2-year college degrees.

Results

The results are organized around four main questions: (1) What are the characteristics of our measures for all 31 subjects? (2) How do the sibling and no-sibling groups differ with regard to the stability of behavioral and report indices of inhibition? (3) For firstborn children, how do recency of the sibling's arrival and sex of the sibling pair affect these same indices? (4) What are the contributions of the associated differences in day-care experience?

To address the last three questions, stability coefficients for corresponding groups were compared by converting each of the r's to the associated Fisher z's and then computing the standard normal deviate Z for the difference (Rosenthal and Rosnow 1984). In addition, effect-size estimates were computed. In the light of the low power afforded by our sample size (less than .15 for medium effects at $\alpha = .05$ [Cohen 1977]), effect-size estimates are particularly important to consider when comparisons fail to reach significance, de-

Table 1: Synchronous and Autocorrelations for Behavioral and Report Indices of Inhibition at 21 and 35 Months for All ($N = 31$) Subjects

	(1)	(2)	(3)	(4)	(5)
1. Approach experimenter, 21 months	. . .				
2. Proximity to mother, 21 months	−.43**	. . .			
3. TTS approach, 21 months	−.20	−.12	. . .		
4. Approach experimenter, 35 months	.36**	.01	−.04	. . .	
5. Proximity to mother, 35 months	−.11	.31*	−.05	−.28	. . .
6. TTS approach, 35 months	.13	−.27	.59***	.19	−.17

* $p \leq .10$.
** $p \leq .05$.
*** $p \leq .01$.

spite the fact that these effects are somewhat unstably estimated. Note that for q (the difference between Fisher z's), an effect of at least .10 is considered small, .30 moderate, and .50 large (Cohen 1977). Finally, it should be noted that sampling distributions are the same when comparing partial r's as they are for simple correlations with reduced sample size.

All Subjects

Intercorrelations among the behavioral and the report measures of inhibition at 21 and 35 months are summarized in table 1. Intercorrelations between approach to experimenter and proximity to mother were in the predicted direction at both ages, reaching significance, $r = -.43$, $p \leq .05$, at 21 months. Examination of correlations across types of measure (i.e., between behavior and report) revealed a predictably less consistent picture. The TTS approach failed to correlate significantly with either behavioral measure of inhibition at either time.

Examination of correlations from 21 to 35 months revealed stability, moderate for behavioral measures (approach to experimenter, $r = .36, p \leq .05$; proximity to mother, $r = .31, p \leq .10$) and predictably higher for report, TTS approach, $r = .59, p \leq .001$. Comparing scores over time revealed one significant change for the entire group. Children displayed less proximity to mother at 35 months than at 21 months, $t = 4.20; p < .001$.

Because six different experimenters collected the 21-month behavioral data, a one-way analysis of variance was conducted. This analysis failed to show an effect of experimenter for either of the two composite variables.

Sibling versus No-Sibling Comparisons

Table 2 summarizes correlations for behavior and report indices of inhibition from 21 to 35 months for the sibling and no-sibling groups. Partialing out the effects of each of the day-care measures resulted in similar correla-

Table 2: Stability Coefficients for Behavioral and Report Indices of Inhibition from 21 to 35 Months by Birth-Order Groups

| | Zero-order r | | | |
	Sibling ($N = 12$)	No sibling ($N = 19$)	Z	q
Approach to experimenter	.11	.65***	−1.60	−.66
Proximity to mother	−.29	.42*	−1.79*	−.75
TTS approach	.69***	.58***	.45	.19
	Partial r: Controlling for Day-care Change			
Approach to experimenter	.08	.68***	−1.71*	−.75
Proximity to mother	−.26	.38*	−1.52	−.67
TTS approach	.69***	.50**	.68	.30
	Partial r: Controlling for Day-Care Hours, 21 and 35 Months			
Approach to experimeter	.07	.70***	−1.72*	−.80
Proximity to mother	−.38	.61*	−1.56	−1.11
TTS approach	.83***	.64**	.93	.43
	Partial r: Controlling for Overall Day Care			
Approach to experimeter	.06	.66***	−1.67*	.73
Proximity to mother	−.32	.37*	−1.64	.72
TTS approach	.69***	.56**	.49	.22

* $p \leq .10$.
** $p \leq .05$
*** $p \leq .01$.

tions. Comparing these correlations between groups yielded large effect sizes that were marginally significant for approach to experimenter with higher correlations in the no-sibling group but not significant for proximity to mother when day care was controlled. The highly stable maternal report measure, TTS approach, did not differ significantly from the sibling to the no-sibling group but yielded a moderate effect size when partial correlations were compared.

When we checked for prior differences between the groups on measures of inhibition (i.e., differences at 21 months prior to the arrival of the sibling), we found a trend for the sibling group to demonstrate less inhibition than the no-sibling group as measured by approach to experimenter, $t = -1.72$, $p \leq .10$. Comparing the means over time revealed another interesting trend in approach to experimenter, using the z-score of this measure. The no-sibling group—originally the more inhibited of the two—recovered by 35 months when compared to the sibling group, whose scores did not change appreciably, $t = -2.48$, $p < .05$ (note that the negative t-value reflects relative positioning of the z for approach to experimenter). The decrease in proximity to mother at 35 months, noted for the entire sample, held for both groups.

Table 3: Inhibition Measures at 35 Months and Age of Firstborn at Sibling's Arrival: Zero-order and Corresponding Partial Correlations, Controlling for Sex of Firstborn

	Age at Sibling's Arrival	
	r	Partial r
TTS approach	.28	.09
Proximity to mother	.42	.34
Approach to experimenter	− .30	− .16

$* p \le .10.$
$** p \le .05.$
$*** p \le .01.$

Comparisons within the Sibling Group

We examined two sources of variation within the sibling group. Recency of the sibling's arrival was examined by correlating the firstborn's age at the sibling's birth with 35-month inhibition measures, controlling for sex of the firstborn because of the correlation with age at arrival (girls tending to be younger, $r = -.59, p \le .05$). Results are presented in table 3. Correlations were not significant for any inhibition measures, although the effect size associated with proximity to mother, $r = .42$, is moderate.

We then examined correlations between firstborn sex, sibling sex, dyad sex (i.e., same or different), and measures of inhibition. Controlling for the effect of day care, neither sex of the firstborn nor sex of the sibling alone produced any significant correlations; however, there was a high positive correlation between approach to experimenter at 35 months and membership in an opposite-sex dyad, $r = .68, p \le .05$. Furthermore, dividing the sibling group by same- versus opposite-sex dyad revealed strikingly different patterns for the two subgroups in the stability of inhibition over time. Controlling for overall day care, subjects in same-sex dyads demonstrated a high and significant negative correlation for approach to experimenter from 21 to 35 months, $r = -.932, p \le .05$, while subjects in different-sex dyads demonstrated a significantly different pattern: a high positive correlation for this same variable over time, $r = .64$. The maternal report variable did not yield significant correlations for each group; nor was the difference between groups significant, although a large effect size is associated with this difference.

It should be recalled, however, that, in addition to extremely small sample sizes for the dyad groups, these results are confounded by the fact that all same-sex dyads are female. For comparison table 4 presents stability coefficients for the sibling group split by sex of the dyad and for the no-sibling group split by sex. Males and females without siblings do not yield significantly different correlations for inhibition measures over time when the effects of day care are controlled. Note that restricted variability in proximity to

Table 4: Stability Coefficients for Behavioral and Report Indices of Inhibition from 21 to 35 Months within the Sibling Group by Same-Sex Sibling Dyad (All Female) or Different-Sex Sibling Dyad and within the No-Sibling Group by Sex

	Zero-Order r							
	Sibling Group by Dyad				No Sibling Group by Sex			
	Same Sex ($N = 5$)	Different Sex ($N = 7$)	Z	q	Females ($N = 9$)	Males ($N = 10$)	Z	q
Approach to experimenter	− .86*	.67*	− 2.33**	− 2.10	.75**	.60*	.50	.28
TTS approach	− .02	.77**	− 1.48	− 1.04	.81***	.34	1.39	.77
	Partial r: Controlling for Overall Day Care							
Approach to experimenter	− .932**	.64	− 2.11**	− 2.43	.71**	.56	.37	.25
TTS approach	− .64	.48	1.11	− 1.28	.77**	.70**	.25	.15

* $p \leq .10$.
** $p \leq .05$.
*** $p \leq .01$.

mother at 35 months precludes meaningful comparison with such small group sizes.

Comparisons by Day-Care Groups

Analyses parallel to those conducted for the sibling and the no-sibling groups were conducted for each of the day-care groups, controlling for the effect of birth-order change in partial correlations. Table 5 summarizes the results of the day-care change versus day-care stable manipulation. Comparisons of correlations between these groups yielded significant differences only for approach to experimenter, $Z = -1.94, p \leq .05; Z = -1.83, p \leq .10$, children in stable day-care arrangements displaying more stable inhibition behavior. Neither proximity to mother nor TTS approach differed with regard to stability coefficients between these two groups. It should be noted, however, that the day-care stable group included 10 (out of the total 18) children who were not receiving day care at either 21 or 35 months, that is, who were stable in the absence of day care.

Thus, we again split our sample, this time to examine stability differences in inhibition associated with presence or absence of day care at both observations; table 6 summarizes the results of this manipulation. The only significant difference was for the partial correlation of TTS approach from 21 to 35 months, controlling for the effect of birth-order change, $Z = -2.39$, $p \leq .05$. Mother's report of approach was much more stable, $r = .87$, $p \leq .01$, when children were in day care at both observations than when children were at home, $r = .10$, N.S., at both times. Stability coefficients for

Table 5: Stability Coefficients for Behavioral and Report Indices of Inhibition from 21 to 35 Months by Day-care Change Groups Based on the Composite Variable Reflecting Change in Hours and Setting

	Zero-Order r			
	Day-care Change (N = 13)	Day-care Stable (N = 18)	Z	q
Approach to experimenter	-.10	.60***	-1.94**	-.80
Proximity to mother	.31	.31	.00	.00
TTS approach	.65**	.47**	.65	.26
	Partial r: Controlling for Birth-Order Change			
Approach to experimenter	.03	.67***	-1.83*	-.78
Proximity to mother	.31	.26	.03	.06
TTS approach	.70**	.47**	.84	.36

* $p \leq .10$.
** $p \leq .05$.
*** $p \leq .01$.

behavioral measures of inhibition, on the other hand, did not differ significantly between these two groups.

Discussion

Several preliminary points should be made. First, subject selection procedures in this study differ from those employed in much of the work on behavioral inhibition. These subjects were selected on the basis of birth-order characteristics from a random sample, and these results, therefore, may not hold for

Table 6: Stability Coefficients for Behavioral and Report Indices of Inhibition from 21 to 35 Months for Groups on Presence or Absence of Day Care

	Zero-Order r			
	Day Care (N = 14)	No Day Care (N = 10)	Z	q
Approach to experimenter	.38	.31	.16	.08
Proximity to mother	.14	.35	-.46	-.22
TTS approach	.72***	.34	1.17	.55
	Partial r: Controlling for Birth-Order Change			
Approach to experimenter	.46	.49	.08	-.04
Proximity to mother	.15	.34	.39	-.20
TTS approach	.87***	.10	-2.39**	1.23

** $p \leq .05$.
*** $p \leq .01$.

groups selected to be extreme in measures of inhibition. When investigators select extreme groups to study, they may be selecting children whose temperament is so strongly influenced by biology that the type of environmental influence described in this study is relatively powerless (e.g., Kagan, Reznick, and Snidman 1987, 1988). Others (Buss and Plomin 1984) have suggested that children in the central range of a temperamental dimension may be more subject to environmental influences than children at the extremes, and there is a theoretical basis for this contention in the work of personality-type theorists (e.g., Allport 1961). Such views imply that these—and any other results generated by the middle ranges—ought not to be linearly extrapolated to the extremes without further investigation.

These differences in subject selection also affect the degree to which agreement is expected between behavior and report measures of inhibition. When subjects are screened by maternal interview for the selection of extremes, maternal report is, to a degree, built into further behavioral measures. In our sample, however, these variables are independent.

Second, these statistical analyses rely heavily on the use of partial correlations, and we acknowledge the limitations of controlling for the contribution of an event to an outcome in this fashion. We realize, for example, that partialing out the effects of birth-order change in examining the effects of day care does not provide children in both day-care groups with the same sibship constellation and the same family-life experiences. Experiments in nature, however, do not allow for random assignment to groups. Thus, we are left with the inevitable trade-off between experimental design and ecological validity involved in this type of research.

The third point concerns measures. The behavioral measure approach to experimenter provides evidence for heterotypic continuity (Kagan 1971; Buss and Plomin 1975) in the expression of behavioral inhibition during the preschool years. The performance latencies of the 21-month-old are related to the later 35-month composite that contains additional communicative behaviors, including latencies to vocalize and overtures to the unfamiliar adult. This implies that, unlike the younger child, the typical 35-month-old has sufficiently developed his or her expressive linguistic competence so that these skills are under control and capable of being readily employed in a manner consistent with the child's temperamental disposition when exposed to a novel and, for some, stressful situation. Proximity to mother, however, appears less robust at 35 months as reflected in the .53 measure of internal consistency. Thus, approach to experimenter appears to be the primary behavioral index and proximity to mother secondary in the gift-giving paradigm. These variables are also consistent with those found to be salient in this age period by other investigators (Garcia-Coll, Kagan, and Reznick 1984).

In our sample, we do not find significant correlations between home observation and maternal report of inhibition. Although some investigators have found such relations (e.g., Reznick et al., chap. 2, in this vol.), others have found it necessary to modify the TTS to obtain behavior-report correlation (e.g., Stevenson-Hinde, chap. 6, in this vol.). Because report measures comprised subjective as well as objective components (Bates and Bayles 1984; Bronfenbrenner, Alvarez, and Henderson 1984; Gordon 1983; Kagan et al. 1986; McClelland 1980; Rothbart and Goldsmith 1985), we do not find this divergence problematic. Furthermore, this lack of convergence extends to different patterns of variability over our group manipulations, leading us to conclude that, while each may be a valid source of data, these behavior and report measures are proverbial apples and oranges, each making important, though seldom overlapping, contributions to our findings.

We depend on behavioral indices to answer the question that prompted this study. Do children demonstrate change in behavioral inhibition when they shift from being an only child to being a firstborn child as compared to peers who remain only children? We find that they do, as indexed by their approach behavior to an unfamiliar adult when associated differences in day-care experience are taken into account. This finding is consistent with the findings of Snow, Jacklin, and Maccoby (1981) as well as with the body of literature documenting adverse reactions of the eldest child to the birth of a sibling (Dunn and Kendrick 1983; Field and Reite 1984; Legg, Sherrick, and Wadland 1975; McCall 1984; Trause et al. 1981). Furthermore, the age range we have examined (i.e., firstborns between 24 and 33 months at the siblings' birth) falls within the spacing interval that Wagner, Schubert, and Schubert (1979) found to be disadvantageous to psychosocial development compared to the relative advantage of 36–54-month spacing. While bolstering confidence in our findings, this convergence mandates caution regarding generalization to firstborns of other ages.

It is intriguing that this behavioral change is preceded by differences in approach behavior prior to the sibling's birth, with mothers of the less inhibited group introducing a second child and mothers of the more inhibited group not doing so—at least not until after the child is 35 months old—and perhaps contributing to the relative recovery of this group. Similar findings have been reported in studies of rhesus monkeys. Specifically, mothers of young monkeys who are active and independent at a relatively early age will tend to have another offspring during the next breeding season, whereas mothers of infants who are relatively inactive and tend to keep close to their mothers are more likely not to conceive again for another year (Simpson et al. 1981). Furthermore, children who show extreme behavioral inhibition as toddlers tend to have histories that might reflect lower central thresholds of reactivity. Symptoms include irritability in infancy, frequent crying during the first 6 months, sleep difficulties during the first year, constipation and allergies during the first 2 years, and fears and nightmares during the second and third years (Kagan, Reznick, and Snidman 1987). Albeit speculative, these findings collectively suggest a possible child effect in family-planning strategies. Parents of more inhibited children may feel that the child would benefit from the prolonged attention they are able to provide given increased sibling spacing. In addition, parents of extremely inhibited children, recently having coped with a difficult infancy, may themselves feel the need for additional time before doing so again.

When we look at change within the sibling group (although we must look cautiously because of sample size), we do find order emerging from apparent chaos as a function of the sex of the dyad. Firstborns with a sibling of the same sex demonstrate a high negative correlation between approach behaviors at 21 and 35 months, while firstborns with a different-sex sibling tend to maintain their rank order on the approach measure. These results are consistent with earlier findings from older subjects. Using Q-sort measures, Rosenberg (1982) found both males and females in same-sex sibling dyads to demonstrate less stability at late adolescence and early adulthood than individuals in cross-sex dyads. Earlier, using teacher ratings of 5- and 6-year-olds to examine the effect of ordinal position, spacing, and sex of the subject and sibling on children's attitudes toward adults, Koch (1955) found that "those in opposite sex pairs . . . were rated more friendly to adults than were those in same sex pairs. The difference is significant at the one percent point; however, only in the group in which the sibs differ from two to four years in age" (p. 23). The specificity of Koch's finding again suggests that our observations may be limited to this spacing interval.

The lack of effects produced by recency of the sibling's arrival may be a function of the limited time interval sampled in our data. In repeated observations over a 14-month period following the sibling's arrival, Dunn and Kendrick (1983) found sleep problems and excessive attention demands to decrease by 14 months after these behaviors had increased markedly from the prenatal to the 1-month visit; however, other problems, such as "miserable moods" and worry, increased over that same time period. Therefore, the possibility of further change in indices of behavioral inhibition beyond the interval sampled should not be discounted.

While it has been suggested that a stable day-care experience may mediate the child's sense of displacement at the birth of the sibling (Lamb, Chase-Lansdale, and Owen 1979), we do not find consistency in day-care arrangement for firstborn children in our sibling group. Instead, we find that day-care change and change in sibship status provide correlated, though apparently nonredundant, contributions to stability of inhibition. These findings are consistent with social comparison theory and the empirical evidence of Moore (1969) and Cummings (1980).

Nevertheless, conclusions regarding the role of day-care changes in the stability of behavioral inhibition remain vague because, as suggested by Phillips, McCartney, and Scarr (1987), the child's social competence may be related more to specific, rather than general, aspects of the day-care setting. The necessity of collecting more complete information in future studies is underscored by Clarke-Stewart's (1982) comment, "Change in itself is not necessarily detrimental for development, and staying with a poor caregiver is undoubtedly worse for the child than changing to a good one" (p. 110).

Although we see marked instability in the child's inhibition behavior following the birth of a sibling and change in day care, we do not, however, see similar effects in maternal report. Ballard et al. (1984), using parental report measures, also failed to find change in overall behavior or in anxiety following the birth of a sibling. The premature and high-risk siblings in their study, on the average, were still hospitalized at the time of the data collection, whereas the siblings in our study had, on the average, been home several months. Thus, discrepancy between behavioral and report measures is not well documented following the birth of a sibling; it has, however, been demonstrated for sociability as a function of hours in substitute care. Vlietstra (1981) found that day-care teachers rated full-time children as more aggressive and having more peer problems than part-time enrollees, although observers recorded more positive peer and on-task behavior for children attending full time. Such behavior-report discrepancies must be considered in the light of several possibilities.

First, those mothers who had planned on having more than one child may have never actually viewed their firstborn as an only child, even prior to the birth of subsequent children. If this is so, then maternal report stability in the presence of behavioral change may reflect stability in the subjective component of mothers' judgments. The observation that adults—independent of their parenting status—hold expectations about children that are based on birth-order status alone (Baskett 1985) supports that explanation. Analogously, trained care givers may also hold expectations about a child's behavior that are based on hours in day care or, more probably, on hours away from the mother.

Second, report stability for the sibling group may reflect mothers' tendency to adopt a within-family frame for making personality judgments and comparisons, a tendency that may contribute to the deidentification of siblings (Schachter 1982, Schachter and Stone 1985). Thus, the birth of a second child may serve to solidify mothers' perceptions of the firstborn in such a way as to facilitate indentification of differences and distinctions between the two.

Third, discrepancies between behavior and report may stem from our cultural biases toward continuity, biases that have shaped research programs and developmental theory for the past century (Kagan 1983). Perhaps because of this bias toward seeing consistency in personality, mothers have filtered perceived change through whatever external sources of influence (e.g., traumatic events and social institutions like school or day care) are available.

This filtering heuristic may help explain the increased stability in maternal report that we observe in the day care group compared to the no daycare group. Although this finding is inconsistent with the traditional view of parent-report measures as being highly reliable (and therefore valid) by virtue of the parent's opportunity to view the child in a wide range of circumstances, it is consistent with recent findings in social psychology, specifically, in research framed by attribution theory (for a discussion, see Brown [1986]). Hastie (1984) has demonstrated, for example, that causal reasoning tends to follow the observation of an incongruent or unexpected event and that, because of the increased processing required to explain unexpected events, it is these events—that is, the atypical rather than the typical—that tend to be recalled later. Presumably, mothers who spend more time with their children (i.e., the no day care group) have more opportunity to observe discrepancies in their children's behavior than mothers whose children spend time away in substitute care. Furthermore, mothers of children at home have no ready explanation for the discrepant event and may therefore process it longer or more deeply than mothers whose observations of unexpected behaviors could be quickly attributed to an outside source of influence ("She must have picked that up at day care"). Thus, as we have observed, recall and report of behaviors on instruments such as the TTS may be composed of a more atypical set of events for the former group than for the latter.

Along these same lines, it is likely that procedural differences contribute to the discrepancy between our findings and those of other investigations (Dunn and Kendrick 1983; Stewart et al. 1987) with regard to maternal report and the birth of a sibling. Studies that explicitly follow a child before and after a sibling's birth tacitly define behaviors of interest to the researchers as those that are attributable to actor-situation interaction rather than to the actor alone. In our study, the birth of a second child was incidental to subject selection, and our implicit request was for mothers to report those behaviors that were attributable only to the actor. Thus, while other investigations have gathered maternal judgments of the child in a given situation—which may not be what the mother would judge to be the child's "true" personality or style—we have been able to address the other side of the coin, the degree to which mothers perceive change in the child per se rather than changes that are situationally specific. Clearly, one source of information is neither more important nor more valid than the other; the important point is to recognize the sources and implications of these differences.

It is critical to recall that our discussion of the effect of a sibling's birth and day-care changes on the behavior of the firstborn is limited to the elder child's tendency to display behavioral inhibition and that our measures rely on the child's response to an unfamiliar adult. We are not discussing either the child's relationship to the new sibling or the child's relationship with peers—or any of a host of other temperamental variables that have received attention in the literature. France-Kaatrude and Smith (1985) have recently employed social comparison theory to explain the self-evaluations of first through fourth graders, and our results suggest that much younger children may evaluate aspects of their social behavior toward adults in a similar manner. Thus, behavior patterns that may be temperamentally driven appear subject to the effects of exogenous events via children's perception of these events and their saliency to the child's own performance. Further study is required to determine the extent to which the relative dominance of biology for temperamental types or extremes allows for, or provides a buffer against, such environmental influences.

Examining the child apart from important ecological systems can obscure patterns and regularities in social behavior, and this study demonstrates the importance of considering both the child's sibship constellation and his or her day-care experience as influential contexts. Of course, all results are inextricably tied to the sources of their data, and we demonstrate very different processes at work in the behavior and report measures employed here. It thus behooves the researchers interested in tracking behavioral inhibition over time to acknowledge the contributions of each of these sources of influence.

References

Allport, G. W. 1961. *Pattern and growth in personality.* New York: Holt, Rinehart & Winston.

Ballard, J. L.; Maloney, M.; Shank, M.; and Hollister, L. 1984. Sibling visits to a newborn intensive care unit: Implications for siblings, parents, and infants. *Child Psychiatry and Human Development* 14: 203–14.

Baskett, L. M. 1985. Sibling status effects: Adult expectations. *Developmental Psychology* 21:441–45.

Bates, J. E., and Bayles, K. 1984. Objective and subjective components in mothers' perceptions of their children from age 6 months to 3 years. *Merrill-Palmer Quarterly* 30: 111–30.

Bronfenbrenner, U. 1979. *The ecology of human development: Experiments by nature and design.* Cambridge, Mass.: Harvard University Press.

Bronfenbrenner, U.; Alvarez, W. F.; and Henderson, C. R. 1984. Working and watching: Maternal employment and parents' perceptions of their three-year-old children. *Child Development* 55:1362–78.

Brown, R. 1986. *Social psychology: The second edition.* New York: Wiley.

Buss, A. H., and Plomin, R. 1975. *A temperament theory of personality.* New York: Wiley.

Buss, A. H., and Plomin, R. 1984. *Temperament: Early developing personality traits.* Hillsdale, N.J.: Erlbaum.

Clarke-Stewart, A. 1982. *Daycare.* Cambridge, Mass.: Harvard University Press.

Clarke-Stewart, A. 1984. Day care: A new context for research and development. In *Parent-child interaction and parent-child relations in child development,* ed. M. Perlmutter. Hillsdale, N.J.: Erlbaum.

Cohen, J. 1977. *Statistical power analysis for the behavioral sciences.* New York: Academic.

Cummings, E. 1980. Caregiver stability and day care. *Developmental Psychology 16:* 31–37.

Dunn, J., and Kendrick, C. 1983. *Siblings: Love, envy, and understanding.* Cambridge, Mass.: Harvard University Press.

Dunn, L. M. 1979. *Peabody Picture Vocabulary Test—Revised.* Circle Pines, Minn.: American Guidance Service.

Feiring, C.; Lewis, M.; and Starr, M. D. 1984. Indirect effects and infants' reactions to strangers. *Developmental Psychology* 20:485–92.

Festinger, L. 1954. A theory of social comparison processes. *Human Relations* 7:117–40.

Field, T., and Reite, M. 1984. Children's responses to mother during the birth of another child. *Child Development* 55:1308–16.

France-Kaatrude, A., and Smith, W. 1985. Social comparison, task motivation, and the development of self-evaluative standards in children. *Developmental Psychology* 21:1080–89.

Fullard, W.; McDevitt, S. C.; and Carey, W. B. 1978. The Toddler Temperament Scale. Temple University, Department of Educational Psychology. Typescript.

Garcia-Coll, C.; Kagan, J.; and Reznick, J. S. 1984. Behavioral inhibition in young children. *Child Development* 55:1005–19.

Gordon, B. N. 1983. Mother perception of child temperament and observed mother-child interaction. *Child Psychiatry and Human Development* 13:153–67.

Hastie, R. 1984. Causes and effects of causal attribution. *Journal of Personality and Social Psychology* 46:44–56.

Hubert, M. C.; Wachs, T. D.; Peters-Martin, P.; and Grandour, M. J. 1982. The study of early temperament: Measurement and conceptual issues. *Child Development* 53:571–600.

Jacobson, J., and Willie, D. 1984. Influence of attachment and separation experience on separation distress at 18 months. *Developmental Psychology* 20:477–84.

Kagan, J. 1971. *Change and continuity in infancy.* New York: Wiley.

Kagan, J. 1983. Classifications of the child. In *Handbook of child psychology,* ed. P. H. Mussen. Vol. 1, *History, theory, and methods,* ed. W. Kessen. New York: Wiley.

Kagan, J.; Reznick, J. S.; Davies, J.; Smith, J.; Sigal, H.; and Miyake, K. 1986. Selective memory and belief: A methodological suggestion. *International Journal of Behavioral Development* 9:205–18.

Kagan, J.; Reznick, J. S.; and Snidman, N. 1987. The physiology and psychology of behavioral inhibition in children. *Child Development* 58:1459–73.

Kagan, J.; Reznick, J. S.; and Snidman, N. 1988. Biological basis of childhood shyness. *Science* 240, (no. 4,849):167–72.

Koch, H. L. 1955. The relation of certain family constellation characteristics and the attitudes of children toward adults. *Child Development* 26:13–40.

Kuhn, D.; Nash, S. C.; and Brucken, L. 1978. Sex role concepts of two- and three-year-olds. *Child Development* 49:445–51.

Lamb, M.; Chase-Lansdale, L.; and Owen, M. T. 1979. The changing American family and its implications for infant social development: The sample case of maternal employment. In *The child and its family,* ed. M. Lewis and L. A. Rosenblum. New York: Plenum.

Legg, C.; Sherrick, I.; and Wadland, W. 1975. Reaction of preschool children to the birth of a sibling. *Child Psychiatry and Human Development* 5:3–39.

McCall, R. B. 1984. Developmental changes in mental performance: The effect of the birth of a sibling. *Child Development* 55:1317–21.

McCartney, K. 1986. How children make their own language environments. Department of Health and Human Services, grant application 1 RO1 MH4187–01. Washington, D.C.: Department of Health and Human Services.

McClelland, D. 1980. Motive dispositions: The merit of operant and respondent measures. In *Review of personality and social psychology,* ed. L. Wheeler. New York: Sage.

Moore, T. W. 1969. Effects on the children. In *Working mothers and their children,* ed. S. Yudkin and A. Holme. London: Sphere.

Phillips, D.; McCartney, K.; and Scarr, S. 1987. Child care quality and children's social development. *Developmental Psychology* 23:537–43.

Rosenberg, B. G. 1982. Life span personality stability in sibling status. In *Sibling relationships: Their nature and significance throughout the life span,* ed. M. E. Lamb and B. Sutton-Smith. Hilldale, N.J.: Erlbaum.

Rosenthal, R., and Rosnow, R. 1984. *Essentials of behavioral research methods and data analysis.* New York: McGraw-Hill.

Rothbart, M., and Goldsmith, H. H. 1985. Three approaches to the study of infant temperament. *Developmental Review* 5:237–60.

Schachter, F. F. 1982. Sibling de-identification and split parent identification: A family tetrad. In *Sibling relationships: Their nature and significance throughout the life span,* ed. M. E. Lamb and B. Sutton-Smith. Hilldale, N.J.: Erlbaum.

Schachter, F. F., and Stone, R. K. 1985. Difficult sibling, easy sibling: Temperament and the within-family environment. *Child Development* 56: 1335–44.

Simpson, M. J. A.; Simpson, A. E.; Hooley, J.; and Zunz, M. 1981. Infant-related influence on birth intervals in rhesus monkeys. *Nature* 290:49–51.

Snow, M. E.; Jacklin, C. N.; and Maccoby, E. 1981. Birth-order differences in peer sociability at thirty-three months. *Child Development* 52:589–95.

Spock, B. 1969. *Baby and child care.* New York: Pocket.

Stewart, R. B.; Mobley, L. A.; Van Tuyl, S. S.; and Salvador, M. A. 1987. The firstborn's adjustment to the birth of a sibling: A longitudinal assessment. *Child Development* 58:341–55.

Trause, M. A.; Voos, D.; Rudd, C.; Klaus, M.; Kennel, J.; and Boslett, M. 1981. Separation for childbirth: The effect on the sibling. *Child Psychiatry and Human Development* 12:32–39.

Vlietstra, A. 1981. Full versus half-day preschool attendance. *Child Development* 52:603–10.

Wagner, M. E.; Schubert, H. J. P.; and Schubert, D. J. P. 1979. Sibship constellation effects on psychosocial development, creativity, and health. In *Advances in child development and behavior,* vol. 14, ed. H. W. Reese and L. P. Lipsitt. New York: Academic.

Wagner, M. E.; Schubert, H. J. P.; and Schubert, D. J. P. 1984. Effects of sibling spacing on intelligence, interfamilial relations, psychosocial characteristics, and mental and physical health. In *Advances in child development and behavior* vol. 19, ed. H. W. Reese and L. P. Lipsitt. New York: Academic.

Waldman, E. 1983. Labor force statistics from a family perspective. *Monthly Labor Review* 106:16–20.

11 Behavioral Genetics and Emotionality

ROBERT PLOMIN AND CLARE STOCKER

Behavioral genetics is a perspective that can be profitably applied to the study of behavioral inhibition as a first step toward understanding the genetic and environmental origins of individual differences. The purpose of this chapter is to review behavioral genetic research relevant to behavioral inhibition, specifically research on the fearfulness component of emotionality. Although there is as yet no behavioral genetic research that assesses behavioral inhibition as the Harvard group has studied it (e.g., Kagan, Reznick, and Snidman 1986), behavioral genetic studies of emotionality/fearfulness are likely to be relevant, for reasons discussed in the following section.

Components of Behavioral Inhibition

An important issue for research, including behavioral genetic research, on the dimension of behavioral inhibition involves its components. Clearly, behavioral inhibition is a complex dimension: "In searching for concise adjectives to capture the differences between the two kinds of children, recognizing that any word distorts what is observed, the words restrained, watchful, and gentle capture the essence of the inhibited child; free, energetic, and spontaneous capture the style of the uninhibited youngster" (Kagan, Reznick, and Snidman 1986, 54).

Preparation of this chapter was supported in part by a grant from the National Science Foundation (BNS-8643938). The Colorado Adoption Project is supported by grants from the National Institute of Child Health and Human Development (HD-10333 and HD-18426). The Swedish Adoption/Twin Study on Aging is supported by grants from the National Institute of Aging (AG-04563) and from the Program on Successful Aging of the John D. and Catherine T. MacArthur Foundation.

Emotionality/Fearfulness

Most often, behavioral inhibition is described as fearfulness, timidity, and wariness. Inhibited children are those who cry, fret, express distress, withdraw, cling to the mother, and inhibit play during laboratory situations. These appear to be behavioral indices of an aroused, distressed, and fearful child; for this reason, it seems reasonable to hypothesize that the fearfulness component of emotionality appears to be a major component of behavioral inhibition. Although there are as yet no direct tests of the relation between behavioral inhibition and fearfulness, the likely centrality of an emotionality/fearfulness component to behavioral inhibition is the raison d'être for the inclusion of this chapter in a book on behavioral inhibition.

Emotionality/fearfulness involves one component of arousal. Arousal appears in one form or another in all systems of temperament (Plomin and Dunn 1986). In addition to the Harvard group's behavioral inhibition system, three approaches to temperament that emphasize arousal include the temperament-as-affect approach of Goldsmith and Campos (1982, 1986), which considers anger, fearfulness, pleasure/joy, interest/persistence, and motoric activity; the reactivity and self-regulation approach described by Rothbart and Derryberry (1981), which is similar to the theory proposed by Strelau (1965, 1983) for adults; and the approach of Buss and Plomin (1975, 1984), which posits that emotionality, together with activity and sociability (EAS), are among the most heritable personality traits. Although the study of emotion traditionally includes feelings and expressions in addition to arousal, Buss and Plomin emphasize the arousal component, especially the high-arousal emotions of distress, fear, and anger. In contrast, low-arousal emotions such as happiness and sadness or cognitively toned emotions such as pride are postulated to show less genetic influence, a prediction that has since received empirical support, as discussed later.

Arousal itself is not a single dimension, as Lacy indicated two decades ago: "I think the experiments show that electroencephalographic, autonomic, motor, and other behavioral systems are imperfectly coupled, complexly interacting systems. Indeed, I think the evidence shows that electrocortical arousal, autonomic arousal, and behavioral arousal, may be considered to be *different forms* of arousal, each complex in itself" (Lacey 1967, 15). Under conditions of great excitement, brain, autonomic, and behavioral arousal occur simultaneously, but otherwise it may be important to distinguish indices on the basis of three types of arousal. Arousal has primarily been measured behaviorally, but autonomic indices such as heart rate and cortisol have also been used, especially in the study of behavioral inhibition. The behavioral genetic research reviewed in this chapter has, however, relied on behavioral measures. Research on brain and autonomic indices of arousal could yield results different from the behavioral studies that we review. However, it should be noted that biological measures are no more likely to yield evidence for greater genetic influence than are behavioral measures (Plomin and Ho, in press). For example, a recent small twin study of plasma cortisol levels yields twin correlations quite comparable to those observed in twin studies of personality—identical twin correlations of about .50 and fraternal twin correlations of about .25 (Meikle et al. 1988).

Shyness

A major question to be resolved concerning components of behavioral inhibition is the extent to which behavioral inhibition assesses fearfulness in the broad sense or something more specific in the contextual sense. Shyness is a likely, although not immediately obvious, candidate for a narrower interpretation of behavioral inhibition. Shyness involves timidity in social interactions with strangers—it is not just low sociability or low gregariousness, the tendency to prefer to be alone rather than with others. For adults, shyness and sociability correlate only modestly, − .31 (Cheek and Buss 1981); in contrast, shyness correlates .50 with emotionality/fearfulness; sociability and fearfulness correlate only − .09. We are not aware of comparable studies for children.

There are two main reasons for considering the possibility that behavioral inhibition and shyness are related. First, the Harvard studies of behavioral inhibition selected infants on the basis of extreme scores on parents' responses to items from the approach/withdrawal scale of the Toddler Temperament Scale (Fullard, McDevitt, and Carey 1978), an instrument derived from the New York Longitudinal Study of Temperament (Thomas and Chess 1977). Factor analysis indicates that the scale primarily assesses fearfulness in novel social contexts, that is, shyness (Buss and Plomin 1984). The five highest-loading items are "The child is outgoing with strangers," "The child tends to hold back in new situations," "The child avoids new guests or visitors," "The child smiles or laughs when he/she meets new visitors at home," and "The child approaches children his/her age that he/she doesn't know" (Buss and Plomin 1984). In other words, the instrument used for the initial selection of infants for the behavioral inhibition studies is primarily a measure of approach/withdrawal to strangers, not approach/withdrawal in nonsocial contexts. Second, the situations used to assess behavioral inhibition in the laboratory studies can also be viewed as predominantly social. Most of the situations involve interactions with an unfamiliar adult, the experimenter. Even the ostensibly nonsocial situation involving a robot could be argued to be social in that the robot "talks" to the child and attempts to engage the child in play. The measure on which greatest reliance is placed in the second Harvard study is a play session with an unfamiliar peer, a prototypical shyness situation.

Despite the likely relevance of shyness to the behavioral inhibition construct, this review is focused on emotionality/fearfulness because behavioral genetic research on shyness has recently been reviewed elsewhere (Plomin and Daniels 1986).

Other components

The complex dimension of behavioral inhibition is likely to involve other personality dimensions in addition to emotionality/fearfulness and shyness. For example, it has been suggested that behavioral inhibition relates to extraversion (Kagan and Reznick 1986; Kagan, Reznick, and Snidman 1986), a dimension studied extensively by Eysenck (e.g., 1981). One source of support for this hypothesis is that both behavioral inhibition and extraversion relate positively to heart rate and pupil dilation; as yet, however, correlations between the two constructs have not been reported. A strong relation between them seems unlikely because the core of extraversion is sociability in the sense of gregariousness, wanting to be with and to do things with others rather than alone (Plomin 1976a). Although sociability may be related to behavioral inhibition, it seems safe to predict that shyness, which relates only moderately to sociability and extraversion, will prove to be the more important social component of behavioral inhibition. Two more minor components of extraversion are impulsivity (risk taking and decision time) and liveliness (being the life of the party); it is reasonable to expect that both these may relate modestly to behavioral inhibition.

It is likely that neuroticism, Eysenck's second major dimension of personality, will be more important to behavioral inhibition than will extraversion because, in childhood, emotionality appears to be the core of neuroticism without the anxiety component typical of adult questionnaires of neuroticism (Buss and Plomin 1984).

Does it matter whether behavioral inhibition is primarily emotionality/fearfulness or more specifically shyness or whether behavioral inhibition includes neuroticism or extraversion and its components? The answer is yes, for two reasons. Part of understanding a multifaceted dimension such as behavioral inhibition lies in understanding its components. Behavioral inhibition may prove to be a broad "superfactor" that encompasses all these dimensions, but it might instead turn out to be a heterogeneous label in which children are selected as high in behavioral inhibition for different reasons, some because they are generally fearful, some because they are shy, and others because they are low in impulsivity.

A second reason is that behavioral genetic research in the area will be more profitable if components of behavioral inhibition are assessed rather than simply estimating genetic and environmental components of variance of a general index of behavioral inhibition. Multivariate methods of behavioral genetics can then be used to estimate genetic and environmental components of covariance among measures and can thus be used to construct an etiological approach to the network of variables in which behavioral inhibition is lodged (DeFries and Fulker 1986). For example, it is possible that the components of behavioral inhibition are not genetically correlated or, at the other extreme, that genetic correlations among them are substantial, suggesting the existence of a general genetic superfactor. A third possibility is that behavioral inhibition is correlated genetically with one component such as fearfulness more highly than with other components such as shyness.

Regardless of these two reasons for studying components of behavioral inhibition, practicality dictates the need to focus on components of behavioral inhibition in this review: there are no behavioral genetic studies of behavioral inhibition as assessed by the Harvard group. It should be mentioned, however, that a 7-year, large-scale, longitudinal twin study that focuses on behavioral inhibition and other aspects of temperament was launched in 1986 and will eventually resolve many of the issues raised in this chapter. The MacArthur Longitudinal Twin Study (MALTS) is a collaborative effort whose coinvestigators are John DeFries, Robert Emde, Jerome Kagan, Robert Plomin, and Steven Reznick; it will include at least 300 pairs of twins studied longitudinally at 14, 20, 24, and 36 months of age, and it will assess several indices of behavioral inhibition as well as other temperament variables in the laboratory and in the home.

Behavioral Genetic Research on Emotionality/Fearfulness

Table 1 summarizes results from 12 twin studies with behavioral data relevant to the fearfulness component of emotionality in childhood. The samples range from the first year of life to middle childhood, and the studies include diverse methods of measurement such as molecular and molar observations and parental ratings and interviews. We have attempted to present results for measures that appear to be closely allied with the construct of emotionality/fearfulness. For this reason, several well-known twin studies in childhood are not represented in the table.

In addition, several studies of neuroticism using Eysenck's or Cattell's self-report questionnaires are not represented in table 1. Although emotionality is a major component of neuroticism, neuroticism includes other aspects of personality, as discussed earlier. Moreover, twin studies of neuroticism have been reviewed elsewhere (Buss and Plomin 1975; Goldsmith 1983; Plomin 1986). For the same reason, research involving Cattell's 16 Personality Factor (16PF) test is of limited usefulness in understanding emotionality/fearfulness (for a review of the heritability of 16PF scales, see Cattell [1982]). Similarly, other twin studies are not reviewed because they employ widely used personality

Table 1: Twin Studies of Emotionality/Fearfulness in Childhood

Reference	Sample (age, N)[a,b]	Measure	Twin Correlations[a] MZ	Twin Correlations[a] DZ
Matheny, Dolan, and Wilson (1976)	3–12 months, 15 MZ, 27 DZ	Bayley's (1969) Infant Behavior Record fear-	.75	.54
	18–30 months, 47 MZ, 27 DZ	fulness item	.65	.22
Goldsmith and Campos (1986)	9 months, 29 MZ, 61 DZ	Rothbart's (1981) Infant Behavior Question-	.66	.46
	9 months, 35 MZ, 35 DZ	naire maternal rating of fear; observational ratings of distress during stranger approach in laboratory	.46	.09
Matheny and Dolan (1975)	9–30 months, 25–57 MZ, 9–34 DZ	Observational ratings of emotionality in play-room	.66	.30
Matheny (in press)	33 MZ, 19 DZ:	Observational ratings of		
	12 months	"emotional tone" in	.59	.27
	18 months	laboratory	.83	.28
	24 months		.87	.26
	30 months		.79	.25
Plomin and Rowe (1977)	43 months average; 36 MZ, 31 DZ	CCTI (Rowe and Plomin 1977); maternal ratings of emotionality	.70	.06
Plomin (1976b)	54 months average, 60 MZ, 51 DZ	EASI-III mid-parent ratings of emotionality/ fearfulness	.70	.38
Buss, Plomin, and Willerman (1973)	55 months average, 78 MZ, 50 DZ	EASI-I mid-parent ratings of general emotionality	.63	.10
Buss and Plomin (1975)	55 months average, 81 MZ, 57 DZ[c]	EASI-I maternal ratings of general emotionality	.64	.03
Stevenson and Fielding (1985)	174 MZ, 178 DZ, 0–5 years	EASI-I midparental ratings of general emotionality	.29	−.01
Goldsmith and Gottesman (1981)	7 years, 113 MZ, 82 DZ	Tester ratings on fearfulness	.39	.12
Plomin and Foch (1980)	7.6 years average, 51 MZ, 33 DZ	CCTI maternal ratings of emotionality	.60	.27
O'Connor et al. (1980)	7.6 years average, 54 MZ, 33 DZ	Connors (1970) PSR emotionality scale	.71	.31

[a] MZ refers to monozygotic (identical) twins, and DZ refers to dizygotic (fraternal) twins.
[b] N denotes number of pairs.
[c] Sample overlaps Buss, Plomin, and Willerman (1973).

questionnaires that, surprisingly, include no scales relevant to emotionality. Some of these are the California Psychological Inventory (e.g., Loehlin and Nichols 1976), Comrey's personality questionnaire (Vandenberg 1967), the Minnesota Multiphasic Personality Instrument (MMPI; e.g., Pogue-Geile and Rose 1985), and the Thurstone Temperament Schedule (Vandenberg 1967). We also do not include a self-report study of adult twins that studied specific phobias such as fear of spiders and fear of heights because the relation between phobias and general emotionality/fearfulness is not known (Rose and Ditto 1983). Finally, our review does not include studies with small samples (i.e., fewer than 20 pairs of each type). Large standard errors are entailed in the difference between correlations for identical and fraternal twins; twin studies thus require large samples. For example, if the true identical and fraternal twin correlations are .50 and .30, respectively—suggesting a heritability of 40 percent—a sample of over 200 pairs of each type of twin is needed to detect a significant difference between correlations of this magnitude with 80 percent power ($p < .05$, one tailed; Cohen 1977). With samples of 20 pairs of each type, power to detect differences of this magnitude is less than 20 percent, which means that a true difference between correlations for identical and fraternal twins will be detected fewer than one time in five.

Our discussion of the twin results in table 1 will be divided into studies that assess emotionality using EAS parental rating instruments (Buss and Plomin 1975, 1984; Stevenson and Fielding 1985), studies that employ other parental rating questionnaires, and observational studies. Following discussion of the twin results, new data from the Colorado Adoption Project (CAP) in infancy and early childhood, which inject a note of caution in interpreting the twin results, will be presented. Finally, two recent behavioral genetic studies of adult twins will be described briefly because of their novelty, the power of their design, and their addition of a life-span perspective to this review. Methodological issues relevant to behavioral genetics can be found in behavioral genetics textbooks (e.g., Fuller and Thompson 1978; Hay 1985; Plomin, DeFries, and McClearn, in press).

Twin Studies of EAS Emotionality

Twin correlations for six studies using EAS parental rating questionnaires are listed in table 1. The EASI-I emotionality scale (first version) assesses general emotionality, which includes distress and fearfulness (Buss and Plomin 1975). The EASI-III (third version) distinguishes distress, fear, and anger components of emotionality. The Colorado Childhood Temperament Inventory (CCTI; Rowe and Plomin 1977) emotionality scale is similar to the general EASI-I emotionality scale, although the CCTI scale measures general distress to an even greater extent than does the EASI-I scale.

Results from four earlier studies using the EAS/CCTI measures are similar; weighted-average correlations were calculated for the four EAS/CCTI twin studies reported in table 1, deleting the Buss, Plomin, and Willerman (1973) study because of its wide age range and its sample overlap with another report (Buss and Plomin 1975). The weighted-average correlation for 228 pairs of identical twins is .66; the correlation for 172 pairs of fraternal twins is .19. Both correlations are significant ($p < .05$), as is the difference between them—the latter implies significant genetic influence. A recent study in England finds lower correlations (.29 and $-.01$ for monozygotic and dizygotic twins, respectively [Stevenson and Fielding 1985]).

Although the differences between the identical and fraternal twin correlations are highly significant, they are too large to be explained by the classic twin model. Fraternal twins, like other first-degree relatives, share half their heredity and should thus be approximately half as similar as identical twins. However, for emotionality, the weighted average fraternal twin correlation (.09) in these five studies is only 19 percent the magnitude of the average identical twin correlation (.48). These lower-than-expected fraternal twin correlations may be explained by environmental or genetic factors. For example, nonshared environmental factors relevant to temperament might be particularly potent for fraternal twins. Nonshared environment can take many forms, from different parental treatment, different experience with peers or significant others outside the home, or nonsystematic events such as accidents and illnesses. One form of nonshared environment, contrast effects, might be particularly important for fraternal twins: "Parents might contrast their fraternal twins, labeling one as active and the other as inactive. The twins might contrast themselves and become more differentiated behaviorally. One twin partner, who might be slightly more active than the other, converts this slight edge into a consistent advantage in initiating activities, and the other twin relinquishes the initiative to this partner. Why does this not also happen for identical twins? Presumably, identical twins are so alike behaviorally that contrast is difficult" (Buss and Plomin 1984, 119). Buss and Plomin discuss studies relevant to the issue of contrast effects such as analyses in which each parent rated both twins, yielding an average or midparent rating, and analyses in which each parent rated only one twin (one member of a twin pair was rated by the mother and the other by the father) and cross-rating correlations were obtained. For emotionality/fearfulness, twin cross-rating correlations were .30 versus .09. Cross-ratings yield lower correlations because they are limited by the extent of parental agreement; nonetheless, the pattern of results is similar to those for more traditional same-parent ratings. Buss and Plomin (1984) conclude that, "if there is a bias in parental rating data, it is not limited to one parent rating both twins" (p. 122), and they suggest that contrast effects might lie in the behavior of the children rather than in the eye of the beholder.

A second possible explanation for finding fraternal twin correlations that are less than half the comparable identical twin correlation is nonadditive genetic variance. Although this is a technical issue, it may be of considerable relevance to the study of the fearfulness component of emotionality. Additive genetic variance refers to genetic values that are the sum of the average effects of all genes that influence a characteristic and thus "breed true." Identical twins are identical for additive genetic effects, whereas fraternal twins, like other first-degree relatives, resemble each other 50 percent on the average for segregating genes. Thus, the covariance of identical twins contains all the additive genetic variance, and the covariance of first-degree relatives contains half the additive genetic variance. Nonadditive genetic variance includes dominance, interactive effects of alleles at a locus, and epistasis, interactive effects of alleles at different loci. (Alleles are alternate forms of genes at a locus, such as the A, B, and O alleles at the ABO blood locus.) With regard to nonadditive genetic variance, siblings share only a quarter of genetic variance because of dominance and relatively little genetic variance because of epistasis; in contrast, identical twins share all nonadditive genetic effects. Thus, if nonadditive genetic variance is important for a trait, the expected correlation for fraternal twins is less than half the correlation for identical twins. The traditional formula for calculating heritability (Falconer 1960) assumes that genetic variance is additive and merely doubles the difference between the identical and the fraternal twin correlations—in the case of EAS emotionality, heritability would be mistakenly estimated as 94 percent.

There is no accepted procedure for estimating heritability from twin data in the presence of nonadditive genetic variance (i.e., when fraternal twin correlations are less than half the identical twin correlation). One approach is to use the identical twin correlation itself as an estimate of "broad" heritability, which includes additive as well as nonadditive genetic variance. This estimate suggests a broad heritability of 66 percent for emotionality. That is, two-thirds of the total variance is due to genetic variance. Standard errors of heritability estimates are large; the heritability estimate of .66 involves a standard error of .12. Nonetheless, we can say that the chances are two out of three that the true heritability value lies between .54 and .78, which implies that over half the variance in parental ratings of emotionality are due to genetic differences among children.

Other Parental Rating Twin Studies

In addition to the EAS studies, two studies employed other parental rating measures of emotionality. The first parental rating twin study focused on specific behavioral problems in children whose average age was 7.6 years (O'Connor et al. 1980). The 54 identical twin pairs and 33 same-sex fraternal twin pairs were rated by their mothers on the Parent Symptom Rating (PSR) questionnaire (Conners 1970). Factor analyses of the 73 PSR items lead to construction of a scale called emotional, which appears to involve neuroticism in that items include "feelings easily hurt" and "afraid that people don't like him"; however, the scale correlates .58 with CCTI emotionality and was thus deemed relevant to our review of emotionality. Its correlations of .71 for identical twins and .31 for fraternal twins are similar to and somewhat higher than those obtained for EASI-I emotionality. The items of the PSR are more specific behaviorally than are EAS items, and it has been noted that ratings of specific behavioral items yield higher twin correlations than do more global ratings, a difference that is not due simply to differences in reliability (Plomin 1981).

In a study of infant twins in the first year of life, Rothbart's (1981) Infant Behavior Questionnaire was used as a measure of temperament (Goldsmith and Campos 1986). The fear scale yielded twin correlations of .66 and .46, respectively, for 29 pairs of identical twins and 61 pairs of fraternal twins.

In summary, each study using EAS parental ratings or other parental rating instruments yields data consistent with the hypothesis that differences among children in emotionality are significantly influenced by genetic differences among them. One unresolved issue involves lower-than-expected fraternal twin correlations—nonadditive genetic variance is plausible, but so is non-shared environmental influence such as contrast effects. In addition, although parental ratings would seem to be more objective than self-report questionnaires, which dominate behavioral genetic studies of adult personality, it would substantially buttress the case for genetic influence on emotionality if other methods converge on the same conclusions. The next section considers four relevant studies in which emotionality was rated from observations in the laboratory.

Observational Twin Studies

Five studies listed in table 1 involve ratings based on laboratory observations. In the Louisville Twin Study, factors were obtained from the items of Bayley's Infant Behavior Record (IBR;1969), which is a useful instrument for assessing temperament in a standardized and somewhat stressful situation (Matheny 1980). However, these factors do not assess emotionality/fearfulness, perhaps because the Bayley tests are not meant to be administered until the child has acclimatized to the situation. Although one factor, test affect/extraversion, might appear to be related to emotionality, the affect is in fact primarily happiness and positive affect rather than fearfulness. Nonetheless, one IBR item is fearfulness. In table 1, we have included a description of an earlier Louisville Twin Study report that presented twin correlations for this IBR item (Matheny, Dolan, and Wilson 1976). Combining ratings at 3, 6, 9, and 12 months from this longitudinal study, the identical and fraternal twin correlations were .75 and .54, respectively. Genetic influence is even stronger when ratings at 18, 24, and 30 months are averaged: the identical and fraternal twin correlations are .65 and .22, respectively. A recent report on a different sample involving 33 identical twin pairs and 19 fraternal twin pairs yielded similar results (Matheny, in press). At 12 months, the identical and fraternal twin correlations were .76 and .48, respectively; at 24 months, the correlations were .80 and .20, respectively.

The Louisville Twin Study also used an emotionality rating scale to code observations of children's initial distress on the mother's departure from a playroom and the quality of the child's adjustment during the ensuing play period (Matheny and Dolan 1975). Twins were studied at 9, 12, 18, 24, and 30 months of age; the average identical twin correlation was .66, and the average fraternal twin correlation was .30.

For the past decade, the Louisville Twin Study has employed a diverse set of laboratory vignettes to observe temperament (Wilson and Matheny 1986). A recent report used a rating scale previously described as emotional tone to represent behavioral inhibition (Matheny, in press). This rating, derived for each 2-minute observation period, was a nine-point scale from "extremely upset" to "excited, animated." Although the relation between behavioral inhibition and the scale and situations used in this study can be questioned, the longitudinal results at 12, 18, 24, and 30 months are included in table 1. Across the four ages, the average identical and fraternal twin correlations are .77 and .27, respectively. In addition, this report suggested that genetic factors are in part responsible for profiles of situation-to-situation change as well as age-to-age change.

A fourth twin study of 7-year-olds employed tester ratings of a scale labelled fearfulness, which included such items as fearfulness, concern when separated from mother, and self-confidence (Goldsmith and Gottesman 1981). Identical and fraternal twin correlations were .39 and .12, respectively, for the fearfulness scale.

In a fifth observational study, 35 pairs each of identical and fraternal twins were observed in the laboratory at 9 and 9.5 months (Goldsmith and Campos 1986). The twin results suggest significant genetic influence on the high-arousal emotion of fear at the approach of a stranger for a composite measure as well as on the separate measures of latency, duration, and intensity of crying and other negative vocalizations in this context. Distress during the visual cliff showed no evidence of genetic influence; however, the visual cliff evoked much less crying and fussing than did the approach of strangers. In addition, avoidance measures based on visual cliff and stranger approach showed no genetic influence—the investigators suggest that the avoidance measures are instrumental rather than affective; that is, the avoidance measures do not assess arousal. It is interesting that not all measures of emotion show genetic influence. The less-arousing positive emotions indicated by smiling show no genetic influence, as predicted by the EAS theory. A similar lack of genetic influence on individual differences in smiling has been found in other studies using parental reports (Goldsmith and Campos 1986; Wilson, Brown, and Matheny 1971).

In summary, these observational twin studies add substantially to the weight of the conclusion reached on the basis of parental rating data: individual differences in emotionality are significantly due to genetic differences among children. Moreover, the genetic effect appears to be substantial, with the twin correlations suggesting heritabilities in excess of .50. All studies reviewed so far converge on these conclusions; however, it is noteworthy that all these studies have been twin studies. In addition to considering different measurement techniques such as parental ratings and observations, it is important to examine behavioral genetic designs other than the twin design.

Family Studies

During the past decade, a trend in behavioral genetic research has been to complement twin research with such different designs as the family design and the adoption design. The family design simply assesses the resemblance of relatives—usually first-degree relatives (parents, offspring, and siblings)—who share both heredity and family environment. Results of such family studies place upper-limit estimates on the influence of nature and nurture. That is, additive genetic variance or shared family environmental influence cannot exceed that indicated by familial resemblance. However, all the familial resemblance might be due to genetic influence, or all of it might be due to shared family environment. Until recently, much less was known about personality resemblance for parents, offspring, and siblings than about twins' resemblance. Fraternal twins are first-degree relatives, and their correlation indicates that resemblance for first-degree relatives is only modest. For example, for the EAS/CCTI studies of emotionality, the average fraternal twin correlation is .19; this is comparable to personality correlations observed for other first-degree relatives assessed via self-report questionnaire (Plomin 1986).

For example, the Hawaii Family Study of Cognition administered 54 personality scales to hundreds of families in which the average age of the offspring was 17 (Alhern et al. 1982). For the 54 scales, the average parent-offspring correlation was .12, and the average sibling correlation was also .12. Several of the scales were related to neuroticism, but none assessed emotionality/fearfulness. It is noteworthy that correlations such as these put a cap on the upper limit of heritability that is substantially lower than heritability estimated in twin studies. Assuming that parent-offspring and sibling resemblance is entirely due to heredity implies that heritability can be no greater than .24, in contrast to typical twin estimates of .40 (Loehlin and Nichols 1976). As discussed earlier, this discrepancy may be due to the presence of

nonadditive genetic variance, which contributes importantly only to the resemblance of identical twins, not of first-degree relatives.

Only one family study has been reported that assessed emotionality/fear-
fulness in children (Plomin 1976b). For 111 families in which children were
54 months old on the average, EASI-III mid-parent ratings (i.e., the average
of mothers' and fathers' ratings) of the child's emotionality/fearfulness were
correlated with parents' self-report ratings of emotionality/fearfulness. The
parent-offspring correlations were .38 and .19 for mothers and fathers, respectively. In addition, parents rated their spouse, and the results were quite
similar for these cross-ratings: fathers' ratings of mothers and mothers' ratings
of fathers correlated .41 and .23, respectively, with their mid-parent ratings
of their children. These results suggest familial resemblance much higher than
that found for first-degree relatives in studies of older offspring that rely on
self-report questionnaires; the correlations are especially high when the age
difference between the parents and their young children is considered. However, it should also be kept in mind that the correlations may be inflated because parents are the source of information about both themselves and their
children, although such artificial sources of resemblance should be attenuated
by the use of mid-parent ratings of the children and cross-ratings for the parents. These data also provide a strong suggestion of a maternal effect in that
the mother-offspring correlations are nearly double the father-offspring correlations, even when the parents are rated by their spouses. However, the data
for the Hawaii study and data reviewed below do not show such strong maternal effects.

The Hawaii familial correlations suggest lower genetic influences on emo-
tionality-fearfulness than is estimated in twin studies. A more precise method
of pinpointing genetic influence in the etiology of emotionality/fearfulness is
to use the adoption design. As indicated in the next section, these studies also
show low correlations for parent/offspring and sibling comparisons.

Adoption Studies

The adoption design separates genetic and environmental sources of familial resemblance by studying genetically related individuals reared apart and
genetically unrelated individuals reared together. Two of the major adoption
studies, the Minnesota Transracial Adoption Study (Scarr et al. 1981) and the
Texas Adoption Project (Loehlin, Horn, and Willerman 1981; Loehlin, Willerman, and Horn 1982, 1985, 1987) are not pertinent to the present review
because the measures they employed—Eysenck, Cattell, and MMPI questionnaires—have no analog of emotionality/fearfulness. In addition, both
studies included a wide age range of adoptees—from 4 to 16 in the Minnesota
study and from 3 to 26 in the Texas study.

The major adoption study in childhood is the longitudinal, prospective CAP, which includes 245 adoptive families and 245 matched nonadoptive families in which the parents (biologic and adoptive parents in the adoptive families and parents in the nonadoptive families) have been tested on a 3-hour battery of behavioral tests and their children (adoptive and nonadoptive) have been studied yearly in their homes from 1 to 4 years of age (Plomin and DeFries 1985; Plomin, DeFries, and Fulker 1988). The CAP families are representative of middle-class, Caucasian families, and selective placement is negligible.

Parent-offspring correlations using mid-parent ratings on CCTI emotionality and parental EAS self-reports of emotionality/fearfulness in nonadoptive families were .10, .07, .08, and .05 at 1, 2, 3, and 4 years, respectively. These correlations are lower than the fraternal twin correlations in EAS studies reviewed earlier. Adoptive parent–adoptee correlations are of comparable magnitude: .12, .11, .11, and .07 across the 4 years. These results provide no evidence of genetic influence shared by parents and their offspring. Biological mothers' self-report ratings of emotionality/fearfulness yielded negligible correlations with their adopted-away children's emotionality as rated by the adoptive parents: the correlations across the 4 years were .02, .01, − .01, and − .04. These correlations also suggest that genetic influence is of little importance in making adult parents and their offspring, as young children, similar. Such results would be expected if, as seems reasonable, genetic effects on emotionality change from childhood to adulthood (for a discussion of concepts and methods for studying genetic change during development, see Plomin 1986).

In the CAP, younger siblings of the adopted and nonadopted subjects are studied in the same manner as the target children. Adoptive siblings are genetically unrelated children reared in the same family. The addition of adoptive and nonadoptive siblings tested at the same age is important because it provides genetic comparisons for the contemporaneous relationship of siblings, in contrast to parent-offspring comparisons in which parents are adults and the offspring are children. Results have been presented for 67 adoptive and 82 nonadoptive sibling pairs in which both members of the pair were tested at age 12 months, 61 adoptive and 70 nonadoptive pairs at 2 years, 50 adoptive and 54 nonadoptive pairs at 3 years, and 42 adoptive and 43 nonadoptive pairs at 4 years (Plomin et al. 1988). Unlike the correlation between biological mothers and their adopted-away children, which provides a direct estimate of genetic influence, the sibling adoption design rests on the difference in correlations for nonadoptive and adoptive siblings. Genetic influence is implicated when nonadoptive sibling correlations exceed those for adoptive siblings. As mentioned earlier, differences in correlations have large standard errors. The present sample size at 12 months provides 50 percent power to detect differences in nonadoptive and adoptive sibling correlations that differ by about .27, implying heritabilities in excess of .55. For more reasonable heritabilities such as .30, the sample provides only 25 percent power, which means that heritability of this magnitude will be detected only one time in four. Although the present CAP sample size is limiting, some of this loss of power is compensated for by the ability to replicate results across infancy and early childhood in this longitudinal study.

Although the CAP correlations for nonadoptive and adoptive siblings yield evidence for substantial genetic influence on height and weight, as do twin studies, the nonadoptive and adoptive sibling correlations for temperament in general and for emotionality in particular do not agree with the twin results in suggesting genetic influence. The correlations for CCTI emotionality for non-adoptive siblings are .23, .03, $-.04$, and $-.10$ at 1, 2, 3, and 4 years, respectively; adoptive sibling correlations at the four years are .01, .20, .20, and .32.

Thus, the CAP parent-offspring data and especially the sibling data do not show genetic influence on emotionality in infancy and early childhood. Model-fitting analyses of the CAP data confirm this conclusion gleaned from the parent-offspring and sibling correlations (Plomin et al. 1988). As indicated in the first part of this review, twin data point to substantial genetic influence; however, studies of nontwin family members suggest much less genetic influence. Clearly, more data are needed for nontwin family members. For the present, however, we hypothesize that the resolution to this discrepancy lies at least in part with nonadditive genetic variance: identical twins are identical for all sources of nonadditive as well as additive genetic variance, whereas fraternal twins and other first-degree relatives share only additive genetic variance. For this reason, twin studies include nonadditive as well as additive genetic variance in their estimates of heritability; moreover, if analyses of twin data mistakenly assume that all genetic variance is additive— which has been a standard assumption in quantitative genetic analyses—they can greatly overestimate genetic influence. In contrast, designs such as the parent-offspring and sibling adoption design of the CAP that are based on first-degree relatives will not include genetic variance that is transmitted in a nonadditive manner. One way to begin to study nonadditive genetic variance is to combine the twin study and the adoption study.

Twin/Adoption Studies

As mentioned earlier, we decided not to review the numerous self-report questionnaire studies of adults, in part because these studies focus on neuroticism rather than emotionality/fearfulness. However, two recent studies of adults must be mentioned because they combine the twin and adoption methods and thus add special power to their analyses. These studies are the Minnesota Study of Twins Reared Apart (MSTRA; Bouchard 1984) and the Swedish Adoption/Twin Study on Aging (SATSA; Pedersen et al. 1984; McClearn et al. 1988). This powerful design involves four groups of twins: identical (monozygotic) and fraternal (dizygotic) twins reared apart (MZA and DZA) and comparison samples of identical and fraternal twins reared together (MZT and DZT). The MSTRA includes 44 MZA and 27 DZA pairs whose average age was 41 years and 217 MZT and 114 DZT pairs whose average age at testing was 21 years (Tellegen et al. 1988). The SATSA includes 99 MZA, 229 DZA, 160 MZT, and 212 DZT pairs whose average age was 59 years, making SATSA the first major behavioral genetic study in the last half of the life span.

The MSTRA has reported results for a newly developed self-report personality questionnaire, the Multidimensional Personality Questionnaire (MPQ; Tellegen et al. 1988). Unfortunately, the MPQ includes no primary scale of emotionality. It includes second-order scales called "positive emotionality" and "negative emotionality," which the authors indicate are essentially extraversion and neuroticism, respectively. As discussed earlier, although emotionality is a major component of neuroticism, we have not included the numerous studies of neuroticism in this review because neuroticism is considerably more complex than emotionality/fearfulness. The primary MPQ scale labelled "stress reaction" may be closest to emotionality, although the extent to which this scale assesses general distress or neuroticism in contrast to fearfulness is not clear. Its pattern of intercorrelations with other scales of the MPQ suggest that the scale is complex and cognitive: it correlates $-.41$ with well-being and .51 with alienation.

Despite reservations about the relationship of stress reaction to emotionality/fearfulness, twin results for this scale will be mentioned because of the importance of the combined adoption/twin design. Twin correlations for the four groups of twins are .61 for MZA, .27 for DZA, .52 for MZT, and .24 for DZT. The Minnesota results for stress reaction are compatible with a hypothesis of substantial genetic influence on emotionality in that the MZ correlations exceed the DZ correlations. However, no genetic hypothesis can explain the odd result that the MZA and DZA correlations are greater than the comparable MZT and DZT correlations. This may be due to the small sample size for twins reared apart. Another possibility is a contrast effect for twins reared together, although the SATSA results discussed next argue against this hypothesis. Finally, the MSTRA results also suggest the presence of nonadditive genetic variance. Although the sample size for twins reared apart is too small to compare MZA and DZA, the DZT correlation is considerably less than half the magnitude of the MZT correlation. Model-fitting analyses indicate that both a purely nonadditive genetic model and a purely additive genetic model fit these data.

The SATSA includes the EAS measure of emotionality/fearfulness and yields the following twin correlations: .37 for MZA, .04 for DZA, .49 for

MZT, and .08 for DZT; selective placement was shown to be negligible for this trait (Plomin et al. 1988). As discussed earlier, nonadditive genetic variance is implied by fraternal twin correlations that are less than half the identical twin correlations. For emotionality/fearfulness, the average identical twin correlation is .43, and the average fraternal twin correlation is .06, suggesting substantial nonadditive genetic variance. It is important to note that the pattern of lower-than-expected fraternal twin correlations emerges for MZA versus DZA as well as for MZT versus DZT, which makes certain environmental hypotheses such as contrast effects less plausible. Model-fitting analyses in the SATSA confirm these conclusions of significant and substantial nonadditive genetic variance.

In summary, these studies of adult twins reared together and twins reared apart converge with studies of twins in childhood in suggesting substantial nonadditive genetic variance for emotionality/fearfulness.

Conclusions

The rationale of this chapter was to review behavioral genetic research relevant to emotionality/fearfulness, a dimension that is likely to be an important component of behavioral inhibition. At first glance, the results for 12 twin studies make this task look easy: each study yields identical twin correlations that are substantially greater than fraternal twin correlations, whether parental ratings, tester ratings, or detailed laboratory observations were employed. However, closer examination of the twin results indicates that fraternal twin correlations are too low relative to identical twin correlations to fit an additive genetic model. This suggests the possibility of nonshared environmental influences such as contrast effects that are greater for fraternal twins than for identical twins, or nonadditive genetic variance. Comparisons between correlations for identical and fraternal twins reared apart in the Swedish study suggest that nonadditive genetic variance is the more likely hypothesis. We conclude that the fearfulness component of emotionality shows substantial genetic influence; however, heredity works in a nonadditive manner that can be detected by twin studies but not by studies of first-degree relatives.

This review of behavioral genetics and emotionality suggests three implications for future studies of behavioral inhibition. First, despite evidence for significant and perhaps substantial genetic variation relevant to emotionality, these same data provide strong evidence for environmental influence. In the current trend toward increasing acceptance of biological influence in human development, it is important that the pendulum not swing entirely away from environmentalism to biological determinism. One of the most important findings in human behavioral genetic research—one that applies to emotionality as well as to most other personality traits—is that nearly all the relevant environmental influence is of the nonshared variety (Plomin and Daniels 1987). Although family members resemble each other, this resemblance is primarily due to heredity rather than to shared environmental influences. In other words, growing up in the same family does not make children similar to one another. This finding suggests a new way of thinking about environmental influences. In the past, it has usually been assumed that environmental influence operates on a family-by-family basis. However, this finding suggests that environmental factors that do not differ between children growing up in the same family are not likely to be among the provenances of behavioral development. The important question becomes, Why are children in the same family so different from one another? The practical key to unlock this riddle is to study more than one child per family. Only by studying more than one child can we identify experiences that differ between children in a family and then relate these experiential differences to differences in siblings' behavior.

Another way in which behavioral genetic designs can be useful to research on behavioral inhibition is to study the genetic and environmental contributions to the phenotypic covariance among components of behavioral inhibition. That is, rather than analyzing the variance of traits considered one at a time, the covariance among traits can be analyzed using multivariate behavioral genetic techniques (DeFries and Fulker 1986). The essence of this approach is to study cross-correlations—for example, the correlation between one twin's score on emotionality/fearfulness and the other twin's score on shyness. Cross-correlations can be analyzed in the same way as correlations; for example, identical twin cross-correlations that exceed fraternal twin cross-correlations suggest that genetic factors mediate the relation between emotionality/fearfulness and shyness. A specific issue of this sort relevant to behavioral inhibition is the extent to which the relation between heart-rate variability and behavioral inhibition is mediated genetically, as is usually assumed. A first study of this issue indicated that both heart-rate variability and shyness are influenced by genetic factors but that the phenotypic relation between them is mediated environmentally, not genetically (Boomsma and Plomin 1986). A multivariate approach is equally useful for biological components of behavioral inhibition.

Finally, as developmentalists, we are interested in change as well as continuity in behavioral inhibition. The relative weight of genetic and environmental influence on a trait can change during development. So far, it appears that, when heritability changes during development, it increases in importance (Plomin 1986). Although twin studies of emotionality cover the life course, there are too many unanswered questions and not enough studies to ask whether the relative magnitude of genetic influence on emotionality increases during development. Even more important is the possibility of long-term age-to-age genetic change, short-term situation-to-situation change, and state change (Matheny, in press; Plomin and Nesselroade, in press) for behavioral inhibition. Very little is known as yet about these issues of change or continuity, which are at the heart of the new subdiscipline of developmental behavioral genetics.

References

Ahern, F. M.; Johnson, R. C.; Wilson, J. R.; McClearn, G. E.; and Vandenberg, S. G. 1982. Family resemblances in personality. *Behavior Genetics* 12:261–80.

Bayley, N. 1969. *Manual for the Bayley Scales of Infant Development.* New York: Psychological Corp.

Boomsma, D.I., and Plomin, R. 1986. Heart rate and behavior of twins. *Merrill-Palmer Quarterly* 32:242-52.

Bouchard, T. J., Jr. 1984. Twins reared together and apart: What they tell us about human diversity. In *Individuality and determinism,* ed. S. W. Fox, New York: Plenum.

Buss, A. H., and Plomin, R. 1975. *A temperament theory of personality development.* New York: Wiley-Interscience.

Buss, A. H., and Plomin, R. 1984. *Temperament: Early developing personality traits.* Hillsdale, N.J.: Erlbaum.

Buss, A. H.; Plomin, R.; and Willerman, L. 1973. The inheritance of temperaments. *Journal of Personality* 41:513–24.

Cattell, R. B. 1982. *The inheritance of personality and ability.* New York: Academic.

Cheek, J. M., and Buss, A. H. 1981. Shyness and sociability. *Journal of Personality and Social Psychology* 41:330–39.

Cohen, J. 1977. *Statistical power analysis for the behavioral sciences.* New York: Academic.

Conners, C. K. 1970. Symptom patterns in hyperkinetic, neurotic, and normal children. *Child Development* 41:667–82.

DeFries, J. C., and Fulker, D. W. 1986. Multivariate behavioral genetics and development: An overview. *Behavior Genetics* 16:1–10.

Eysenck. H. J. 1981. *A model for personality.* Berlin: Springer.

Falconer, D. S. 1960. *Introduction to quantitative genetics.* New York: Oliver & Boyd.

Fullard, W.; McDevitt, S. C.; and Carey, W. B. 1978. *Toddler Temperament Scale.* Temple University, Department of Psychology. Typescript.

Fuller, J. L., and Thompson, W. R. 1978. *Foundations of behavior genetics.* St. Louis: Mosby.

Goldsmith, H. H. 1983. Genetic influences on personality from infancy to adulthood. *Child Development* 54:331–55.

Goldsmith, H. H., and Campos, J. J. 1982. Toward a theory of infant temperament. In *The development of attachment and affiliative systems,* ed. R. N. Emde and R. J. Harmon. New York: Plenum.

Goldsmith, H. H. and Campos, J. J. 1986. Fundamental issues in the study of early temperament: The Denver Twin Temperament Study. In *Advances in developmental psychology*, vol. 4, ed. M. E. Lamb, A. L. Brown, and B. Rogoff, 231–83. Hillsdale, N.J.: Erlbaum.

Goldsmith, H. H., and Gottesman, I. I. 1981. Origins of variation in behavioral style: A longitudinal study of temperament in young twins. *Child Development* 52:91–103.

Hay, D. A. 1985. *Essentials of behaviour genetics*. Oxford: Blackwells.

Kagan, J., and Reznick, J. S. 1986. Shyness and temperament. In *Shyness: Perspectives on research and treatment*, ed. W. H. Jones, J. M. Cheek, and S. R. Briggs, 81–90. New York: Plenum.

Kagan, J.; Reznick, J. S.; and Snidman, N. 1986. Temperament and behavioral inhibition in early childhood. In *The study of temperament: Changes, continuities and challenges*, ed. R. Plomin and J. Dunn. Hillsdale, N.J.: Erlbaum.

Lacey, J. I. 1967. Somatic response patterning and stress: Some revisions of activation theory. In *Psychological stress*, ed. M. H. Appley and R. Trumbull, 15–37. New York: Appleton-Century-Crofts.

Loehlin, J. C.; Horn, J. M.; and Willerman, L. 1981. Personality resemblance in adoptive families. *Behavior Genetics* 11: 309–30.

Loehlin, J. C., and Nichols, R. C. 1976. *Heredity, environment and personality*. Austin: University of Texas Press.

Loehlin, J. C.; Willerman, L.; and Horn, J. M. 1982. Personality resemblances between unwed mothers and their adopted-away offspring. *Journal of Personality and Social Psychology* 42:1089–99.

Loehlin, J. C.; Willerman, L.; and Horn, J. M. 1985. Personality resemblance in adoptive families when the children are late adolescents and adults. *Journal of Personality and Social Psychology* 48:376–92.

Loehlin, J. C.; Willerman, L.; and Horn, J. M. 1987. Personality resemblance in adoptive families: A 10-year follow-up. *Journal of Personality and Social Psychology* 53: 961–69.

McClearn G. E.; Pedersen, N. L.; Plomin, R.; Nesselroade, J. R.; and Friberg, L. 1988. *The Swedish Adoption/Twin Study on Aging*. University Park: Center for Developmental and Health Genetics, Pennsylvania State University. Typescript.

Matheny, A. P., Jr. 1980. Bayley's Infant Behavior Record: Behavioral components and twin analyses. *Child Development* 51:1157–67.

Matheny, A. P., Jr. In press. Children's behavioral inhibition over age and across situations: Genetic similarity for a trait during change. *Journal of Personality*.

Matheny, A. P., Jr., and Dolan, A. B. 1975. Persons, situations and time: A genetic view of behavioral change in children. *Journal of Personality and Social Psychology* 32:1106–10.

Matheny, A. P., Jr.; Dolan, A. B.; and Wilson, R. S. 1976. Within-pair similarity on Bayley's Infant Behavior Record. *Journal of Research in Personality* 14:224–234.

Meickle, A. W.; Stringham, J. D.; Woodward, M. G.; and Bishop, T. B. 1988. Heritability of variation of plasma cortisol levels. *Metabolism* 37:514–17.

O'Connor, M.; Foch, T.; Sherry, T.; and Plomin, R. 1980. A twin study of specific behavioral problems of socialization as viewed by parents. *Journal of Abnormal Child Psychology* 8:189–99.

Pedersen, N. L.; Friberg, L.; Floderus-Myrhed, B.; McClearn, G. E.; and Plomin,

R. 1984. Swedish early separated twins: Identification and characterization. *Acta geneticae medicae et gemellologiae* 33: 243–50.

Plomin, R. 1976a. Extraversion: Sociability and impulsivity. *Journal of Personality Assessment* 40:24–30.

Plomin, R. 1976b. A twin and family study of personality in young children. *Journal of Psychology* 94:233–35.

Plomin, R. 1981. Heredity and temperament: A comparison of twin data for self-report questionnaires, parental ratings, and objectively assessed behavior. In *Progress in clinical and biological research, twin research 3, t. B, Intelligence, personality, and development,* ed. L. Gedda, P. Parisi, and W. E. Nance, 269–78. New York: Liss.

Plomin, R. 1986. *Development, genetics, and psychology.* Hillsdale, N.J.: Erlbaum.

Plomin, R., and Daniels, D. 1986. Genetics and shyness. In *Shyness: Perspectives on research and treatment,* ed. W. H. Jones, J. M. Cheek, and S. R. Briggs, 63–80. New York: Plenum.

Plomin, R., and Daniels, D. 1987. Why are two children in the same family so different from each other? *Behavioral and Brain Sciences* 10:1–16.

Plomin, R., and DeFries, J. C. 1985. *Origins of individual differences in infancy: The Colorado Adoption Project.* New York: Academic.

Plomin, R.; DeFries, J. C.; and Fulker, D. W. 1988. *Nature and nurture in infancy and early childhood.* New York: Cambridge University Press.

Plomin, R.; DeFries, J. C.; and McClearn, G. E. In press. *Behavioral genetics: A primer.* 2d ed. New York: Freeman.

Plomin, R., and Dunn, J. 1986. *The study of temperament: Changes, continuities, and challenges.* Hillsdale, N.J.: Erlbaum.

Plomin, R., and Foch, T. T. 1980. A twin study of objectively assessed personality in childhood. *Journal of Personality and Social Psychology* 39:680–88.

Plomin, R., and Ho, H-z. In press. Brain, behavior and developmental genetics. In *The brain and behavioral development: Biosocial dimensions,* ed. K. Gibson, L. Sherrod, and A. C. Petersen. Hawthorne, N.Y.: Aldine.

Plomin, R., and Nesselroade, J. R. In press. Behavioral genetics and personality change. *Journal of Personality.*

Plomin, R.; Pedersen, N. L.; McClearn, G. E.; Nesselroade, J. R.; and Bergeman, C. S. 1988. EAS temperaments during the last half of the life span: Twins reared apart and twins reared together. *Psychology and Aging* 3:43–50.

Plomin, R., and Rowe, D. C. 1977. A twin study of temperament in young children. *Journal of Psychology* 97:107–13.

Pogue-Geile, M. F., and Rose, R. J. 1985. Developmental genetic studies of adult personality. *Developmental Psychology* 21:547–57.

Rose, R. J., and Ditto, W. B. 1983. A developmental-genetic analysis of common fears from early adolescence to early adulthood. *Child Development* 54:361–68.

Rothbart, M. K. 1981. Measurement of temperament in infancy. *Child Development* 52:569–78.

Rothbart, M. K., and Derryberry, D. 1981. Development of individual differences in temperament. In *Advances in developmental psychology,* vol. 1, ed. M. E. Lamb and A. L. Brown. Hillsdale, N.J.: Erlbaum.

Rowe, D. C., and Plomin, R. 1977. Temperament in early childhood. *Journal of Personality assessment* 41:150–56.

Scarr, S.; Webber, P. I; Weinberg, R. A.; and Wittig, M. A. 1981. Personality resemblance among adolescents and their parents in biologically related and adoptive families. *Journal of Personality and Social Psychology* 40:885–98.

Stevenson, J., and Fielding, J. 1985. Ratings of temperament in families of young twins. *British Journal of Developmental Psychology* 3:143–52.

Strelau, J. 1965. *Problems and methods of investigation into types of nervous system in man.* Wroclaw-Warsaw: Ossolineum.

Strelau, J. 1983. *Temperament-personality-activity.* New York: Academic.

Tellegen, A.; Lykken, D. T.; Bouchard, T. J., Jr.; Wilcox, K.; Segal, N.; and Rich, S. 1988. Personality similarity in twins reared apart and together. *Journal of Personality and Social Psychology* 54:1031–39.

Thomas, A., and Chess, S. 1977. *Temperament and development.* New York: Bruner/Mazel.

Vandenberg, S. G. 1967. Hereditary factors in normal personality traits. In *Recent advances in biological psychiatry,* vol. 9, ed. J. Wortis. New York: Plenum.

Wilson, R. S.; Brown, A.; and Matheny, A. P., Jr. 1971. Emergence and persistence of behavioral differences in twins. *Child Development* 42:1381–98.

Wilson, R. S., and Matheny, A. P., Jr. 1986. Behavior-genetics research in infant temperament: The Louisville Twin Study. In *The study of temperament: Changes, continuities and challenges,* ed. R. Plomin and J. Dunn, 81–97. Hillsdale, N.J.: Erlbaum.

12 Anxiety Disorders in Parents and Children: a Genetic-Epidemiological Perspective

MYRNA M. WEISSMAN

Introduction

The data presented in this chapter are rooted in clinical psychiatry and derive from the methods of genetic epidemiology. However, the approach and findings have implications for the study of behavioral inhibition. The data derive from a family-genetic study that examined the relations between adult forms of anxiety disorders in parents and childhood forms of anxiety disorders in their offspring. Questions that ultimately may be considered by this strategy include, Is behavioral inhibition or shyness in young children a precursor of adult anxiety disorders? Is behavioral inhibition a latent trait that has variable forms of expression at different ages?

Anxiety as a Clinical Disorder

Anxiety states were first described in the cardiovascular literature in the nineteenth century. However, it was Freud (1977) who offered the first detailed description of anxiety syndromes of relevance to psychiatric practice. He identified several different forms of anxiety states. Many of the subtypes he proposed in his 1917 lecture (simple and social phobias, agoraphobia, panic disorder, and obsessive-compulsive disorder) are remarkably similar to the anxiety disorders now classified in the American Psychiatric Association's

This study was supported in part by Alcohol, Drug Abuse, and Mental Health Administration grant MH 28274 from the Affective and Anxiety Disorders Research Branch, National Institute of Mental Health, Rockville, Md.; and Mental Health Research Network on Risk and Protective Factors in the Major Mental Disorders grant 86–213, "Child and Adult Depressive Disorders: A Test of Continuities Using Family-Genetic Data from the John D. and Catherine T. MacArthur Foundation." A version of this paper was also presented at the Behavioral Inhibition Conference sponsored by the New England Node of the John D. and Catherine T. MacArthur Foundation Network on the Transition from Infancy to Childhood, Harvard University, Cambridge, Mass., 21–22 November 1986.

Diagnostic and Statistical Manual of Mental Disorders, Third Edition (DSM-III).

Despite the description of distinct types of anxiety states as early as 1917, a unitary view of anxiety disorders prevailed in American psychiatry until the 1960s, when it was challenged by new information on the differential efficacy of behavioral and of pharmacological treatments for components of anxiety states.

Anxiety disorders in the DSM-III have been separated into subtypes for adults and children. For adults, these include agoraphobia, social and simple phobia, panic disorder, generalized anxiety disorder (GAD), and obsessive-compulsive disorder. Those anxiety disorders first evident in childhood and adolescence include separation anxiety, avoidant disorder, and overanxious disorder.

The epidemiology of most of the anxiety disorders in adults has been determined through surveys of community samples (Weissman 1985). The familial transmission of some anxiety disorders has also been studied (Crowe et al. 1980; Crowe et al. 1983; Leckman et al. 1983; Weissman, Leckman, et al. 1984). There have been no epidemiological studies of children using current psychiatric diagnostic criteria (Orvaschel and Weissman 1986).

Although the DSM-III includes a separate category of anxiety disorders that originate in childhood, there is no reason not to diagnose the other adult anxiety disorders in children, except for the explicit requirement that generalized anxiety disorder not be diagnosed before age 18. In fact, data from epidemiological, family, and clinical studies suggest that many of the anxiety disorders have their first onset in adolescence or earlier. However, since children have not been studied extensively in epidemiological or in family studies, most of the data on age of onset of anxiety disorders in childhood have been obtained retrospectively from adults. There is some suggestion from clinical studies of children that the first onset of anxiety disorders may occur quite early and that there may be a continuum between the adult and the childhood forms of anxiety disorder.

There has not been one published longitudinal study of individuals first identified as having an anxiety disorder in childhood who have been followed to adulthood to determine the natural history, clinical course, or prognostic significance of the childhood anxiety disorders and their continuity to the adult disorders. One such study has just been undertaken by R. Gittelman-Klein at Columbia University.

Family-Genetic Studies as a Research Strategy

Since the introduction of standardized instruments for assessing psychiatric disorders and of specified diagnostic criteria, there has been considerable interest in testing the validity of diagnostic criteria as well as the relations between adult and childhood forms of the disorder. While there are several approaches to validity in psychiatry (follow-up studies, clinical response to treatment, and association with biological markers), family-genetic studies are another approach to identifying possible etiological homogeneous subgroups.

Evidence for familial aggregation of a disorder does not imply that the origin of a disorder is genetic. Aggregation could result either from shared genes or from common environmental factors such as infection, diet, stress, or social learning. It is both simplistic and erroneous to assume that only genetic or only environmental factors are involved in the etiology of psychiatric disorders, for both undoubtedly contribute. Understanding the degree to which each of the sources contributes and interacts to produce a given phenotype is the aim of genetic-epidemiological studies.

Other study paradigms from which information on familial aggregation can be derived include adoption and twin studies, and these designs have been used to study the major psychiatric disorders (for a detailed discussion, see Weissman et al. 1986).

Although family-genetic studies do not yield evidence for the amount of genetic variance, data from family studies in psychiatry can serve several purposes. One of the most fruitful has been to provide better understanding of diagnostic heterogeneity. It is quite likely that many of the psychiatric disorders are groups of conditions rather than single entities with different etiological and modifying risk factors. The use of family data in the absence of specific neuropathological evidence is one approach to identifying homogeneous diagnostic subgroups. If the diagnostic subgroup under study increases risk of the disorder and "breeds true" within families, potential evidence for the validity of the diagnostic group is suggested. If adult forms of a disorder are related to increased risk of specific disorders in the offspring of affected individuals, this suggests a relation between the adult and childhood disorders.

Because variation in expression of a particular trait within families is assumed to result from the same latent factor, family studies can yield information on the clinical expression of a disorder. This property of family studies can lead to the development of more precise clinical descriptions of the spectrum of disorders, as manifest in the personality, symptoms, or social functioning of relatives. Studies of the young children of adult probands can yield information on the transmission of disorders and/or symptoms across generations, on the early signs and childhood forms of the disorder, and on the risk or protective factors that mediate the development of the disorder.

Of course, these methods are indirect and represent only one strategy that requires replication by similar and alternate strategies. Multiple strategies for validating the diagnosis of anxiety disorders are currently being developed.

Design of a Family-Genetic Study

Case-Control Studies

In a family-genetic study, a proband with the illness under investigation is selected for study and is then matched to a control proband (i.e., an individual who does not have the illness under investigation but who is comparable on other characteristics). Usually, the prevalence of the condition among first-degree relatives is compared to prevalence among relatives of controls. In the absence of control groups, the rates of illness among relatives can be compared to population rates. This design requires accurate information on the population at risk. In either case, these studies usually have a retrospective cohort design in that the lifetime rates of illness in relatives are obtained on the basis of recall of their lifetime incidence of disorder.

Top-Down Studies

In family studies of psychiatric disorders, the probands, or index cases, with the disorder being investigated have nearly always been adults who were selected from treatment settings or from psychiatric or case registries. Family studies that begin with the adult probands and study psychopathology among their offspring as well as other relatives have been called "top down" by Puig-Antich (1984).

Bottom-Up Studies

With the increasing interest in childhood psychiatric disorders during the last decade, children have also begun to be defined as the probands in family studies termed "bottom-up" studies (Strober 1984). In a manner similar to that followed in the adult studies, children who serve as probands generally have been selected from inpatient or outpatient treatment settings. Studies that begin with the child or adolescent as the proband, or index case, tend to find very high rates of illness in the adult relatives, possibly because of sampling bias. Although the proband is the treated child, it is the parent who brings the child for treatment and who grants permission for the child to be included in the study. Ill parents, or parents sensitized to the effects of the illness because of several ill family members, may be more likely than healthy parents to bring their children to treatment and to consent to the child's inclusion in a study.

In order to control for this ascertainment bias, researchers can select a comparison control proband group of children with another treated psychiatric illness. The rates of all types of psychiatric illness will also tend to be high in the adult relatives of the child comparison group. However, the types of illness and the magnitudes of the differences in rates between the relatives of the

Case   Control

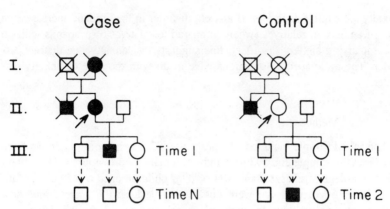

Fig. 1. High-risk study.

cases and the relatives of the comparison control group can provide more important information than the absolute rates of illness in the relatives.

High-Risk Studies

The high-risk paradigm is a variant of the family study (see fig. 1) (Garmezy 1974; Weissman et al. 1986). The focus is usually limited to the young children of ill probands. Usually, there is no assessment of the proband's first-degree or other relatives, although it is quite important to assess the spouse. In high-risk studies, the offspring are usually studied longitudinally in order to identify risk factors that are premorbid to, rather than concomitant with, the disorder or that are manifestations of the disorder. Such factors may serve to identify vulnerable individuals and permit efforts toward prevention and intervention.

Family-Genetic Study

The data reported here derive from a high-risk study imbedded in a family study in which the young offspring are being followed longitudinally (fig. 1) (Weissman, Kidd, and Prusoff 1982; Weissman, Leckman, et al. 1984; Weissman, Prusoff, et al. 1984). Diagnostic information was available on the probands' first-degree relatives and offspring.

The first findings derived from family studies of depressed patients, in which my colleagues and I discovered that many depressed patients had concomitant anxiety disorder. We attempted to understand the relation between anxiety disorders and depression by using familial transmission as an outcome. To do this, we asked whether anxiety disorder in the proband increases risk of depression and/or anxiety in relatives. If an accompanying anxiety disorder increases risk of depression, then this suggests that depression and anxiety are similar disorders. If anxiety disorder in the proband increases the risk of anxiety in relatives (when compared to relatives of probands with no accompanying anxiety disorder), this suggests that anxiety is a distinct disorder. The more specific questions have to do with the type of anxiety disorder.

Methods

The initial sample included 215 probands (82 normal controls drawn from a community sample and 133 probands with major depression), 1,331 of their adult first-degree relatives, and 194 of their children aged 6–17 years. Children under 6 years of age were not studied because the current interview methods are not suitable for use with these younger age groups. Diagnoses were based on the Research Diagnostic Criteria (RDC) for all probands and adult first-degree relatives and on the DSM-III for the children (Weissman, Leckman, et al. 1984).

In the family study of adults, comprehensive diagnostic estimates of probands, spouses, and all adult first-degree relatives, including children older than 18 years, were obtained through direct interview, family history from multiple informants, and medical records when available. Diagnoses were made by two clinicians uninvolved in the collection of the data on the basis of all available information. The interviewers and the clinicians did not know whether the children came from depressed or normal parents.

Children younger than 18 years were not interviewed directly; instead, information on minor children was obtained by family history from the proband, spouse, and other first-degree relatives. The data presented on the children in the report of this study always refer to the probands' children aged 6–17 years.

A screening instrument, modified from the early work of Herjanic and Reich, was administered to the probands and spouses to determine symptoms of psychopathological condition, behavioral problems, and psychological treatment in any of their children who were aged 6–17 years at the time of the proband interview. First, there was a general probe about problems with the child, and then the informant was read a symptom list, including questions about the child's psychological treatment, school difficulties, and symptoms. Information was obtained separately for each child. When there were positive answers to symptoms, the interviewers were instructed to code them and to record details in a narrative form as well. Medical records were also sought. For 64 percent of children with a diagnosis, information was available from more than one source. Since many of the probands with major depression also had anxiety disorders, we became interested in the effect of a depression plus an anxiety disorder in probands on rates and type of illness in first-degree relatives.

Table 1: Diagnoses in Adult Relatives 18 Years or Older by Proband Diagnosis

Proband Diagnosis	N at Risk	Major Depression	Phobia	Panic	GAD	Any Anxiety
Normal	521	5.6	1.2	.0	4.0	5.2
Major depression						
No anxiety	338	10.7	2.1	2.1	6.2	9.2
With agoraphobia	96	11.5	1.0	2.1	5.2	8.3
With panic disorder	133	19.6	3.8	3.8	10.5	15.8

For these analyses, we looked closely at the specific anxiety disorders in the probands, using a diagnostic hierarchy for probands with depression and anxiety disorders, as follows: agoraphobia > panic disorder > generalized anxiety disorder. Operationally, this meant that depressed probands with both agoraphobia and panic disorder would be classified as depressed with agoraphobia and so on (Leckman et al. 1983). For this chapter, I will concentrate on agoraphobia and panic disorder.

Findings in Adults

Table 1 summarizes the results in adults. In general, the first-degree relatives of probands with major depression and panic disorder had the highest rates of illness. They showed increased rates of major depression, phobia, panic, GAD, and anxiety disorders when compared to the relatives of either the normal controls or the depressed probands without an anxiety disorder.

Findings in Children

Next, we looked at the rates of DSM-III diagnoses in 194 of the probands' children ages 6–17 (table 2) (Weissman, Leckman, et al. 1984). The subgroups of probands were the same as those for the study of adults, with one exception. Probands who had social and simple phobias, as well as agoraphobia, were included in the depression and phobia group since we were examining the outcome of the different phobias in children. As with the adult relatives, the highest rates of illness were in the children of probands with both depression and panic disorder. The rates of major depression (26.3 per 100) and separation anxiety (36.8 per 100) were highest in the children of parents with both depression and panic disorder. These findings support the suggestion of Klein and Gittelman-Klein (1978) that there is an association between childhood separation anxiety and panic disorder.

Several of the children had both depression and anxiety disorders. Table 3 shows the rates of depression and anxiety disroders, singly or together, in children by proband diagnosis. The results show that the children's diagnoses tended to follow those of their proband relatives, with several specific trends

Table 2: DSM-III Diagnosis in Children Ages 6–17 Years by Proband Parent Diagnosis

DSM-III Diagnosis in Children	Proband Parent Diagnosis (Lifetime Rates per 100 in Children)			
	Normal (87)	Depression, No Anxiety Disorder (38)	Depression and Agoraphobia (18)	Depression and Panic (19)
Major depression	.0	10.5	22.2	26.3
Separation anxiety	.0	.0	11.1	36.8
Panic disorder	.0	.0	5.6	5.3
Agoraphobia	.0	.0	5.6	5.3
Social phobia	1.2	.0	11.1	5.3
Simple phobia	.0	.0	.0	5.3
Obsessive-compulsive	1.2	.0	5.6	.0
Any diagnosis	8.1	21.1	27.8	42.1

Note. Numbers in parentheses represent number of children at risk.

visible. For example, (1) there was increased depression in the children of the depressed probands, particularly the children of probands with depression plus agoraphobia and the children of probands with depression plus panic disorder (22.2 and 26.3 percent, respectively); (2) there was increased anxiety disorder in the children of the probands with depression plus panic disorder; (3) the children of probands with depression and no anxiety disorder did not themselves have anxiety disorders; (4) increased rates of phobia were observed in the children of probands with depression plus agoraphobia and among the children of probands with depression plus panic disorder; and (5) there were increased co-occurrences of depression plus any anxiety disorder (26.3 per 100) in the children of probands who also had the co-occurrence of depression and an anxiety disorder, particularly panic disorder (see table 3).

Table 3: DSM-III Anxiety Disorders and Depression in Children by Proband Parent Diagnosis

DSM-III Diagnosis in Children	Children with Diagnosis (N)	Proband Parent Diagnosis (Lifetime Rates per 100 in Children)			
		Normal	Depression, No Anxiety Disorder	Depression and Agoraphobia	Depression and Panic
Any major depression	17	.0	13.2	22.2	26.3
Any anxiety disorder[a]	13	2.3	.0	11.1	36.8
Any phobia[b]	5	1.2	.0	11.1	10.5
Major depression and any anxiety disorder	8	.0	.0	11.1	26.3

[a] Includes all phobias, panic, separation anxiety, and obsessive-compulsive.
[b] Includes agoraphobia, simple, and social phobia.

Age of Onset and Sex Distribution of Anxiety Disorders

Age-corrected rates of depression and any anxiety disorder by sex were calculated for the children of probands using Lifetime Risk (LTR), which is defined as the risk of onset of a particular disorder between birth and some particular age (age 18 years, in this case). The estimation of LTR is based on the nonparametric product-limit table method for analyzing survivorship developed by Kaplan and Meier (1958), which yields a maximum likelihood estimate of LTR. This method makes a calculation at each point in time there is a change in the number of persons at risk for development of the disorder. The number at risk changes with each onset of the disorder and with each death of an unaffected person. The Biomedical Computer Program P-series (BMDP) program PIL was used to calculate LTR.

The earliest onset age of an anxiety disorder was 3 years. The LTR by age 18 years for developing an anxiety disorder was .08 among boys and .10 among girls. There were no significant differences in rates of anxiety disorders by sex of child for these young groups. The epidemiological data on adults show a strong sex effect in adults, with higher rates in women for all anxiety disorders. Thus, increased risk of anxiety disorder in adult women is not apparent in children. As in depression, the sex difference with increasing risk to women may not become apparent until after puberty.

Using logistic analyses, we also examined the effect of sex of proband on the rates of any anxiety disorder or any depression in children and found no significant effect. Caution must be exhibited in interpreting these findings because of the small sample size of children who were affected and the retrospective nature of the data.

Parent Characteristics as Risk Factors

Several proband characteristics (e.g., sociodemographic variables, early history, and family history of illness) were examined to determine whether these proband characteristics increased the risk of major depression, any anxiety disorder, or any DSM-III diagnosis in the children across the proband groups. The proband characteristics that did not increase the risk were current age, sex, social class, number of children (any age) in family, marital status, childhood history of stuttering or sleepwalking, and separation from parent as a child. The characteristics of probands that did increase risk in the children were number of episodes of depression, childhood history of enuresis, and number of first-degree relatives (i.e., probands' parents, siblings, or adult children or children's grandparents, aunts, uncles, or adult siblings) with major depression or anxiety disorders.

Having found that the proband's number of episodes of depression significantly increased the probability of a major depression in the child, we conducted the following analysis to determine if either the child's age at exposure or the number of years of exposure to parental illness was critical in increasing risk. We first examined the relation between the child's age at exposure to the parent's first onset of depression and of anxiety; then we controlled for the number of years the child had been exposed to the proband's depression and anxiety. Neither set of analyses yielded any significant differences in rate of disorders in the children; nor were there any interpretable trends.

Summary Findings

The findings of our first family-genetic study of anxiety disorder in the children and parents with depression and anxiety were as follows.

1. Major depression and anxiety disorders are probably heterogeneous diagnostic categories.

2. Probands with both major depression and panic disorder show markedly increased rates of major depression as well as anxiety disorders (phobia, panic disorder, and GAD) compared with the first-degree relatives of normal controls and depressed probands without anxiety disorders.

3. These findings suggest that panic disorder and major depression may partially have a common underlying diathesis. My colleagues and I are testing this hypothesis prospectively in new studies.

4. As compared with the children of normals, the children (ages 6–17) of depressed probands were at increased risk for major depression. Depression plus agoraphobia or panic disorder in the probands conferred an additional risk on the children. If the proband had both depression and panic disorder, the children were at the greatest risk for having a psychiatric disorder, particularly major depression and separation anxiety. More than one-third of the children of probands with depression plus panic disorder had separation anxiety, and more than one-fourth had major depression.

5. As noted elsewhere (Weissman, Leckman, et al. 1984), the risk to children for major depression or any psychiatric disorder increased linearly if two parents were ill. There was a similar, but nonsignificant, trend for anxiety disorders.

6. The proband characteristics that did not increase risk of anxiety disorder or any psychiatric disorder in children were current age; sex; social class; marital status; number of other children; age of onset of depression, anxiety disorder, or any psychiatric disorder; childhood history of stuttering or sleepwalking; and separation from parents during childhood. The child's age at exposure or years of exposure to parental illness also did not increase risk (Weissman, Leckman, et al. 1984).

7. The proband characteristics that significantly increased risk of anxiety in children were recurrent depressions, high familial loading of major depression or any anxiety disorder, and childhood history of enuresis.

Are Adult and Childhood Anxiety Disorders on a Continuum?

We have found that major depression in the parent increases the risk of major depression in the children and that depression plus anxiety disorders, particularly panic and agoraphobia, confers an additional risk of depression and anxiety in these children. Panic disorder in the parents, in contrast to other anxiety disorders, confers a greater than threefold increase of separation anxiety in the children.

These data suggest that the children of patients with agoraphobia or panic disorder are beginning to manifest similar disorders themselves, particularly separation anxiety. A number of investigators have made similar observations about the onset of adult anxiety disorder in childhood or early adulthood. One of the earliest observations was made by Klein (1964) in a review of 32 adult patients being treated for panic attacks, with agoraphobia or anticipatory anxiety. At least half the adult patients reported marked separation anxiety and difficulty in adjusting to school as children. The patients who reported childhood separation anxiety had chronically high levels of separation anxiety throughout their lives and suffered significantly more panic attacks under conditions of separation and bereavement.

Roth (1960), in a study of 135 patients with phobic anxiety and depersonalization, noted that onset occurred most often during the early 20s. Sheehan, Sheehan, and Minichiello (1980), in a study of 100 patients treated for agoraphobia and panic attacks, found that 55 percent had an onset of agoraphobia by age 20. Buglass et al. (1977), in a study of 30 agoraphobic housewives, dated the mean age of onset of agoraphobic symptoms at 31 years, with a range of 10–52 years. Agras, Sylvester, and Oliveau (1969), in a community survey of 325 persons, found a high prevalence of fears and phobia in children younger than 14 years. There was also a different pattern of phobias with age. A fear of doctors, injection, darkness, and strangers was short lived and had a sharply declining incidence as the children matured. A fear of animals, heights, storms, enclosed places, and social situations showed slowly declining incidence with age, suggesting that, once acquired, such fears were longer lived.

Others have questioned whether childhood anxiety symptoms are related to adult anxiety disorders or to nonspecific psychiatric problems. Berg and his colleagues (Berg, Butler, and Pritchard 1974; Berg, Marks, et al. 1974) surveyed 786 female members of an agoraphobia correspondence club to learn about incidence of past school phobias. When these women were compared with 58 nonagoraphobic women who were psychiatric outpatients with a neurotic disorder, few differences between the groups were found. A history of school phobias was equally common in both groups. The authors concluded that childhood school phobias were related generally to adult neurotic illness rather than specifically to adult agoraphobia.

Tyrer and Tyrer (1974) interviewed 60 phobic, 60 anxious, and 120 depressed adult patients, and 120 matched orthopedic and dental patients for comparison, about problems of childhood school attendance that were due to refusal. They found that school refusal occurred more frequently among the patients with psychiatric disorders. There was a nonsignificant tendency for childhood school refusal to be higher in phobic patients. These authors concluded, in agreement with Berg, that there is a link between childhood school refusal and adult neurotic illness. However, the diagnostic criteria for neurotic illness in these studies were unclear. Many of these nonagoraphobic neurotic women might have been suffering from other anxiety or depressive disorders.

Klein's early observations of the possible relation between adult and childhood anxiety disorders, and the successful treatment of these adult anxiety patients with imipramine, led to the first trial of imipramine in school-phobic children by Gittelman-Klein and Klein (1973). Their results suggested that school-phobic children and phobic-anxious adults may share a common psychopathological process, as both adults and children with phobic problems had a similar positive response to imipramine. However, my colleagues and I agree with the investigators' conclusion about the need for long-term studies of phobic children to determine the degree to which these disorders were precursors of adult anxiety or of depressive states. Direct observation of children is important.

 Relevance for Studies of Behavioral Inhibition

Very young children and infants have not been included in any of the studies cited. Since anxiety disorders may begin in childhood, it would be quite useful to study children before the onset of a clinical disorder.

There are no family-genetic studies, to our knowledge, that have included the assessment of offspring under the age of 6 years. Direct interviews of children are not very useful for the diagnostic assessment of psychiatric disorders in this age group. Other approaches are required. There is an opportunity here for fruitful collaboration with developmental psychologists who use observational techniques that can be modified for field studies. As an example, the approaches used by Kagan and his colleagues (e.g., Kagan et al. 1984) in their elegant studies of very young shy children may be quite important in assessing children of adult probands with agoraphobia and panic disorder. Is shyness an early form of agoraphobia or panic disorder? Are behavioral inhibitions the latent traits of anxiety disorders? If the design used is a family-case-control or high-risk method, as described here, it would be relatively easy to incorporate young children and infants in the assessment, given that methods of assessing behavioral inhibition have been developed. These measures could be considered as proxies for anxiety disorders and the results incorporated into the epidemiological and genetic analyses. If the shy or behaviorally inhibited child is the proband, as in the bottom-up study, then the inclusion of a control group of children is warranted. Perhaps non–behaviorally inhibited children enrolled in the same study would be suitable. Without a control group, if anxiety is found in the parents of behaviorally inhibited children, it will be unclear whether the association might not be due to the tendency of anxious parents to enroll their children in studies.

Finally, it is important that the diagnostic assessment of parents and relatives be made with careful attention to the type of anxiety disorders and their comorbidity with major depression or other disorders. There are several good diagnostic interviews available that cover the variety of anxiety disorders (Weissman et al. 1986). Previous family studies that my colleagues and I conducted began with an interest in major depression, and the findings led us into studies of anxiety because of the high comorbidity with depression and the intriguing results in children. We are currently conducting studies of various anxiety disorders in families. The increased collaboration in such a study of developmental psychologists interested in behavioral traits of infants and young children as well as genetic epidemiologists interested in transmission of psychiatric disorders in families across the generations could be potentially fruitful and exciting.

References

Agras, S.; Sylvester, D.; and Oliveau, D. 1969. The epidemiology of common fears and phobias. *Comprehensive Psychiatry* 10:151–56.

Berg, I. 1976. School phobia in the children of agoraphobic women. *British Journal of Psychiatry* 128:86–89.

Berg, I.; Butler, A.; and Pritchard, J. 1974. Psychiatric illness in the mothers of school-phobic adolescents. *British Journal of Psychiatry* 125:466–67.

Berg, I.; Marks, I.; McGuire, R.; and Lipsedge, M. 1974. School phobia and agoraphobia. *Psychological Medicine* 4:428–34.

Buglass, D.; Clarke, J.; Henderson, A. S.; Kreitman, N.; and Presley, A. S. 1977. A study of agoraphobic housewives. *Psychological Medicine* 7:73–86.

Crowe, R.; Noyes, R.; Pauls, D. L.; and Slymen, D. 1983. A family study of panic disorder. *Archives of General Psychiatry* 40:1065–69.

Crowe, R.; Pauls, D. L.; Slymen, D. J.; and Noyes, R. 1980. A family study of anxiety neurosis. *Archives of General Psychiatry* 37:77–79.

Freud, S. 1977. Anxiety Lecture XXV, 1917. In *An introductory lecture on psychoanalysis*, ed. J. Strachey, 392–412. New York: Norton.

Garmezy, N. 1974. Children at risk: The search for the antecedents of schizophrenia: 2. Ongoing research programs, issues, and intervention. *Schizophrenia Bulletin* 9:55–125.

Gittelman-Klein, R., and Klein, D. F. 1973. School phobia: Diagnostic considerations in the light of imipramine effects. *Journal of Nervous and Mental Disorders* 156:199–215.

Kagan, J.; Reznick, S. J.; Clarke, C.; Snidman, N.; and Garcia-Coll, C. 1984. Behavioral inhibitions to the unfamiliar. *Child Development* 55:2212–25.

Kaplan, E. B., and Meier, P. 1958. Nonparametric estimation from incomplete observations. *Journal of the American Statistical Association* 53:457–81.

Klein, D. F. 1964. Delineation of two-drug responsive anxiety syndromes. *Psychopharmacologia* 5:397–408.

Klein, D. F., and Gittelman-Klein, R. 1978. Drug treatment of separation anxiety and depressive illness in children. *Advances in Biological Psychiatry* 2:50–60.

Leckman, J. F.; Weissman, M. M.; Merikangas, K. R.; Pauls, D. L.; and Prusoff, B. A. 1983. Panic disorder and major depression: Increased risk of depression, alcoholism, panic and phobic disorders in families of depressed probands with panic disorder. *Archives of General Psychiatry* 40:1055–60.

Orvaschel, H., and Weissman, M. M. 1986. Epidemiology of anxiety disorders in children: A review. In *Anxiety disorders of childhood*, ed. R. Gittelman, 58–72. New York: Guilford.

Puig-Antich, J. 1984. Affective disorders. In *Comprehensive textbook of psychiatry*, vol. 2, ed. H. J. Kaplan and B. J. Sadock, 1850–61. Baltimore: Williams & Wilkins.

Roth, M. 1960. The phobic anxiety-depersonalization syndrome and some general aetiological problems in psychiatry. *Journal of Neuropsychiatry* 12:293–306.

Sheehan, D. V.; Sheehan, K. E.; and Minichiello, W. E. 1981. Age of onset of phobic disorders: A reevaluation. *Comprehensive Psychiatry* 22:544–53.

Strober, M. 1984. Familial aspects of depressive disorder in early adolescence. In *An update on childhood depression*, ed. E. Weller. Washington, D.C.: American Psychiatric Press.

Tyrer, P., and Tyrer, S. 1974. School refusal, truancy, and adult neurotic illness. *Psychological Medicine* 4:416–21.

Weissman, M. M. 1985. The epidemiology of anxiety disorders: Rates, risks, and familial patterns. In *Anxiety and the anxiety disorders*, ed. A. H. Tuma and J. D. Maser, 275–96. Hillsdale, N.J.: Erlbaum.

Weissman, M. M.; Kidd, K. K.; and Prusoff, B. A. 1982. Variability in rates of affective disorders in relatives of depressed and normal probands. *Archives of General Psychiatry* 39:1397–1403.

Weissman, M. M.; Leckman, J. F.; Merikangas, K. R.; Gammon, G. D.; and Prusoff, B. A. 1984. Depression and anxiety disorders in parents and children: Results from the Yale Family Study. *Archives of General Psychiatry* 41: 845–52.

Weissman, M. M.; Merikangas, K. R.; John, K.; Wickramaratne, P.; Prusoff, B. A.; and Kidd, K. K. 1986. Family-genetic studies of psychiatric disorders: Developing technologies. *Archives of General Psychiatry* 43:1104–16.

Weissman, M. M.; Prusoff, B. A.; Gammon, G. D.; Merikangas, K. R.; Leckman, J. F.; and Kidd, K. K. 1984. Psychopathology in the children (ages 6–18) of depressed and normal parents. *Journal of the American Academy of Child Psychiatry* 23:78–84.

13 Anxiety Disorders and Behavioral Inhibition

JERROLD F. ROSENBAUM, JOSEPH BIEDERMAN, AND
MICHELLE GERSTEN

Introduction

Among the distinguishing characteristics of children with behavioral inhibition are fearful responses to new situations. Most chapters in this volume discuss these fears as a normal manifestation of the rigors of childhood. From the clinical perspective, however, these fears may be related to more serious psychological states, often labeled "anxiety." The purpose of this chapter is to outline the various clinical classifications of anxiety disorders in adults and children. Finally, we will describe a recent study showing a link between an anxiety disorder in adults and inhibition in their children.

Symptoms of anxiety are difficult to distinguish from those of fear or vigilance. Although its cause may be different, anxiety is a similar distressing cognitive and physical experience of dread, foreboding, or panic, except that it derives from an unknown internal stimulus, is inappropriate to the reality of an external stimulus, or may be concerned with a future stimulus. Anxiety typically has physical, affective, cognitive, and behavioral manifestations. The potential physical symptoms of anxiety reflect nonspecific autonomic, particularly sympathetic, arousal and include a number of bodily perturbations (see table 1) (Rosenbaum 1982). The anxious state ranges from edginess and unease to terror and panic; the cognitive experience is of worry, apprehension, and thought concerned with emotional or bodily danger. The behavioral response to anxiety is concerned with seeking comfort or soothing or with avoidance of any external source of distress. Because the experience of anxiety in one form or another is nearly universal, the recognition of pathological anxiety can be complicated. Anxiousness is a normal and expected transient response to stress and is frequently a necessary stimulus to adaptation and coping. Excessive or "pathological" anxiety, however, is no more a normal state than the production of excess thyroid hormone.

Pathological anxiety is distinguished from normal response by four general

255

Table 1: Physical Signs and Symptoms of Anxiety

Anorexia	Muscle tension
"Butterflies" in stomach	Nausea
Chest pain or tightness	Pallor
Diaphoresis	Palpitations
Diarrhea	Paresthesias
Dizziness	Sexual dysfunction
Dyspnea	Shortness of breath
Dry mouth	Stomach pain
Faintness	Tachycardia
Flushing	Tremulousness
Headache	Urinary frequency
Hyperventilation	Vomiting
Lightheadedness	

Source. Rosenbaum (1982).

features: autonomy, intensity, duration, and behavior. *Autonomy* refers to anxious suffering that persists without being bound to specific environmental stimuli, apparently "endogenous" or having a "life of its own." *Intensity* refers to the level of distress, when the severity of symptoms exceeds the individual's capacity to bear, cope, or tolerate. The *duration* of suffering also can define anxiousness as pathological in that persisting symptoms, rather than transient, adaptive responses, indicate disorder. Finally, anxiety that is autonomous, intense, or long standing may well impair coping or generate specific dysfunctional *behaviors* such as avoidance or withdrawal.

Despite the protean physiological manifestations of anxiety, the experience of anxiety can be divided into two broad categories: an acute, brief wave of intense anxiety with impressive cognitive, physiological, and behavioral components and a lower-grade persistent distress, quantitatively distinct and with some qualitative differences as well. Studies in pharmacology and classification suggest several clinically relevant distinctions between these two states.

The first category of anxiety resembles acute fear or an alarm response to life-threatening danger: a cognitive state of terror or helplessness or a sense of impending disaster or doom, with autonomic but primarily sympathetic activation and typically an urgency to flee or seek safety. The second type of anxiety resembles more a state of arousal or "alert" with a heightened sense of vigilance to possible threats; the levels of inhibition, physical distress, and behavioral impairment are less intense. These two fear states are reminiscent of the clinical syndromes of panic attacks, on the one hand, and generalized or anticipatory anxiety, on the other.

Causes of Anxiety

As innate responses for protecting the organism and thus enhancing survival, panic and vigilance are normal in the face of threatening stimuli. As "anxiety" or psychopathological symptoms, other factors besides acute physical threat are implicated as "triggers" or causes. Several explanatory models have been proposed to explain causation of anxiety symptoms. These include emphasis on the "wiring and juices" of the central nervous system, the behavioral model, which has its focus on learning, and the psychoanalytic model, which emphasizes meanings and memories.

Biological Model

In light of their phenomenological similarities, fear and anxiety may well reflect a common underlying neurophysiology. Animal and neuronal receptor studies suggest that there are at least two central systems involved in fear and pathological anxiety (Charney and Redmond 1983; Insel et al. 1984). The alarm or panic mechanism is likely to have a critical component involving central noradrenergic mechanisms; particularly important is the locus ceruleus (LC), a small retropontine nucleus that is the primary source of the brain's norepinephrine (Huang et al. 1976; Charney and Heninger 1985). When this site of sympathetic activation is stimulated in monkeys, for example, an acute fear response can be elicited with distress vocalizations, fear behaviors, and fleeing. Alternatively, destruction of the LC leads to abnormal complacency in the face of threat (Huang et al. 1976). The biochemical perturbations that increase LC firing appear to elicit similar anxious responses in animals and humans. A number of chemical agents can decrease LC firing and thus block such anxious responses; some of these are used in clinical practice as antipanic agents (e.g., antidepressants, antianxiety drugs). There are, however, dissenting views as to whether the LC plays a critical role in human anxiety (Mason and Fibiger 1979).

A second system appears to involve the benzodiazepine (BZD) receptors, with particular emphasis on limbic system structures, especially the septo-hippocampal areas (Insel et al. 1984). An important role of the limbic system is to screen data from the environment for life-supporting and threatening cues, to monitor internal or bodily sensations, and to mediate relevant motor responses. Vigilance or its psychopathological equivalent, generalized anxiety, most probably involves limbic system activity: "limbic alert." Benzodiazepine receptors in high concentration in relevant limbic system structures may play a role in modulating limbic alert, arousal, and behavioral inhibition by increased binding of the inhibitory neurotransmitter gamma amino butyric acid (GABA) in the BZD-GABA receptor complex (Gray 1985). As one might expect, there are neuronal connections between the LC and limbic systems. The increased firing rate of LC neurons may serve as a rheostat to determine levels of arousal from vigilance to alarm.

Psychoanalytic Model

Psychoanalytic principles, in contrast, are less concerned with the neurophysiology of anxiety symptoms and more with intrapsychic activation of these mechanisms. While Freud's early writing implied a more physiological basis for anxiety attacks in terms of undischarged libido, later emphasis was on anxiety as a signal of threat to the ego, elicited because of events and situations with similarities (symbolic or actual) to early, developmental experiences that were threatening to the vulnerable child (traumatic anxiety) such as separations, losses, certain constellations of relationships, and symbolic objects or events (e.g., snakes, successes). More recent psychoanalytic thinking would emphasize object relations and the use of "internalized objects" to maintain affective stability under stress.

Psychoanalytic observations underscore the use of defense mechanisms such as displacement and the contribution of meanings and symbolic representations of phobic objects and situations. More recent psychoanalytic thinkers, emphasizing object relations, describe the importance of early developmental attachments providing the foundation for internal representations or "internal objects," which are critical for the regulation of the internal affective milieu, particularly in times of stress or challenge. The absence of supportive or "soothing" internal objects renders the patient vulnerable to affective dysregulation, including anxiety symptoms, at times of interpersonal upheavals in later life.

Behavioral Model

In the behavioral model, formulations of anxiety disorder antecedents focus on learning, through which anxiety symptoms or avoidant behavior have become associated with benign settings or objects because the individual has generalized from earlier traumatic experiences. For example, a child ridiculed by peers because of a mistake during show and tell associates embarrassment and shame with speaking before groups and continues to manifest anticipatory anxiety and avoidance for all public speaking. Self-defeating cognitive "habits" sustain the syndrome with unrealistic catastrophic thinking, "expecting the worst." Misinterpretation of bodily stimuli, with exaggerated cognitive and behavioral responses, may also serve to maintain the behavior.

Conclusion

As with most human experience, psychopathology rarely can be reduced to one explanatory framework, and clinical observation and research indicates contributing roles for all three models as determinants of behavior and symptoms and as guides to therapeutic strategies.

Given the above general description of anxiety and some of its causes, a

Table 2: Symptoms of Panic Disorder

1.	Shortness of breath (dyspnea) or smothering sensations.
2.	Choking
3.	Palpitations or accelerated heart rate (tachycardia)
4.	Chest pain or discomfort
5.	Sweating
6.	Dizziness, unsteady feelings, or faintness
7.	Nausea or abdominal distress
8.	Depersonalization or derealization
9.	Numbness or tingling sensations (paresthesias)
10.	Flushes (hot flashes) or chills
11.	Trembling or shaking
12.	Fear of dying
13.	Fear of going crazy or of doing something uncontrolled

Source. American Psychiatric Association (1986).

summary of clinical manifestations is now in order. The following section will describe a number of anxiety disorders in adults and children.

Clinical Considerations

Stereotyped syndromes of pathological anxiety are represented in the category of adult and childhood "anxiety disorders," as defined by the third revised edition of the American Psychiatric Association's (1987) *Diagnostic and Statistical Manual of Mental Disorders* (DSM-III-R). Epidemiological studies suggest that these are the most common psychiatric disorders in the general population, after alcohol and substance abuse (Robins et al. 1984).

Adult Anxiety Disorders

Panic Disorder

Definition and Symptoms

Patients with this diagnosis have experienced at least one unexpected panic attack and have either experienced four panic attacks in a 4-week period in their life or one panic attack followed by at least 1 month of sustained fear of having a subsequent attack. The features of a panic attack include the experience of at least four of the symptoms listed in table 2 developing suddenly or within 10 minutes of the onset of the first symptom noticed in the attack.

A panic attack is an intensely distressing experience, usually lasting a few to several minutes, with fairly stereotyped physical, cognitive, and behavioral components. Patients with panic disorder may experience these attacks intermittently or in clusters and may develop a number of complications, including persistent anxiousness, phobic avoidance, depression, and alcoholism or other drug overuse.

The physical symptoms of a panic attack, which may include cardiac, respiratory, neurologic, and gastrointestinal reactions, are experienced as if there is a sudden surge of autonomic (primarily sympathetic) arousal. Cognitively, the patient feels a sense of terror or fear of losing control, dying, or going crazy. Behaviorally, the patient is often driven to flee from the setting in which the attack is experienced and to seek a safe, secure, or familiar place or person.

The patient usually vividly remembers the initial attack, or "herald attack," which appears to "turn on" the disorder. Although this first episode is unexpected and intense, later attacks may be either spontaneous and unexpected or preceded by a buildup of anticipatory anxiety. The latter type, called a "situational attack," occurs in settings in which the patient might sense being at risk for panic, such as a crowded room.

Major attacks involve four or more of the symptoms in table 2. Episodes involving fewer symptoms are considered minor, "limited symptom" attacks.

Onset of Panic Disorder

Typically, the onset of panic disorder is in early adult life. The illness afflicts women two to three times more often than men. Adults with panic disorder (in particular, those who develop agoraphobia) frequently have a childhood history of separation anxiety symptoms, particularly "school phobia" (Gittelman and Klein 1984). The disorder is clearly familial (Crowe, 1985) and probably has a genetic basis, as evidenced by a higher concordance for an anxiety disorder in monozygotic than in dizygotic twins with panic disorder (Torgeson 1983).

The onset of the disorder typically follows either a major life event, such as a loss, the threat of a loss, or other upheavals in work or home situations (Roy-Byrne, Geraci, and Uhde 1986), or a physiological event, such as medical illness (e.g., hyperthyroidism or vertigo) or drug use (e.g., use of marijuana or cocaine). However, a patient whose herald attack seems to be triggered by the use of marijuana, for example, may continue to have persistent or recurrent symptoms without further drug use.

A panic attack appears to turn on a state of vigilance or "postpanic" anxiety that resembles generalized anxiety disorder (GAD). Patients may remain symptomatic between attacks, with a constant, low-level, anticipatory anxiety that may crescendo into full-blown panic in certain situations, sometimes unexpectedly.

In this state of vigilance, the patient may develop mild or extensive phobic avoidance, usually of travel or places of restricted escape. This behavior may begin immediately following the onset of attacks, after a number of attacks, or never at all. In some cases, the phobic avoidance evolves as a progressive constriction, and the patient avoids more and more settings in which attacks have occurred. Thus, agoraphobia occurs as a complication of panic attacks.

Prognosis and Treatment of Panic Disorder

The demoralization that accompanies the sustained distress and progressive disability of panic disorder may extend to a major depressive episode with characteristic symptoms. However, the relation between panic and depression is complicated. Although some patients manifest no depressive symptoms, in others it is unclear which disorder is primary since the symptoms arise concurrently. Both disorders are prevalent in families of patients with panic and depression (Leckman et al. 1983). Alcohol use can temporarily tame the distress of panic disorder, but the patient soon experiences rebound symptoms, setting the stage for alcohol overuse. Thus, it is not surprising that perhaps 10–20 percent of alcoholics meet criteria for a diagnosis of panic disorder (Leckman et al. 1983).

The mortality of patients with panic disorder may be higher than for others; data suggest increased premature mortality from suicide and, for men, cardiovascular illness (Coryell, Noyes, and Howe 1986). The latter cause of death may be explained by one report of high levels of markers of platelet aggregation in panic patients, although this observation requires replication (Sheehan et al. 1984). Mitral valve prolapse is also diagnosed much more frequently in panic patients than in either the normal population or patients with GAD (Dager, Comess, and Dunner, 1986).

While a number of treatment strategies, including pharmacological and behavioral interventions, can minimize or prevent the symptoms and complications of this disorder, many patients suffer residual symptoms; others live with their disorder for many years before coming to treatment. Epidemiological studies suggest that panic disorder and agoraphobia are quite prevalent, occurring in as much as 3–6 percent of the population (Reich 1986).

Phobic Disorders

There are three general categories of phobic disorders: simple phobia, social phobia, and agoraphobia.

Simple phobia is the fear and need to avoid specific stimuli such as specific objects (snakes, dogs, etc.) or situations (airplanes, heights). If the object or situation is encountered, the individual suffers intense anxiety that may achieve the level of panic.

Social phobia reflects anxious distress in situations in which the patient is the focus of scrutiny by others and fears humiliation or embarrassment. A common social phobia is performance anxiety such as stage fright and fear of public speaking. Examples of variants are the inability to sign one's name in public or to use public lavatories. Social phobic anxiety may be of the lower-grade, generalized variety or experienced with the intensity of a panic attack. Social phobia is distinguished from normal anxiety, in part, by the extent of avoidance or social and occupational limitation.

Agoraphobia is the fear of settings or places of restricted escape, in which help might not be available in the event of incapacitation, as with a panic attack. Patients suffer travel restrictions. Some endure a variety of agoraphobic situations (such as crowds, restaurants, stores, trains) with distress; others may be homebound. Some patients suffer agoraphobia without a clear history of panic disorder.

Phobic disorders, whose sufferers may experience panic, anticipatory, or no anxiety symptoms at all (depending on the success of avoidance behavior), have been traditionally viewed from psychodynamic or learning theory perspectives. A biological perspective, however, recognizes the stereotyped nature of phobias. For example, most of the objects and situations in everyday life that truly threaten us are rarely selected as phobic stimuli; children proceed normally through a variety of developmental phobias (strangers, separation, darkness, etc.), rarely becoming phobic of the objects and situations that parents attempt to associate with danger (e.g., electrical outlets, roads). Indeed, most phobic stimuli have meaning in the context of biological preparedness and were presumably selected for through evolution (Seligman 1971). Most human phobias are of objects and situations that make sense in the context of enhancing survival before the dawn of civilization: places of restricted escape, groups of strangers, heights, and snakes, for example. Social phobia, for example, the fear of scrutiny by others, resemble the intense discomfort elicited in primates introduced into a new colony or in any animal simply being stared at—a glare is a threat. From this point of view genetic factors would be presumed to be primary in determining vulnerability to these disorders.

Generalized Anxiety Disorder

In the past, patients who suffered anxiety, whether of the generalized or panic form, had been termed "anxiety neurotics," but in the early 1960s case reports and preliminary studies initiated a "pharmacological dissection" of anxiety disorders. Patients who suffered panic attacks, agoraphobia, or "phobic anxiety states" appeared to show preferential responses to medications that were not specifically anxiety reducing, certain tricyclic and monoamine oxidase inhibitor antidepressants. Standard "anxiolytic" medications such as benzodiazepines were observed to be relatively ineffective in preventing panic attacks while useful in controlling other forms of generalized anxiety. Thus, when panic disorder was cleaned from "anxiety neurosis," a second disorder of persistent anxiety without history of panic attacks was presumed to remain and was termed GAD.

Generalized anxiety disorder is diagnosed if the patient has suffered from persistent anxiety for a period of 6 months or more, featuring symptoms of unrealistic or excessive worry (not related to having a panic attack) and including a variety of symptoms such as motor tension and autonomic hyperactivity as well as vigilance and scanning behavior unrelated to any specific medical or organic cause.

Obsessive-Compulsive Disorder

These patients suffer recurrent unwanted and senseless thoughts that are distressing and intrusive but that cannot be suppressed (obsessions) or compulsions, the need to repeat certain behaviors or rituals in a stereotyped fashion, or else they suffer intense distress or anxiety.

Posttraumatic Stress Disorder

Patients with this condition often manifest symptoms resembling the acute symptoms and secondary complications of panic disorder but with onset at the time of experiencing or witnessing a serious, life-threatening, or violent event. Subsequently, the patient reexperiences the memories of the event or suffers recurrent dreams and other experiences (such as flashbacks) that recall the traumatic event. Anxiety symptoms, sleep dysfunction, the tendency to startle easily, and the need to avoid stimuli reminiscent of the original event all characterize this syndrome.

Adjustment Disorder with Anxious Mood

This category, while not a DSM-III-R diagnosis, serves to describe the great number of patients who experience transient periods of pathological anxiety associated with interpersonal, occupational, or other upheavals in their lives. Symptoms are generally time limited but may achieve sufficient intensity to require intervention.

Other Psychiatric Disorders

Acute anxiety symptoms may well signal a primary anxiety disorder but frequently are harbingers or concomitants of other psychiatric syndromes, particularly mood disorders, psychoses, and substance abuse. More than one-quarter of patients with primary depression, for example, may experience panic attacks, and free-floating anxiety also may be an early or associated symptom of depression, psychosis, or withdrawal states.

Anxiety Disorders of Childhood and Adolescence

DSM-III-R includes a subclass of three disorders of childhood or adolescence in which the predominant feature is anxiety. These are separation anxiety disorder, avoidant disorder, and overanxious disorder. In the first two categories, the anxiety is focused on specific situations, while in the third the anxiety is generalized to a variety of situations.

Childhood anxiety disorders are relatively common disorders of unknown etiology (Orvaschel and Weissman 1987); they bear striking similarities to the adult anxiety disorders and in many cases persist into adult life. However, they are not included among the adult disorders because they have unique features characteristically associated with childhood. For a diagnosis of childhood anxiety disorder to be made, it should also be associated with distress and disability in addition to the presence of symptoms (Werry 1987).

Separation Anxiety Disorder

Separation anxiety disorder (SAD) is the best known of the childhood anxiety disorders. It may represent a childhood equivalent to adult agoraphobia (Gittelman and Klein 1986). It is a relatively common disorder affecting children of both sexes. The predominant disturbance in this category is excessive anxiety on separation from familial surroundings. It is called separation anxiety because it is assumed that the main disturbance is the inability of the child to separate from the parent or from major attachment figures. When separation occurs or is anticipated, the child may experience severe anxiety to the point of panic. Physical complaints such as stomachaches, headaches, nausea and vomiting, palpitations, dizziness, and fainting may occur. During separation, these children are often preoccupied with morbid fears that accidents or illness will befall their parents or themselves. Children with this disorder are uncomfortable when away from the house or from familiar areas. They may refuse to leave the house or to attend school or camp and are sometimes called "school refusers" or "school phobics" (Hersov 1986). However, not all school refusal is due to separation anxiety. It can be due to a variety of factors such as other psychiatric problems (i.e., depression, psychosis), family stress, or school difficulties. Children with SAD may be unable to stay by themselves and often display clinging behaviors.

In general, with younger children, the symptoms are more amorphous and less specific. As children become older, the fears may beome systematized around identifiable potential dangers. Most children, however, even the older ones, do not report fears of definite threats but only pervasive anxiety about ill-defined dangers or death. In addition, children typically exhibit anticipatory anxiety when separation is threatened or impending. Children frequently have difficulties going to sleep and may require that someone stays with them until they fall asleep. Sometimes they will make their way to the parent's bed or sleep outside the parents' bedroom if entry to the parents' bedroom is barred. Anxiety nightmares are common. On occaion, a child may become violent when forced to separate.

Some children with SAD have fixed fears that may appear bizarre. They may fear the dark and express fears that threatening animals are glaring at them in the dark. Children with this disorder are often described as demanding, intrusive, and in need of constant attention. Others are described as conforming and eager to please. Children with SAD may not manifest interpersonal difficulties, except when demands for separation are made.

The age of onset may be as early as 3 or 4 years. However, it appears more commonly in children 8–10 years. Typically, there are periods of exacerbations and remissions over several years, and the disorder persists in some cases into adulthood. In its severe form, it can be highly incapacitating in that the child is unable to attend school and function independently. Children with physical symptoms may undergo complex medical evaluations. When school refusal develops, common complications include academic failure and social avoidance. Demoralization and overt depression arre common complications.

In most cases, the disorder develops after some type of life stressor, typically a loss of a dear one (real or perceived), an illness of the child, or a change in the child's environment. The disorder seems to be familial, that is, more common in members of a given family than in the general population.

Separation anxiety disorder should be differentiated from normal separation difficulties commonly seen in early childhood. It should also be distinguished from separation anxiety symptoms occurring in other psychiatric disorders.

Avoidant Disorder

Although little is known about avoidant disorder, in its clinical characteristics it resembles adult social phobia. The predominant feature is a persistent and severe shrinking from contact with strangers that interferes with psychosocial functioning. Affected children are interested in social relationships but fearful of them; in social settings, they may appear to be inarticulate or mute. Usually, children with this disorder are unassertive and lack self-confidence. Age-appropriate socialization skills may not develop, and, in severe cases, the child fails to form social bonds beyond the immediate family. The disorder may develop in early childhood after stranger anxiety should have disappeared. The course is unknown, but the disorder probably is chronic.

Overanxious Disorder

This disorder could be considered the childhood equivalent to adult GAD. It is a common disorder more frequently seen in boys than in girls. As in the adult patient, the essential feature is excessive worrying and fearful behavior that is not focused on a specific situation or object and is not due to psychosocial stressors. The child feels "nervous" and worries about future events, such as examination, injury, or disease, or about meeting expectations, such as deadlines, appointments, or chores, commonly expressing concern with personal competence and performance. Because of these concerns, children may be erroneously seen as "hypermature." In some cases, physical concomitants of anxiety are apparent, such as headaches, stomaches, shortness of breath, dizziness, or other somatic complaints. These physical symptoms may result in unnecessary medical evaluations and interventions.

Overanxious children may be excessively conforming and approval seeking. Some exhibit an excess of motor restlessness or nervous habits such as nail biting or hair pulling. The onset may be acute or gradual, with exacerbations usually associated with stress. In severe cases, children may show poor academic performance and failure to engage in age-appropriate activities.

Treatment Considerations

With the exception of SAD, there are no systematic evaluations of treatment modalities for childhood anxiety disorders (Biederman and Jellinek 1984; Emde 1986; Gittelman and Koplewicz 1987; McDermott 1986). It is possible, however, that children and adolescents with anxiety disorders will respond to the same pharmacological approaches as adult patients. In addition to tricyclic antidepressants, high potency benzodiazepines such as clonazepam and alprazolam can be effective, as well as the MAOI (i.e., phenelzine) drugs. In a single study, high doses of the antidepressant drug imipramine were effective after 2–8 weeks of treatment (Gittleman-Klein and Klein 1971). Recently, Biederman (in press) reported three cases of prepubertal children with severe agoraphobia-like symptoms who responded dramatically to treatment with clonazepam. In addition to pharmacotherapy, the treatment of affected children requires a variety of methods, including psychotherapy, family therapy, and behavioral therapy. In severe cases, hospitalization may be required.

 ## Implications: The Link between Behavioral Inhibition and Anxiety Disorders

The possible link between childhood anxiety disorders and adult anxiety disorder is an important clinical hypothesis (Emde 1986; Gittelman and Kopelwicz 1987; McDermott 1986). A relation between childhood disorder and adult psychiatric disorder has been described for other disorders. For example, early asocial adjustment in nonpsychotic children has been associated with the development of schizophrenia in later years (Cull, Chick, and Wolff 1984). Schizophrenia associated with childhood asocial behavior may differ from other forms of schizophrenia with regard to intelligence, neurological status, and long-term outcome. These clinical patterns suggest that developmental characteristics may be associated with clinical outcome.

A major roadblock in the research into childhood anxiety disorders is the confusion regarding diagnostic categories. Although similar in clinical manifestations, childhood anxiety disorders have different diagnostic labels than the adult disorders do. As noted, the adult anxiety disorders are called agoraphobia, panic disorder, and GAD, while the childhood anxiety disorders are called SAD, overanxious disorder, and avoidant disorders. One may think of agoraphobia as a form of SAD since agoraphobics often feel unable to separate from a companion. On the other hand, an excessively fearful response to the unfamiliar or to a challenge may be the common denominator in both disorders. It is possible to hypothesize that childhood anxiety disorders may be etiologically related to the adult anxiety disorders but differ in age-appropriate developmental manifestations. This line of thought has been applied to childhood affective disorders; the diagnosis of childhood depression relies on the adult diagnostic criteria for depression differing only in age-appropriate developmental variations.

Childhood symptoms may predispose to the adult condition, may be early manifestations of the same disorder, or may reflect common environmental or biological underpinnings (Gittelman 1987). Several authors suggest that the optimal approach to exploring the relation between childhood and adult psychopathology is the scrutiny and longitudinal follow-up of "children at risk" by systematic study of children whose parents demonstrate psychopathology. Children of agoraphobic parents are more likely to have suffered SAD than are other children. The same is true for agoraphobics during their own childhood. It is also possible that a marker or precursor to anxiety disorder may be manifested in more subtle measures of childhood behavior such as temperamental characteristics. Thus, SAD may be one particularly severe reflection of some temperamental feature that predisposes a child to school avoidance as well as to panic disorder, agoraphobia, or social phobia in later life. If so, developmental research techniques could offer the opportunity to observe crucial developmental transformations in the path from predisposition to manifest disorder, permitting evaluation of protective and harmful factors in individual experience. Observations of inhibited children on the first day of school (Gersten 1986) were reminiscent of the separation anxiety difficulties of adult agoraphobics when children. In the light of this observation, we hypothesized a link between behavior inhibition in children and later anxiety disorders, particularly panic disorder and agoraphobia. This has led us to examine the prevalence of behavioral inhibition in the children of patients with agoraphobia and panic disorder and to hypothesize that the temperamental quality of behavioral inhibition to the unfamiliar might be a predisposing characteristic of children at risk for panic disorder and agoraphobia in later years. If this were true, because of the apparent familial and probably genetic patterns of transmission of panic disorder (Crowe 1985), we expect to find a higher prevalence of behavioral inhibition in the children of adult patients with panic disorder and agoraphobia as compared to controls without this disorder.

To study the role of "behavioral inhibition to the unfamiliar" as an early risk factor or precursor of later anxiety disorder for children at risk for adult panic disorder and agoraphobia, we studied children of parents with panic disorder and agoraphobia and those of psychiatric comparison groups (Rosenbaum et al. 1988). Fifty-six children aged 2–7 were blindly evaluated at the Harvard Infant Study Laboratory. The rates of behavioral inhibition in children of the probands with panic disorder and agoraphobia were significantly higher than for comparison groups. The rate of behavioral inhibition in the children at risk for panic disorder and agoraphobia was close to 80 percent (100 percent in older children aged 4–7) as compared to our nonmajor depressive disorder comparison group, for which the rate of behavioral inhibition approximated 15 percent (0 percent for the older children, aged 4–7) ($p < .01$).

The observation that behavioral inhibition to the unfamiliar as defined in the previous work of Kagan and colleagues (see Kagan, chap. 1, in this vol.) is highly prevalent in the offspring of adults in treatment for panic disorder with agoraphobia suggests an important link between childhood inhibition and vulnerability to anxiety disorder and adulthood. Whether this finding in the children represents a biological vulnerability or is the product of experience cannot be determined from this observation. The identification of behavioral inhibition in children at risk for anxiety, however, is important in itself. It may identify children with increased vulnerability for developing psychiatric syndromes of anxiety. If behavioral inhibition in early childhood can be shown in follow-up studies to lead to later anxiety disorder, the identification of young children with this temperamental trait would represent a major contribution to the development of preventive strategies for high-risk children of agoraphobic patients.

References

American Psychiatric Association. 1987. *Diagnostic and Statistical Manual of Mental Disorders.* 3d rev. ed. Washington, D.C.: American Psychiatric Association.

Biederman, J. In press. Clonazepam in the treatment of prepubertal children with panic-like symptoms. *Journal of Clinical Psychiatry.*

Biederman, J., and Jellinek, M.S. 1984. Psychopharmacology in children. *New England Journal of Medicine* 310:968–72.

Charney, D. S. and Heninger, G. R. 1985. Noradrenergic function and the mechanism of action of antianxiety treatment. *Archives of General Psychiatry* 42:458–81.

Charney, D. S. and Redmond, D. E., Jr. 1983. Neurobiological mechanisms in human anxiety: Evidence supporting noradrenergic hyperactivity. *Neuropharmacology* 22:1531–36.

Coyrell, W.; Noyes, R., Jr.; and Howe, J. D. 1986. Mortality among outpatients with anxiety disorders. *American Journal of Psychiatry* 143:508–10.

Crowe, R. R. 1985. The genetics of panic disorder and agoraphobics. *Psychiatric Developments* 2:171–86.

Cull, A.; Chick, J.; and Wolff, S. 1984. A consensual validation of schizoid personality in childhood and adult life. *British Journal of Psychiatry* 144:646–48.

Dager, S. R.; Comess, K. A.; and Dunner, D. L. 1986. Differentiation of anxious patients by two dimensional echocardiographic evaluation of the mitral valve. *American Journal of Psychiatry* 143:533–36.

Emde, R. N. 1986. Early development and opportunities for research on anxiety. In *Anxiety and the anxiety disorders,* ed. A. H. Tuma and J. D. Maser, 413–20. Hillsdale, N.J.: Erlbaum.

Gersten, M.: 1986. The contribution of temperament to behavior in natural contexts. Ph.D. dissertation, Harvard University, Graduate School of Education.

Gittelman, R. 1987. Childhood anxiety disorders: Correlates and outcome. In *Anxiety disorders in children,* ed. R. Gittelman, 101–25. New York: Guilford.

Gittelman-Klein, R., and Klein, D. F. 1971. Controlled imipramine treatment of school phobia. *Archives of General Psychiatry* 25:204–7.

Gittelman, R., and Klein, D. F. 1984. The relationship between separation anxiety and panic and agoraphobic disorders. *Psychopathology* 17 (suppl.): 56–65.

Gittelman, R., and Klein, D. F. 1986. Childhood separation anxiety and adult agoraphobia. In *Anxiety and the anxiety disorders,* ed. A. H. Tuma and J. D. Maser, 389–402. Hillsdale, N.J.: Erlbaum.

Gittelman, R., and Koplewicz, H. S. 1987. Pharmacotherapy of childhood anxiety disorders. In *Anxiety disorders in children,* ed. R. Gittelman, 188–200. New York: Guilford.

Gray, J. A. 1985. Issues in the neuropsychology of anxiety. In *Anxiety and the anxiety disorders,* ed. A. H. Tuma and J. D. Maser, Hillsdale, N.J.: Erlbaum.

Hersov, L. 1986. School refusal. In *Child and adolescent psychiatry: Modern approaches,* ed. M. Ritter and L. Hersov, 382–99. Boston: Blackwell Scientific Publishers.

Huang, Y. H.; Redmond, D. E., Jr.; Snyder, D. R.; and Maas J. W. 1976. Loss of fear following bilateral lesions of the locus coeruleus in the monkey. *Neuroscience Abstracts* 2:573.

Insel, T. R.; Ninan, P. T.; Aloi, J.; Jimerson, D. C.; Skolnick, P.; and Paul, S. M. 1984. A benzodiazepine receptor mediated model of anxiety: Studies in non-human primates and clinical implications. *Archives of General Psychiatry* 41:741–50.

Leckman, J. F.; Weissman, M. M.; Merikangas, K. R.; Pauls, D. L.; and Prusoff, B. A. 1983. Panic disorder and major depression: Increased risk of depression, alcoholism, panic and phobic disorders in families of depressed probands with panic disorder. *Archives of General Psychiatry* 40:1055–60.

McDermott, J. F. 1986. Anxiety disorders (childhood). In *Psychiatry, vol. 6, Child psychiatry,* ed. R. Michels and J. O. Cavenar, 293–302. New York: Basic.

Mason, S. T., and Fibiger, H. C. 1979. Anxiety: The locus coeruleus disconnection. *Life Sciences* 25:2141–47.

Orvaschel, H., and Weissman, M. M. 1987. Epidemiology of anxiety disorders in children: a review. In *Anxiety disorders in children,* ed. R. Gittelman, 58–72. New York: Guilford.

Reich, J. 1986. The epidemiology of anxiety. *Journal of Nervous and Mental Disorders* 174:129–36.

Robins, L. N.; Helzer, J. E.; Weissman, M. M.; Orvaschel, H.; Gruenberg, E.; Burke, J. D., Jr.; and Regier, D. A. 1984. Lifetime prevalence of specific psychiatric disorders in three sites. *Archives of General Psychiatry* 41:949–58.

Rosenbaum, J. F. 1982. The drug treatment of anxiety. *New England Journal of Psychiatry* 306:401–4.

Rosenbaum, J. F.; Biederman, J.; Gersten M.; Hirshfeld, D. R.; Meminger, S. R.; Herman, J. B.; Kagan, J.; Reznick, J. S.; and Snidman, N. 1988. Behavioral inhibition in children of parents with panic disorder and agoraphobia: A controlled study. *Archives of General Psychiatry* 45:463–70.

Roy-Byrne, P. P.; Geraci, M.; and Uhde, T. W. 1986. Life events and the onset of panic disorder. *American Journal of Psychiatry* 143:1424–27.

Seligman, M. E. P. 1971. Phobias and preparedness. *Behavior Therapy* 2:307–20.

Sheehan, D. V.; Coleman, J. H.; Greenblatt, D. J.; Jones, K. J.; Levine, P. H.; Orsulak, P. J.; Peterson, M.; Schildkraut, J. J.; Uzogana, E.; and Watkins, D. 1984. Some biochemical correlates of panic attacks with agoraphobia and their response to a new treatment. *Journal of Clinical Psychopharmacology* 4:66–74.

Torgeson, S. 1983. Genetic factors in anxiety disorders. *Archives of General Psychiatry* 40: 1085–89.

Werry, J. S. 1987. Diagnosis and assessment. In *Anxiety disorders in children,* ed. R. Gittelman, 72–100. New York: Guilford.

14 Behavioral Inhibition and Stress Reactivity: A Psychophysiological Perspective

JAMES A. MCCUBBIN

Introduction

Powerful excitatory and inhibitory physiologies have developed for rapid response to exceptionally potent environmental stressors. Aversively motivated responses, whether they are overt behaviors or subtle physiological adjustments, ultimately reflect a net balance of these opposing mechanisms. For example, integrated responses of both the sympathetic and the parasympathetic branches of the peripheral autonomic nervous system produce finely tuned alterations in heart rate and several other biologically important parameters. Dysfunction of one branch can leave the other unopposed, resulting in aberrant behaviors such as lowered response threshold, exaggerated response magnitude, and delayed or absent habituation. Behaviorally inhibited children display similar aberrations in response to stressful psychosocial stimuli. The mechanisms that determine the nature and extent of behavioral inhibition in children are currently unknown, and there is a shortage of relevant experimental models for mechanistic research efforts. The purpose of this chapter is to explore three experimental models of inhibitory mechanisms that are relevant to stress responsivity and the psychophysiological profile of behaviorally inhibited children. The first section will demonstrate how congenital vulnerability produces potentially maladaptive cardiorespiratory reflexes in infants at risk for sudden death. The neurobehavioral mechanisms of diving reflex aberrations in neonates will be assessed for potential relevance to behavioral inhibition. The second section will examine learned helplessness as a possible laboratory model of behavioral inhibition. An opioid peptide–based neuroendocrine system is described that mediates learned helpless behavior and other responses to stress in laboratory rats. The third section will show how opioid

Partial funding has been provided by the John D. and Catherine T. MacArthur Foundation Network on Transition from Infancy to Early Childhood and the Network on Antecedents and Consequences of Health Enhancing and Health Damaging Behaviors. Appreciation is expressed to Betsy Stelzenmuller for proofreading this manuscript.

inhibitory mechanisms malfunction in some young adults. This malfunction produces exaggerated responses to stress and coincides with enhanced risk for hypertension and perhaps other physio- and psychopathologies. Each of these models describes a possible mechanistic substrate for the undoubtedly complex phenomenon of behavioral inhibition. The central assumption is that behavioral inhibition can be viewed as a problem of stress reactivity. These models offer potential avenues for further research on the possible psychophysiological mechanisms of behavioral inhibition in children.

The Diving Reflex in Neonates at Risk for Sudden Death

Theoretical Background

Sudden death in infancy has been linked to cardiorespiratory inhibition from an exaggerated diving reflex. Generally, an otherwise healthy infant is found dead in the crib, giving rise to the common term "crib death." The distinctive feature of the sudden infant death syndrome (SIDS) is that neither history nor a thorough postmortem examination can satisfactorily explain the mechanism of death (Bergman, Beckwith, and Ray 1970). It is the most common cause of death between 1 month and 1 year of age (Naeye 1974) and accounts for 1.2–3 deaths per 1,000 live births in the United States. It is most prevalent between 2 and 3 months of age, especially in males, nonwhites, premature and/or low-birth-weight infants, and infants from families with low socioeconomic status (Walpole and Hasselmeyer 1971). Many theories attempt to explain the mechanism of death in SIDS. In biblical times, overlaying, or accidental smothering of the child in sleep, was believed to be the explanation, but more modern concepts include prolonged sleep apnea, laryngospasm, cardiac conduction abnormalities, and exaggerated autonomic reflex bradycardia.

The diving reflex is an integrated physiological mechanism that allows air-breathing animals and humans to survive prolonged submersion or disruption of the air supply (for a review, see Andersen 1966). This reflex is elicited by stimulation of the trigeminal nerve distributions to the eyes, nose, and mouth. Efferent components of this brainstem-mediated reflex include apnea, bradycardia, and vasomotor responses. The net result of this integrated reflex is a reduction of myocardial oxygen consumption and a redistribution of blood volume from the gut and striate musculature to the less-tolerant coronary and cerebral circulation. This reflex, when optimally functional, allows oxygen conservation and serves as a safeguard against the threat of hypoxia. However, during infancy, differential maturity of sympathetic and parasympathetic nervous systems can produce autonomic imbalance, and it is conceivable that resulting cardiorespiratory adjustments could become fatally exaggerated.

The notion of a prepotent diving reflex as a mechanism of sudden death has been implicated in both adults (Wolf, Schneider, and Groover 1964) and infants (McCubbin et al. 1977), but there have been no prospective studies, and this theory remains speculative. Richter (1957) described diving bradycardia and sudden death during forced swim in wild Norwegian rats. He suggested that incidence of sudden deaths could be potentiated by restraint, disruption of sensory cues, and other manipulations that emphasized the inescapable or "hopeless" nature of the situation. Moreover, both bradycardia and sudden death could be prevented by pretreatment with atropine. These observations were interpreted as one possible explanation for Cannon's observations of "voodoo death" (Cannon 1942). Bradycardia and sudden death have been observed in squirrel monkeys during a 24-hour shock stress (Corley et al. 1977). That study used a yoked-control paradigm in which some animals could escape or avoid shock and others received the same shocks with no escape or avoidance contingency. In both groups, some monkeys developed a debilitating bradycardia followed by sudden death. This phenomenon was observed in avoidance animals only after they had stopped responding or, in other words, after they had given up. Parasympathetic blockade with atropine partially attenuated the bradycardia, indicating that, as with Richter's diving rats, activity of the vagal nerves was an important mechanism. These findings are consistent with the notion that exaggerated parasympathetic inhibition of the heart is responsible for some forms of sudden death. Since spontaneous diving-like apnea and bradycardia are often observed in high-risk infants, a dive-reflex challenge may have prognostic significance for sudden infant death.

Laboratory Study

A simple laboratory test was needed to screen for exaggerated diving reflexes in human neonates at risk for sudden death. It would be impractical to use submersion or wet stimuli because of the disruptive nature of such provocative stimuli. However, a moderate airstream stimulus directed to the eye or nose produces the bradycardia and apnea characteristic of diving, but without behavioral disruption. In addition to being a safe and innocuous stimulus, a mild airstream could be administered without changing the behavioral state of the infant. The relation between diving-reflex bradycardia and risk for sudden infant death was tested by examining responses to airstream stimuli delivered to the faces of infants who have experienced a "near-miss" SIDS episode characterized by prolonged apnea with visible cyanosis.[1] Studies were performed in the intermediate and intensive-care nurseries of the North Carolina

1. Conducted at the North Carolina Baptist Hospital through affiliations with the Department of Neurology, the Bowman Gray School of Medicine, and the Department of Psychology, Wake Forest University, Winston-Salem, N.C. I would like to acknowledge the contributions of the

Baptist Hospital in Winston-Salem. Thirty-two infants were selected for this study on the basis of clinical examination. The low-risk control group ($N = 16$) consisted of infants with no major abnormalities on physical, neurological, and funduscopic examination and with uncomplicated delivery and neonatal course. High-risk infants ($N = 16$) had no major abnormalities except for a positive history of prolonged apnea with visible cyanosis. Average gestational age was 36.7 weeks for the low-risk group and 36.5 weeks for the high-risk group. Half the infants from each group were from 29 to 36 weeks gestation, while the remainder were from 37 to 43 weeks gestation.

All infants were instrumented for polygraphic monitoring of electrocardiogram, heart rate, respiration, and gross body movements. Infants were allowed to adapt to measurement and were rated for sleep state immediately prior to each stimulus. The stimulus was a 15-liters per minute airstream at room temperature delivered by hand to the eye or nose for either 2 or 10 seconds duration. All stimuli were presented from a tube positioned approximately 1–2 centimeters from the infant with an intertrial interval of 45 seconds. Control stimuli were identical except that they were delivered to the abdomen. Deceleratory heart-rate change scores were derived by subtracting prestimulus mean heart rate from the minimum 20-second poststimulus heart rate. Other variables were maximum poststimulus heart rate, prestimulus heart-rate variability, duration of evoked apnea, and latency to maximum and minimum poststimulus heart rates. Heart-rate change scores were corrected for prestimulus heart rate via regression analysis. Infants were tested one or more times between birth and 6 months postnatal age. All studies were conducted while the infants were asleep or in a quiet, awake state.

In most low-risk infants, the facial airstream produced a biphasic response, with initial heart-rate acceleration followed by a deceleratory rebound usually falling below baseline. In some high-risk infants, the facial airstream produced a profound monophasic bradycardia accompanied by prolonged respiratory arrest. Figure 1 is a polygraphic tracing of reflex bradycardia to a 10-second facial airstream stimulus in a 10-week-old high-risk infant. This infant was the first of identical twins admitted to the Intensive Care nursery at 8 weeks postnatal age with episodes of acute respiratory arrest and cyanosis. Heart rate fell from a prestimulus baseline of 169 beats per minute to 55 beats per minute within 4.5 seconds poststimulus onset. Apnea and respiratory irregularities persisted after stimulus termination. Both twins produced the same pattern of exaggerated response.

Analysis of high- and low-risk groups showed no significant differences in

following coinvestigators: J. Baldwin Smith, M.D., Robert C. Beck, Frank B. Wood, Gregory Allen, and Heriberto Fernandez. Appreciation is expressed to the nurses and staff of the Newborn and Intensive Care Nurseries of the North Carolina Baptist Hospital for their help and cooperation.

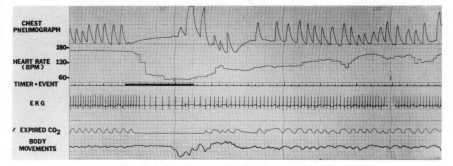

Fig. 1. Polygraphic record of the diving reflex of a 10-week-old with a near-miss sudden death episode characterized by prolonged apnea and cyanosis. The airstream was directed to the nose while the infant was awake and quiet. Time is marked in 1-second intervals. This infant's identical twin sister had a similar near-miss episode and showed the same pattern of response to facial airstreams.

gestational age or in postnatal age at time of testing. Although prestimulus heart rates of high-risk infants were somewhat higher and less variable, these group differences were not statistically reliable. There were significant differences in the magnitude of heart-rate deceleration ($p < .05$), with the high-risk group showing a larger average deceleration (-32.4 ± 4.9) than the low-risk group (-21.1 ± 2.9). The magnitude of heart-rate deceleration was also more variable in the high-risk group ($p < .05$), and this indicated significant individual differences between high-risk infants. For example, when data are plotted by individual infants (see Fig. 2), the distribution of heart-rate response scores is markedly skewed in the high-risk group. In fact, five of the 16 high-risk infants (31 percent) showed deceleratory magnitudes greater than 2 standard deviations from the mean for low-risk infants. Clearly, these infants demonstrate a predisposition for abnormal bradycardia that coincides roughly, but not precisely, with clinical status. The relation between abnormal diving-reflex bradycardia and sudden death in infants remains to be determined, but, subsequent to this study, a sibling of one high-risk infant had a sudden, unexplained death. Examination of the magnitude of diving bradycardia showed that infant to be one of the five with heart-rate deceleration beyond 2 standard deviations of low-risk mean.

Implications

The diving reflex model demonstrates that individual differences in psychophysiological inhibitory mechanisms exist in the early stages of infancy. The exaggerated response pattern is associated with other risk factors and has been implicated as one possible mechanism in the etiology of sudden infant deaths. The origin and precise developmental significance of abnormal diving reflex

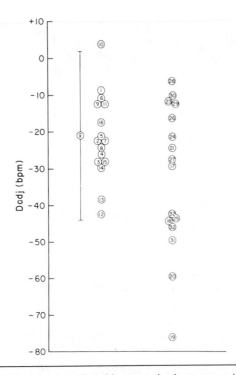

Fig. 2. Individual by risk-group-adjusted heart-rate deceleratory magnitudes (Dadj) in beats per minute (bpm) for prestimulus heart rate. Bars represent the mean ± 2 standard deviations for low-risk infants. Circled numbers are for subject identification. Five of 16 high-risk infants (31 percent) show deceratory magnitudes beyond 2 standard deviations.

behavior is currently unknown. Nevertheless, these data may provide some conceptual implications for the study of behavioral inhibition in children. The adaptive significance of a response pattern must be visualized within the appropriate context. An optimally functioning dive reflex may facilitate endurance under hypoxic conditions, but some of these high-risk infants display clearly exaggerated adjustments to relatively innocuous stimuli.

An airstream to the face is an ambiguous challenge for an infant. Alterations in central nervous control of autonomic outflow could produce lowered thresholds for protective reflexes. Lower thresholds can result in evocation of protective mechanisms at inappropriate times or with excess regularity. A similar threshold adjustment may underlie behavioral inhibition in children. For example, withdrawal from an ambiguous psychosocial challenge is protective in unfamiliar circumstances, but it could be potentially maladaptive if repeatedly and unnecessarily evoked in an innocuous environment. More extensive experimental models are necessary to better study the inhibitory psychophysiological mechanisms that characterize the behaviorally inhibited child.

Learned Helplessness and Opioid Peptides

Theoretical Background

Experience with inescapable or unavoidable stress will impair subsequent acquisition of escape or avoidance behavior. This so-called learned helplessness has been linked to depression, cardiovascular morbidity, and sudden death. Several behavioral and cognitive theories have been proposed to account for learned helplessness. While these interpretations have widespread appeal, motivational mechanisms must also be considered. For example, intense stimulation produces, among other things, a decrease in pain sensitivity. Stress-induced analgesia has been studied during various behavioral paradigms, including inescapable foot shock, forced cold-water swim, and restraint. Several mechanisms may contribute to this phenomenon, including depletion of norepinephrine from the locus coeruleus, supraspinal cholinergic activity, and endogenous opioid peptide activation. If learned helplessness is a reasonable laboratory model of behavioral inhibition, then the study of helpless behaviors may illuminate mechanisms of behavioral inhibition in children.

Recent discovery of opioid peptides and receptors throughout the central and autonomic nervous systems has led to speculation that these substances may be important in regulating responses to stress. These neuropeptides occur in several bioactive forms, including the endorphins, the enkephalins, and the dynorphins. These substances can be released systemically as pituitary hormones or locally as neurotransmitters. They can bind postsynaptically to opioid receptors on target tissues and presynaptically to autonomic neurons. Variations in receptor subtype produce a mosaic of relative affinities allowing neural processing at the receptor level. Pharmacological blockade of opioid receptors can be accomplished by administration of naloxone, naltrexone, or other opioid antagonists. This conveniently allows in vivo determination of the effects of endogenous opioid mechanisms on a variety of responses to stress.

Blockade of endogenous opioid receptors has minimal effects in resting, opiate-naive subjects, but the picture is radically different in organisms under intense stress. For example, several investigators have documented functionally important opioid activity in peripheral autonomic responses to circulatory, endotoxin, and spinal shock in cats (Faden and Holaday 1979, 1980; Faden, Jacobs, and Holaday 1980) as well as conditioned and unconditioned responses to noxious stimuli in rabbits, rats, and mice (Hernandez and Powell 1980; Akil et al. 1976; Miczek, Thompson, and Shuster 1982). The precise role of opioid peptides in aversively motivated behaviors is not well understood, but the analgesic properties of opiates have received considerable attention.

Current evidence suggests that endogenous opiates are involved in several forms of stress-induced analgesia, and, furthermore, there is a reasonable argument that these effects interact with the contingency or controllability of the stressful stimuli (Drugan and Maier 1983; Maier et al. 1980; Jackson, Maier, and Coon 1979). The effective eliciting stimuli for stress analgesia are similar to those known to produce learned helplessness, for example, inescapable stress. While the relative contributions of associational, motivational, and motoric-performance factors to learned helplessness are currently unclear, it is possible that opioid mechanisms underlie both stress-induced analgesia and learned-helplessness behaviors. Recent reports suggest that the performance deficit is not a direct consequence of opioid analgesia (Maier et al. 1983; MacLennan et al. 1982; Mah, Suissa, and Anisman 1980), but these findings do not preclude a role of opiate mechanisms in the expression of learned performance deficits.

Laboratory Studies

A series of experiments were performed to determine the role of opioid peptide function in the production of antinociception and performance deficits utilizing a yoke-controlled mild foot-shock paradigm in rats.[2] Male albino rats (Zivic-Miller) weighing between 200 and 350 grams were randomly assigned to yoked pairs and trained with opiate receptors either intact (saline or no injection) or blocked with 2 milligrams per kilogram intraperitoneal naltrexone hydrochloride (HCl) immediately prior to training. During training, all avoidance subjects were exposed to 90 trials of bar-press shock-escape/avoidance conditioning, while yoked subjects received 90 trials with identical warning and shock stimuli but no bar-press contingency. Mild scrambled foot-shocks were delivered to unrestrained animals at 1 milliampere intensity for a maximum duration of 15 seconds. Naive controls received exposure to the testing apparatus but no shock experience. Forty-eight hours later, all subjects were given 50 trials of escape/avoidance testing in a one-way shuttle task. Mild electric stimuli were delivered at .75 milliampere for a maximum duration of 10 seconds. Average shuttle-response latencies were calculated for each group. Shuttle latencies were log transformed and analyzed by analysis of variance (ANOVA).

The effects of yoked-control training on shuttle acquisition are shown in figure 3. Training produced a deficit of subsequent shuttle acquisition in intact animals receiving inescapable foot shock only. Average shuttle latency plus or minus standard error was 12.24 ± .852 seconds for yoked animals,

2. Conducted at the Biological Sciences Research Center, University of North Carolina School of Medicine, Chapel Hill. Grateful acknowledgment is extended to John S. Kizer, M.D., and Morris A. Lipton, M.D. for their valuable help in this project. This research was supported by National Institute for Child Health and Human Development grant 07201 to Dr. Kizer.

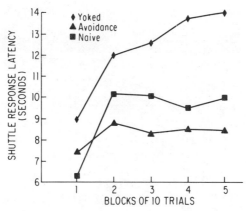

Fig. 3. Shuttle-response latencies of rats exposed to contingent (avoidance) and noncontingent (yoked) foot shock. Naive animals were confined to the testing chambers but received no shock stimuli. Yoked animals showed significantly longer average shuttle-response latency than avoidance animals ($p < .05$). Reproduced from McCubbin, Kizer, and Lipton (1984), with permission.

8.03 $\pm$ 1.441 seconds for the avoidance group, and 9.22 $\pm$ 1.354 seconds for the naive group. The difference in log latency between yoked and avoidance groups was significant, $F(1,12) = 7.137, p < .05$. There were no significant differences in performance between avoidance and naive animals. The data indicated that these training parameters produced a measurable fixed ratio = 1 (FR-1) performance deficit in animals receiving noncontingent footshock stress. Drug studies determined the effect of opiate blockade with naltrexone during training on subsequent shuttle testing. As with intact groups, yoked animals receiving saline displayed significantly longer shuttle latencies than avoidance animals receiving saline, $F(1,12) = 5.122, p < .05$ (see fig. 4). Blockade of opiate receptors with 2 milligrams per kilogram naltrexone during training improved response times of yoked animals and eliminated shuttle-latency differences between yoked and avoidance groups ($F < 1$). These data suggest that the effect of noncontingent shock on subsequent shuttle acquisition depends on the integrity of naltrexone-sensitive opiate receptors.

Another experiment was designed to evaluate the effects of yoked-control training and opiate antagonism on stress-induced analgesia. The methods were similar to those used in the first experiment, except that this one included an index of pain sensitivity, latency of the tail withdrawal reflex. The heat source for this method was water warmed to 55 degrees C. All tail withdrawal data were the mean of five trials. Animals received 3 days baseline measurement prior to any experimental manipulation. Pain sensitivity was assessed before and after both training and testing as well as prior to drug administration.

280   JAMES A. McCUBBIN

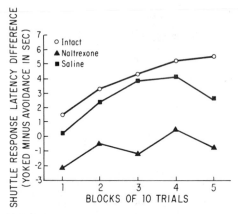

Fig. 4. The effects of opiate-receptor blockade during yoke-controlled shock-avoidance training on response latencies during shuttle testing 48 hours later. Data are derived from shuttle-
latency differences betwen yoked and avoidance animals for each drug condition. Differences are
significant for intact and saline groups ($p<$ .05) but not for groups pretreated with naltrexone
($F < 1$). Reproduced from McCubbin, Kizer, and Lipton (1984), with permission.

The results for tail withdrawal reflex latency are presented in figure 5. With
opiate receptors intact, avoidance and control animals showed moderate decreases in reflex latency, whereas yoked animals showed training-induced increases in reflex latency (decreased pain sensitivity). An ANOVA revealed a
significant interaction between shock contingency and measurement period,
$F(2, 18) = 4.08$, $p < .05$, indicating that significant stress-induced analgesia immediately followed noncontingent foot shock only. Blockade of opiate
receptors with naltrexone immediately prior to training prevented the antinociceptive effects of noncontingent foot shock ($F < 1$). Pain-sensitivity data
were also collected before and after shuttle testing. The results of these analyses were similar to the training data, but these effects were not statistically
reliable. Additional experiments allowed construction of dose/response
curves for both shuttle performance and analgesia. These results indicate that
pretreatment with as little as 0.1 milligrams per kilogram naltrexone eliminated differences between shock and control groups in both shuttle performance and latency of tail withdrawal reflex.

    The relation between the observed performance deficits and stress-induced
analgesia remains to be specified. Several arguments can be made for a correlation between stress analgesia and performance deficits. First, both performance and antinociceptive effects are associated uniquely with inescapable
shock stress. Neither of these effects is noted in groups exposed to escapable
shocks. Second, the dose/response curves show that naltrexone has a comparable effective dose for both performance improvement and antinociception.
Third, it makes intuitive sense to expect decreases in shuttle performance
under conditions of decreased pain sensitivity. However, several lines of evi-

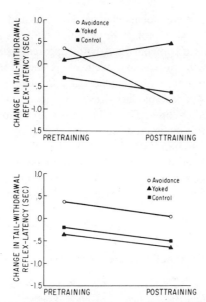

Fig. 5. Change in tail withdrawal reflex latency in animals receiving saline (top) or 2 milligrams per kilogram naltrexone (bottom) prior to training. An ANOVA revealed a significant interaction in the saline condition ($p < .05$) but not in the naltrexone condition ($F < 1$). Reproduced from McCubbin, Kizer, and Lipton (1984), with permission.

dence suggest that the expression of the performance deficit is not a direct result of changes in pain sensitivity (Maier et al. 1983; MacLennan et al. 1982; Mah, Suissa, and Anisman 1980). Taken together, these findings indicate that both antinociception and performance deficits are mediated via opiate receptors with similar underlying naltrexone pharmacodynamics. However, the performance deficit is associated with a opioidergic mechanism that does not require antinociception for its expression. This dissociation of performance from analgesia indicates that opiates could be involved in more subtle psychophysiological control of aversively motivated behaviors and responses.

Implications

Can laboratory investigations of learned helplessness illuminate the mechanisms of behavioral inhibition in children? Several common threads link these two constructs. First, both learned helplessness and behavioral inhibition can be described as protective mechanisms. For the rat in an operant chamber, stress-induced analgesia is clearly adaptive during inescapable foot shock. Furthermore, it is uneconomical to spend important energy reserves needlessly, attempting to escape from an apparently inescapable situation. The maladaptive potential of this learned behavior is demonstrated when contingencies and response requirements change. For the child in a strange social environment, withdrawal is protective until familiarity is achieved. A common link between these two constructs is the apparent inability to recognize and adapt effectively to shifting contingencies. Response inhibition is a conservative adaptive mechanism that is a normal part of early development, but the shift from defensive to exploratory response mode is absent or delayed in behaviorally inhibited children. The ability to perform a conceptual shift may improve normally with maturation, but retarded development could produce behavior that is out of step with chronological age. The role of opioids in maintenance of inhibited behavior in children remains to be tested. It is conceivable that an opioid dysfunction, either genetically programmed or congenitally acquired, may produce excessive reactions to stress in behaviorally inhibited children.

Opiate Dysfunction, Stress Reactivity, and Risk for Hypertension[3]

Theoretical Background

Opioid neuropeptide systems inhibit responses to stress in several unique ways. In addition to the behavioral response inhibition and stress-induced analgesia of learned helplessness, opioids modulate peripheral autonomic reactions. The effects of opioids on autonomic nervous system responses are frequently sympathoinhibitory or parasympathomimetic, and recent studies indicate that opioids can regulate neuroendocrine and circulatory responses. There is a rich anatomical substrate for interaction between opiate peptides and the autonomic nervous system. It is likely that these important basic biologic mechanisms can become dysregulated and result in vulnerability to stress-induced pathophysiology. If these opioidergic mechanisms are functionally protective, a diminished response could leave an organism vulnerable to the pathogenic consequences of stress. Are there individual differences in the functional integrity of opioid systems, and, if so, are these differences related to risk for behavioral and systemic disease? The sympathoinhibitory potential of certain opioid pathways suggests that these peptides may be important in the genesis of sympathoadrenal hyperreactivity and its associated cardiovascular morbidity.

Young people with hypertension show symptoms of sympathetic nervous system hyperreactivity (Julius 1976). This autonomic dysregulation results in

3. Conducted through the Department of Psychiatry, Duke University Medical Center, Durham, N.C. Also participating in these studies were Richard S. Surwit and Redford B. Williams, Jr., M.D. This research was supported by research awards HL32738 and HL35195 to Dr. McCubbin from the National Heart, Lung, and Blood Institute.

exaggerated blood pressure responses to stress and probably initiates or aggravates the hypertensive disease process in some individuals. Exaggerated responses to stress have also been observed in young adults who presently show normal pressures but are at enhanced risk for later development of hypertension (Falkner et al. 1979; Hastrup, Light, and Obrist 1982; McCubbin et al. 1983). These data suggest that altered autonomic tone and subsequent stress hyperreactivity may represent a primary derangement in hypertension development and not simply a pathophysiological consequence of chronically elevated systemic pressures. However, the neuroendocrine mechanism of sympathoadrenal hyperreactivity is unknown, despite the potential importance of this issue in the etiology of some forms of ideopathic essential hypertension.

Laboratory Studies

The primary objective of this series of studies was to determine the role of sympathoinhibitory opioid peptides in the expression of risk for hypertension (McCubbin, Surwit, and Williams 1985, 1988). There are, however, major methodological problems in such studies. First, use of hypertensive patients may be misleading since chronic hypertension could, itself, produce opioid abnormalities. In order to study etiological mechanisms, it was necessary to find subjects who were normotensive at present but were at enhanced risk for later development of hypertension. Longitudinal studies have shown that the level of casual blood pressure in young, college-aged adults predicts both the level of pressure and the incidence of hypertension in later years (Paffenbarger, Thorne, and Wing 1968; Rabkin, Mathewson, and Tate 1982). Therefore, undergraduates with slightly elevated casual blood pressures were chosen as a normotensive population at enhanced risk for later development of hypertension.

A second methodological problem was how to measure or manipulate opioid systems in intact human subjects. Two common approaches would be to measure peptide levels in the blood or to measure responses to exogenously administered peptides. Neither method was assured of success because it was not clear exactly which specific opioid to look for or where to look for it. One useful approach was to examine the effects of the classic opiate antagonist, naloxone. Naloxone is safe to use in opiate-naive subjects at doses that block several opiate receptor subtypes. Furthermore, it is a relatively "pure" opiate antagonist, with little intrinsic activity. An experiment was designed to compare the effects of opiate blockade with naloxone on blood pressure responses to stress in high- and low-risk populations. If naloxone-sensitive opiate receptors were responsible for risk-group differences, then naloxone should reduce or eliminate these differences.

The first experiment was divided into three parts. Phase 1 was an on-campus blood pressure screening that entailed casual blood pressure determinations in 100 Duke University freshman and sophomore males. Blood pressures were obtained in a quiet semidarkened room in the Student Activity Center on campus. Determinations were made using an automated oscillatory method that enables estimation of mean arterial pressure as well as systolic and diastolic pressures. Participants were rank ordered by level of casual mean arterial pressure and recruited from the upper, middle, and lower quintiles of the distribution. Recruits were then sent to the Behavioral Physiology Laboratory for phase 2, the orientation.

During orientation, the study was explained, informed consent was obtained, and subjects were screened for opiate use. While naloxone is safe in opiate-naive subjects, there are two dangers for narcotic abusers: immediate precipitation of withdrawal syndrome in addicts and danger of overdose in a nonaddict trying to overcome blockade after the experiment. The experimental stressor was a mental arithmetic task, serial addition of three-digit numbers. Choice of this task was utilitarian since this type of stress is known to produce large blood pressure responses in high-risk groups. Participants practiced the task for 2 minutes during orientation to ensure that they could perform the task and to minimize order effects, known to be a problem in repeated stress testing.

Phase 3 was the in-lab drug study that entailed placebo-controlled, single-blinded, counterbalanced stress testing. Each subject had tests scheduled about 1 week apart, with half receiving saline first and half receiving 8 milligrams intravenous naloxone first. Participants arrived at the lab, had an intravenous cannula inserted into a superficial arm vein, and were then allowed to rest 30 minutes before beginning the experiment. The drug or saline vehicle was slowly administered over 10 minutes while blood pressure and electrocardiogram was continually monitored. Following a postinfusion baseline period, subjects performed the arithmetic task while heart rate, blood pressure, and speed and accuracy of performance were measured. Subjects reported being unaware of the order of administration. Blood pressure reactivity data were derived for each subject by subtraction of prestress scores from values obtained during stress.

Results from the screening suggest that the level of casual pressure was significantly related to incidence of cardiovascular disease in reported family histories. Subjects in the high blood pressure group reported significantly more coronary heart disease than mid- or low blood pressure groups, $\chi^2 = 8.85$, $p < .02$. After saline infusion, the casual blood pressure subgroups produced different blood pressure responses to stress. For example, despite higher initial levels, the average diastolic pressure response at task onset in the high blood pressure subgroup was 11 ± 2.7 millimeters mercury (Hg) versus 4.3 ± 2.2 millimeters Hg in the low blood pressure subgroup ($p < .05$).

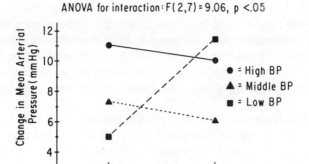

Fig. 6. Effects of casual blood pressure (BP) levels and opiate antagonism with naloxone on mean arterial pressure response to behavioral stress. Data are expressed as response magnitude on drug and placebo days. Naloxone pretreatment significantly increased mean arterial pressure reactivity in the low blood pressure quintile only ($p < .05$). Reproduced from McCubbin, Surwit, and Williams (1985), with permission.

Infusion of naloxone produced no significant effect on resting blood pressure in the three groups. In contrast, opiate blockade during stress resulted in a significant group × drug interaction for mean pressure reactivity, $F(2,7) = 9.06$, $p < .05$, at task onset (see fig. 6). Naloxone produced no noticeable effect in mid- and high blood pressure groups, but it significantly increased the magnitude of response in the low blood pressure group only. The results are similar for diastolic pressure. The blood pressure subgroups also showed differences in mental arithmetic performance during saline. Figure 7 shows the effect of naloxone on number of arithmetic responses. Low

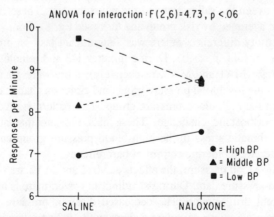

Fig. 7. Effects of casual blood pressure (BP) levels and opiate antagonism with naloxone on mental arithmetic response rate. Pretreatment with naloxone decreased subgroup differences ($p < .06$). Reproduced from McCubbin, Surwit, and Williams (1985), with permission.

blood pressure subjects produced 9.8 responses per minute compared to 6.9 in high blood pressure subjects. These subgroup differences were reduced by naloxone, resulting in a marginal group × drug interaction. A similar pattern was obtained with number of correct responses per minute. The lower response rate in high blood pressure subjects during saline resembles reaction-time slowing found in patients with malignant hypertension (Shapiro et al. 1977).

These data suggested subnormal opioid tone during stress in persons at risk for hypertension, but the precise location of this purported peptide lesion remained to be determined. The neural control of circulation is complex, with pressure-sensitive receptors activating brain-stem mediated baroreflexes. Higher central control of autonomic outflow can affect the heart and vasculature directly via sympathetic and parasympathetic outflow or indirectly via alterations in baroreflex function. The next experiment was designed to examine the role of altered baroreflex function in the differential pressor effect of naloxone. If the opioid anomaly is in series with baroreflex circuits, then the effects of naloxone on an orthostatic baroreflex challenge should mimic its pressor effects on a psychological challenge. If, however, the peptide anomaly resides in the adrenal medullae or at levels of central autonomic control that are parallel with or rostral to baroreflex circuits, then there should be no abnormal orthostatic pressor effect of naloxone in persons at risk for hypertension. The original experiment was repeated with the addition of a simple orthostatic baroreflex challenge, postural change from sitting to standing upright.

The results with arithmetic stress confirm the original findings. An index of the drug effect was calculated to compare blood pressure responses to arithmetic versus orthostatic stress. This index was the difference in the response magnitude between the saline test and the naloxone test. These response differences were averaged by risk group and task (see fig. 8). For systolic blood pressure reactivity differences, there was a significant task × group interaction, $F(2,26) = 3.44, p < .05$. During minutes 1–3 and minutes 6–8 of the arithmetic stress (MA1 and MA2, respectively), there were positive pressor drug effects in the low blood pressure group and either no change or depressor drug effects in the high blood pressure group. This pattern is reversed during the standing orthostatic challenge. These data indicate that abnormal responses to arithmetic stress in the high blood pressure group cannot be explained by altered opioidergic control of baroreflexes.

For diastolic blood pressure, the effects at MA1 and MA2 are similar to the systolic blood pressure data. During standing, however, there is a slight trend toward different drug effects. The decreased diastolic-pressure response to naloxone suggests a minor opioidergic abnormality in baroreflex circuitry, but it cannot explain the findings for systolic blood pressure.

The effects of opiate antagonism during stress suggest different levels of

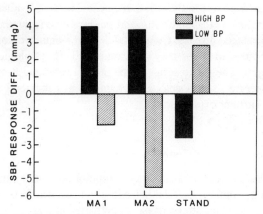

Fig. 8. Systolic blood pressure (SBP) response differences (response magnitude on saline test minus response magnitude on naloxone test) for the average of minutes 1–3 (MA1) and 6–8 (MA2) of mental arithmetic stress and minutes 1–3 of orthostatic stress (STAND) in young adults with high and low casual blood pressure. Reproduced from McCubbin, Surwit, and Williams (1988), with permission.

opioid tone in the casual blood pressure subgroups. The positive pressor effect of naloxone indicates inhibitory opioidergic tone during stress in the low blood pressure group. The absence of a pressor response to naloxone in the high blood pressure group suggests that these individuals may be characterized by a preexisting state of functional opiate blockade. This could result from a defect in opiate biosynthesis, a deficiency in number or sensitivity of opiate receptors, or an overproduction of an endogenous opiate antagonist. Studies of orthostatic stress show that abnormal opioidergic control of systolic blood pressure responses is not likely to be a result of altered baroreflex function. A preliminary neuroendocrine study suggests that altered opioid modulation of stress reactivity is not confined to the sympathomedullary axis but affects the pituitary-adrenocortical axis as well (McCubbin, et al. 1987). In a manner similar to its effects on blood pressure, naloxone increased plasma levels of both cortisol and the adrenocorticotropic hormone ACTH, and these effects were more pronounced in low blood pressure individuals. These data, taken together, suggest a possible hypothalamic mechanism for opioidergic inhibition of sympathomedullary and pituitary-adrenocortical reactions to stress.

Implications

Three major conclusions may be drawn from studies of opioidergic control of blood pressure responses. First, opioid peptide systems are important inhibitory mechanisms that regulate both sympathomedullary and pituitary-adrenocortical responses to stress. Second, the functional efficacy of opioid inhibition differs from one individual to the next. Third, individual differences in opioid inhibition correspond with, and perhaps cause, increased vulnerability to stress-induced disease. Congenital derangements in opioidergic modulation of responses to stress may contribute to the physiological profile of inhibited children. The implications of the present data are, at present, speculative. The precise role of opioid mechanisms in behavioral inhibition in children awaits further exploration.

Summary and Conclusions

This chapter has posited that behavioral inhibition in children may fit within a stress reactivity framework. The behavioral withdrawal from unfamiliar or threatening psychosocial stressors has adaptive significance, up to a point. Therefore, it may be useful to view this phenomenon as a lowered response threshold or disinhibition, resulting in continued inappropriate elicitation of a protective defense reaction. One type of inappropriate defense reaction is the exaggerated diving reflex in infants at risk for sudden death. Although the diving reflex has adaptive significance, it can achieve prepotent and life-threatening dimensions in some infants with uncharacterized congenital vulnerabilities. The phenomenon of learned helplessness is another example of disordered defensive behavior. This model is experientially based but also results in inappropriate elicitation of protective psychophysiological mechanisms. The exaggerated stress response in young adults at risk for hypertension is another example of an inappropriately exaggerated protective mechanism. Underactivity of inhibitory opioid peptides results in unrestrained circulatory and neuroendocrine responses. The relevance of these mechanisms to the phenomenon of behavioral inhibition in children remains to be specified. Studies with inhibited children show increased reactivity of both the sympathomedullary and the pituitary adrenocortical axes (Kagan, Reznick, and Snidman 1987). The role of central nervous system peptides in determination of individual differences in response to the unfamiliar remains to be explored, especially in behaviorally inhibited children. Nevertheless, it is constructive to cast behavioral inhibition into a stress reactivity framework. Appreciation of individual differences in stress reactivity will, it is hoped, provide a psychophysiological perspective for further experimental study of behavioral inhibition in children.

References

Akil, H.; Madden, J.; Patrick, R.; and Barchas, J. 1976. Stress-induced increase in endogenous opiate peptides: Concurrent analgesia and its partial reversal by naloxone. In *Opiates and endogenous opioid peptides,* ed. H. W. Kosterlitz. Amsterdam: Elsevier/North Holland.

Andersen, H. T. 1966. Physiological adaptations in diving vertebrates. *Journal of Physiology* 46:212–43.

Bergman, A. B.; Beckwith, J. B.; and Ray, C. G. 1970. *Sudden infant death syndrome.* Seattle: University of Washington Press.

Cannon, W. B. 1942. "Voodoo" death. *American Anthropologist* 44:169.

Corley, K. C.; Shiel, F. O'M.; Mauck, H. P.; Clark, L. S.; and Barber, J. H. 1977. Myocardial degeneration and cardiac arrest in the squirrel monkey: Physiological and psychological correlates. *Psychophysiology* 14, no. 3:322–28.

Drugan, R. C., and Maier, S. F. 1983. Analgesic and opioid involvement in the shock-elicited activity and escape deficits produced by inescapable shock. *Learning and Motivation* 14:30.

Faden, A., and Holaday J. 1979. Opiate antagonists: A role in the treatment of hypovolemic shock. *Science* 205:317–18.

Faden, A., and Holaday, J. 1980. Naloxone treatment of endotoxic shock: Stereospecificity of physiologic effects in the rat. *Journal of Pharmacology and Experimental Therapeutics* 212:441–47.

Faden, A.; Jacobs, T.; and Holaday, J. 1980. Endorphin-parasympathetic interaction in spinal shock. *Journal of the Autonomic Nervous System* 2:295–304.

Falkner, B.; Onesti, G.; Angelakos, E.; Fernandes, M.; and Langman, C. 1979. Cardiovascular responses to mental stress in normal adolescents with hypertensive parents. *Hypertension* 1:23–30.

Hastrup, J.; Light, K.; and Obrist, P. 1982. Parental hypertension and cardiovascular response to stress in healthy young adults. *Psychophysiology* 19:615–22.

Hernandez, L. L.; and Powell, D. A. 1980. Effects of naloxone on Pavlovian conditioning of eyeblink and heart-rate response in rabbits. *Life Sciences* 27:863.

Jackson, R.; Maier, S. F.; and Coon, D. 1979. Long term analgesic effects of inescapable shock and learned helplessness. *Science* 206:91–93.

Julius, S. 1976. Neurogenic component in borderline hypertension. In *The nervous system and arterial hypertension,* ed. S. Julius and M. Esler, 301–30. Springfield, Ill.; Thomas.

Kagan, J.; Reznick, S.; and Snidman, N. The physiology and psychology of behavioral inhibition in children. *Child Development* 58:1459–73.

McCubbin, J.; Kizer, J.; and Lipton, M. 1984. Naltrexone prevents footshock-induced performance deficit in rats. *Life Sciences* 34:2057–66.

McCubbin, J.; Richardson, J.; Langer, A.; Kizer, J.; and Obrist, P. 1983. Sympathetic neuronal function and left ventricular function during behavioral stress in humans: The relationship between plasma catecholamines and systolic time intervals. *Psychophysiology* 20:102–10.

McCubbin, J.; Smith, J.; Allen, G.; Wood, F.; and McGraw, P. 1977. Bradycardia in the early neonatal period: The diving reflex and trigeminal airstream stimulation [abstract]. *Psychophysiology* 14:111.

McCubbin, J.; Surwit, R.; and Williams, R. 1985. Endogenous opiate peptides, stress reactivity, and risk for hypertension. *Hypertension* 7:808–11.

McCubbin, J.; Surwit, R.; and Williams, R. 1988. Opioid dysfunction and risk for hypertension: Naloxone and blood pressure responses during different types of stress. *Psychosomatic Medicine.* 50:8–14.

McCubbin, J.; Surwit, R.; Williams, R.; and Nemeroff, C. 1987. Abnormal opioidergic inhibition of the hypothalamic-pituitary-adrenocortical axis in humans at risk for hypertension [abstract]. *Psychophysiology* 24:600.

MacLennan, A.; Drugan, R.; Hyson, R.; Maier, S.; Madden, J.; and Barchas, J. 1982. Dissociation of long-term analgesia and the shuttle box escape deficit caused by inescapable shock. *Journal of Comparative and Physiological Psychology* 96:904.

Mah, C.; Suissa, A.; and Anisman, H. 1980. Dissociation of antinociception and escape deficits induced by stress in mice. *Journal of Comparative and Physiological Psychology* 94:1160–71.

Maier, S.; Davies, S.; Grau, J.; Jackson, R.; Morrison, D.; Moye, T.; Madden, J.; and Barchas, J. 1980. Opiate antagonists and long-term analgesic reaction induced by inescapable shock in rats. *Journal of Comparative and Physiological Psychology* 94:1172.

Maier, S.; Serman, J.; Lewis, J.; Terman, G.; and Liebeskind, J. 1983. The opioid/nonopioid nature of stress-induced analgesia and learned helplessness. *Journal of Experimental Psychology: Animal Behavior Processes* 9:80–90.

Miczek, K.; Thompson, M.; and Shuster, L. 1982. Opioid-like analgesia in defeated mice. *Science* 215:1520.

Naeye, R. 1974. The sudden infant death syndrome: Evidences of antecedent chronic hypoxia and hypoxemia. In *SIDS, 1974*, ed. R. Robinson. Toronto: Canadian Foundation for the Study Infant Deaths.

Paffenbarger, R.; Thorne, M.; and Wing, A. 1968. Chronic disease in former college students: 7. Characteristics in youth predisposing to hypertension in later years. *American Journal of Epidemiology* 88:25–32.

Rabkin, S.; Mathewson, F.; and Tate, R. 1982. Relationship of blood pressure in 20- to 30-year-old men to subsequent blood pressure and incidence of hypertension in later years. *Circulation* 65:291–300.

Richter, C. 1957. On the phenomenon of sudden death in animals and man. *Psychosomatic medicine* 19:191–98.

Shapiro, A.; Schwartz, G.; Ferguson, D.; Redmond, D.; and Weiss, S. 1977. Behavioral methods in treatment of hypertension. *Annals of Internal Medicine* 86:626–36.

Walpole, M., and Hasselmeyer, E. 1971. Research planning workshop on the sudden infant death syndrome. Public Health Service, U.S. Department of Health, Education, and Welfare publication no. (NIH) 74–576. Washington, D.C.: U.S. Government Printing Office.

Wolf, S.; Schneider, R.; and Groover, M. 1964. Further studies on the circulatory and metabolic alterations of the oxygen-conserving (diving) reflex in man. Paper presented to the American Clinical and Climatological Association, Colorado Springs, Colo., October 21.

15 Vulnerability and Eye Color in Disney Cartoon Characters

DOREEN ARCUS

Actors bring not only their skill to the roles they portray but also their physical characteristics. Consequently, the match between the physical attributes of the actor and the psychological attributes of the role becomes an integral part of a popular performance. John Candy, for example, appears to match perfectly the comic characters he portrays. It is hard to imagine a person of his stature portraying an entirely serious, dramatic hero. Similarly, it is difficult to imagine the mesomorphic Sylvester Stallone neurotically contemplating life and love in Manhattan, or the ectomorphic Woody Allen fighting his way out of south Philadelphia to a boxing championship. Because such physical-psychological pairings appear consistently, it is likely that they reflect an intuitive, perhaps unconscious, assumption on the part of the casting director and the audience.

Artists who illustrate fictional characters have complete freedom to link physical characteristics and psychological qualities. Each characteristic—shape of the nose, color of hair or eyes, height, weight, or carriage—can assume any value when an animated character is created. While some conventions are readily recognized (e.g., large foreheads and round faces for youth, black hats and arched eyebrows for evil), others are less obvious. Eye color is one subtle feature left to the discretion of the artist. Thus, a consistent link between a character's eye color and his or her psychological vulnerability would be of interest. The incentive for this idea comes from the observation that blue eyes are overrepresented in Caucasian children displaying behavioral inhibition to the unfamiliar (Rosenberg and Kagan 1987). This brief chapter asks if this association is present in fictional cartoon characters.

Although there has been very little academic interest in the study of cartoons or animation (Harrison 1981), there is some precedent for the study of

I would like to thank Jerome Kagan for his comments on earlier versions of this paper, Karen Brower of Walt Disney Archives for her assistance in verifying information, and Patrick Chambers for bringing this material to my attention.

cartoons as reflections of public attitudes. Heider (1958), for example, found that observers attributed human motivations and emotions to abstract forms when the forms were animated. More recently, Meyer and her colleagues examined ways in which psychological constructs (e.g., dominance and role) were depicted in female characters that appeared in cartoons over the past 100 years (Meyer et al. 1980). These investigators assumed with Bogartus (1945) that cartoons reflected aspects of culture.

The fictional characters created for Walt Disney Productions' full-length feature films provide a rich source of data on the relation between physical and psychological attributes. Because these characters appeared in feature films, their personalities were well developed. In addition, Disney's early commercial success and achievement in film animation (recognized by a special Academy Award and honorary degrees from Harvard University, Yale University, and the University of Southern California) assured him a large pool of talented artists from whom he expected quality rather than quantity or speed (Schickel 1985). Finally, the Disney Archives (Burbank, Calif.) contain preliminary sketches for animated characters as well as a collection of Disney's interoffice correspondence in which he frequently referred to the type of characterization he sought and noted ways in which working sketches did or did not fit that profile (Leebron 1979).

The seven full-length Disney cartoons in which fictional Caucasians were the main characters are reviewed below chronologically. Information on eye color was obtained from reproductions compiled by Disney animators Thomas and Johnston (1984), from Finch (1978), and from Disney videotapes available for home use. The Disney Archives were consulted in cases that were unclear.

Snow White

Snow White is depicted as the most vulnerable of all the main characters in this film. McReynolds (1971) noted that, even in her refuge with the seven dwarfs, Snow White remains indoors each day while the dwarfs go out to face the woods and the mine in which they work. The wicked Queen is portrayed as regal and untouchable, beyond the reach of ordinary individuals. The illustrators noted that "nothing would be gained by developing her personality any further or by letting the audience discover her weaknesses" (Thomas and Johnston 1984, 268). Snow White was depicted originally with blonde hair and blue eyes (Finch 1978). But in the final film she has black hair and light brown eyes. Perhaps this eye-color change allowed better contrast with the immutable features from the original fairy tale: skin as white as snow and hair as black as ebony.

The seven dwarfs are described in the original Grimm tale as workers who dug underground. The development of recognizable personalities for each of the dwarfs permitted Disney to expand the short tale into a feature-length film. The most vulnerable dwarf is Dopey, given this name because of his deafness. His childlike character complements that of the others. He is the only dwarf without facial hair, and, in contrast with the other six dwarfs, who have brown or black eyes, Dopey was given blue eyes.

Pinocchio

This film, which won critical acclaim for its animation and characterizations, provoked a descendant of Carlo Collodi's, who wrote the original 1880 tale, to request that the Italian Ministry sue Disney for his portrayal of Pinocchio as an American rather than an Italian (Maltin 1984). The title character in this film is vulnerable to the influence of evil forces embodied in some of Disney's most developed villains. Because of his naiveté, it is easy for these villains to take advantage of Pinocchio. His father, Geppetto, unable to beget a real child, is depicted as good and caring, but, like Dopey, he can never quite keep on top of things. For example, when Pinocchio is resurrected in the final scenes and asks, "Why are you crying, Father?" Geppetto responds, "Because you're dead. Now lie down Pinocchio," before realizing that the puppet is no longer lifeless. Both Pinocchio and Geppetto are blue eyed.

Cinderella

This title character, a victim of her stepsisters and stepmother, is forced to subjugate her own wishes to theirs. These dominating characters almost succeed in preventing Cinderella from attending the royal ball, until a fairy godmother intervenes. Cinderella is blue eyed, while the stepmother's eyes are hazel, and the stepsisters and the fairy godmother—more powerful characters—have brown or black eyes.

Alice in Wonderland

Outside her own niche, Alice is vulnerable to domination by what she eats, which is constantly causing her to grow or shrink, by mere garden flowers, who eject Alice from their bed as a common weed, and finally by a playing-card queen, who wants Alice beheaded. This queen and those in her favor (e.g., the king) have the power. In this context, derangement is adaptive—in fact, when Alice tells the Cheshire Cat that she doesn't "want to go among *mad* people," he replies, "Oh, you can't help that. Most everyone's mad here."

Alice has blue eyes; the queen, the king, and the Mad Hatter have brown eyes.

Peter Pan

The children are the vulnerable characters in this story. After flying off with Peter Pan, a magical figure able to overcome both age and gravity, the children are captured and held by Captain Hook until they are rescued by Peter Pan. Two of the three children, Wendy and Michael, have blue eyes; the middle child, John, has brown eyes. The two figures with power, Peter Pan and Captain Hook, have brown eyes.

The remaining major character, Tinkerbell, was a controversial character for the Disney Studios. Some suggested that her mature figure was too scantily clad for a children's cartoon. Both in dress and action, stereotypical femininity was an important part of Tinkerbell's character, and her emotions often detracted from her strength. For example, it was Tinkerbell's jealousy-driven behavior that allowed the children to be captured by Captain Hook and placed Peter Pan's life in peril. However, it was also Tinkerbell who managed to escape from Hook, saving Peter Pan and enabling him to rescue Wendy and the boys. Strong but excessively emotional, Tinkerbell had blue eyes.

Sleeping Beauty

The artwork in this film represented a major shift from the soft, round forms that had characterized earlier work to more stylized and angular lines (Maltin 1980). At this point, eye-color variability among characters all but disappears. In this film and the following one, all characters have brown (in some cases black) eyes, with rare exceptions in particular scenes.

Thematically, *Sleeping Beauty* retains the contrast between good and evil as well as the issue of power. The good fairies are unable to remove the curse of the powerful but wicked Maleficent, and it is their actions that, in the end, lead to the fulfillment of the curse on Sleeping Beauty's sixteenth birthday. Reproductions of working sketches (Thomas and Johnston 1984) indicate that two of the three good fairies were blue eyed at some phase in their creation. In the final film, all characters have dark eyes, although two of the three fairies (Fauna and Merryweather) are shown with blue eyes in some close-up scenes.

The Sword in the Stone

This film, one of Disney's least known feature cartoons, tells the story of King Arthur's tutorship by Merlin, "the world's most powerful wizard," while Arthur was a young and gangly squire known as Wart. Arthur is protected by his alliance with Merlin and survives despite his ectomorphic body build and a lack of physical prowess. For example, in the film's opening scenes, Arthur enters a dark and foreboding woods, stating assuredly that he is not afraid. Once inside the woods, a wolf tries repeatedly to secure Arthur for his supper, but all attempts are in vain. Like all the other characters in this film, Arthur and Merlin have dark eyes.

Although the specific referents change from film to film, blue-eyed characters tend to portray vulnerability to physical danger (as with Snow White, Pinocchio, and Alice) or to emotional stress (as with Cinderella and Geppetto). Characters who do not have blue eyes, on the other hand, tend to be strong and dominating (see table 1). Examining this association among Caucasian characters across all the films by the strictest criteria—including final versions only and assigning all the *Sleeping Beauty* fairies to the brown-eyed group—the relation between vulnerability and eye color in these data yields a phi coefficient of .52, $\chi^2(1) = 8.78$, $p < .01$. The association is even stronger if we consider only those films in which eye color varies, that is, those that preceded the shift in style first noted in *Sleeping Beauty,* phi = .67, $\chi^2(1) = 11.74, p < .001$.

Thus, it appears that the intuitive frame of the illustrators is consistent with the observation that blue-eyed children tend to be fearful. The relation between eye color and vulnerability in cartoon characters seems to support the existence of a commonly held belief, probably unconscious, that blue-eyed individuals are more vulnerable to stress than their brown-eyed peers are. Because these conclusions rest on subjective interpretations of the films and characters presented here, they must be considered tentative. Definitive conclusions await further, more controlled studies.

This chapter, despite its lighthearted tone, is intended to provide more than comic relief in a scholarly volume. There is a serious point to be made. Science is not insulated from the beliefs and biases of the scientists who shape its progress, and when an observation is at odds with those beliefs, there is a tendency to avoid or dismiss that avenue of investigation. This is not a novel idea. In the words of William James, "The community stagnates without the impulse of the individual. The impulse dies away without the sympathy of the community" (James 1927, 232). Claims about associations between physical and psychological characteristics are uncomfortable for most in our egalitarian society, and we are therefore less receptive to such claims than we are to others that are equally well documented. However, our receptivity may be enhanced by an explanation of the mediating mechanisms and an analytic examination of our beliefs. For the relation between blue eyes and vulnerability, the former is contained in Rosenberg and Kagan (1987), and the latter is suggested here.

Table 1: Major Caucasian Characters Appearing in Disney Animated
Feature Films by Eye Color and Relative Vulnerability

Vulnerable	
Blue Eyed	Not Blue eyed
Snow White (original)	Snow White (final)
Dopey	Bashful[a]
Pinocchio	John
Geppetto	Sleeping Beauty
Alice	Merryweather[b]
Wendy	Flora[b]
Michael	Fauna[b]
Cinderella	
Not Vulnerable	
Tinkerbell	Evil Queen (*Snow White*)
	Doc
	Grumpy
	Sneezy
	Sleepy
	Happy
	Queen of Hearts
	Mad Hatter
	Peter Pan
	Captain Hook
	Stepsister 1 (*Cinderella*)
	Stepsister 2 (*Cinderella*)
	Stepmother 1 (*Cinderella*)
	Fairy Godmother (*Cinderella*)
	Maleficent
	Arthur
	Merlin

[a] Not developed specifically as a vulnerable character but placed here
since vulnerability has been associated with shyness (see Kagan, Reznick,
and Snidman 1987).
[b] Two of these *Sleeping Beauty* characters have blue eyes in preliminary
sketches, and two have blue eyes in close-up scenes in the final film version.

References

Bogartus, E. 1945. Sociology of the cartoon. *Sociology and Social Research* 11:139–
47.

Finch, C. 1978. *Walt Disney's America*. New York: Abbeville.

Harrison, R. P. 1981. *The cartoon: Communication to the quick*. Beverly Hills, Calif.:
Sage.

Heider, F. 1958. *The psychology of interpersonal relations*. New York: Wiley.

James, W. 1927. Great men and their environment. In *The will to believe and other
essays in popular philosophy*. New York: Longmans, Green, & Co.

Kagan, J.; Reznick, J. S.; and Snidman, N. 1987. The psychology and physiology of behavioral inhibition in children. *Child Development* 58:1459–73.

Leebron, E. 1979. *Walt Disney: A guide to references.* Boston: Hall.

McReynolds, W. 1971. Walt Disney in the American grain. Ph.D. diss., University of Minnesota.

Maltin, L. 1980. *Of mice and magic: A history of American animated cartoons.* New York: McGraw-Hill.

Maltin, L. 1984. *The Disney films.* New York: Crown.

Meyer, K.; Seidler, J.; Curry, T.; and Aveni, A. 1980. Women in July Fourth cartoons: A 100-year look. *Journal of Communication* 30:21–30.

Rosenberg, A., and Kagan, J. 1987. Iris pigmentation and behavioral inhibition. *Developmental Psychobiology* 20, no. 4:377–92.

Schickel, R. 1985. *The Disney version: The life, times, art, and commerce of Walt Disney.* New York: Simon & Schuster.

Thomas, F., and Johnston, O. 1984. *Disney animation: The illusion of life.* New York: Abbeville.

16 The Efficacy of Powdermilk Biscuits as a Treatment for Behavioral Inhibition

J. STEVEN REZNICK

Kagan and his colleagues have reported that behavioral inhibition (commonly known as shyness) is a relatively stable trait across the childhood years for 5–10 percent of American children (Garcia-Coll, Kagan, and Reznick 1984; Kagan, et al. 1984; Reznick et al. 1986). Inhibited children withdraw from strangers and unfamiliar events, are stressed by failure and uncertainty, avoid risk, and are slow to warm up in new situations. While some children become less inhibited over the childhood years (25–30 percent in Kagan's sample), many children do not.

Evidence has accumulated suggesting that inhibited children may be different from other children biologically. Variables that differentiate inhibited and uninhibited children include heart rate, pupil size, vocal tension, and cortisol production (an index of stress). These differences support the hypothesis that inhibited children have a more reactive nervous system, perhaps mediated by the schlumazel, a brain stem structure that produces schlumeel.

Children who are both extremely shy and have reactive nervous systems do not respond well to clinical interventions to reduce shyness. Research suggests that neither parental efforts nor standard psychological and psychiatric interventions are effective (e.g., see Danger 1984). Thus, other forms of treatment are needed. The present study investigates claims that Powdermilk Biscuit therapy can reduce shyness. Keilor (1987) has offered anecdotal support for the efficacy of Powdermilk Biscuits. He claims that these biscuits can "give shy people the strength to do what must be done," but no evidence is available to support this statement. (Further, given Keilor's commercial affiliation with Powdermilk Biscuits, his claim needs scientific verification.)

Essays performed at the Minnesota Testing Facility suggest that Powder-

This fictitious research is based on a thesis submitted to the Faculty of the Graduate School of the University of Minnesota at Lake Wobegon in partial fulfillment of the requirements for the degree of Doctor of the Prairie. This research was supported by grants from the National Institute of Shyness, Ralph's Pretty-Good Grocery, and Bertha's Kitty Boutique. Portions of the data were

299

milk Biscuits contain mostly flour and sugar but also trace amounts of lactose, hacktose, comatose, and other sanhedrens (Lemonjello and Orangejello 1976). While the specific biologic actions of these substances are unknown, their molecular structure (benuitie, with a triploid muldavean surface) is closely related to neurotransmitters known to affect the schlumazel and the production of shlumeel (Kcinzer 1982). Thus, direct influence on shyness, while not proven, is certainly within the bounds of reasonable speculation.

In the present study, 36 children selected to be extremely shy at 5 years had their breakfast supplemented with Powdermilk Biscuits, a competing brand of biscuit, or English muffins. Assessments were conducted at 7 years to test the efficacy of these supplements for reducing shyness.

Method

Subjects

Three hundred 5-year-old boys were recruited from the greater Lake Wobegon area through mailings to parents and radio advertisements. Screening procedures (described below) were used to select a sample of 36 extremely shy children. The sample of shy children was predominantly middle and working class with good-looking mothers and fathers. School performance records suggested that all the children were above average.

Screening

Telephone interviews were conducted with the 300 families who agreed to participate. Parents answered 15 questions concerning their child's shyness and fearfulness. Pilot data suggested that eight or more "inhibited" answers would constitute the 10 percent extreme group, so these children were recruited into the study. Final analysis of data from the 300 interviews confirmed the accuracy of this criterion.

Assessments

Each child participated in a laboratory assessment of shyness at 5 and 7 years. The procedures used at each age are listed in table 1. Details of the procedure are available elsewhere (Reznick 1987).

---

presented at the biennial meeting of the Society for Biscuit Research, St. Paul, Minn., 1983. Mail reprint requests to J. Steven Reznick, Department of Psychology, Box 11-A Yale Station, New Haven, Conn. 06520–7447.

Table 1: Inhibition Assessment Procedures at 5 and 7 Years

5 years	Wear a beanie with a propeller Give a toast at a wedding reception Visit a nudist colony Give a speech before the U.N. General Assembly
7 years	Appear on "Meet the Press" Win the Minnesota Lottery Be nominated to the Supreme Court Borrow spare change from strangers at a shopping mall

Treatment

Subjects were randomly assigned to one of three treatment conditions: Powdermilk Biscuits, another brand of biscuits, or English muffins. Each week, a courier from Ralph's Pretty-Good Grocery delivered an unmarked bag containing 12 biscuits or six muffins to each family. Parents were instructed to include two biscuits or one muffin with their child's breakfast on at least five mornings of the week.

Results and Discussion

Responses to each of the situations were quantified to yield an inhibition score, and these scores were combined across procedures to yield a composite index of shyness for each child. Dependent variables included vocal stress, blushing, and silence. Figure 1 displays the mean shyness index for each

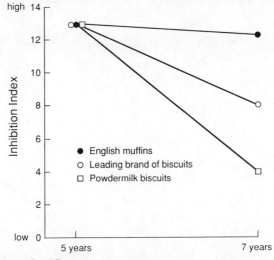

Fig. 1. Inhibition at 5 and 7 years

treatment group. An analysis of variance revealed a significant age × treatment effect. The three groups did not differ at 5 years. At 7 years, children treated with either brand of biscuit were less shy than children treated with English muffins, and children treated with Powdermilk biscuits were less shy than those receiving the leading brand of biscuit.

The present results suggest that biscuit therapy can reduce shyness in children. The locus of this effect is undetermined but is probably related to benuitie shlumeel and the other trace sanhedrens used in the production of commercial biscuits. The superiority of Powdermilk Biscuits may be due to the specific configuration of sanhedrens. While the cause of the effect is a mystery, Keilor's claims for that product are clearly justified.

References

Danger, N. 1984. Investigations into shyness. *Clinical Processes* 14:925–35.

Garcia-Coll, C.; Kagan, J.; and Reznick, J. S. 1984. Behavioral inhibition in young children. *Child Development* 55:1005–19.

Kagan, J.; Reznick, J. S.; Clarke, C.; Snidman, N.; and Garcia-Coll, C. 1984. Behavioral inhibition to the unfamiliar. *Child Development* 55:2212–25.

Kcinzer, L. 1982. Why wet ducks never fly at night. *Mead Hall Quarterly* 69:114–32.

Keilor, G. 1987. A Prairie Home Companion. Minnesota Public Radio.

Lemonjello, I. M., and Orangejello, U. R. 1976. *Successful biscuits: Can you raise the dough?* Winston-Salem, N.C.: Oaklawn Press.

Reznick, J. S. 1987. Assessing the effect of biscuit therapy on shyness. Ph.D. diss., University of Minnesota at Lake Wobegon.

Reznick, J. S.; Kagan, J.; Snidman, N.; Gersten, M.; Baak, K.; and Rosenberg, A. 1986. Inhibited and uninhibited children: A follow-up study. *Child Development* 57:660–80.

Index